MARKETING TOURISM

A PRACTICAL GUIDE

Alan Jefferson and Leonard Lickorish

LONGMAN

Longman Group UK Limited, Longman Industry and
Public Service Management Publishing Division
Westgate House, The High, Harlow, Essex, CM20 1YR

First published 1988
Second edition 1991

A catalogue record for this book is available from the British Library

ISBN-0-582-09506-9

Photosetting by Tradeset Photosetting Limited, Welwyn Garden City
Printed and bound in Great Britain by
Biddles Limited, Guildford and King's Lynn

Contents

List of figures and tables

Abbreviations

AEA	Association of European Airlines
ATI	Aviation and Tourism International
BTA	British Tourist Authority
BUAC	British Universities Accommodation Consortium
CBI	Confederation of British Industry
COMO	Committee of Marketing Organisations in Britain
CRS	Computerised Reservation System
CTT	Council for Travel and Tourism
DEA	Department of External Affairs (Canada)
ECU	European Currency Unit
EC	European Community
EFTA	European Free Trade Association
EIU	Economist Intelligence Unit
ETAG	European Tourism Action Group
ETB	English Tourist Board
ETC	European Travel Commission
ETY	European Tourism Year
GDP	Gross Domestic Product
GIT	Group Inclusive Tour
GNP	Gross National Product
IATA	International Air Transport Association
ICAO	International Civil Aviation Organisation of the United Nations
ICCA	International Congress of Convention Associations
ICOMOS	International Council on Monuments and Sites
IHA	International Hotel Association
IPS	International Passenger Survey
ITA:UK	Incentive Travel Association of the United Kingdom
IUOTO	International Union of Official Tourist Organisations
LNER	London North Eastern Railway
LTB	London Tourist Board
NBT	Netherlands Board of Tourism
NTO	National Tourist Organisation
OECD	Organisation for Economic Co-operation and Development
RIBA	Royal Institute of British Architects
SITE	Society of Incentive Travel Executives
STB	Scottish Tourist Board
THF	Trusthouse Forte
USTTA	United States Travel and Tourism Administration
WTB	Welsh Tourist Board
WTO	World Tourism Organisation

Introduction

Tourism is a market not a single industry, a trade in people and thus a complex phenomenon with important social as well as economic consequences.

Governments, central and local, represent the destination and play a key role in tourist development, not least by ensuring a focal point for co-ordination and, where appropriate, collective action with the large range of interests providing the services, facilities and attractions which make up the whole tourist product.

An explanation of the principles of tourism and its marketing characteristics should provide the essential framework for marketing planning and operation by all tourist interests in the public and private sectors. Full understanding of the role of the public sector tourist organisations representing the destination is fundamental, as they are responsible for the essence of the 'product' and act as the key focal point. This is the reason for concentrating on their proper function which needs industry partnership and influence for success.

While many of the examples of operation are taken from Britain, the principles apply widely and generally to the international movement. Many of the case studies and statistics relate to the international field. Although international action is more difficult and complex than the domestic market functions, the same guidelines and practices apply domestically as internationally, though the scale of activity may often be modest in the local areas. However, the links to the wider universe must be in place for full development.

This book has not been written specifically for the hotelier, transporter or tour operator, though many of the principles apply to their marketing operation. It has been written as a practical guide for those concerned with marketing the tourist destination, whether in the public or commercial sector.

The help and assistance of many leading personalities in the industry is acknowledged and in particular thanks are due to the British Tourist Authority for allowing access to material and publications and to W. S. Richards who kindly read the manuscript and made a number of useful suggestions.

1 Travel and the tourist

Concept, definitions and statistics

Tourism is a movement of people, a demand force and not a single industry. It embraces the temporary movement of people to destinations outside their place of permanent residence, involving transport, accommodation, activities at the destination visited, and a vast range of services making the visit possible. Thus tourism covers all the aspects of the 'mobile' as opposed to the residential population for which government and their communities normally cater. It is important to treat the 'mobile' community as a separate concept since there are many substantial differences.

Recent years have witnessed unprecedented technological changes, and in no sector more dramatically than in communication and mobility. The world is on the move, travel is very much part of modern living, with far reaching economic and social consequences.

Definition of tourism

Tourism covers all movements of people outside their own community for all purposes except migration or regular daily work. In many ways 'travel' is a better word to describe the concept since although the most common reason for trips outside the area of permanent residence is holiday taking, business journeys and visits for specific purposes eg health, religion (pilgrimages), education and study, sport and cultural activity are all important elements in the total movement. There is, however, a distinction for practical and important economic reasons between international and domestic journeys.

'Tourism' is a relative newcomer to the English language. It was at first used to define pleasure travel only, and in particular, the early package ('Cooks') tours. Even today the words 'travel' and the 'traveller' are respected descriptions whereas 'tourists' can still be considered in the abstract as either amusing, comical and even objects of doubt or suspicion.

The Swiss professors Walter Hunziker and Kurt Krapf published their general theory of tourism in 1942 and defined the subject as 'the totality of relationships and phenomena linked with the stay of foreigners in a locality provided they do not exercise a major, permanent or temporary remunerated activity'.[1] Professor Medlik of the University of Surrey put forward the following definition – 'the phenomenon arising from temporary visits (or staying away from home) outside the normal place of residence for any reason other than following an occupation remunerated from within the place visited'.[2] This fits well with the official international definitions and is suitable for international and national studies.

In 1968 the Statistical Commission of the United Nations approve the following:

> for statistical purposes the term 'visitor' describes any person visiting a country other than that in which he has his usual place of residence for any reason other than following an occupation remunerated from within the country visited.[3]

The International Union of Official Tourist Organisations (IUOTO), later to become the World Tourist Organisation (WTO) supported this description, but recommended that the term 'visitor' should be divided into two categories, 'tourists' to include visitors making at least one overnight stay, and 'excursionists' or in other words, day visitors.[4]

> Tourist, i.e. temporary visitor staying at least twenty-four hours in the country visited, the purpose of whose journey can be classified under one of the following headings:
>
> 1. Leisure (recreation, holiday, health, study, religion and sport)
> 2. Business, family, mission, meeting.
>
> Excursionist, ie temporary visitor staying less than twenty-four hours in the country visited (including travellers on cruises). The statistics should not include travellers, who in the legal sense do not enter the country (air travellers who do not leave an airport's transit area and similar cases).[5]

These definitions were intended for use in measuring international travel and fitted into the police, immigration and frontier control systems. But they are basically economic and also work well for domestic travel, at least in theory. The key feature is the expenditure by the visitor at the destination, which represents an injection of revenue (income) from outside the territory ie region, town or resort. Thus the essential concept of tourism is economic. It can best be seen, studied and worked at as a market, as an economic entity which gives the activity its identity.

There are social, political and other important aspects of tourism apart from its economic implications. But it is as a trade that the activity has its unity and power. There are many other definitions, which may relate to certain market segments such as youth, social, cultural, rural and educational tourism. Provided that the terms are precisely explained they have their place. However, it would be more efficient and businesslike to recognise the segments or the specialist streams of traffic for what they are, and avoid careless and often confusing terminology. Jargon can obscure. In recent years reference is sometimes made to the management of tourism. Taken literally this would suggest demand management, or market control, which in practice is the rather unsuccessful economics of the planned or communist societies. In fact what is meant is the management of tourism resources, and includes the indirect role of public bodies, notably the local authorities, with their substantial interventionist powers, both in planning controls and in investment and operating tourist 'plants' (theatres, conference halls, sports, entertainment and catering facilities). Even in such cases the market will dictate to any and all managers. In tourism the consumer is king — at least in the longer term. The trade is vast, highly competitive and with a truly world market place.

Movement of people on a vast scale represents a major economic activity. Indeed it has been estimated that tourism is now the largest single item in world trade, and for many countries a major factor in their national economy. Visitor spending creates massive wealth, sustains large numbers of jobs and offers many other important benefits, such as prosperity for regions with poor physical resources, or in the restoration of cities, towns and regions with declining trades.

International travel has a special significance. Firstly, it plays a major part in international trade, giving rise to massive foreign currency earnings and expenditures. Social consequences can be substantial, usually beneficial, as potentially travel represents the most powerful form of personal communication and face-to-face contact. Habits and customs can be affected, new markets created in fashions and consumer goods. Food and drink are obvious examples. But there can be unwelcome side effects, sometimes, distorted or used for political ends such as the vilification of multi-national companies invited to develop new areas. The errors may not be in tourism itself, indeed often there are no alternative resources or other options for development on a large and rapid scale. The fault lies in the management of resource, the lack of clear planning, and basic errors in definition and concept. That is why the principles of tourism are worth careful study and analysis. Clearly the trade does not take place in a vacuum. There will be geographic, environmental and social impacts, and cost benefits, as there are with any other business. But travel is a trade in people, where contacts and communication are vital elements. It is a trade without chimneys or dark satanic mills. Carefully developed visitor spending can conserve and sustain the best in the environment, finance amenities for the local community and provide a basis through allied transport and services for the growth of secondary and indigenous trades, increasing the wealth of the area directly and indirectly in a unique way.

Let us now consider some of the principal elements, firstly, the product and secondly, the component businesses. There is much confusion over the definition of the product. Tourism is not a sunny beach, a grand hotel, a flight or indeed any particular attraction. It is a satisfying activity at a desired destination. The two features must be present together. From this it can be seen that the complexities of tourism are substantial because a vast range of options, services and suppliers are involved. Furthermore, although in creating any one tourism product many interests are involved which are interdependent, they are also independent of each other and often in competition.

The product can take a variety of forms, but this is the basis of creativity in marketing, leading to product presentation and product development. The desired activity may be business or pleasure, a special interest (hobbies or sports), health or education, or social, uniting of friends and relatives. The place may be a resort or a town. Indeed it can be truly said in this age of mass mobility that no place is without some visitor appeal, and no season is a total off-season. For many countries, including Britain, movement should be created on a twelve-month basis and failure to achieve this is the failure of the destination marketers. Seasonality is an opportunity not a problem.

Every product must have its market. There is a vast range of products, and so also complex segmentation of the total market. There are specialist markets, mass markets and mini-mass markets. The range is great. This makes it all the more necessary to insist on precise definitions and market analysis. Recently in Britain large industrial cities have sometimes to their astonishment found a niche in the tourism movement. Bradford surprised many by its initiative and success resulting in considerable national publicity. This can present a false picture. Cities have always attracted travel movement. Large communities always do, for business, social and cultural reasons. They have good basic primary tourist trades – hotels, transport, restaurants and a wealth of cultural, sporting and other amenities such as shops. They are not in competition with seaside resorts as they offer quite different attractions, many indoor and weather proof. Over twenty-five years ago some outstanding marketers in tourism, particularly in the hotel and transport business examined the product market fit situation to deal with their own trading problems. Cities dealing with business men had large surplus hotel and other 'tourist' capacity at weekends and in high summer (August). Grand Metropolitan hotels were one of the first in the field with London winter weekends attracting both British and foreign guests. Transport companies – rail, air and sea ferries joined in. Trusthouse Forte and the other large groups, including the brewers' hotel chains were soon offering breaks in town and country, where capacity existed, with great success. Sheffield in the early 1960s was one of the first industrial cities to develop what might be called 'complementary' tourism, using surplus resources.

Nevertheless, the potential was limited. The business was quite different in scale, scope and marketing and development needs from that of the major tourist resorts. Failure to recognise this is a major marketing error.

Clearly then, destinations vary as do the tourism products. A clear and businesslike analysis is a first requirement to avoid raising false hopes for the ordinary everyday industrial town. They are not prime tourism destinations. The great resorts and spas and their hinterland have a theatrical quality and a scale of trade peculiar to themselves. This brings attendant benefits, problems and opportunities.

There is a life cycle in tourism products and destinations. Some are just starting out, some are mature, some, without a relaunch or rebuild, are approaching the end. Some will never grow but can be content with a limited flow of business as an ancillary trade.

As in nature there are many crops, so also in the tourist market. Historically, the great resorts in Britain and Europe knew this instinctively. They were natural marketers, even if they never used the word, and adapted their attractions and appeal (the product) to a chosen clientele – most successful product market fit. Some sought the carriage trade eg Eastbourne, some the popular, cheerful, gregarious movement in which Blackpool excelled. It may be forgotten that, together with the railways, which were directly related, Britain led Europe in resort development. Even today some famous British centres, notably Brighton and Harrogate, have successfully restructured their facilities and approach to new markets. But too many have not, principally because they could not identify and define changing market trends and find their place in the new travel world, missing opportunities many times greater than in their heyday.

Many new market segments, such as conferences, exhibitions, and large specialist gatherings for sport, arts and entertainment offer immense scope, but only with the necessary capital investment.

Statistics

Statistics of tourism are often criticised. They may not be comprehensive. Analysis may be limited particularly in regard to seasonal information. There are often bureaucratic delays and errors in description so that interpretation and use are difficult. Furthermore, system errors and statistical errors are quite common. Nevertheless statistics, however limited, are necessary, and useful if the figures are correctly described. There are ways of supplementing official data from trade information and through periodic sampling. Full knowledge of what figures are available, how to use them and how to be numerate, is an essential part of the marketing art.

The principal definitions of tourism have already been described.

These are the bases for effective statistical systems. The key element in the generally accepted definition is the temporary stay, normally more than twenty-four hours and less than one year (after which the visitor is assumed to be a resident), and no income earned at the destination visited. In other words, the visitor spend represents an injection of external 'income'.

Definitions also take account of day visits. These are important in domestic tourism but difficult to define and measure. In some countries (eg the USA) distances of one hundred miles have been taken as the dividing line between local and 'tourist' journeys. This may be arbitrary; the economic distinction is again a visit outside the area of residence involving spending of money not earned in the place visited. Commuters are clearly not tourists, even if they commute one hundred miles, as some do.

Official records may not conform to the agreed 'official' definitions, because the governmental systems of measurement are usually based on police controls at frontiers (immigration), or through hotel registration. The latter is common practice in many European countries where massive cross border flows make a full count impractical. Clearly hotel checks are unsatisfactory in many ways because they may not cover visits to camping sites, self-catering establishments, staying with friends and relatives etc. In other words fifty per cent or more of the traffic may not be measured. There are even more problems with value measurements to report tourist expenditure. The most effective method is through sample surveys, either at the frontier, at the destinations or through household surveys. Such surveys are difficult and expensive. So many countries resort to broad estimates based on bank records of foreign currency exchanged. The results are often substantially inaccurate.

In spite of many technical problems official figures can be helpful. Sometimes cross checks are possible, for example the US government Department of Commerce and other agencies report American visitor spending in European countries which can be compared with the figures produced by European governments. Provided definitions used, and limitations are carefully and exactly reported, the regular series of international and national travel statistics can be put to practical marketing use.

Categories of tourist statistics
There are four basic categories of measurement:

1.   Traffic movement (volume) and visitor expenditure (representing economic value).
2.   Information on the stock (capacity) and development of services and facilities for travellers.
3.   Market research and intelligence, analysing demand and demand trends.

4.   Checks and tests of effectiveness in operations. This would cover occupancy rates, load factors but also sales and marketing activity.

Statistical information needed
Commonly the basic unit of measurement is the 'visit', although some countries and some trades use the 'visitor night' ie one night stay by one person, as the standard. If the number of visitors is known then tourist nights are reported by length of stay checks. In practice many figures are reported as 'visitors' when the measure is in fact one person making one visit. A considerable number of travellers make a number of journeys. Some business men, for example, almost 'commute' across the Atlantic. Official records for foreign visitors to Britain are in fact separate visits and not people. For certain types of movement this distinction could be important in promotion and sales plans. The official records clearly aim to report visits to the destination concerned (the country, region, city or resort). Information is needed on:

1.   the place of permanent residence of the visitor;
2.   country, region or town (resort) visited;
3.   purpose of visit (business, pleasure, health, education etc), the more detailed the classification the better, as this assists in valuable segmentation exercises;
4.   length of stay in country, region or town (resort);
5.   basic socio-economic information (age, sex, status, nationality, occupation). There is a limit to the detail, but for market research purposes education, income and indications of behaviour or 'life style' groups can be very useful.

There is inevitably a conflict between the desire to facilitate travel, especially across frontiers, and to remove tiresome official checks and the desire to collect data. If basic volume and value checks are carried out much of the detail can be collected through sampling. This can be very expensive in tourism, and is often best done as explained later through cooperative action with the trades concerned.

Statistical methods
Principal methods can be summarised as follows:

1.   Household sample surveys, at the visitors' place of residence (before, but more usually, after the journey).
2.   International frontier or port surveys, counting or sampling visitors on arrival or departure. This is the principal means of collecting Britain's official international travel records.
3.   Traffic counts, sampling travellers en route, at termini or at traffic cordons.
4.   Surveys in the destination (resort) areas during their stay.

5.   Accommodation records and sampling at visitors' place of stay (hotels etc).

6.   Trade information. This can take many forms, most commonly sales analysis. It also includes informative data from in flight surveys on airlines, hotel occupancy data, and although not much used, travel agent and tour operator information.

Statistics – improving techniques and sources

The classic statistical systems based on police controls (immigration checks at the frontier or accommodation registers) are gradually disintegrating in the industrialised countries with the removal of frontier formalities and the expansion of mass travel. The meek do indeed inherit the earth and swamp the control systems. After the introduction of the Single Market in 1992, the European Community intends to create a borderless Europe. In practice some controls for health and security are likely to remain.

Official statistics based on the United Nations Statistical Commission's recommended definitions (see above) are the basis for most government attempts to measure travel. Thus the statistics are on a national or country basis, although definitions used may vary from country to country. Statistics collected by inter-governmental bodies (WTO, OECD, EC) from national governments can be compared provided they are properly labelled in detail. The international organisations are basically editors and commentators. They are not producers or sources of much original material.

Expenditure figures are increasingly suspect where these are based on bank reporting methods. The only reasonable results are those obtained from sample surveys of visitors either entry/exit or household surveys. Governments are interested in global figures, and data for balance of payments purposes, but operators need more detail especially for marketing planning. There are many problems. Information collected is often out of date when published, too limited in scope, and not comparable or compatible with other countries' data or other national series. The failings often lie in the methods used which are a by-product of the state's control systems. Thus official statistics cannot easily respond to changes in tourism flows, and the development of a number of mini mass markets, each with distinct behaviour patterns and demands.

The OECD in its recent reports on government tourism policies stressed the importance of expertise and effective management in policy making, and the necessary access to and provision of information and statistics. They report 'the state's role in tourism will be increasingly judged on its ability to provide industry and other levels of government with the information they need to draw up their own investment and communication strategies'.

Such information is fundamental in marketing the destination, where the public authority does not have the discipline of profit and loss to chart progress.

The lack of qualitative information is compounded by differences in definitions used. Usually official statistics record visits, not individuals travelling. Where frequent travellers are substantial in number, the records will fail to guide the market plan. Some figures are on a nationality and not country of residence basis as they should be. Many countries do not measure fare payments. But these can be large. In 1989 credits and debits in fares paid by travellers to and from the UK amounted to a total turnover of nearly £4 billion.

Most countries collect statistics on incoming not outgoing movement, since their controls were introduced to check immigration. Outward travel by residents and domestic tourism is not measured on a regular and compatible European or international basis. Fortunately the necessity to obtain data for major operations in the travel trades has encouraged the introduction of new techniques, largely through traffic or household sample surveys by a number of non-government producers and sources. In fact there is now more information coming from institutions and non-government sources than from the official statistical offices. Problems remain, because much of the new material is not compatible with official data, irregular in timing, varies considerably in scope, and may not be freely available to the public.

These difficulties are now widely recognised. Recently the European Community (Eurostat) and the World Tourist Organisation have started major reviews in consultation with industry groups. The original United Nations definitions (see above) are still generally valid, and apply also to domestic travel if the concept of 'visiting an environment different from that of permanent residence' is used. The key elements are the incidence of the mobile, not the resident population, in any given areas, and the injection of external revenues through visitor spending in the (local) economy.

Sampling techniques, although expensive if used on a mass scale, can apply such definitions to any tourist market segment, including day trips which have been largely ignored. There is no agreement on the standards for measurement. Most surveys use either a time or a distance characteristic or both (ie a trip which exceeds three hours away from home, or a distance travelled of more than 50 or 100 miles). It may be desirable to include more than one measure, and to analyse by distance, as results vary quite substantially according to distance, reflecting any given community's recreational behaviour. In rural areas journeys may be much longer than in conurbations.

A new addition to the useful annual reports on tourism trends has been published by Eurostat (EC) *Tourism in Europe – Trends 1989*[6]. These collections of national official figures, with all their faults are useful to the marketer, if used in conjunction with National Tourist Office or other industry-based data. The Eurostat publication given an overview for the twelve member countries. Tourist 'nights stayed' are given for ten member countries, together with changes on the previous year (1988) showing seasonal flow trends. Total 'nights stayed' increased by 1.2 per cent, domestic nights by 2.1 per cent, and non-resident nights by 3.2 per cent. Mediterranean countries registered a decrease in non-resident nights (Spain by 11 per cent) but the more Northern countries did well. Reasons for changing trends are given.

Balance of payments information is shown in detail for both receipts and expenditures. Receipts rose to 75.3 billion Ecus in 1989, by 9.5 per cent. Expenditure increased by 9.1 per cent to 72.8 billion Ecus. The rapid growth in outward travel from the EC countries is eroding the now modest surplus in the travel account with the rest of the world.

The publication includes more detailed information on each of the member countries. There are deficiences. Volume figures in terms of arrivals of visitors can be more useful than 'nights stayed'. Comparison should be made between the two sets of data. Qualitative information necessary for segmentation study is poor, simply because the official national systems which are the basis of the report are weak.

A number of countries now produce good complementary information through sample surveys, whether on incoming visitors' behaviour (where they travel during their stay, what they purchase etc.) or on outward and domestic travel. The BTA and the Tourist Boards for England, Scotland and Wales publish annually the *British National Travel Survey*[7] and the *United Kingdom Tourism Survey*[8], measuring British residents' travel abroad, and domestic movement within the country in great detail (see Appendix to chapter 4), with valuable information for marketers. There are some problems of definition, for example the failure to classify hotels, guest houses and other forms of accommodation separately. They represent very different trades for promotion purposes.

The intergovernmental reviews (WTO and EC) will be examining classification and nomenclature in the hope of extending tourism data to national accounts, which could be useful for macro analysis and long term planning.

A valuable new survey in Britain carried out by the Department of Employment *Leisure Day Visits Survey 1988/9*[9] examined day trips in depth for the first time. The WTO's guidelines define an excursionist as 'any person travelling . . . to a place other than that of his usual environment, and the main purpose of whose visit is other than the exercise of an activity remunerated within the place visited, and who does not spend the night in the place or country visited'.

This is a reasonable basis, but there needs to be some simple additional criteria. The British survey used the limits of 'over three hours' and 'twenty miles away from home'. There is clearly a need for international consistency.

The importance of the day visit traffic was established. Spending on day trips by residents in the UK was £5 billion or twenty per cent of total tourism spend, based on 630 million visits according to the definition used. There were also 900,000 day trips, including business trips by overseas visitors. The number of visits and expenditure were also analysed on a limitation of forty rather than twenty miles, which reduced the totals by nearly forty per cent (ie from 630 million to 379 million trips). Thus the criteria are vital, and so is a classification by range of time and distance for marketing purposes.

Major sample surveys of tourist flows are carried out from time to time in the principal countries; Germany (*Reiseanalyse* – annually), Netherlands, Austria, and France. In fact most of the European countries provide useful sampling data. The USA is rich in such material. An annual digest *Travel Industry Yearbook – The Big Picture* by Somerset Waters offers a mine of information[10]. Survey material for Japan is improving rapidly.

The *European Travel Monitor* is a new and interesting development in Europe[11]. This is a continuous survey measuring all overnight trips by the adult population of each of the 18 West European countries and since 1990, six of the most important East European countries. It was started in 1988 after extensive pilot work and is co-ordinated by the Luxembourg based European Travel Data Center. Fieldwork is carried out by leading opinion polling institutes in each country. In most countries interviewing is carried out every two months with samples of at least 2,000 adults aged 15 and over, totalling 12,000 interviews per country per year. Information is collected on destination countries, season, purpose of travel, length of trip, method of transport, accommodation used, method of booking (package/independent) and on the socio-demographic characteristics of trip takers.

The results for 1990 were available in March 1991 and the following resume indicates the kind of useful information available. Full results are available only to subscribers. Similar information is available from studies in the USA and Japan.

Table 1.1 – European outbound travel 1990

Number of trips	205 million + 2.7%
Number of nights	1,944 million + 0.4%
Turnover	134 billion Ecu + 9.3%
Purpose of trip	Business 15%
	Pleasure 85% (short trips 18%)

Source: ETM.
Note: Exchange rate £1 – Ecu (1991) = approximately 1.43

This information can be broken down by nights spent and area of origin of traffic, with results available for 100 West European regions separately (and thirty-two East). For example North Rhine Westphalia accounts for seventeen per cent and Greater London for eleven per cent of all West European outgoing trips. Similarly destination trips are indicated, for example in 1990 the Mediterranean area (excluding France) had a thirty-six per cent share of West European outbound travel.

In addition to regular reports for subscribers, the ETM produces a series of Special Publications on market segments such as Business Travel.

Such tourism surveys are complemented by useful information from sector organisations, both public and private. Air travel is well documented by IATA[12] and AEA[13], with their regular and timely information on traffic by routes and regions. The International Hotel Association (IHA) has commissioned strategic long term studies. Research and consultancy organisations, such as the EIU, publish studies and client reports from time to time. Howarth Consulting regularly publish both an international and a UK report on hotel trends, giving occupancy, sales and profitability data.

There is better access to data from research libraries, through National Tourist Offices[14] and universities[15] specialising in research. The European Travel Commission[16] carries out cooperative research with industry and publishes detailed results on major markets, such as the *French Outward Travel Movement, Incentive Travel, Senior Citizen Movement*, and marketing studies in North America.

The regular annual reports of the official international organisations (WTO[17], OECD[18]), for all their problems remain very useful, if used in conjunction with new sources described. The European Commission[19] has produced some interesting source material in 1985, and plans greater activity in the travel sector.

Summary

Tourism is a movement of people, a demand force and not a single industry. Tourism covers all movement by people outside their own community for all purposes except migration or regular daily work. In 1968 the Statistical Commission of the United Nations approved the following: 'For statistical purposes the term "visitor" describes any person visiting a country other than that in which he has his usual place of residence for any reason other than following an occupation remunerated from within the country visited. The same concept applies to the measurement of domestic tourism . . . .'.

The tourist 'product' is a satisfying activity at a desired destination. Every product must have its market. There is a vast range of products and so also complex segmentation in the total market. There are specialist markets, mass markets and mini mass markets.

Management of tourism is a confused concept since in tourism the consumer is king, but management of tourism resources is a practical and essential task.

References

1 Lickorish, L J, *Reviews of United Kingdom Statistical Sources*, Vol. IV, *Leisure and Tourism*. Heinemann Educational Books p 7.

2 Lickorish, L J, *ibid*, p 7.

3 Lickorish, L J, *ibid*, p 28.

4 Lickorish, L J, *ibid*, p 28.

5 Lickorish, L J, *ibid*, p 27.

6 *Tourism in Europe – Trends 1989*. Commission of the European Communities (Eurostat), Brussels (annual).

7 *British National Travel Survey* (BNTS). British Tourist Authority (annual).

8 *United Kingdom Tourism Survey*. English, Scottish, Wales and Northern Ireland Tourist Boards (annual).

9 *Leisure Day Visits Survey 1988–9* Employment Gazette May 1991. Department of Employment (annual).

10 Waters, S, *Travel Industry Year Book – The Big Picture*. Child and Waters Inc (annual).

11 *European Travel Monitor*. European Travel Data Centre, IPK, Munich.

12 *IATA World Transport Statistics*. Geneva (annual).

13 *Association of European Airlines Year Book*. Brussels (annual).

14 *Digest of Tourist Statistics*. British Tourist Authority (annual).

15 *Computerised Database on Tourism*. Centre des Hautes Etudes Touristiques, University of Aix en Provence, France. *Annals of Tourism Research*. University of Wisconsin-Stout, USA.

16 *European Incentive Travel Survey* (ETC, ETAG, IHA) undertaken and published by Touche Ross, London.

17 *Yearbook of Tourism Statistics*. WTO, Madrid (annual). *Current Travel and Tourism Indicators*. WTO, Madrid (annual).

18 *OECD Tourism Policy and International Tourism in OECD Member Countries*. Paris (annual).

19 *Europeans and their Holidays*. Commission of the European Communities, Brussels 1986.

2 The tourist service trades

These are the trades that provide the visitor with his essential needs. They are separate industries in their own right, and usually will have their own distinct 'markets' selling to residents and visitors alike. Although independent of each other and often fiercely competitive, they are also interdependent, at least in so far as tourism is concerned. This gives rise to special needs and problems.

Primary trades are transport, accommodation and catering; visitor servicing, principally by travel agents and tour operators, information agencies (public and private) and guiding staffs; entertainment and specialist activities for visitors in visitor destinations.

Secondary trades range from shops, personal services, such as banking, hairdressing, laundering and a considerable range of businesses supplying tourist enterprises, such as building, maintenance, light and heat and professional services including the tourism marketers.

This broad division can only be indicative, since inclusion of businesses or institutions in the tourism category depends so much on the incidence and impact of tourism in their area of business, and the proportion of their trade that is with visitors.

The primary trades themselves can be effectively subdivided into a number of separate industries often in competition with each other. Transport covers movement by air, sea, rail and road, and the latter, by far the largest element, must be further subdivided into public and private (buses, coaches and private cars and cycles). Accommodation and catering likewise take a number of quite different forms. The classic hotels and restaurants, although serving the major part of the top end of the market, in fact cater for a minority of the total tourist movement. Pleasure travellers are much more likely to use guest houses, holiday apartments, villas, cottages and a variety of other types of self-catering accommodation, including a substantial camping and caravan sector. Private accommodation, friends and relatives and bed and breakfast (B&B) is a further major element straddling the commercial and non-commercial field.

While the service trades are easier to define and recognise, they also have their sub-divisions. The travel trade proper (travel agents and tour operators) is relatively small. But as with the cheaper forms of accommodation there is a vast tail with many retail businesses and voluntary organisers on the fringe. For years newsagents have sold coach tickets and many other high street retailers have shown an interest in the travel business. In certain countries (Australia for example) the banks are active in selling travel.

From the earliest days institutions have played a very substantial part in their own specialist field. Thomas Cook started with the temperance movement. Poly Travel was an offshoot of the Polytechnic movement, an early initiative of the educational interests which are today one of the most powerful forces in travel. The Churches have always been active since the medieval days of pilgrimages. Today religious pilgrimages are probably greater in volume than ever, for example to Lourdes, the Holy Land, Mecca.

Clearly guides and servicing staff from both the commercial and public sectors, tourist boards, local authorities and institutions (such as historic properties, museums and art galleries), make an important contribution to the tourist trade. In fact, in Britain domestic movement largely bypasses the travel trade and is assisted by public sector information services and the great army of tourist auxiliaries, many from voluntary institutions. There is a great lack of marketing organisation and help. It is hardly surprising that travel spend abroad by the British public is greater than total domestic holiday spend. This is not due to the absence of hot sunny beaches in Britain. Over fifty per cent of British travellers abroad do not go to hot beaches. Climate is not necessarily the principal motivator.

The secondary and tertiary trades can be subdivided infinitely. Just as there is hardly a destination that cannot offer some visitor satisfaction, it is difficult to think of an industry that does not benefit from tourism. Steel for cars and cutlery, carpets and curtains for hotels, china and glass for restaurants are obvious examples. Insurance, banking, telecommunications, quantity surveying are perhaps not so obvious.

An understanding of the make up of the principal tourist trades and their products is fundamental to successful marketing and to the product market fit (see chapter 10). There has to be joint working and cooperation, but there is inevitably, and rightly, competition too. Finding the true dividing line between the competitive and cooperative operations is a great, but necessary, art and essential for successful promotion and development of great streams of traffic.

Statistics of the tourist service trades

These are tools of the trade. The discipline of profit and loss and financial history and experience cannot be the only guide in the world market, nor can financial analyses by themselves identify trends, forecast the future and determine product presentation and development. It is often said of statistics, apart from jokes about accuracy, that there are too many figures and that they are never the figures that are wanted. This is more a criticism of the managers and marketers whose job it is to employ and instruct the statisticians and market researchers. Accordingly, a clear understanding of statistical and market research sources and resources is both necessary and rewarding.

Some twenty-five to thirty per cent of visitor expenditure (excluding day trips, foreign visitors and international transport) is on accommodation. Thus the accommodation industry is not only a vital primary trade but a major economic sector and income generator in its own right.

The Development of Tourism Act 1969 defined tourist accommodation as 'hotels or other establishments at which sleeping accommodation is provided by way of trade or business'. There is a broad range of services and facilities which can be described as follows:

1. Hotels: hotels, inns, motels providing overnight accommodation with food and service.
2. Guest or boarding houses and hostels which may not offer a full meal service (for example bed and breakfast).
3. Holiday camps, holiday or leisure centres, holiday villages, offering catering and other services for their residents. These establishments will often operate only in the season and for longer stays (eg one week on a pre-booked inclusive service basis).
4. Bed and breakfast accommodation. This 'tail' of the industry is very large, on the border of private and commercial premises, and capable of quickly responding to fluctuating (seasonal) demand. It is largely a British invention, and generally not well organised or marketed, but some enterprising developments have taken place in recent years.
5. Cruise ships.
6. Self-catering accommodation. This is again large, usually seasonal, responds quickly to demand changes, and increasingly takes a number of separate forms. It is an area of considerable experimentation and enterprise, and responsive to promotion. The main forms are as follows:

(a) camping and caravan sites;
(b) chalets, holiday cottages or other purpose built tourist accommodation (villas, hostels, apartments etc.);
(c) a growing specialist sector embraces boats on inland waterways and the sea;
(d) new forms of self-catering continue to come into the market, the latest large scale innovation is time share, where tourists buy, by providing a capital sum, the right to use the holiday accommodation for a given period (one, two or more weeks in the year) for a long future period – a life time or more.

7. An important category of accommodation for seasonal use only can be described as institutional, particularly educational premises, including universities, where tourism provides a 'double' use during

Table 2.1 – Accommodation used on holiday 1989 by UK residents

All holiday trips	All holiday trips					1 to 3 night holiday trips					4 or more night holiday trips				
	United Kingdom 64.5m. %	England 50.5m. %	Scotland 6.0m. %	Wales 6.5m. %	Northern Ireland 1.0m. %	United Kingdom 30.5m. %	England 25.0m. %	Scotland 2.0m. %	Wales 2.5m. %	Northern Ireland 0.5m. %	United Kingdom 34.0m. %	England 25.5m. %	Scotland 4.0m. %	Wales 4.0m. %	Northern Ireland 0.5m. %
Hotel/motel/guest house	21	21	30	13	8	21	21	30	15	8	22	21	31	13	9
Paying guest in:															
– farmhouse	1	1	1	1	1	1	*	1	1	1	1	1	1	2	1
– other private house/ bed & breakfast establishment	3	3	5	2	4	3	3	3	3	3	3	2	6	2	4
Self catering in rented:															
– flat/apartment	3	3	2	3	2	1	1	1	1	1	5	5	3	5	3
– house/chalet/villa/ bungalow	6	5	7	11	3	2	1	2	5	*	10	9	9	15	6
– hostel/university/ school	2	2	3	2	1	2	2	5	2	1	2	2	2	2	2
Friends'/relatives' home	37	39	39	25	51	44	45	42	30	55	31	32	37	23	45
Own second home/ timeshare	2	2	2	2	4	2	2	1	4	7	1	1	2	1	1
Holiday camp/village:															
– self catering	2	2	1	4	*	1	1	*	1	*	4	4	2	5	*
– serviced	1	1	*	*	*	*	1	*	*	*	2	2	*	1	1
Camping	5	6	4	7	5	6	6	2	5	2	5	5	4	8	9
Caravan:															
– towed	6	7	5	6	4	6	6	3	7	4	6	7	6	5	4
– static owned	6	6	5	12	8	9	8	8	18	11	4	4	3	7	5
– static not owned	6	5	5	12	10	2	2	3	6	8	9	8	6	16	13
Boat(s)	1	1	1	1	*	1	1	*	1	*	1	1	1	1	*
Sleeper cab of lorry/truck	*	*	*	*	*	*	*	*	*	*	*	*	*	*	*
Other transit	1	1	2	*	1	*	*	1	*	*	1	1	2	*	1

Source: UKTS.

Note: Columns may add to more than 100% because more than one type of accommodation may be used on some holidays.
* less than 0.5%.

students' vacations. This can be practical and profitable for certain kinds of traffic such as conferences. There are many opportunities to turn 'spare' accommodation to tourist use, bearing in mind the specialist and seasonal flows of traffic which might not sustain development of purpose built accommodation. Some forms of specialist travel require, or call into service, the necessary ancillary facilities at, for example, religious and pilgrimage centres, or for special events such as festivals, where private accommodation is sought, and indeed should be professionally organised, on a temporary special need basis.

An interesting accommodation development in Britain was the use of steeplechase race courses, in the peak summer weeks, as touring camping and caravan sites. Their facilities (hard stands, water, sanitation and other services) and expertise in handling large crowds and numbers of vehicles provided ideal 'alternative' facilities for a growth sector, but where the short season would not justify permanent investment in infrastructure.

Statistics are imprecise but the following figures give at least the order of magnitude of the accommodation industry in Britain. The industry is clearly highly segmented in structure and use in most countries. Although there is in recent years a well established trend in the richer countries for trading up in standards and facilities, favouring the traditional hotel sector, over half of overseas visitors to Britain, and three-quarters of domestic travellers and holiday makers do not stay in hotels. The breakdown is as follows:

Table 2.2 – Accommodation used by overseas visitors to London summer 1979 to 1989

Base:	1979 (1,201) %	1982 (1,114) %	1985 (1,085) %	1987 (1,174) %	1988 (1,126) %	1989 (1,166) %
Licensed hotel	35	30	40	33	43	38
Unlicensed hotel/guest house/pension	14	20	16	15	18	15
Friends'/relatives' home	24	25	21	24	20	22
Youth/student hostel/ university/school	8	12	8	10	7	11
Rented house/flat	4	4	4	6	4	5
Paying guest in private house	5	4	4	8	4	4
Camping/caravanning	4	3	2	2	2	3
Other	1	*	1	*	2	1
Not stated	3	*	2	2	*	*

Source: UKTS.

Note: The proportions refer to the type of accommodation used in London on the night prior to the interview. Results for 1979 are not quite comparable because they include details of accommodation used regardless of whether the previous night was spent in London. In Summer 1989 3% of visitors had not spent the previous night in London (although they had spent at least one night in London earlier in their visit).

* less than 0.5%.

However, proportions can be misleading. Marketers need to study segments. Business travellers are heavy hotel users; first class and up market international travellers are mainly hotel clients. In many resorts purpose built holiday hotels, often served by charters and tour operators accommodate the majority of a resort's visitors. Hotels with their superior facilities and substantial investment in service and comfort are inevitably more costly than simple provision. They also account for a substantial proportion of total spending. Furthermore, many of their clients are frequent and year-round patrons. City centre hotels for example, may enjoy high occupancy (in London seventy per cent or more compared with about fifty per cent for the national average in Britain and scarcely thirty per cent for seasonal services).

The marketer will need to study the industry sector by sector and the following special characteristics.

1.   Distribution of accommodation is uneven and reflects historic use. The nature of the traffic will vary considerably. Cities, attracting business and pleasure movement, enjoy a long season, with good prospects of expansion. The types of traffic may well be complementary evening out peaks and troughs. At the other end of the scale the resort hotel, especially in the historic seaside towns, has a highly seasonal business and may face declining trade. Their tide has indeed been on the ebb and the marketing challenge is great. The spas in Britain have done better.
2.   Occupancy is a vital consideration. Low seasons or troughs represent compelling marketing challenges. The trends in modern tourism, in an age of mobility strongly favour the introduction of new appeals, new services and new products. In most parts of Britain there should be a twelve month season, as the attractions are often specialist, indoor or sheltered, and not dependent on hot sunny beaches where the seasonal problem is often more acute and difficult to remedy.
3.   Structure and scale. In Britain more so than in many European countries there are a number of large scale operators. At the end of the 1970s thirty hotel companies, each with more than 1,000 rooms operated some 1,000 hotels (90,000 rooms). Six of these companies operated over half of this large capacity.[1]

Integration with the other trade sectors has tended to diminish rather than grow, apart from the traditional link between the brewers and inns and hotels in Britain. This on the whole has been beneficial for Britain's tourism. Railway hotels are now in private sector and competitive ownership. A European trend earlier in the century for government intervention has been reversed, although schemes of government subsidy are fairly common. There are special cases, some very successful, such as the *paradores* in Spain and the *pousadas* in Portugal, often using historic buildings and heritage sites.

A post war trend of airline incursion into hotel building and operation

has been reversed. The American chains, notably Hilton and Intercontinental, have been sold by their airline parents to British hotel companies.
The original reason for intervention was a shortage of destination
accommodation for international airline passengers, especially high
tariff business travellers.

The large hotel companies have marketing resources to join with
other trade sectors and destination interests to promote and create new
business, often by creating new products. It was the hotel groups in Britain working with the BTA in the first instance, which created off peak
breaks (for example, London winter weekends), bringing business to
many city centres. The famous veteran car race from London to
Brighton was a hotelier's invention. There are many other examples of
successful resort initiative to lengthen the season.

The International Hotel Association with the European Travel Commission organised seminars on seasonality over three years in the
Mediterranean islands of Malta, Cyprus and Rhodes. Extension of the
season notably by attracting senior citizens seeking a change and relaxation in a marginally better climate has in some cases been quite dramatic. Innovation and experiment are expensive, and need to be sustained
over a period, perhaps three years. So the larger groups with their bigger
resources are often the only trade partners who can finance such essential promotional and traffic creating experiments.

Within the accommodation sector there has been an encouraging
growth of consortia and cooperative marketing organisations. Best
Western for example, groups some 300 independent hotels of similar
standard in Britain and abroad, enabling them to carry out effective sales
(reservations), promotional and product presentation schemes, thus
providing these separately owned hotels with some of the advantages
of the chain. As information technology and reservation techniques
develop these marketing cooperatives will become even more significant.

The destination interests have an important role to play in providing a
cooperative marketing forum at the city, resort and regional level, but
are often under resourced in skills and finance to do the job. Tourism
marketing is a creative function designed to produce more profitable
business: it is a cooperative process with all key interests involved.

Accommodation interests cannot and should not be expected to do
the whole job. They have their competitive as well as their cooperative
promotional role, necessary for efficiency and expansion. The distributive channels, usually referred to as the travel trades (retail and
wholesale agents or tour operators), working in harmony with the destination interest (tourist boards or marketing cooperatives), should be in
the lead. They can be inefficient – promotion or product presentation
may be poor, relationships ineffective. The majority of international standard hotels pay travel agents' commission, but it was not so long ago

that a substantial proportion of these establishments did not. Furthermore, the introduction of credit cards some two decades ago was strongly resisted, on the grounds that these promotional sales services were not needed. The advent of the larger groups with their marketing skills changed that outlook.

There are other important characteristics: for example classification of grading schemes, public and private. Many of these, especially in Europe were not intended as marketing aids, but rather as a system of control for government regulation and intervention, not least in fiscal matters, providing a basis for taxation. Even today the argument for or against government intervention is obscure. There is often an unwillingness to accept the market's disciplines, or to examine market demands. In the USA and Germany, two successful tourism countries, there is no state system of registration or control. In Britain the motoring organisations have operated the well known star system for hotels for years. Their efforts are supplemented by quality guides (for example, Michelin, Egon Ronay and the Good Food Guide for restaurants). However, these systems concentrate on the top range of hotel establishments. It is in the budget and lower price categories that the need is greatest (bed and breakfast for example). The destination interests, the resort or municipal authority, the regional tourist organisations, are in a position to do this for good marketing reasons rather than bureaucratic control reasons, such as price regulation. It may not be profitable, and thus not practical, for the trade to do this, and yet to create business it must be easy for the tourist to assess and buy the product, and it must be easy for the packagers, to offer the total service. It is not essential for state tourist organisations to grade internationally known chain hotels, such as the Hiltons, but it is essential, although difficult, unglamorous and commercially not directly profitable to operate at the other end of the scale.

Transport, together with accommodation, are the principal primary trades in tourism, and account for approximately fifty per cent of total tourist expenditure, although the proportion varies considerably. Nevertheless, they represent the controlling trades in essential services and in the shaping and development of tourism flows, with a key role in the marketing and creation of tourism products.

The principal forms of transport, road, rail, sea and air represent separate trades in themselves, often competitive, but nearly always complementary in part. Furthermore, in most cases passenger transport is not the sole business. For many transport organisations freight may be as important, or more important, than passengers. For some, social and basic communication transport is the main purpose of the operation and tourism may be insignificant. However, in most cases where there is spare capacity, tourism flows and the creation of new traffic which will normally only be possible through tourism, will become important and profitable.

There is massive public sector investment in costly infrastructure. Since the communication systems have a fundamental effect on the national economy government intervention and control is the norm. Although there has been a trend towards liberalisation and even privatisation in recent years in most countries, including the industrialised western countries, the major public networks of road, rail and air are government owned or controlled. In Britain, bus and coach transport and air transport has recently been privatised, but strict government controls on routes and many other aspects of air travel remain. So also does international regulation in spite of many efforts to deregulate air travel in Europe following the example of the USA. Sea transport has remained largely in private hands although some routes are subsidised.

State control may limit competition on routes or capacity and regulate prices. Thus marketing takes place in an imperfect market. On the other hand public transport can be highly productive. Capacity can respond to demand changes rapidly with little extra investment. Where there is surplus capacity, which is normal over the year, creation of new tourism business may be very profitable at relatively low prices. The growth of charter travel, which now accounts for the larger part of the massive north–south flow of recreational travel in Europe, from the northern industrial cities to the Mediterranean beaches, is a good example. The importance of each type of transport varies considerably according to markets, market segments and routes. Tables 2.3 –2.7 illustrate the differences.

Domestic travel for business or pleasure is heavily private car dominated, although domestic air services, which tend to be expensive in Europe, have a substantial business clientele. Generally speaking the longer the journey, the greater the use of public transport. Air travel dominates long distance and intercontinental travel. As a broad rule of thumb, the longer the distance and the greater the cost of the journey to the destination, the greater the length of stay and expenditure at the destination.

For most routes and destinations a trinity of market forces operate in determining choice of transport. These are time, price and convenience (or comfort and appeal). Any transport mode offering advantages in two of the three elements will normally capture the market, but it must be remembered that choice varies considerably by market segment. Discrimination in the market is necessary and commonplace; one plane on one route will offer a variety of fares. It has been said jokingly that on some flights no two passengers pay the same fare for an apparently identical service. The challenge of filling spare capacity without endangering regular 'full' or high price travel is a continuing one in passenger transport and can lead to substantial price reductions and innovation to the benefit of the traveller.

The International Civil Aviation Organisation recorded over one billion passengers on scheduled trips in 1987 for the first time.

Table 2.3 – Main method of transport used to reach the destination on holidays of 4+ nights in Great Britain 1971 to 1989

Base	All holidays																	Main holidays	Additional holidays
	1971 %	1974 %	1975 %	1976 %	1977 %	1978 %	1979 %	1980 %	1981 %	1982 %	1983 %	1984 %	1985 %	1986 %	1987 %	1988 %	1989 %	1989 %	1989 %
Car	69	69	71	69	71	72	71	71	69	68	72	69	71	72	73	74	74	72	77
Bus/Coach	15	14	12	13	12	11	12	12	12	15	12	15	14	15	14	13	13	15	12
Train	13	13	11	11	13	11	13	13	13	12	10	11	10	8	8	8	8	9	7
Other	3	4	3	4	4	4	4	4	5	3	5	4	4	4	5	4	4	5	4

Source: BNTS/BTSY.

Note: In 1972 and 1973 information on transport used was not collected in the BNTS.
Figures may not add up to 100% because of rounding and because of a proportion of people who could not recall method of transport used.

The above statistics do not include charter traffic which in Europe in 1986 accounted for no less than forty-six per cent of the total. Furthermore, the Association of European Airlines reports that four-fifths of all passengers (scheduled and charter together) benefit from an average price reduction of fifty per cent on the normal published full economy fare.

The investment and expansion programmes of air carriers is massive. In 1987 nearly 800 new commercial jet aircraft were on order. Although some represent replacements, a substantial proportion represent expansion. In addition many new aircraft are either larger or more efficient which further effects total capacity.

The ten year annual average international traffic growth was five per cent in the decade 1976–86. IATA forecasts 3.5 per cent for the North Atlantic in 1989 and 1990, 5.0 per cent in Europe in 1989 and 1990. Since the world average in this period is put at 5.5 per cent faster rates of growth are anticipated in Asia and the Far East. Many experts consider these forecasts are on the low side.

The tourist product is a satisfying activity at a desired or acceptable destination. Thus after accommodation and transport the activity which represents the reason for the visit involves the third primary trade, often a combination of specialist services centred on entertainment, sport, health, culture or business (for example, conferences and trade fairs). The activity sector will often embrace resort services, and municipal authorities or regional government may be the key investor, planner and operator of many of these services.

This complex of trading services representing the attractions is not clear cut, and many traders may be on the margin. It depends on the incidence of demand. In tourist resorts the main business of the place, and the main use of amenities, including museums, art galleries and theatres, heritage buildings and centres, leisure and sports centres, depends on tourism. These services are in effect primary trades. In industrial and non-tourist towns similar trades cater for the residential community although their tourist development may be limited.

A fourth primary trade can be described as the distributive service, relatively small compared with the other sectors but vital, and heavily market orientated. This includes retail travel agents, wholesale agents, tour operators and a wide range of specialist operators, embracing educational and religious and other voluntary bodies where travel is linked to their own community's activities.

The traders and tour organisers are supported by a substantial number of information and servicing staff, guides and couriers. Information centres are usually operated by local authorities or tourist boards; many run reservation services and sales activities for local attractions and entertainments. These facilities can effectively put a service on the market, like goods on the shelf in a shop. For many, especially if the

Table 2.4 – Overseas visitors to UK: method of transport (by market countries/areas) 1976 to 1989

Country of permanent residence	Number of visits ('000) 1976			Number of visits ('000) 1983			Number of visits ('000) 1989			Expenditure (£m.) 1976			Expenditure (£m.) 1989		
	Air	Sea**	Total	Air	Sea**	Total	Air	Sea**	Total	Air	Sea**	Total	Air	Sea**	Total
United States	1,269	316	1,585	1,805	512	2,317	2,407	435	2,842	244	44	288	1,299	142	1,441
Canada	428	80	508	442	77	519	557	82	639	87	11	97	243	16	259
North America	1,697	396	2,093	2,247	589	2,836	2,964	517	3,481	330	55	385	1,541	159·	1,700
Belgium/Luxembourg	172	572	744	129	301	430	243	375	618	18	38	56	53	52	105
France	403	875	1,278	483	1,033	1,516	853	1,408	2,261	37	64	101	225	199	424
West Germany	476	728	1,204	490	884	1,374	924	1,103	2,027	55	66	121	237	172	410
Italy	246	61	307	355	103	458	544	164	708	33	6	39	249	42	291
Netherlands	327	580	907	247	488	735	458	482	940	36	63	99	95	83	178
Denmark	117	92	209	109	110	219	173	86	259	17	9	26	51	16	68
Irish Republic	319	385	703	283	625	908	759	543	1,302	30	29	59	202	143	345
Greece	54	10	64	78	7	85	114	14	128	15	4	19	85	6	91
Spain	212	57	269	249	50	298	525	96	622	41	11	51	249	31	279
Portugal	46	5	51	46	9	55	90	5	95	6	1	7	38	1	39
Western Europe EEC†	2,372	3,365	5,736	2,469	3,609	6,078	4,684	4,276	8,960	297	300	597	1,506	766	2,272
Yugoslavia	30	6	36	13	11	24	25	5	31	7	*	7	9	1	10
Austria	60	29	89	64	24	88	105	43	148	8	4	11	44	24	68
Switzerland	203	60	263	253	56	310	374	50	424	31	10	41	151	18	169
Norway	142	86	228	159	35	194	232	55	287	29	12	41	89	18	107
Sweden	216	112	328	156	133	288	321	160	481	32	13	45	129	51	180
Finland	44	6	50	43	19	62	152	13	166	7	*	7	65	6	70
Gibraltar/Malta/Cyprus	34	4	38	69	4	73	108	3	111	7	1	7	45	*	46

Others	50	2	48	20	2	18	81	10	71	47	7	40	48	8	40
Western Europe non-EEC	699	118	581	180	43	137	1,728	339	1,389	1,086	290	796	1,080	311	769
Middle East	500	9	491	220	17	203	457	16	442	616	46	570	395	41	354
North Africa	89	1	88	32	2	31	93	7	87	125	7	118	91	12	79
South Africa	84	14	69	31	4	27	145	17	128	147	27	120	141	25	116
Rest of Africa	328	7	321	77	4	73	310	12	298	376	17	360	217	20	197
Eastern Europe	43	9	35	8	3	5	165	43	122	50	11	39	63	31	32
Japan	247	9	238	24	4	20	505	22	483	170	19	151	129	20	109
Australia	347	56	291	97	26	70	535	107	428	331	81	249	382	127	255
New Zealand	73	15	58	16	4	11	123	32	91	76	25	52	65	20	45
Commonwealth Caribbean	42	*	41	11	*	11	70	3	67	48	6	42	47	4	43
Latin America	106	22	83	43	7	37	179	63	116	109	28	82	169	42	127
Others	415	38	377	48	4	44	586	56	530	415	49	366	200	25	175
Rest of World	2,274	181	2,093	606	75	531	3,168	377	2,792	2,464	315	2,148	1,899	367	1,532
All Countries†	6,945	1,224	5,721	1,768	472	1,296	17,338	5,509	11,829	12,464	4,803	7,661	10,808	4,438	6,370

Source: International Passenger Survey

Note: Figures are rounded, so that component figures may not add up to totals.

*Less than £0.5m.

**Visits by road and rail across the border with the Irish Republic are included with the sea routes, as are travellers by hovercraft and jetfoil.

†Includes expenditure of overseas visitors in the Channel Islands.

Table 2.5 – US trip profile 1988

(Base: 1,232.5 million person-trips to places 100 miles or more from home)

Category	Percentage of trips
Round trip distances:	
200–299 miles	22
300–399 miles	16
400–599 miles	17
600–999 miles	13
1,000–1,999 miles	15
2,000 miles or more	12
Outside US	6
	100
Average distance (miles) 950	
(Domestic travel only)	
Mode of transportation:	
Auto/Truck/RV	77
Airplane	19
Bus	1
Train	1
Other	2
Trip duration:	
No. nights	13
One night	13
2 or 3 nights	37
4 to 9 nights	27
10 nights or more	11
Average nights	4.9
Type of lodging:	
Friends', relatives' homes	39
Hotel or motel	43
Rented cabin or condo	3
Owned cabin or condo	3
Camper, trailer or RV	5
Other	2
No overnight stay	13
Primary purpose of trip:	
Visit friends, relatives	35
Outdoor recreation	16
Entertainment	25
Business	12
Convention	5
Other	9
Vacation travel:	**67**
Weekend travel:	**45**

Source: US Travel Data Centre

Table 2.6 – Transportation means by Europeans

	Car	Train	Plane	Boat	Bicycle/ motorbike	Other	TOTAL
Belgium	77	6	10	1	2	7	(1)
Denmark	59	14	18	11	3	4	(1)
Germany	61	16	17	3	1	7	(1)
Greece	78	4	13	25	1	–	(1)
Spain	70	16	5	2	–	12	(1)
France	81	15	6	2	2	7	(1)
Ireland	51	11	31	18	1	6	(1)
Italy	73	15	5	5	2	11	(1)
Luxembourg	62	10	19	4	–	15	(1)
Netherlands	70	8	14	5	6	14	(1)
Portugal	76	17	3	3	1	16	–
United Kingdom	59	11	24	8	–	14	(1)
CE 12*	68	14	13	5	1	10	(1)

Total may exceed 100% because some respondents used different means of transportation.
*Twelve member countries of EEC.
Source: Europeans and their holidays (Commission of the European Communities Brussels 1986)

Table 2.7 – Development of world air transport 1972 to 1989

	1972	1974	1976	1978	1980	1982	1983	1984	1985	1986	1987	1988	P 1989
Scheduled international and domestic													
Passengers carried (millions)	450	514	576	679	748	766	798	848	899	960	1,027	1,080	1,100
Passenger load factor %	57	59	60	65	63	64	64	65	66	65	67	68	68
Scheduled international													
Passengers carried (millions)	88	102	118	143	163	170	173	185	194	198	222	243	260
Passenger load factor %	54	56	57	62	61	62	63	65	65	63	67	68	68
Scheduled domestic													
Passenger carried (millions)	362	412	458	536	585	596	625	663	705	762	805	837	840
Passenger load factor %	59	62	62	67	65	65	65	64	66	66	67	67	68

Source: International Civil Aviation Organisation.
Note: Figures are rounded, so that component figures may not add up to totals.
P = provisional.

price is low and the distribution very local, there is no other viable way. Since a large proportion of all tourists in Britain and in most other tourist locations (with the exception of sunny beaches, special events or bargain offers) travel independently, such services, in making travel arrangements easy to identify and to buy, play a vital role. Eighty per cent of all overseas leisure travellers to Britain are independent and in spite of mass package tours to the sun over half of all British travellers abroad travel independently. Over two-thirds of European holiday makers travelling outside their own country are not packaged, since they rely on the private car, and the bulk of domestic travel in Europe and in North America moves independently.

This is no way belittles the role of the travel agent. About eighty per cent of American visitors to Europe use agencies' services, and the majority of international travellers in Europe, other than by private car, buy through agents. But the proportions illustrate the importance of the auxiliaries – the tourist information staff, the voluntary bodies and the specialist organisers. Many of these are inefficient, but change is coming fast, not only as a result of the entry of new competitors (large retail organisations) but the introduction of new business and communication techniques as well as information technology.

The retail and wholesale trade is likely to respond as forcefully and dramatically as it has done in the past. The rate of expansion in past years however may not be sustained. British travel abroad has increased by over 300 per cent in little more than a decade from twelve million overseas visits to twenty-one million. Package trips have been skilfully marketed by British tour operators and the number of package tours abroad sold in Britain has risen from five million in 1970 to fourteen million in 1987. Unfortunately this efficient sales force imports foreign leisure services and in a fiercely competitive free international market Britain's resort and tourist interests have been less and less successful in selling local manufactures to the resident natives. Clearly, the entre-preneurial role in this whole servicing field is immense. Tour operators create products, packages and business. The product will often be the package, the brochure the goods on the shelf.

Secondary tourist trades are sometimes defined as those selling to the tourist supplier and not directly to the visitors. These include a whole range of providers to hotels, transport organisations and visitor attrac-tions, from the farmers, food providers, builders, bankers, laundries and public utilities, in short all the goods and services needed for the resident community.

The retail shopping trade has a larger share of overseas visitor spend-ing in Britain than any other single sector, larger even than accommoda-tion or transport. However, the spending is heavily concentrated on tourist centres. The great bulk of the retail trade is outside the tourist industry. Shopping is a tourist attraction in its own right. The souvenir business, often regarded with little favour, is enormously important. The trade can introduce foreigners to local and national products, and return-ing visitors' travellers' tales, the free harbinger of international market-ing, eases the difficult and expensive task of breaking into foreign mar-kets. But, generally speaking, the tourist is not well served. For a trade that lives by selling, its horizon is local, and not international. Visi-tors want to buy local products, but there are too many stories of imported goods replacing local crafts.

This is a field for new marketing endeavour, and new enterprise, and a matter of interest to both the public and private sector and to all the primary tourist service and trading sectors.

Summary

The tourist service trades provide the visitor with his essential needs. Primary trades include transport, accommodation, catering and visitor servicing (including travel agencies) and specialist activities for visitors (eg entertainment) in tourist resorts.

Secondary trades range from shops, personal services (banking, laundry) and a wide spectrum of trades and services supplying or supporting tourist enterprises (eg building, utilities, professional services). There must be cooperative activity between the trades as well as competition. They are interdependent as well as independent of each other. This broad division can only be indicative since inclusion of businesses in the tourism category depends on the incidence of tourism, and the proportion of total trade with visitors. Thus in resort areas a majority of trades may be tourist trades.

The primary trades can be subdivided into separate industries often in competition. Much accommodation and transport is provided on a private basis. In fact only a minority of visitors stay in commercial hotels. Public sector services and voluntary institutions play an important role. A clear understanding of statistical and market research sources is necessary and rewarding. As the product has an important and perishable time element, measures of use (load factors) and occupancy rates are vital. The marketer must study the component industries sector by sector and take account of market segmentation.

Destination interests have an important role to play in providing a cooperative marketing forum at the city, resort and regional level. Massive public sector investment, notably in transport, may be accompanied by state control and the establishment of an imperfect market regulated by state intervention, a common practice in public transport. Generally speaking the tourist can be better served by the travel distributive trades. There is a great field for marketing endeavour and new enterprise.

Reference

1 Burkart, A J, and Medlik, S, *Tourism: Past, Present and Future,* 2nd edition. Heinemann. London 1981 p 159.

3 The marketing concept

Marketing is not a precise science. There are too many variables for that. Neither is it an art. Marketing is concerned with research which is the foundation for organised planning; with accounting which measures the success of the marketer's skills and enterprise and with the purchase of raw materials and adding value to those materials. So marketing is concerned with production and pricing and promotion and not least profits. The marketer is concerned with the coordination of the roles of experts, each in their field. The marketer is like the impresario, who brings together experts in design and scene building, lighting and choreography, singers and dancers. Marketing is the concern of the whole organisation – the entire executive hierarchy. Above all, marketing is common sense applied to a coordinating function. The success of all marketing operations depends on the effective and efficient coordination of all those elements which it embraces and all those tools which are at the disposal of the marketer.

It is also an attitude of mind of the management of an organisation. The marketer should have a large say in the goods which are produced, the prices charged, the way they are distributed, and he is, of course, responsible for promoting and selling them at a profit.

Unless the organisation has knowingly accepted the marketing concept it is unlikely that the marketer will be able to influence those areas of the operation which are outside his immediate control. The marketing oriented organisation on the other hand ensures that marketing is involved in all the operations – from the process of creating the product to consumption by the ultimate consumer.

For a long time marketing was regarded as an art practised by those with intuitive judgement or hunch, often based on years of experience which, when successful, was hailed as inspiration but when a failure, was written off as bad judgement. There was a period when marketers were inclined to the view that all decisions had a scientific basis, that research was the panacea and analysis an end in itself. Research techniques and theoretical concepts were quickly developed and just as quickly went out of fashion, only to be replaced by others. It is true that marketing must use scientific theories and techniques: the behavioural sciences, statistics and modelling, logic and analysis. Yet the interaction of the variables, the complexity of the consumer, the dynamics of the marketplace, make it quite impossible to bring scientific precision to bear on the marketing problem. A scientific approach in marketing can never be exact or precise. There is never a single right answer to a marketing problem.

Research can certainly help to indicate the right solution and so guide the marketer to do a better job. No research can be completely accurate but if the marketer is able to reduce the odds research is worthwhile; if it helps him in analysing the problem it has played a crucial role. Nonetheless, risk is an integral part of marketing, creativity is an essential part of marketing, intuition is vital. The marketer uses scientific techniques and theories to try to minimise that risk through careful analysis and planning. The marketer is guided towards his decision, possibly using a computer model, but at the end of the day the most sophisticated models can never be perfect and are only as good as the data put into them. No matter how much science is invested in the marketing decision process, there remains an ultimate need for intuitive judgement, for creativity, for art. Science can very often only tell you how much you don't know. Art is a creative activity and aims to change the world. So does marketing. That is why it is neither science nor art but rather a blend of both.

So marketing is comprehensive coordination, part science and part art; scientific yet creative and above all dynamic. It is not easy to define so complex a concept precisely. Definitions have depended on where the marketer stood in the operational spectrum – as a theoretician or a practitioner.

The American Management Association uses the following definition: 'Marketing is the management function which organises and directs all those business activities involved in assessing and converting customer purchasing power into effective demand for a specific product or service and in moving the product or service to the final customer or user so as to achieve the profit target or other objectives set by the company'.

There are other more succinct definitions – that marketing is concerned with providing the right product at the right price in the right place and the right time. The Committee of Marketing Organisations in Britain (COMO) defines marketing as 'the management process responsible for identifying, anticipating and satisfying customer requirements profitably' and goes on to suggest that marketing consists of 'two essential and inter-related elements:

(a)   a concept which focuses the company at all levels upon meeting the identified and anticipated requirements of customers as indicated in the definition above, and . . .

(b)   a range of techniques which assist the company in determining customer requirements and meeting these'.

Theodore Levitt said: 'selling focuses on the need of the seller' . . . that marketing is concerned 'with the idea of satisfying the needs of the customer by means of the product and a whole cluster of things associated with creating, delivering and finally consuming it'.[1]

Perhaps the best definition is that devised by Philip Kotler, Professor of Marketing at Northwestern University, in his book 'Marketing Management – analysis, planning and control'. He claims that 'marketing is the analysing, organising, planning and controlling of the firm's customer impinging resources, policies and activities with a view to satisfying the needs and wants of chosen customer groups at a profit'.[2]

In this one statement Kotler underlines the comprehensive coordination role, embraces the scientific aspects of analysis, planning and control, the need for organisation of the marketing function, the concept of market segmentation ('chosen customer groups') and the marketing mix ('customer – impinging resources, policies and activities'). Above all it suggests that the customer is king: it is the customer's needs and wants which have to be satisfied. Customer satisfaction is the keystone of marketing; attention to customer needs is the basis of product development, product presentation and the lodestone in guiding the marketer into the right techniques in reaching the customer. A marketing organisation sees things through the customer's eyes, the product, the advertising, the promotion, the print.

Marketing is an organisational attitude of mind as well as a function within the organisation; an attitude of mind where all members of an organisation try to look at their role in terms of the customer and customer satisfaction and are prepared to adapt to changes in the marketplace.

While marketing has a comprehensive coordinating role in the business it does not, and should not, take over all the management functions. This is an extreme position which will undoubtedly lead to a great deal of antagonism and an uncooperative attitude from colleagues. Sufficient that customer satisfaction should permeate the corporate thinking at every level. This is particularly important in mass consumer markets. There will be a different emphasis in capital goods type selling. Thus marketing should be a functional activity, a coordinator and an attitude of mind for the whole organisation.

This single minded approach to marketing which Kotler commends certainly would make sense in an hotel group. Indeed, it can be best seen in an hotel, where most of the departments interface with the customer, where customer wants and needs are the key to the operation and where customer satisfaction provided at a profit is the recipe for success. Segmentation can also be clearly demonstrated in an hotel – the business traveller, the leisure traveller, the convention delegate, the guest at a banquet or a function. All have their different wants and needs, and all these needs must be satisfied profitably for the hotel to succeed. Certainly, customer satisfaction should be an objective for the whole organisation from kitchen porter to chef, from chambermaid to housekeeper, receptionist to general manager.

All very well – but does it, can it work for a tourist destination? Is marketing a product not very different from marketing a country or even a resort? Consideration of the history of Britain's spas and some British seaside resorts will demonstrate what Theodore Levitt called 'marketing myopia'. In his classic essay on the subject he claims that 'every major industry was once a growth industry but many decline simply because they fail to look to satisfying the wants and needs of the consumer'. They fail to recognise what business they were in. He cites a number of examples – the American railroads and the Hollywood film industry. 'The railroads did not stop growing because the need for passenger and freight transportation declined. That grew. The railroads are in trouble today not because the need was filled by others (cars, trucks, airplanes, even telephones) but because it was not filled by the railroads themselves' and he concludes that 'they assumed themselves to be in the railroad business rather than in the transportation business . . . they were product-oriented instead of customer-oriented'.[3] Similarly he demonstrates how Hollywood was almost killed off because it defined its business incorrectly. 'It thought it was in the movie business when it was actually in the entertainment business.'[4] Hollywood in the early days of the medium set its face against television instead of recognising it as a new opportunity rather than a threat. Detroit's motor industry with all their research budgets almost failed to recognise that customer wants and needs were changing until it lost millions of dollars worth of business to the manufacturers of small cars. They allowed Volkswagen to take their market. Detroit was researching the wrong thing and concentrating on customer preferences between those lines and models which it had already decided to offer, rather than going back to basic needs.

In Britain after the 1939–45 war the railways were nationalised. At that time they owned the biggest hotel chain, British Transport Hotels, Thomas Cook, Dean and Dawson and Pickfords (the top travel operators) as well as a shipping line. British Transport Hotels was the only chain not to build anew during the great 1970s boom. Now they have all gone their separate ways because the public sector management failed to find their way in deciding what business they were in.

Britain's resorts and spas lost their way too. By the middle of the seventeenth century spas like Bath were beginning to be popular among sick people seeking a cure and over the next century Bath's popularity grew apace, rapidly accelerating as a result of royal patronage. Fashion is a key motivator. The curative properties of the water were not a new discovery – the Roman baths are testimony to this. It was rather the rediscovery by leaders of society which brought with it the development plans for the ancillary entertainment complex – the pleasure domes of yesteryear. Beau Nash brilliantly exploited the resort, for that is what it had become in the first half of the eighteenth century, as master of ceremonies and organising genius.

The product was a smart watering place patronised by royalty and the beau monde, and others sought to emulate the success of Bath. The 'me too' plagiarists existed even then. The original reasons for the visit were perhaps lost sight of as the entertainment complexes and the divertissements grew apace but the product was the promotion. Fortunately, and not least because of fashion following royal patronage, people did want to visit the spa town for the resources that it offered, or perhaps they went simply because it was fashionable to do so.

Success was shortlived. Seaside resorts became fashionable and the development of the railways considerably helped to increase their popularity. Sea bathing became the fashion and the popularity of the inland spa towns waned. The coastal resorts in their turn declined in popularity as air travel became cheaper and seaside holidays with 'guaranteed' sunshine became a reality. Yet the marketers of many British resorts continued to promote in advertisements and in posters, in brochures and guide books, a product-oriented resource. They lost their way because they failed to find out what the wants and needs of the customer were; they were product oriented instead of customer oriented.

A new generation of resort marketers began to ask 'who are the potential customers and what are their wants and needs?' They had the courage and the conviction. Markets were segmented and researched, feasibility studies carried out, new products developed, old products restored and revitalised, and they are succeeding. Others, still selling only bucket and spade holidays, will surely fail and wither away.

Scheveningen, the Dutch North Sea spa town, could well have withered away but instead the Steigenberger Kurhaus Hotel redevelopment and reopening in 1979 marked the beginning of a new era in the history of this famous resort, which has had so many changes of direction in its short history. In 1818 Jacob Pronk built a wooden bathhouse and in 1828 the town opened a municipal bathhouse which was later enlarged and remodelled. A few years later the splendid Kurhaus bath hotel was opened only to be destroyed by fire two successful seasons later. It was rebuilt and the resort prospered – the Kurhauszaal became a popular international music centre attracting the great orchestras of the day. After the war the Kurhaus installed central heating to provide all year round bathing (one of the first controlled climate leisure complexes?) and the Kurhauszaal became the centrepiece of the Holland Festival. Just as British resorts reeled from the competition of the Mediterranean and Adriatic resorts, so did Scheveningen and in 1972 the Kurhaus was forced to close. Phoenix-like it has risen from the ashes again with a leisure complex – indoor pool with wave machine, saunas, solariums, gymnasium and a casino. Scheveningen has been reborn as an all year round resort, taking advantage of the new wants and needs of the customer and his preoccupation with health and fitness.

Thistle Hotels opened a leisure club at their Gosforth Park Hotel in Newcastle-upon-Tyne in 1981. They recognised the new potential and developed new markets best illustrated by the growth in weekend occupancy patterns. In November 1980 Friday/Saturday occupancy was forty-seven per cent and in November 1981 it was eighty-two per cent. In February 1981, Friday/Saturday occupancy was forty-four per cent and in February 1982 this had been increased to eighty-nine per cent. Since then many hotels have followed suit and the new generation of hotels in this country are being developed with leisure facilities, and many older ones have been redeveloped to include leisure centres.

Increasingly, resort tourist officers and national tourist offices are turning away from the product to the potential visitor to the destination. The product increasingly is being developed to meet the wants and needs of the potential visitor.

A resort tourist office, and even more so a national tourist office, is in many ways not able to embrace the marketing concept totally. There are some important fundamental differences between marketing a tourist destination and marketing consumer goods or services. These differences need to be recognised and addressed in their different ways.

The marketer of a resort, city or country has no control over the brand name. When Ford failed with the Edzel or the Classic models they were able to drop the brand name and neither has been resurrected. The brand name of the British Tourist Authority's product is Britain. It cannot be changed. What can and must be protected is the brand image. A tourist office must be constantly vigilant in ensuring that the brand image attaching to the name is the best possible and that, if the image does become tarnished, steps are taken immediately to correct the situation. Protection of the image is a key role for a national tourist office, but the organisation must also be the 'patron' of the product, and directly concerned with product development.

On the other hand resorts and regions *can* be branded and this will serve to distinguish them from someone else's products. In time the brand will become a valuable asset. There are many examples of branding in tourism – the Cote d'Azur in France, the Costa del Sol in Spain, the English Riviera (Torbay Tourist Board) in England, Surfers' Paradise in Australia. To survive though the brand must be 'protected' by ensuring consistent quality and value.

Standards, strategies for growth, product initiation and innovation, and the establishment of partnerships and new enterprise are all part of the destination tourist organisation's job, notably by the provision of a focal point for the doers to pursue the necessary collective, as well as their own competitive trading. In their formative years the famous resorts of Britain and Europe achieved this difficult task with great distinction. Blackpool knew it should create a cheerful, bright, breezy, zestful and gregarious place. Eastbourne was grander and sedate, and Frinton quiet. Never did nor should the Frinton man meet the Blackpool man.

A tourist office can rarely research a consumer need and then develop a product from scratch. To a very large extent the product is inherited – the climate, geography, history, culture and traditions. It can be modified and the infrastructure can be developed. Above all it can be presented in an appealing and appetising way through themes, specially created events, or simply by making it easier for the consumer to buy.

The major strategy areas are product, price, promotion and market place. Yet the national tourist office has little control over product as we have seen, and in most countries no control over prices charged either. There is a considerable influencing role through its marketing resources as well as in product development and especially in product presentation, and to some extent in pricing policies as well through its advisory committee structure (see chapter 14).

The resort tourist officer is often responsible for entertainment, catering and in some cases conference facilities and so does have some control over price, depending on the delegated authority vested in him by his local authority. Municipalities have substantial powers to invest, to plan, to lay down strategy, to form trading partnerships and to trade on their own. They have a vital role to play and have often failed in recent years in Britain to seize their opportunities, to have vision for the future and the confidence to embark on restoration and rejuvenation to meet changing needs. Their tide of prosperity has waned, often through their own lack of necessary municipal leadership and enterprise. They own many attractions and entertainments, sporting facilities (swimming pools, tennis courts, golf courses, leisure and health centres), parks and gardens, piers and ballrooms, theatres, conference centres and many other facilities. Brighton is an outstanding example of saving its future, which at one stage looked most unpromising, by foresight, confident investment in a major conference centre, marina, hotels and skilful planning and marketing.

The tourist resort is theatrical, as indeed is tourism by its very nature. An attractive resort is the stage, the basis of the product, but there has to be a show, with skilled impresarios and performers. This demands a key marketing role. The resort offers capacity and shelter and indoor accommodation for large groups when an increasing number of people want to travel more frequently. There is a vast community, often ageing, frustrated, bored and lonely needing new activity in this mobile and leisure age. They need amusing all year round. This should be the age of the resort.

The national tourist officer can have only minimal control over channels of distribution, but depending on the market characteristics and segmentation analyses, he can have a powerful influencing role without becoming involved in the selling arena.

Finally, where the national tourist office is government funded, budgets are not ultimately determined by the agency and in some cases this has given rise to stop–go marketing policies, changes in direction and enforced cuts which have not been in the long term interests of the country. They have invariably been achieved at the cost of a loss in brand share. This is very clearly illustrated in the histogram which demonstrates how Britain, through consistent and persistent marketing in the USA, has overtaken France and Italy. Both were ahead of Britain in tourism dollar earnings. By 1985 Britain earned more than France and Italy combined. Alas, Britain has lost share since then.

Table 3.1 – Britain: now biggest earner in Europe from US travel

		1960
Switzerland	$53,000,000	
West Germany	$83,000,000	
Britain	$116,000,000	
France	$118,000,000	
Italy	$122,000,000	

		1967
Switzerland	$67,000,000	
West Germany	$104,000,000	
France	$119,000,000	
Italy	$148,000,000	
Britain	$190,000,000	

		1970
Switzerland	$99,000,000	
West Germany	$126,000,000	
France	$169,000,000	
Italy	$178,000,000	
Britain	$334,000,000	

		1975
Spain	$135,000,000	
West Germany	$174,000,000	
Italy	$194,000,000	
France	$226,000,000	
Britain	$404,000,000	

		1980
Spain	$173,000,000	
West Germany	$322,000,000	
Italy	$360,000,000	
France	$383,000,000	
Britain	$903,000,000	

		1985
Switzerland	$369,000,000	
Italy	$619,000,000	
West Germany	$672,000,000	
France	$770,000,000	
Britain	$1,645,000,000	

Source: US Department of Commerce.

Furthermore, while a commercial organisation is very often required to secure an immediate return on investment, a national tourist office should be the trail blazer in developing new markets, new segments and new techniques, where the trade will follow once the missionary work has been done. The return on investment is in the longer term and marketing in these conditions becomes something of an act of faith, difficult to measure in the short term. It is important though that marketing budgets fully take this need into account, both at the stage of compilation of budgets and allocation by market and segment.

Nevertheless, the marketing concept can and must be embraced by all organisations engaged in tourism, whether they are commercial or governmental. Tourism is a demand force, not a single industry. The principles of marketing apply and good marketing must be the goal of well led management teams and an attitude of mind. Marketing concerns itself with what customers want and are prepared to buy and this is as vital to a tourist office as it is to a commercial organisation.

Summary

Marketing is neither pure science nor pure art. It is common sense applied to a coordinating function, involving all the operations from the creation of the product to consumption by the ultimate customer. Marketing is a range of techniques which are concerned with identifying consumer needs and meeting them. Customer satisfaction is the keystone of marketing and the marketing oriented organisation sees things through the eyes of the consumer. Marketing is a functional activity, a multi-faceted discipline requiring many skills. It should also be the common purpose of all departments in an organisation.

References

1 Levitt, T, *1964 Modern Marketing Strategy*, edited Bursk and Chapman. The New English Library Ltd, p 35.
2 Kotler, P, *1967 Marketing Management*, Prentice Hall Inc p 12.
3 Levitt, T, *ibid.* p 24.
4 Levitt, T, *ibid* p 25.

4 Market research

The broadest definition of market research is the systematic collection of information about supply and demand in tourism to guide the formulation of policies, strategies and plans for those concerned with the management of tourism interests, including government. Research is an essential advisory function but its value will depend on clear instruction from managers on the information needed.

To some extent, in view of the wide range of tourism interests, much economic and social research will be involved. The four general categories listed for statistics in tourism apply also to research in general:

1. Measurement: traffic volume and expenditure. Forecasts and potential estimates.
2. The product: resources in plant, facilities and attractions, existing and potential. Occupancy and load factors are involved in resource analysis as they are in effectiveness tests.
3. Market analysis including segmentation and motivation.
4. Performance. Appraisals of marketing effectiveness and review of product. Both supply and demand should be subject to performance against objective tests.

There is a mass of information at both national and international levels, which is sometimes unused or misinterpreted. Governments, trade bodies and large organisations can make a great deal of useful information available. So the first task of the researcher is desk research, collecting available information and presenting this in a useful form for management and operations. This will involve analysis and interpretation.

The best research and usually the most accurate is understandable, free from jargon, confusing econometric equations or theoretical diagrams, which do not guide the action. Communication is fundamental in marketing. This means above all else being understood, but the requirement works in both directions. Researchers must be given a clear brief. In some cases their task will be to prove a hypothesis, to confirm the marketers' inspired judgement about market movements. The competent manager will know a great deal about his business (usually more than the researchers). There is, of course, a field for academic, institutional and theoretical research, which deserves and often gets industry support, but market research is above all action orientated.

Desk research must start with the basic measurement function – monitoring trends and checking short and long term forecasts which will be important elements in both market and production planning. To an extent these go together, and the time scale can be similar. Tourism is essentially market orientated so the production plans must be firmly market based.

Traffic flow measurement

The first task is to measure and monitor traffic flows and expenditures both at national and regional levels and relate these to the specific interest. This may be a destination, a product or a service, for example, hotels or transport. For many interests an international scale may be important.

Primary information is generally provided on a national basis by governments, state tourist organisations, supplemented by national institutions, regional and local authorities and industry. In Britain the principal source of regular information on international travel is the International Passenger Survey (IPS) carried out for the Department of Employment by the Government Statistical Service. The results are published regularly in the Business Monitor and monthly press reports are issued by the Department. The survey is probably the most complete regular measurement of international traffic flows of any country in the world, covering movement into and out of the country, broken down by country of residence, and with estimates of expenditure both by foreign visitors and British residents travelling abroad. Although the figures are often reported as visitors they represent visits ie one person making one journey into and out of the country. Multiple visits are important to researchers and to the trade. Clearly, a considerable part of the flow out of the country by residents is made up of frequent travellers. Traffic statistics are based on country of residence and not nationality, an important consideration in marketing. For example as much as ten per cent of 'American visitors to Britain' are not American citizens. There are a large number of British expatriates coming home for business and pleasure and to see family and friends. Similarly in Germany the British forces are counted as residents of Germany. The survey's figures are based on interviews within a stratified random sample of passengers leaving the United Kingdom on the principal sea and air routes.

Travellers passing through the immigration controls are randomly selected for interview. In 1987 some 175,000 interviews were made, so that the survey is a large continuous exercise. Day visitors are included provided they get off the ship, but migrants and other non 'tourists' are excluded. The results report visits, length of stay and expenditure, main purpose of visit and mode of transport. Useful seasonal information is available by month and by quarter.

An indication of the comprehensive range of the information can be

Table 4.1 – International tourism volume and value

YEARLY TRENDS OF INTERNATIONAL TOURISM TO THE UK							
AREA OF ORIGIN			PURPOSE OF VISIT				TOTAL
Western Europe	English speaking	Rest of the world	Holiday	Business/ Conference	Friends or relatives	Other reasons	Visits
TRIPS MILLIONS							
1978	7.87	3.07	1.71	5.88	2.30	2.19	2.28	12.65
1979	7.87	2.84	1.77	5.53	2.40	2.25	2.31	12.49
1980	7.91	2.72	1.80	5.48	2.57	2.32	2.06	12.42
1981	7.06	2.61	1.79	5.04	2.45	2.29	1.68	11.45
1982	7.08	2.70	1.85	5.27	2.39	2.41	1.57	11.64
1983	7.16	3.39	1.91	5.82	2.56	2.56	1.53	12.46
1984	7.55	4.06	2.03	6.39	2.86	2.63	1.77	13.64
1985	7.87	4.50	2.08	6.67	3.01	2.88	1.89	14.45
1986	8.35	3.54	2.00	5.92	3.29	2.95	1.75	13.90
1987	9.32	4.18	2.07	6.83	3.56	3.18	2.00	15.57
1988	9.67	4.04	2.09	6.68	4.10	3.16	1.85	15.80
NIGHTS MILLIONS							
1978	72	46	31	63	16	36	35	149
1979	75	45	35	63	15	37	39	155
1980	73	41	32	58	17	38	33	146
1981	65	38	33	56	15	35	29	135
1982	65	39	32	57	15	37	27	136
1983	67	45	32	61	15	40	28	145
1984	69	52	34	67	17	41	29	154
1985	74	58	35	70	18	46	33	167
1986	75	50	33	63	19	45	31	158
1987	86	56	36	73	19	50	36	178
1988	86	52	35	68	24	48	33	173
SPENDING £ MILLIONS							
1978	1,054	710	743	1,139	530	378	432	2,507
1979	1,207	730	860	1,235	600	415	544	2,797
1980	1,248	740	973	1,258	735	457	508	2,961
1981	1,114	801	1.055	1,276	763	442	484	2,970
1982	1,161	907	1,119	1,386	794	484	518	3,188
1983	1,400	1,272	1,331	1,711	961	639	687	4,003
1984	1,563	1,642	1,409	2,052	1,091	706	759	4,614
1985	1,822	2,089	1,531	2,379	1,293	853	908	5,442
1986	2,207	1,848	1,498	2,228	1,552	844	917	5,553
1987	2,551	2,176	1,533	2,695	1,644	910	1,001	6,260
1988	2,532	2,025	1,528	2,447	1,826	903	898	6,085

Source: International Passenger Survey, Department of Employment.
Area of origin of visitors is defined by their country of residence; 'English Speaking' are those resident in Australia, Canada, New Zealand, South Africa and the USA. BTA Annual Report for 1988/89.

seen in table 4.1 from the BTA Annual Report for the financial year covering 1988/89.

Since the survey has been in operation for a number of years there is now a good time series for analysis of trends, market variations, and comparisons with other countries to indicate market share. The sample is capable of considerable analysis, and from time to time it is possible to add questions to investigate other features, such as accommodation used or regional spread, showing movement to regions of Britain which is part of the national tourism strategy. Information on key market segments, travel for conferences or visits to exhibitions for example, can also be measured. In many cases information gathered over a considerable field of interest even if infrequent can provide useful and practical supplementary information. The statistics will in any case provide a base for many supplementary surveys by institutions. Complementary enquiries by foreign countries (the USA and some European countries) can offer useful checks and additions.

There are few statistical series on an international basis. Primary sources are in the majority of cases countries or national governments. A number of international organisations publish useful compilations of national series providing helpful comparisons for international market analysis. However since the data is on an individual country basis, the figures are not always strictly comparable. But order of magnitude information can be used by skilled researchers in marketing planning.

There are two principal sources. Firstly, the World Tourist Organisation, which normally publishes annually, but with a considerable time lag, the *Regional Breakdown of World Travel and Tourism Statistics*. This covers most countries in the world, in a time series (ie four years) by geographic region and by country, arrivals and/or tourist 'days', receipts and expenditures by region, accommodation capacity, but with a limited commentary on trends. Secondly, the Organisation for Economic Cooperation and Development (OECD) produces an annual report, usually in September each year. *Tourism Policy and International Tourism*. This is one of the most professional of international studies, and essential for the researcher, as it covers the twenty-four leading tourism countries, the industrialised world, responsible for over eighty per cent of world travel, both as receiving and originating countries.

A full commentary on tourism trends accompanies detailed tables giving data on the principal generating markets in terms of expenditure, arrivals or tourist 'nights'. Useful information is given in real prices thus making comparison easier and more accurate. There is much additional data of considerable value, on capacity, length of stay, occupancy, international fare payments, trends in tourism prices, and transport. There is also data on formalities (visas etc) and currency controls which may affect traffic flows.

The European Community has in recent years devoted more time to tourism studies. These include *Europeans and Their Holidays*, a survey conducted in March and April 1986 in the twelve countries of the European Community. This gives considerable detail which can be put to good use in marketing, but with the limitation that it is restricted by sample size and is not a continuing enquiry, so like a synoptic chart it gives a static picture and no trend indication. Detail covers numbers on holiday makers by country, frequency (and reasons for not going away amongst the non-holiday takers), socio-economic data (age, occupation), location, description of main holiday (time, place type, transport used, accommodation, booking patterns etc). This survey provides international comparison, original material, and much socio-economic data which can be used in market planning, including some motivation material. The study repays attention as it represents a move forward on an international basis from straightforward measurement to creative market research.

The second EC study entitled *The Tourism Industry and the Tourism Policies of the Twelve Member States of the Community*[1] has something in common with the OECD annual work, except that it is as yet a 'one off'. However, since the Working Group of the National Tourist Organisations of the EC had previously published similar studies[2] on a two year time interval, there is a basis for trend study.

This is principally an economic and statistical enquiry, but has practical value in policy and strategic planning. Since tourism is all about marketing, demand trends must be the basis for this. Interesting data is given on job generation by categories of tourism spending, receipts in relation to Gross Domestic Product and more relevant in promotional terms, expenditure on international tourism by the member countries as a percentage of (private) final consumption. Trend information of this kind can be an important ingredient in forecasting and studies of market potential. Tourism and the balance of payments is dealt with fully, notably its 'distributive' effects ie reducing the imbalances and relationships to standards of living etc. The study contains an interesting examination of national tourism policies (or lack of them) and the treatment of promotion at home and abroad and intervention in policy 'priority' areas such as social, cultural and rural tourism.

Although the data is very limited in this field it has a special importance in the public sector which is responsible for massive infrastructure spending, and essential promotional spending, which may unwisely be too little in relation to the overall plan and either not linked or linked in too indirect a fashion to changing demand trends. For this reason some of the social tourism agencies, which flourished in the first part of the century, have gone out of business in recent years. Yet strangely the social entrepreneurs in the earlier days of the holiday movement (The Workers Travel Association and its counterparts in European countries) had a firm grasp on the market place and their special relationship to it. They were very businesslike in going about their good works and kept in close touch with the needs and aspirations of their 'customers'. Their successors sometimes forgot the dictates of this specialist market and suffered accordingly.

Other international bodies, regional groupings such as the European Travel Commission (ETC), and trade sectors such as the International Air Transport Association (IATA) and the International Hotel Association (IHA) often produce important series of statistics or reports in depth on traffic flows and market segments. For example IATA's detailed traffic analysis gives early indication of trends, reporting within three months on traffic counts and regional movements. The intercontinental flows are especially relevant to the international marketer. ETC studies often deal with key market segments for example, senior citizens. Over a period of years ETC has published much information on American travel to Europe, including motivation, examining these important movements in depth and offering a mine of information for market analysis of long term trends, and future forecasts.

Increasingly the major countries carry out regular surveys or publish reports of their international travel movement. Some years ago the European Travel Commission recommended to the OECD that statistical systems should be based on inward and outward sample surveys, on a compatible basis, to overcome the deficiencies of traffic counts obtained as a byproduct of frontier controls. As governments responded to the pressures of mass movement, controls have been simplified and formalities either abolished or reduced to limited checks with a corresponding reduction in paper work and statistics. The following examples illustrate the substantial amount of data available for research purposes. In many cases the replacement of the old system by tailor-made surveys has resulted in a higher quality and wider range of information. Surveys often provide socio-economic detail, and offer possibilities of covering special subjects or specific segments from time to time.

The United States Travel and Tourism Administration produces reports on international tourism affecting the USA covering travel to and from the USA. The US Passport Office and the US Immigration and Naturalization Service also provide statistics of travel movement which can often help in market research studies.

In his report *Europeans on Holiday*[3] Professor R Medlik listed a number of travel and holiday surveys in the principal Western European countries. These included Austria, Belgium, Denmark, Finland, France, Germany, Ireland, Italy, Netherlands, Norway, Portugal, Spain, Sweden, Switzerland, and the United Kingdom. Most of these are published on a regular basis, though not all annually, and all are official or officially recognised.

The most sophisticated (and in many ways similar) are the German

Holiday Travel Analysis *(Reiseanalyse)* and the British National Travel Survey which has been carried out for a considerable number of years by the British Tourist Authority.

These surveys have a special value as they cover the domestic holiday (or in some cases the total travel market). A comparison of outward flows can supplement the data collected nationally on the inward movement. Usually the surveys are a much improved basis for market analysis as they will report in considerable detail (socio-economic information, place of residence, purpose of visit, expenditure and detail of trips taken).

The German Survey covers holidays of five days or more away from home, but there is also information on short trips of two to four days, and holiday intentions for the coming year based on a stratified sample of 6,000 individuals. Residents under fourteen years of age and aliens are excluded.

The British National Travel Survey[4] covers holiday trips of four nights or more away from home, by resident adult population (over sixteen years old). Data is also collected on trips abroad of one night or more. The data is drawn from a two stage stratified sample of a basic 3,000 and a supplementary random sample of 4,800.

Since 1985 this study has been merged with the British Home Tourism Survey[5] to give a more detailed picture of the domestic movement. This is a continuous enquiry with interviewing every month. It is a survey on trips taken away from home of one night or more. The survey provides the following information: month the trip started; nights away from home; purpose of trip (including business as well as holiday); regions visited in Britain; accommodation used; number in travelling party; expenditure on trip; mode of transport; trips taken in previous two months.

It will be seen that the British National Travel Survey, now carried out annually by the joint British Tourist Authority/English Tourist Board Research Department, is one of the most complete of its kind in the world, with very detailed data for market researchers. Major interests in Britain's travel and tourism industries support the annual survey and make good use of its findings. The appendix to this chapter gives extracts from the survey to indicate the scope and value of the data.

Inventory of resources

The researcher's first task is to ensure that there is a satisfactory inventory of resources and services for the destination. This is needed on the national, regional and resort or town scale. In fact if marketing is on an international basis, for example, Europe or the Caribbean, then the resource charting must reflect this larger destination area. There are a number of resource classifications. The principal elements should be simple and practical, since the product records will be used as the basis for the product market fit exercises which are the foundation of the marketing programmes.

First, note the natural resources: landscape (scenery, mountains, forest, water, river, sea and beaches). Secondly, list the man-made resources: cities, towns, resorts and spas; cultural amenities – historic buildings, archeology, museums and art galleries, the performing arts (theatre and music); sporting provision, spectator and participatory. Thirdly, examine the tourist service trades: accommodation (subdivided into principal types according to the destination area, ie hotels, guest houses, hostels, apartments, camping and caravan sites etc); transport, again subdivided into principal forms, road, rail, sea, air; specialist recreation or visitor facilities – leisure centres, theme parks, marinas, special interest provision which may be in the educational, health or even religious fields (pilgrim locations).

Product analysis is considered in detail in chapter 5. The mapping or charting must be quantified and classified by type or standard. Furthermore, measurement must take account of seasonal flows. It is estimated that the total capacity of Europe's tourist facilities do not reach fifty per cent occupancy over the year. In other words, more than half of total capacity is unused or in economic terms wasted. This has important operating, economic and financial implications, for unlike physical manufacturing the tourist product cannot be stored. A hotel 'overnight' unused is gone for ever. Revenue cannot be regained but costs continue.

Occupancy and load factors in transport are usually well measured. In Britain the Tourist Boards publish regular reports on hotel occupancy which offer the researcher a great deal of information about the market as well as the product. However, from the resource point of view, and the task of marketing planning, current capacity and its variation over the year is a key factor. Using time series, it is also necessary to know past trends and future forecasts indicating potentials. It may take the suppliers some years to expand capacity where necessary, but it will take as long in many cases to promote new traffic and exploit potentials. In the great hotel building boom from 1970 to 1974 Britain's (and London's) total stock of 'international' standard hotel accommodation ie rooms with bath, doubled through new building. Some 62,000 additional beds were provided. In fact it takes longer to double the market and especially if the market is international and subject to many competitive and other pressures. History shows that, for a variety of reasons, the traffic to Britain did not grow as expected, and the hotel companies experienced a very difficult post 'boom' time.

Tourism although described as an 'invisible' export or service industry with major manpower requirements, is also a heavy infrastructure user.

Airports and planes, ports and ships, roads and road vehicles and facilities, hotel and other accommodation buildings, conference and exhibition halls, entertainment and sporting centres. There are special needs. Firstly, there must be a degree of coordination in expansion by the interests. This is not made easy by the fact that public and private sector development is involved and interdependent, although decision makers may be in competition or disagreement. Currently London is facing a threatened future hotel accommodation shortage. A study for the BTA and the ETB[6] forecast a shortfall of 50,000 beds by the year 2000 if current traffic trends continue.

A key characteristic in tourism development is the uneven 'lumpy' nature of plant and infrastructure growth. There are boom periods for aviation expansion, hotel and resort development. There are many examples of rapid growth when investment in travel or leisure facilities becomes fashionable. There was a period when bowling alleys sprang up all over Britain. Many, very quickly, fell by the wayside. More recently and all over Europe, marinas, water sports, and conference centres have seen massive investment. In these cases substantial long term capital is required, and in many cases public sector support is also needed. The market researcher should play an important role in these developments, since tourism must be market and not product based so far as the future is concerned. The supply and demand equation requires great skill and vision in matching market trends to destination situations.

Planning involves a careful appraisal of what exists, what products are being sold, and can be sold and estimates of potential in relation to national and international markets. The strategies will need to take into account very fully time factors in both construction of physical services and the creation of new or extended markets.

There will be a number of options, with different cost benefit situations. The destination authorities and interests must professionally and objectively examine these options and decide clearly what objectives should be pursued. In other words what kind of tourism is sought, how much and on what time scale. Whatever objectives are chosen there will be a longer term commitment to pursue the agreed strategy and related plans in development and marketing consistently for some years – at the very least three to five.

Market research, analysis, motivation, segmentation

Again, the researcher's first task is desk research, using the regular official and industry statistical series, market intelligence and business information to examine the principal characteristics of the market or markets concerned, and the short and long term trends. The seeds of the future are inevitably in the current movements, so historic patterns which throw light on how we have reached the present position in the markets development are important.

The first basic analysis is concerned with measurement, a full factual description, size in terms of number of visits, purpose of visit, length of stay, period of visit (season) and means of transport. These broad measurements need points of reference, for example, a comparison with world or wider regional figures (in Europe, national figures compared with regional figures). Visitors should then be described in basic socio-economic terms, age, sex, income, occupation, education, family circumstances etc. The national statistics will need breaking down by geographic market, such as North America or Europe, with the major countries analysed separately. Country and place of residence are the dominating characteristics, not nationality, although it may be useful to have nationality information in addition.

There are other important quantitative aspects to be identified before exploring the qualitative elements, such as frequency of travel, type of travel arrangements, eg package tours, organised independent visits, method and time of booking or reservation details. Expenditures will need careful examination not only in total but broken down into separate services (accommodation by type, meals, activities). Details of behaviour, attractions, places visited, will repay surveying in detail.

Research into principal geographic markets with detailed quantitative information needs to be set against the framework of current national and international market conditions. There are important external factors (explained in chapter 9) influencing market development and response, and giving rise to short term distortions in the main trends, for example:

Economic growth rates
Fiscal regulations
Inflation
Exchange rates
Political unrest, health and safety
Fares and relative costs
Competition
Government controls (eg passports and visas, limitations on services such as liquor and gambling restrictions)

An extract from BTA's Marketing Plan 1986/87 dealing with the geographic market Australia and New Zealand illustrates the importance of setting the research data in a broad context.

For major markets more sophisticated information is needed, such as motivation and segmentation studies. US visitors to Europe come in many shapes and sizes, and can be described in a number of different behaviour groups. This is a basis for segmentation studies which in turn enable the marketer to vary the sales approach to suit the differing needs

Figure 4.1 – Australia and New Zealand markets for Britain – key statistics

(i) 1989 % share of world total

Visits	
Australia	3.1%
New Zealand	0.7%
Expenditure	
Autralia	5.4%
New Zealand	1.0%

(ii) 1988–91 index of visits

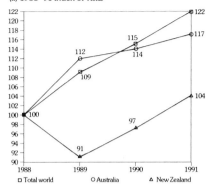

□ Total world   ○ Australia   △ New Zealand

(iii) 1989 purpose of visit

	Visits '000	Expenditure £M
Holiday independent	258 — 39%	178 — 41%
Holiday inclusive	72 — 11%	42 — 10%
Business	71 — 11%	82 — 19%
VFR	182 — 28%	112 — 26%
Miscellaneous	74 — 11%	25 — 6%

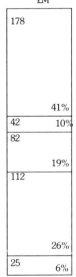

(iv) Mode of transport 1978/1988 (%)

Australia/New Zealand

	Air	Sea
1978	72	28
1988	75	25

World average

	Air	Sea
1978	60	40
1988	69	31

Continued overleaf

Figure 4.1 – Australia and New Zealand markets for Britain – key statistics (*continued*)

(v) Proportion of visits per quarter 1978/1988 (%)

	Australia/New Zealand					World average			
1978	12	26	40	20		16	24	40	20
1988	16	26	36	21		18	25	35	22
	Q1	Q2	Q3	Q4		Q1	Q2	Q3	Q4

(vi) Proportion of nights out of London 1978/1988 (%)

	Australia/New Zealand			World average	
1978	34	66		41	59
1988	31	69		40	60
	London	Outside		London	Outside

Source: British Tourist Authority.

and preferences. In many cases the product must be tailored and presented accordingly in a number of widely differing forms. The most obvious segments are youth, senior citizens, visitors seeking special interest and satisfaction, eg education, training (and in Britain's case, learning English), health and fitness, religion, cultural or sporting attractions, each of which in turn needs further subdivision. One man's sport is another's boredom. Cultural tastes vary greatly. Many come on literary trails, but may not have an ear for music. There is a large and growing business travel segment which has a number of important subsegments needing differing treatment eg conferences, trade fairs, and incentive travel.

The segments representing principal behaviour groups will provide the basis for further research into such items as images, or how the visitors see the destination and its attractions. Since international travel is highly competitive the ranking of the destination in relation to the competition can be vital. Images are linked to the evaluation of satisfaction anticipated and perceived. Value for money will determine future business and recording satisfactions will give a good indication of future visits and potential. There is no more powerful publicity than travellers' tales, and returning visitors will have a major effect on future business. Usually this is favourable, since people like talking about their travels in an exciting and sometimes romantic way. They do not like to admit that the grass was not greener over the hill.

In contrast to quantitative research and surveys, qualitative studies and surveys are difficult. The aim is to explore motivations governing behaviour, attitudes and opinions and so identify behaviour groups and main trends. Results cannot be precise and especially in tourism and leisure when the field covers a vast range of human activity and all the 'nicest' things in life.

There are certain rules. Firstly, the objective must be clear. Research is not undertaken for the sake of research but to guide management in policy, planning and operations for the good of the country or the industry as well as the travellers themselves. Researchers must be careful to ensure objective interpretation. Certain broader motivations will be common to wider market groupings. Sociologists can be helpful. Broad social trends and consumer behaviour in Western industrialised societies will follow similar patterns. These can be applied to leisure and travel spending just as in the many mass markets for consumer goods and services.

Market researchers in tourism can accordingly benefit from cooperative research and need this help since motivation studies can be expensive. The European Travel Commission was one of the first official organisations to develop motivation studies in the American market, examining attitudes, image awareness, and market segments – in depth probing of satisfactions and preferences. One of the early successes in searching for ways of extending the season and creating new off peak transatlantic travel, was the discovery at the beginning of the 1970s of a demand for short visits to Europe for social or cultural reasons in the winter months. The rapid development of the airlines with lower fares together with changing social habits led to the creation almost overnight of a vast off-peak movement, quite different from the existing traditional, grand tour of Europe lasting three weeks or more, mainly on summer package tours.

In recent years greater attention by researchers to motivation and sociology, especially in America, has resulted in some interesting and practical studies charting social change and indicating new trends with major significance for future spending patterns. In short these studies provide guidance to the emerging markets. Some of the descriptive language for these trends, for the segments, and the principal behaviour groups may sound surprising but they illustrate the background to main motivations very clearly. For example, marketers now commonly refer to the 'empty nesters' to describe the position of older parents whose children have grown up and left home. This affects their behaviour, and income since children are no longer dependent. Traditionally in travel two groups, young people before marriage and family, and older people just before retirement, are free from home ties and have relatively high disposable income to spend on themselves. Some researchers refer to the 'me' generation to illustrate an increasing trend to higher personal spending on immediate satisfactions, including travel and leisure, often on credit cards, and less interest in saving to leave an inheritance for their children to ensure a 'better' life for them. The 'singles' market is well established as a concept and has enormous implications for tourism. Many more young people marry later, postpone rearing a family and so have more time and disposable income for travel and leisure. These 'trends' have to be studied carefully. There can and will be exceptions. There will be periods of recession or temporary constraint, but the steady growth of tourism and particularly international travel, has generally approached the optimists, forecasts, and has shown an increasing resilience to adverse factors such as business recession or price changes. Demand elasticity studies, indicating future increases in travel at up to twice the rise in GDP, are significant and clearly involve social factors and attitudes changes as well as expansion in real wealth. One of the more interesting motivation research exercises was carried out by the American Express Company in 1985. This major study[7] examined American travel to Europe and the future challenge in maintaining and expanding the world's most successful long distance route. By 1985, a record year, American visitors to Europe were estimated at over six million visits, with related expenditure of US$6 billion. Nearly all experts consider the potential for future expansion is very considerable, but it is generally the case that growth cannot be taken for granted. New trends emerge, demand can change dramatically and faster than ever before in an age of mass communication. So not every destination or every product will grow even if the market as a whole is expanding massively. There will be winners and losers. The American Express report outlined the challenge to Europe's dominant position in world tourism very clearly and professionally. The following extract from the report indicates a set of behaviour groupings and classifications that motivation researchers can offer and an indication of their practical application in marketing, not only in the USA but in other western industrialised countries.

European travel: the way ahead – by American Express

The maturity of intra-European travel is primarily a result of the slowing down of discretionary income growth (which limits the affordability of increased travel), coupled with an emerging global trend towards long-haul travel, and growing dissatisfaction with peak season, prime destination saturation already in evidence throughout Europe.

Without rapid and effective action Europe may lose share of the prime US overseas travel market because of the following factors: the declining dollar; the perceived risk of travel to some European destinations; evidence of unfriendly attitudes to tourists in some countries; poor knowledge of shoulder season and 'provincial' destination opportunities; the perception of Europe as a 'once in a lifetime' trip by inexperienced travellers; and last but not least the marketing spending by Europe in the USA.

American Express research into US travellers' needs, attitudes and perceptions towards travel in general and European travel in particular, has revealed some significant changes in Americans' approach to travel. In general, Americans believe that vacations are no longer a 'luxury', but a right and no longer a 'once in a lifetime' thrill. Moreover, they perceive travel as 'needed to enhance my life' and use their travel experiences as a type of status badge. More specifically, the research reveals that vacations are really a reflection of a traveller's own beliefs and value. Attitudinally, individuals typically act on vacation with one of three frames of mind:

- 'Survey Tourists' who want to cover as much ground and see as many sites as they can. These people need support, a buffer between themselves and the foreign/unfamiliar.
- 'Aspiring Explorers' who want to be independent, yet privately admit to a desire for some kind of framework or umbilical cord to support them in case of emergencies or difficulties when travelling.
- 'Seasoned Travellers' who have the experience and confidence to be truly independent.

Individuals may exhibit one attitudinal characteristic throughout a vacation, or may adopt more than one, depending on circumstances. Individuals who adopt the 'aspiring explorer' frame of mind offer the most potential for new European travel products. They are eager for experiences, upwardly mobile and have financial resources, but they are not well served by many travel agents and are not sure that any products currently meet their needs.

European markets need to overcome different positioning hurdles if they are to attract more tourists. Individuals build a mental list of places to visit long before they finalise their vacation plans. The key is to get on that list. US consumer attitudes suggest different markets may need to do different things to get on the list, depending upon the awareness and appeal of each destination.

European travel marketing must respond to the needs of a number of distinct segments within American society. At one level American society broadly splits between individuals who have 'traditional' values versus those who have 'contemporary' values. Within the 'traditional' value category, two further segments exist, and while Europe can, and does, attract them, the research suggests that Europeans should be less interested in them. These two segments can be broadly described as:

- 'Stay at Home Americans' whose fear of 'foreignness' outweighs all else. (This group talk of political unrest, terrorism, language barriers and foreign exchange confusion.)

● 'Play it Safe Travellers' to whose values Europeans are unresponsive.

The most attractive segments are those holding 'contemporary' values, namely:

● 'Special Interest Travellers' who go on tours to get the most out of their travel experiences, and tend to choose tours linked to some particular interest they may have.
● 'Adventurers' who are young, 'up-and-coming', travel frequently, and look for immersion in new cultures, experiences and exotica.
● 'Elitists' who are very frequent European visitors and who are very affluent, travel throughout the year, and visit the less traditional European tourist markets.
● 'Grey Panthers' (ie the affluent retired) who have the time, money and inclination to take long European vacations.
● 'Extenders' ie those business travellers who frequently extend their business trips by taking a few days holiday at the same time.

It will be seen that motivation studies have a special significance in guiding marketers in their estimates of future potential and changing demand trends. But there is a more immediate task directly related to the ongoing promotional programmes, this is the study of attitudes and images, both before and after. How does the visitor perceive the destination and its attractions. What are the anticipations, the hoped for satisfactions, the assessment of value for money, and equally important the anxieties or constraints. Surveys of visitors' satisfactions at the destination and on return are also important and practical. Gaps between anticipation and reality must be discovered quickly by the marketers. Worries about price, welcome, standards, health can soon erode a buoyant market. It can take some years and heavy promotion spend to return to profits and meanwhile the lost revenue is very damaging to the maintenance or build up of the tourism infrastructure. Good examples of visitor satisfaction tests are in the annual BTA surveys, Overseas Visitor and London Visitor Surveys.

Motivation studies in their various forms need not be expensive. Principal methods are sample surveys by post, personal interview or by telephone. Group discussions (similar to the Delphi method) can be successful. Apart from direct contact with the traveller much information can be obtained from the trade, if approaches are made on a structured and representative sample basis. This is equally true for quantitative 'factual' and descriptive research as well. In fact the best surveys will combine elements of both which will help the grossing up or the interpretation of the findings and their application to the market as a whole.

Marketing attitude studies

Image and attitude testing are important guides to the marketing operation itself, indicating the messages or creative objectives required. A successful study by the European Travel Commission in 1985[8] examined the off peak potential in the American retired population. There were significant differences in attitude and behaviour compared with the 'average' and this meant determining characteristics in behaviour for this market segment. The trade and destination interests that catered for these special needs would be ahead of the competition and gain market share in a large market with very considerable potential.

The retired American: off-peak travel potential – (ETC 1985)

Economic analyses have documented the economic strength of the older sector of the US population – those over fifty. They own a dominant share of all assets, and a majority of 'discretionary income'. But to provide a pool of off-peak travellers, consumers must have more than economic resources. Also needed are time and seasonal options, unrestricted by constraints of full-time jobs, school or the needs of children.

Those sixty-five and older, 11.5% of the US (28.6 million now and 35 million by the year 2000) are largely retired. Their homes are largely furnished and paid for; their household total discretionary incomes are quite good; their per capita discretionary income is the highest of all age segments. Latest passport application figures show that those sixty-five and over contributed a share of passport applications a bit over their population share ($12^{1}/_{2}$%) and a growth rate nearly twice that of the general population. Their share of travel abroad for vacation – and specifically to Europe – is slightly higher than their population proportion, as is that of those specifically categorised 'retired'.

The study among the retired shows longer periods of stay abroad than among the general population with two-thirds staying in deluxe or first class hotels. A majority of retired travellers indicate past experience with fall/spring stays in Europe; two-thirds would be interested in off-peak trips if offering 'a discount'.

Older Americans go abroad for the same reasons that most American travellers do – to see a different way of life, to view the historical sights they can't see at home. They see it as both exciting and educational; they don't go abroad to rest or relax or because it is less expensive than other places. Like other Americans they worry about being disliked or even mistreated by 'foreigners'. They mistrust the quality of their hotel rooms, fear for the safety of their luggage; they have some concern for threats to their health, high costs, hijacking possibilities and the lack of a travelling partner leading to single supplements or a strange room-mate.

Like their fellow Americans they judge destination countries by the availability of: beautiful countryside, interesting cities and historical places but give greater importance to cultural attractions like museums and cathedrals. They give high marks to good weather, hotels, food and friendly people; are lower than average on 'ease of getting around on one's own'. Retirees show a higher predilection than average for escorted group tours but have only a minor interest in driving abroad.

The most prevalent pattern is still the couple; a small minority go alone; or with friends or 'other relatives'. They look for historical places, cathedrals, museums and good restaurants and have very little interest in nightclubbing. They enjoy sightseeing in cities and the countryside, shopping, taking photographs – and to some extent, meeting the locals. They have minimal interest in spectator or participant sports. Besides requests for lower costs and improvements in the comfort and quality of airline, bus and hotel experiences the retirees are most united in faulting what they perceive as the frenetic pace of most tours – too many activities, too short stays, too many destinations, not enough free time. (Yet a minority ask for more activities suggesting that perhaps tours of different levels of exertion should be made available and clearly labelled.)

There are clearly voiced needs for more information – about the tours and destinations, and an underlying plea for sympathetic understanding from tour personnel; and more help in socialising with what is basically a group of strangers.

Performance tests

There is a wide field for checking performance against objectives, and measuring results, particularly results of marketing operations. In direct commercial operations the discipline of profit and loss is the ultimate, and very efficient measuring system. There can be no better way of appraising effectiveness in business. But in tourism there are many areas of activity and specific operations that cannot be measured in this way. The activities of governments seeking a broad national benefit may not provide trading profits. Destination tourist offices responsible for development and promotion of tourism do not normally trade at all. They may receive some support incidentally from commercial interests for research or cooperative marketing activities, but this is normally small and incidental to the main task. Marketing activity, for example, advertising campaigns, is not always easy to evaluate.

In these cases management will be thrown back on research to check performance against activity, using statistics of visitor movement and spending, length of stay or seasonal and geographic spread to appraise results. For success in this important task, statistics must be available and the marketing plan clear in establishing meaningful and measurable objectives and targets, and a strict and objective assessment of results. Too often these conditions are not met. Marketers and researchers themselves find it difficult to assess failure, but the cost of inadequate testing is high. Marketing failures, however they occur, need to be identified quickly and put right. This tends to happen in the private sector where the discipline of profit and loss is compelling. Public sector operations on the other hand can suffer inefficiencies that are not corrected, sometimes because the appraising systems are poor or the statistics needed inadequate.

Performance testing can be helped by information from the industry. Occupancy rates and load factors have already been mentioned. In addition, it is often possible to obtain information from business, through their retail or other sales audits. Speedy checks of trends may be available in this way as market intelligence to guide current operations.

Broad measurements of major operations in marketing, or development and production, especially in the public sector, will normally require continuous appraisal over a period of time – perhaps two to three years. Time scales in tourism, which involves mass movements, are not short. Even if traditional patterns now change relatively rapidly, measurements will need a two to three year period for reliable assessments.

There are other areas for appraisal notably the marketing operations themselves. It is possible to check on the effectiveness of media, advertising can be checked for coupon returns or other replies, and comparisons made with similar media, or previous campaigns. Respondents can be followed up and surveyed to indicate whether they travelled or purchased the services advertised. Promotional content, copy and illustrations can be checked by sampling methods or group discussions to find out if they are read, understood or led to any specific action. Pretesting of large scale campaigns, rather like the piloting of sample surveys, to ensure that people interviewed understand and are willing to reply, can be a valuable precaution if there are new factors, ie a new market, a new destination, or a special situation. There are examples of expensive travel advertising campaigns which proved to be ineffective, a waste of money, because they were not in line with customer tastes and preferences. This can very easily happen in international trades when there are language and cultural differences in the market place. The use of a humorous approach is particularly risky – wit like some wines does not always travel well.

Studies of booking patterns and use of sample surveys to check visitor reactions can be helpful but there are difficulties. Useful factual information about booking patterns, how long in advance, use of agents, inclusive and independent arrangements can be measured without difficulty and checked against specific marketing or sales action ie price and special offers or special promotions, but qualitative action and motivations are difficult. Tourists do not seem to like to admit acting in a particular way as a result of advertising, or promotional material. They will not always recall or admit seeing or reading specific media. They are more likely to refer to up market or fashionable papers, guides, shows or television programmes than admit to reading or seeing down market ones. It is said that such surveys show that many more people claim to read up market papers than the printed copies would allow. Nevertheless readership surveys have their uses in establishing the audience, factual data about socio-economic characteristics and location. Careful research can add behaviour and motivation information to give some guidance on promotion effectiveness. Clearly in many cases the unfailing commercial tests will suffice, who and how many buy the publication, the travel guide and will advertisers use it.

In spite of problems researchers should continually check and make comparisons on media effectiveness into the audience reached, the message communicated, the style or approach, and the results relative and absolute. Group discussions can be useful for both pre and post testing travel promotional material. The destination tourist organisations can and should act as cooperative agencies and sounding boards for effectiveness testing.

Summary

Market research is the systematic collection of information about the supply and demand in tourism to guide formulation of policies, strategies and plans. There are four general categories of research:

(a) Measurement of traffic volume and expenditures
(b) Resources and capacity in transport, accommodation and facilities
(c) Market analysis including potential, segmentation and motivation
(d) Performance appraisal and effectiveness tests.

Researchers must be given a clear brief. Market research should be action orientated.

Primary information in measuring traffic flows is provided on a national basis by governments, supplemented by state tourist organisations, national institutions and regional and local authorities. A number of international bodies, notably the WTO and OECD, publish useful compilations of travel statistics to enable international comparisons to be made. National statistics are derived from sampling, or police checks at frontiers and hotels. Domestic travel movement, including outward foreign travel, can only be obtained from national sample surveys, a number of which are carried out regularly in European countries and in the USA.

Studies of market potential and forecasting are essential measurements. Principal forecasting methods are extrapolation of trends. Delphi discussion groups, mathematical models. ETC experience suggests a blend of projections, expert group discussion and industry sector expertise produces the best results.

Product research should cover all aspects, including occupancy of accommodation and load factor checks in transport. Mapping and charting must be quantified and classified by type and standard. There must be a degree of coordination in expansion by the interests, public and private sector and even allowing for effective competition.

Research into principal geographic markets needs to be set against national and international market conditions. There are important external factors, economic conditions, fiscal and political situations, exchange rates and relative costs.

Segmentation representing principal behaviour groups will provide the basis for motivation research. In contrast to quantitative research and surveys, qualitative studies are difficult and expensive. There are accordingly benefits in encouraging cooperative research, especially with wider industry and commercial groupings.

The research must cover attitudes and images and visitor satisfaction. There is a wide field for checking performance against objectives and measuring results, including results of marketing operations.

References

1 *The Tourism Industry and The Tourism Policies of the Twelve Member States of The Community.* EEC Brussels 1987.
2 *The Economic Significance of Tourism within the European Community. A fifth report by the working group of the national tourist organisations of the EEC.* BTA London 1983.
3 Medlik, R, *Europeans on Holiday.* Horwath and Horwath. London 1984.
4 *British National Travel Survey* (BNTS). British Tourist Authority (annual).
5 *British Tourism Survey Monthly.* Since 1990 replaced by *United Kingdom Travel Survey* (UKTS). English, Scottish, Wales and Northern Ireland Tourist Boards (annual).
6 *London's Tourist Accommodation in the 1990s.* Horwath and Horwath for BTA/ETB 1986.
7 *European Travel – the way ahead.* American Express Europe Ltd 1985.
8 *The Older American Traveller to Europe.* A report by Mr Ed Berrol for ETC 1985.

Appendix

Tourism in the UK by UK residents 1989

A new survey named the *United Kingdom Tourism Survey* (UKTS)

Table 4.2 – Estimated numbers of trips and nights and estimated expenditure 1989

| | All tourism | | | | | Holiday tourism | | | | |
	United Kingdom	England	Scotland	Wales	Northern Ireland	United Kingdom	England	Scotland	Wales	Northern Ireland
Trips (m.)	109.5	88.5	10.0	9.5	1.5	64.5	50.5	6.0	6.5	1.0
Nights (m.)	443	339	47	43	7	320	238	36	35	6
Expenditure (£m.)	10,865	8,020	1,385	985	165	7,410	5,375	890	760	110

Source: UKTS.

Note: Trips are rounded to 500,000; nights to 1 million; and expenditure to £5 million.
Figures for individual countries may not add up to the totals shown for United Kingdom.
This is due to rounding and the inclusion of Isle of Man and Channel Islands tourism within the UK totals.

replaces the previous domestic tourism survey – the *British Tourism Survey Monthly* (BTSM). It is important to note that, since UKTS incorporates methodological improvements and changes, it is not possible to compare 1989 domestic tourism data with that of previous years.

The UKTS is a continuous survey sponsored by the National Tourist Boards of England, Scotland, Wales and Northern Ireland. It measures all trips away from home lasting one night or more taken by UK residents for the purpose of holidays, visits to friends and relatives, business, conferences or any other purpose except such things as temporary removal, hospital admissions or school visits. The UKTS is conducted monthly and all the UKTS tables in this Appendix are derived from cumulative data for a twelve-month period.

Table 4.3 – Volume and value of tourism in English regions 1989

	All tourism			Holiday tourism		
	Trips m.	Nights m.	Spending £m.	Trips m.	Nights m.	Spending £m.
Cumbria	3.0	11	260	2.5	9	210
Northumbria	3.5	12	260	2.0	8	155
North West	9.0	30	855	5.0	18	515
Yorkshire & Humbs.	9.0	32	840	5.5	23	600
Heart of England	8.5	26	575	4.0	14	255
East Midlands	7.0	25	460	4.0	17	320
Thames & Chilterns	6.0	15	320	2.5	8	120
East Anglia	8.5	34	655	5.0	25	490
London	9.0	24	770	3.0	11	265
West Country	13.5	73	1,790	10.0	62	1,530
Southern	6.5	29	670	4.5	24	530
South East	8.0	28	565	4.5	19	390
England	88.5	339	8,020	50.5	238	5,375

Source: UKTS.

Note: Trips are rounded to 500,000; nights to 1 million; and expenditure to £5 million.

The British on holiday

An annual sample survey of British holiday-makers and their holidays, the *British National Travel Survey* (BNTS) was formerly known as the *British Tourism Survey Yearly* (BTSY) in the years 1985–88 inclusive. It is based on interviews with a sample of adults aged sixteen and over, representative of the adult population of Great Britain.

The survey is concerned only with holiday travel and not with travel for other purposes. 'Holiday' generally refers to a holiday of four nights or more. However, since 1974, information has been collected on all holidays abroad of one or more nights in length and this is shown in table 4.4. Holidays are defined as 'main' or 'additional'. Where only one

Table 4.4 – Estimated number of 4+ night holidays taken by the British population 1965–1989

Year	Britain (millions)	Abroad (millions)	Total (millions)
1965	30.0	5.00	35.00
1966	31.0	5.50	36.50
1967	30.0	5.00	35.00
1968	30.0	5.00	35.00
1969	30.5	5.75	36.25
1970	34.5	5.75	40.25
1971	34.0	7.25	41.25
1972	37.5	8.50	46.00
1973	40.5	8.25	48.75
1974	40.5	6.75	47.25
1975	40.0	8.00	48.00
1976	37.5	7.25	44.75
1977	36.0	7.75	43.75
1978	39.0	9.00	48.00
1979	38.5	10.25	48.75
1980	36.5	12.00	48.50
1981	36.5	13.25	49.75
1982	32.5	14.25	46.75
1983	33.5	14.50	48.00
1984	34.0	15.50	49.50
1985	33.0	15.75	48.75
1986	31.5	17.50	49.00
1987	28.5	20.00	48.50
1988	33.5	20.25	53.75
1989	31.5	21.00	52.50

Source: BNTS/BTSY.

Note: These figures relate to holidays of four nights or more.
They include both holidays taken by adults and holidays taken by children.
The figures are derived from the percentage of the population taking a holiday in each of the years concerned. These percentage figures are, of course, subject to normal sampling error. When applied to large populations, small variations are greatly magnified. These estimates should therefore be regarded as order-of-magnitude figures for individual years; they do not necessarily reflect a precise relationship with the preceding or succeeding year.

is taken, this is the main holiday; when two or more are taken, the main holiday is the longest or, if two or more were of equal length, the one in or nearest to the peak summer period.

The *British National Travel Survey* is carried out for BTA/ETB by NOP Market Research Ltd, from whom subscription details may be obtained.

5   Product analysis

The product is the foundation of the marketing programme, affecting choice of markets and segments, method of distribution, positioning in the market place, promotional media and communications generally. The product/market fit table is the launch pad, inasmuch as it attempts to match the right product with the right market and the right segment within that market. Marketing is concerned with communicating the product to these markets and segments. Consequently, the inventory of resources and a careful analysis of product strengths and weaknesses are fundamental to any marketing planning.

There is an important difference between anticipation and consumption, just as the 'come on' promotional literature is very different from the guide book to action, which explains how to enjoy and make full use of the destination's amenities.

It is not always easy to 'sample' the tourist product and to try out the offer as one might test drive a new car before purchase. There are as a result important marketing implications. To an extent the promotion is the product, the brochure is the package or the goods on the retailer's 'shelf'. Thus natural anxieties about buying 'a pig in a poke' need and repay careful attention. A considerable proportion of holiday visitors return to favoured haunts once discovered. In some cases twenty-five per cent or more of visitors to an hotel, guest house or resort may make a return booking for the following year before leaving on the return journey home.

The tourism product is a collection of physical and service features together with symbolic associations which are expected to fulfil the wants and needs of the buyer. It is a satisfying activity at a desired destination. We have already considered the main suppliers of tourist services in chapter 2, but while transport, accommodation, amenities and attractions are fundamental sub-products, product analysis should extend beyond these sectors to embrace a country's heritage, culture and people.

The history and so the heritage of a nation is inevitably conditioned by the geography of the country and the starting point for any product analysis should be geographical: the position of a country, or indeed a town or resort, relative to its markets; the physical features, the climate, the flora and fauna. It is usual, except in the case of very large countries, to carry out the inventory of the geographical resource at the national level; to analyse a country's strengths and weaknesses relative to its potential markets. The location of the country relative to its major tourist generating markets will determine the time/distance constraint and to some extent the cost of access too. The Australian Travel Commission is investing substantial promotional resources in Japan and South East Asia because these markets offer low cost access in a reasonable time. Australia's location relative to Europe on the other hand means, at least for the foreseeable future, a long journey and high cost. The islands of the Caribbean look mainly to the USA for the same reason. While the short break holiday is the most buoyant sector of Britain's domestic tourism, about two-thirds of those taking them will only travel up to a maximum of 150 miles for such a holiday. Cyprus should not look to north-west Europe to provide a weekend break holiday market.

Geographical position is invariably a determinant of climate and to an extent, the natural resources and physical characteristics of a country. Furthermore, man-made products very often derive from physical and climatic factors, typical examples being ski-lifts, golf courses, hides for observing wildlife and marinas.

Natural resources such as sandy beaches, coral reefs, rivers, mountains, jungles and forests can form the basis of significant tourist attractions but there could well be constraints too, both natural and man-made. Sharks off the sandy beaches, mosquitos or lack of ski resort installations can be powerful deterrents in developing the product potential provided naturally by the physical attributes. All the surveys undertaken by the British Tourist Authority place beautiful countryside very high on the list of things most enjoyed about a trip to Britain. The variety from the gentle Cotswolds to the grandeur of Snowdonia, the rolling South Downs to the majestic Grampians, the moors and the dales, together with the myriad rivers and lakes represents a rich inheritance for British tourism. The mountains of Switzerland and Austria provide the basic resource for both winter and summer tourism. Safaris through the game parks and reserves of Africa, trekking in the foothills of the Himalayas in Nepal, sailing around the islands of Greece and swimming from the beaches of Sardinia all derive from the physical geography and all have been developed sympathetically. There are cases though, where mass tourism has destroyed the environment and yet others, such as the Llanos of Venezuela or the equatorial forests of Brazil, which are yet to be developed (hopefully sympathetically). Green issues are an increasingly important item on the political agenda of national and local governments. Tourism developments, like other developments, must be politically acceptable, socially responsible and environmentally sound. Much of the comment though tends to be very academic and theoretical, eg soft tourism, alternative tourism, ecotourism, reflecting the interest of the commentator, rather than practical. The trades are vitally concerned. Governments cannot act alone.

Award schemes and other motivating programmes affecting the providers and the tourists themselves are important.

A proper balance should be struck between the needs of the tourist and the needs of the residents, including the flora and fauna, in any tourist developments which exploit the physical attractions of an area. Drawing up an inventory of physical resources can be helpful in this respect. Moreover, it should be repeated as an annual exercise and this regular process of re-examination will alert the authorities not just to the obstacles still to be overcome but to the dangers of over exploitation, erosion and decay. The heritage of a country must surely be one of its greatest tourist attractions but again it must be sympathetically treated and presented.

Britain has been endowed more than most countries in terms of its rich heritage: a cradle of Christianity, birthplace of the industrial revolution, the centre of empire, home of colonists, the mother of parliaments. Some newer countries are not able to draw on such treasures but are becoming increasingly conscious of the need to retain the best, or in some cases what is left, of the past – 'The Rocks' in Sydney, Raffles Hotel in Singapore, Ellis Island in New York.

In analysing the range of heritage products it is convenient to group them into sub categories: architectural, industrial, religious, literary, music and the arts and so on. This inventory of heritage products will point up opportunities for developing trails, festivals, special interest packages, anniversary celebrations and theme years (see chapter 19). It is important in drawing up an inventory that it provides not just a listing but details of style, important contents, opening hours, admission charges, group arrangements and special events.

There is nothing new in this inventory compilation. It was first done in Britain 900 years ago, essentially the result of the need of William the Conqueror to know what dues he should receive and indeed what he owned directly in his kingdom. The Domesday Book represents a complete inventory of a country and some of the churches and castles built in the eleventh century still survive today: Rockingham Castle in Northamptonshire is open to the public today and is mentioned in the Domesday Book as 'waste when King William ordered a castle to be built there'.

By the 1830s Britain had developed a complex network of canals and navigable rivers and many canals are still navigable today. The narrow boats or long barges are now used as restaurants, 'floatels' and pleasure boats. The railways brought about greater changes in Britain's landscape with bridges and viaducts, cuttings and embankments and the splendid railway stations and station hotels. A great Victorian railway station has been reborn as Manchester's G Mex exhibition hall. Part of Manchester's Refuge Assurance building – the main clock tower portion of the Grade II listed building – is to become a fifty-five bedroom four star hotel and business centre. Herstmonceux Castle, former home of the Royal

Greenwich Observatory, which was sold in 1988 for £8.1 million, was for sale again in 1990 for more than twice as much, and proposals for the site included a 150 bedroom five star hotel, a twenty-seven hole golf course and clubhouse, sixty lodges, and a conference and health centre. There are plans for a Chinatown development at London's Poplar Docks, hotels at St Pancras and St Marylebone Stations in London, as well as St George's Hospital in London. Liverpool's Albert Dock has seen the transformation of a derelict inner city area into a thriving attraction, drawing millions of visitors a year. Scenic railway lines are being promoted. Marinas and yacht harbours have been developed out of seaports which shipped coal. Portsmouth has developed out of its declining facility a splendid showplace of maritime archaeology. Transport museums, narrow gauge railways, mines, quarries, factories and mills are being reborn as tourist attractions.

It has almost been forgotten that Britain led Europe in resort and spa development. The spas came first, in the 18th century, and to this day provide some of the finest architecture and town planning. Bath is one of the great cities of Europe with its Georgian treasures. The seaside resorts had their own style – wrought iron railings, balconies and piers, theatres and assembly rooms, promenades and pavilions. Much of this historic tourist plant remains. Alas, due to a major strategic marketing error the British spas threw their baby and much prosperity out with the spa water after the war when they surrendered to the National Health policy of hydrotherapy by tap water in town. Now, there is a greater interest in health and health tourism than ever before. Health farms cater for an up-market clientele. To add insult to injury, European spas flourish, attracting many British visitors, and Britain imports billions of gallons of foreign spa water while our native waters languish. The seaside resorts in their heyday of enterprise effectively used the 'marine spa' brand name. 'Dr' Brighton was famous. Most had amongst their largest and best hotels the Hydro (short for hydropathic establishment).

History does repeat itself. Fashions return. Some British resorts, and the public interests that should support them, have lost confidence and the will to enterprise. The marketing task is to examine what exists in 'product' and attractions, to learn from the competition and if need be, to relaunch the product. Britain and indeed northern Europe's resorts should have a twelve month season, freed from the seasonality of the beach holiday. That risk has passed to the Mediterranean. The range of specialist and activity attractions is enormous and the market segments suited to resorts are growing apace. There are many examples of resort relaunch, when their original market has moved on. In Switzerland a number of resorts were mountain health resorts in the first part of the century, with sanatoria not hotels to cure TB. Penicillin killed their business but they recreated trade with new appeals even more successfully.

British genius in art, music, literature and drama represent a rich heritage of enormous appeal, especially to overseas visitors who tend to be well-educated 'culture vultures'. While Britain's best collections of paintings are to be found in the great galleries of London, there are superb collections in many of our provincial galleries and in certain country houses too. Research into the lives of Britain's greatest artists can lead to the development of heritage trails such as 'Constable Country'.

The unequalled genius of Shakespeare has proved to be 'not of an age but for all time' and in the 350 years since his death he has continued to dominate British theatre and literature. His birthplace, the shrine which is Stratford-upon-Avon, is mirrored in other trails and interpretive centres, the Robert Burns Heritage Trail and Sir Walter Scott's Abbotsford in Scotland, Bronte country, Hardy country, Wordsworth's Lake District, Johnson and Milton, Dickens and Dylan Thomas all have their place in attracting tourism.

The English language is perhaps Britain's greatest single resource, more powerful than Mediterranean sunshine as a tourist magnet. Not only does it attract students of all ages to language schools and to many other training and educational establishments (universities and specialist colleges), but as the leading medium of human communication it also embraces meetings, exhibitions, business trips and offers enormous opportunities for exploitation. Too much is taken for granted. Perhaps more important is the continuing promotion for things British. More and more people listen to English and read English. The language establishes cultural roots and poetry and great literature are often associated with Britain's landscape, buildings and towns.

One forgets, in this modern age of conformity when design of buildings follows a common and often uninteresting 'western' pattern, that before the time of mass communication distance may not have had charm but it encouraged local initiative. So buildings, dialect, habits, art and cuisine took their own separate forms. This is most evident for the traveller in architecture. Britain is rich in cathedrals, churches, castles, great houses and great villages and towns (artistically speaking). In Georgian England it seemed as though builders could not put up an ugly construction even if they tried. In the Cotswolds a whole rural region has a distinctive and attractive architectural style that is unique and attractive. Architecture goes with landscape and art and literature. This combination should be unbeatable for Britain's long term future and for many other countries, especially in Europe but it has to be recognised, measured and presented in marketing terms.

Britain's music is translated into a tourism product in two ways – birthplaces and homes of composers like Britten and Elgar and the festivals associated with them (Aldeburgh, Malvern). British musicmakers offer a feast of music at festivals throughout the year, which have enormous appeal for resident and visitor alike.

Britain's religious heritage – the established church, the Roman Catholic, the Free or Non-Conformist churches, as well as Greek Orthodox, Judaism, Hinduism and Islam – is wide-ranging and multi-faceted. The holy places and ecclesiastical buildings, early saints and more recent evangelists, church music and in particular the great cathedrals and the medieval parish churches, are all visitor attractions. What might be termed religious tourism is a force to be recognised and reckoned with. Churches and cathedrals appeal, and many are dependent on the tourist industry for their upkeep. But there is more to it, spiritual centres and pilgrimages are significant. One of the first forms of tourism is brilliantly presented in that classic of English literature, Chaucer's 'Canterbury Tales'.

The movement of pilgrims is now far greater than ever before, and perhaps the need is even greater. Britain has rather lost out, as with spas, in spiritual healing as well. Visitors to Lourdes in France, just one, even if amongst the most famous of Europe's shrines, number several millions a year. The great centre of the Islamic religion, Mecca, still attracts millions of pilgrims each year. One should not forget that tourism started with high endeavour, offering unique and outstanding human experiences. A journey was to be treasured and remembered as a special and important part of life. Religion, education, health and many other serious purposes or deep satisfactions and needs were involved. They still are, and it is the challenge to the marketer to understand, identify and help fulfil these deep seated wishes.

Heritage is one of the major appeals of Britain for overseas visitors as indeed it is for many other countries. In drawing up the product inventory it is necessary to catalogue attractions too – theme parks and entertainment complexes, theatres, concert halls, night-life, festivals, exhibitions, sporting facilities and pageantry, particularly that associated with the Royal Family. It is vitally important to extend the listing to events, the plays, programmes and performances on a regular ongoing basis.

Perhaps the greatest single influence on perceptions of a country or indeed a resort is to be found in the attitude and behaviour of the natives. Some countries and resorts have a reputation for dishonesty, even violence; some for unfriendliness or antipathy towards visitors. Fortunately research consistently shows that overseas visitors to Britain rank the friendliness of the British people highly. A recent survey undertaken by the London Tourist Board showed that generally Londoners were well disposed to tourists, recognising that much of London's 'product' – shops, theatre, transport and attractions – existed for and because of tourists. It is difficult, if not impossible, to change attitudes of the resident population, though attempts have been made from time to time. A number of years ago President de Gaulle attempted to change the attitudes of the French, with limited success. More recently a campaign in Glasgow had much more success. While recognising that local attitudes are not easily changed, the friendliness factor or otherwise should feature among the product strengths and weaknesses.

A friendly local population is very desirable but friendliness among people who meet and serve the visitors, from immigration and customs staff to hotel staff and tourist guides, is vitally important. In Australia, which is enjoying popularity as a tourist destination in Japan currently, the immigration officers are being taught Japanese. In London on the other hand, Japanese visitors perceive a lack of traditional courtesies in the Japanese speaking guides, who have been thought to have become too westernised. Some of the Caribbean islands a few years ago gained an unenviable reputation for theft and muggings which resulted in a downturn of traffic. It is the American traveller who is most likely to be deterred by a perceived lack of welcome and Americans were particularly concerned about the possibility of terrorist attack in Europe in the first half of 1986. They felt isolated and vulnerable but they also felt unwanted and unloved. Consequently, they stayed at home.

The Gulf war in 1991 was even more disruptive causing massive cancellations, deferred decisions, financial problems and collapse of airlines and major tour operators as well as the smaller handling agents. Hotel occupancies dropped dramatically overnight. Some destinations such as Israel and Egypt suffered disproportionately. Post-war crisis marketing came into play with massive reassurance campaigns, discounted prices and increased marketing budgets but some operators could not find the marketing budgets from their much reduced incomes. The lean years should have been anticipated in the good years and marketing funds salted away against such a contingency.

The political stability of a country or an area is an important factor which must be fully taken into account in any product analysis and this highlighting of the problem will enable the marketer to take corrective action so far as it is possible. Unrest in Sri Lanka has brought about a downturn in their foreign visitors. Similarly, unrest and violence in the Punjab has affected traffic through that part of India to Kashmir.

First impressions are vitally important. The British Tourist Authority published a survey in 1986: *Reception of Overseas Visitors Enquiry,*[1] which critically examined welcome and facilities at Britain's seaports and airports – signing and colour, baggage handling, immigration and customs, restaurants, toilet facilities and so on. The marketer must ensure that welcome is writ large. As the report so rightly said. 'People sense an atmosphere very quickly. Bright colours, cleanliness, smiling faces, lack of harassment, immediately make visitors feel wanted.'

Officials in Surfers' Paradise, Queensland, Australia, employ bikini clad meter maids to feed parking meters when a visitor's car has overstayed its time. The welcome *lei* in Hawaii, the welcome orchids in Thailand, the bowl of fruit or the welcome glass of sherry in the hotel, all help those first anxious moments of arrival. So, critical analysis of reception and receptive services is as important as the analysis of physical geography or attractions.

Having persuaded the visitor to come, and hopefully welcomed him, how easy is it for the visitor to get around? It is so important for the marketer always to try and see things through the eyes of the consumer. Are signs in appropriate languages? Is the road and rail network adequate? What about internal air services? Again vitally important, not just from the point of view of identifying product strengths and weaknesses but the cataloguing of this information also ensures the availability of the data for the potential visitor and the actual tourist alike.

This cataloguing of product sectors should be done for all amenities and facilities which have a tourism dimension. Conference centres and exhibition halls, hotels with conference facilities, venues suitable for incentive groups, institutions concerned with management training in the business travel field, sports complexes and facilities for the leisure traveller and the business traveller too, theatres and concert halls, cinemas, nightlife all need to be analysed, catalogued and promoted to the right target segment.

It is always a good idea too to develop a grid of supply and demand for activity holidays, hobby holidays and special interest products, with an indication of whether demand is high, medium or low. The grid will provide an instant analysis and a guide to the marketer in the development of his thinking in terms of segmentation, targeting and communications generally. An example of a simple grid showing Supply and Demand for Activity Holidays in Wales from Scandinavia is shown below.

This sort of grid should be done for hobby holidays or special interest holidays in exactly the same way.

The accommodation sector is fundamental to tourism and should be carefully analysed by type, standard/quality and price. This analysis and cataloguing should be done for serviced accommodation – hotels, inns, farmhouses, bed and breakfast accommodation, and for self-catering including camping and caravanning and boating. The potential visitor will need to know fairly precisely what to expect in terms of facilities, service (even a self-catering cottage is serviced inasmuch as it is cleaned daily or weekly and the potential visitor needs to know this), location and price.

The collection and careful analysis of this data not only allows the marketer to determine the resort or country's strengths and weaknesses current and future, but provides the raw data for communicating the product to the market place and to the right segment in the right markets.

Assessing the accommodation stock in terms of trends, changes in fashion and forecast projections of traffic is vital if the tourist destination is to survive. An area may be losing out on coach touring traffic because there is no suitable hotel capable of taking a coach load in a key touring

Table 5.1 – Activity holidays in Wales and demand from Scandinavian markets

	Coarse fishing	Game fishing	Sea angling	Sailing	Sailing school	Windsurfing	Sub aqua	Golf	Tennis	Pony trekking	Riding	Cycling	Walking	Adventure courses	Football training	Orienteering	Rock climbing	Potholing	Hang gliding	Gliding	Flying	Water skiing	Skiing	Canoeing	Ballooning	Bowls
Wales — Supply / Product / Market	H	H	H	M	M	M	L	H	L	H	M	H	H	H	M	M	H	M	H	L	L	H	L	H	L	H
Sweden	M	M	L	L	L		L	H	M	H	M	H	H	L	H	H								L		
Norway	M	L	L	H	M	L	L	M	L	H	M	H	H	H	H	M								L		
Denmark	L	L	L	L	L	L		M	L	L		H	H	L	M	L								L		

H = High   M = Medium   L = Low

centre. In that case it may well be desirable for the tourist officer to co-operate with a colleague in a nearby town or resort where accommodation is available in a joint promotion to the coach tour operators. The growth in demand for self-catering accommodation is not just on price grounds. Self-catering provides flexibility and a freedom which is not offered in serviced accommodation. Some visitors want the peace and isolation of a country cottage, some seek purpose-built self-catering accommodation, linked to central facilities, which are not weather dependent such as that offered by the very successful Dutch operator Sporthuiscentrum, while others want static caravans and camping.

Market research and forecasting could well point to an imbalance between supply and demand or a potential shortage in the future of accommodation stock generally, in a specific sector of development or in adapting to meet new market needs. Putting this at its simplest, there is an increasing demand for *en suite* facilities and resorts which do not meet this consumer demand should not be surprised when the market starts to decline. Health consciousness manifests itself in a variety of ways from health food shops to aerobics, jogging to leisure complexes and those hoteliers who had the foresight to develop leisure facilities – swimming pool and gymnasium, sauna, jacuzzi and solarium, have watched their occupancy levels grow. Those who have opened the facility to local club membership have found a new market and tapped new profits.

Thorough analysis of the accommodation product together with thorough analysis of changing market needs and growth in traffic flows could well have arrested the decline of many seaside resorts. The marketer should constantly be asking himself 'what is happening in the market place and do I have the right product at the right price to satisfy market demand both now and in the future?' This can only come from careful and continuing product analysis. Product development is a major part of strategic planning and marketing alike. We live in a world of continually changing tastes and constant growth can only result from continuous development of the product to meet changing needs and stay ahead of the game.

No less important is a careful analysis of perceptions of a destination in terms of its product. France has a great international reputation for its cuisine. Belgium's cuisine is probably better, though its reputation is not nearly as great. Britain has an undeservedly bad reputation for cuisine in some overseas markets, though happily it is beginning to change. Marketing can help in accelerating a change in perception, especially through the medium of public relations. The following extract from BTA's 'Strategy for Growth 1986–1990'[2] illustrates the way in which a strengths and weaknesses chart might be developed. Although this example is for Britain, the same exercise could be carried out for any destination.

Britain's major strengths as a destination for domestic and international tourism stem from the country's intrinsic character and unique appeals. Others have evolved as the country has become an increasingly important international tourist destination. These strengths are tabulated on the following pages. Contrasted against the strengths are weaknesses which have hindered and continue to hinder the full realisation of the country's tourism potential. They represent areas for improvement where concerted action is needed.

Strengths

(a) Product Strengths

Politically stable
Internationally recognised
Wide touristic appeal
Many year-round attractions
International communication centre
English is the main international business language
London Heathrow – international gateway for Europe and the world
Links of kinship with many countries
Unique appeal of British countryside
Scenic diversity
London's worldwide repute:
Centre of commerce/business and communications
Entertainment capital of the world
Heritage and culture
Long history
Tradition and pageantry
The Royal Family
Entertainment
Sporting events
Other spectacles
Wide range of accommodation from international chain luxury hotels to bed and breakfast guest houses
Good universities/polytechnics/colleges and English language schools
Good information services in Britain and abroad
Ease of movement around Britain by a variety of transport

(b) Market strengths

Worldwide; EEC and rest of Europe, North America, Australasia, Middle East and Africa, New Markets, eg Far East. A better spread than other European competitor countries.

Productive market segments
Business/business-related especially conference/trade fair/incentive travel
Youth (including education)
Senior citizen
Ethnic
Visits to friends and relatives (VFR)
Specialist with high degree of satisfaction, offering stable and resilient traffic with great world-wide potential.

Weaknesses

Continuing attention to service in view of high international standards
Litter
Image/perception
The Channel: for sea travellers from Europe
Climate
Price; still not regarded as 'good value for money' in some markets
Travel trade not sufficiently committed to British product
Improvements still needed in ease of purchase and information services, especially for independent travellers
Insufficient use of technology
More investment required in capital projects, especially resorts and in hotels of international standard in key visitor centres
More lower-priced accommodation needed in London, York, Bristol and Cambridge
Medium-priced self-catering needed in London
Continuing attention needed to ensure value for money and maintenance of international standards in accommodation sector, especially in self-catering and camping
Access to London's and some other airports and termini needs improvement
Lack of large international exhibition centre
Coach parking problems both at attractions and overnight
Need for attractions and hotels (where appropriate) to stay open longer throughout the year
Need to expand training services in view of job-creating potential
High air fares on certain domestic and European routes
Entry formalities and passenger handling, especially coaches and groups

The marketer must be scrupulously objective in this analysis. This is especially important in competitive situations where switching brands is a real possibility and factors such as food, hygiene, government controls and safety must be measured as accurately and honestly as possible.

The charting of resources, capacity and attractions, together with the catalogue of strengths and weaknesses is the beginning of strategy work and planning. The chapter on market planning develops this, together with market analysis into the concept of Product/Market Fit.

Product analysis should also extend to the producers themselves – the coach operators, the handling agents and the receptive services, including the tourist information providers. This does not just mean the Tourist Information Centres but the transporters and the hoteliers too.

Product presentation is a separate subject but legislation and controls do affect the product and perception of the product and it is incumbent on the marketer to try to bring about a change in the law, if this is thought to be desirable or necessary, or failing that at least a change in perceptions. Sunday trading is a good example. Overseas visitors to Britain claim that there is little to do on a Sunday. The law restricts shopping. However, a careful analysis of the product will show that there are many things which the visitor can do. It is the marketer's job to show the visitor what he can do through the print and PR programmes particularly.

Britain was behind Europe in introducing legislation making it compulsory to use lead free petrol and as a consequence, there was a not unnatural reluctance on the part of the oil companies to provide it at petrol stations. Since many European visitors to Britain travel in their own cars which are increasingly designed to operate only on lead free petrol, there was clearly a danger that this valuable motoring traffic would be lost unless something was done about it. Fortunately the oil

Table 5.2 – Strengths and weaknesses of London's tourist product

Strengths	Weaknesses
Political stability	Perceived terrorism threat
Many year-round attractions	'Closed on Sundays'
International communication centre	Lack of large modern exhibition centre
Large busy airports	Access to airports needs improving
Important for interlining	
World-wide reputation	Litter
Centre of commerce	
Residence of the Queen	
Cosmopolitan	Shortage of foreign language guides of acceptable standard
River Thames	Lack of piers
Entertainment capital of world	Lack of nightlife such as Lido or Moulin Rouge
Centre of international cuisine	
Diversity and quality of shopping	
Wide range of accommodation	Lack of medium priced and budget hotels
Heritage	
Museums and galleries	Coach parking problems at attractions and overnight
Tradition and pageantry	

companies were persuaded to do something about it and it is now widely available.

The characteristics of the product have a substantial influence on the marketing programmes and on strategy, but careful analysis will point up other areas for action as in these two examples of Sunday trading and availability of lead free petrol. Cataloguing and recording are not enough, there must be a careful and honest analysis of product strengths and weaknesses, which for London could look like table 5.2.

Product analysis is the key to market segmentation, to communications strategy (exploit strengths, minimise weaknesses, attempt to change perceptions); the pointer to product presentation (how can it be made to be more attractive, more appealing, easier to buy, and feature more prominently in the operators' brochures?); not least a careful analysis will emphasise any need for change in legislation, product development and improvement or pressure on suppliers whose product has an impact on tourism. The time which the marketer spends on it will repay the investment many times over.

Summary

The product is the foundation of the marketing programme. The product/market fit table is the launch pad for the marketing plan. Analysis of product strengths and weaknesses is fundamental to any marketing planning. The tourism product is a collection of physical and service features together with symbolic associations. Product analysis should include geographical, historical, heritage, the people, political stability or instability, welcome and reception, as well as facilities, infrastructure and the providers (the marketer should highlight unique values). The characteristics of the product have a substantial influence on the marketing programmes and on strategy. Product analysis will point up gaps in the product range or even changes in legislation.

References

1 *Reception of Overseas Visitors Enquiry.* BTA 1986.
2 *Strategy for Growth 1986–1990.* BTA September 1986.

6 Market analysis and segmentation

In tourism there are three distinct markets: the domestic, the international and the day visitor. While the generally accepted definition of the tourist usually excludes the day visitor, the latter is important for the facility provider. Tourism is not a homogeneous movement. Tourism is heterogeneous, individual markets are heterogeneous, segments are heterogeneous. Motivations are complex, operating as they do within the parameters of possibility and impinging in a variety of ways on nationalities, region of residence, social bracket, age or sex groups.

The organisation which analyses its markets and identifies marketing opportunities will have understood the characteristics of individual markets and will have assessed how external factors (or the marketing environment in which the organisation operates) impinge on its marketing. They constitute the forces which determine the marketing opportunities and the constraints. This will be further developed in the marketing planning section of this book. The organisation does have the opportunity to choose markets, and to adapt to the environmental forces, but above all to analyse and segment its markets into meaningful target groups.

All markets are capable of segmentation and this will determine which marketing strategy will be adopted by the organisation. Britain's International Passenger Survey divides each market into the following broad segments: holiday independent, holiday inclusive, business travel, visits to friends and relatives, study and miscellaneous. This is a helpful segmentation analysis in determining trends, the strength or weakness of a particular product sector and indicative of changes in perception. For example, a decline in the number of students attending English language schools, which might point to increased competition from other destinations, price resistance or in some cases a change in government policy in an important source market. When the pound is strong against a major currency such as the American dollar or the Canadian dollar it is often reflected in a move from the holiday independent category to the visiting friends and relatives category.

The more usual methods of touristic segmentation are as follows:

(a)   Socio-demographic characteristics, which are all used in the
      Reiseanalyse survey conducted in Germany annually, referred to
      in chapter 4. These are age, sex, family size and social level,
      occupation, education, region of residence, religion and net family
      income.
(b)   Socio-economic, which is not perhaps as popular as it was,
      subdivides the population into groups which are indicative of
      occupation and income – A, B, C1, C2, D and E. Economists still
      refer to the ABC1 group or, at the other end of the spectrum, the
      DEs.
(c)   Travel motivation, which will be considered in chapter 8.
(d)   Travel patterns of behaviour or psychographic groups which will
      be considered further. Such factors as suitability of the climate,
      need for rest and relaxation, interest in different cultures, liking for
      adventure or experimenting with new and different things.

   In segmenting the market it is relatively straightforward to obtain data
on age, sex, income groups and regions of residence; however, it is
much more difficult to identify meaningful market segments using travel
motivations or psychographics as the criteria. The marketer must determine whether the segment is measurable, in terms of being able to
quantify it, and meaningful, in terms of it representing a discrete group
which can be fairly precisely targeted using relevant media. It is not very
sensible to mount a campaign to reach a market segment only to find
that there is considerable expense involved in reaching that segment
through a large number of people who do not 'belong' to it. So apart
from being measurable, it must allow for cost effective marketing. Segmentation relates to mass or mini mass markets and while the aim is to
identify the larger target audiences of potential customers, one cannot
take the divisions as definitive for all clients. There will be specialist
needs. One person may belong to several groups. Behaviour may vary
over a lifetime, or according to the travel party. Families and friends may
move together and include some diverse interests. But there will be
common motivators. Philip Kotler in 'Marketing Management' says:

> The seller who is alert to the needs of different market segments may gain in
> three ways. First, he is in a better position to spot and compare marketing
> opportunities . . . Second, the seller can use his knowledge of the marketing
> response differences of the various market segments to guide the allocation
> of his total marketing budget. The ultimate bases for meaningful segmenta-
> tion are differences in customer response to different marketing tools. Third,
> the seller can make finer adjustments of his product and marketing appeals.[1]

   Certainly socio-demographic segmentation is immensely useful to
the tourism marketer, providing as it does levels of net income, age and
social class. Generally speaking American visitors to Britain are ABC1,
with high school or college education, in a managerial or professional

job and with a household income of US$30,000 plus. It is this sort of data which enables the marketer to select appropriate media. It is helpful too to know what the regional distribution of the target market is. Again, using American visitors to Britain as our example, there has been a shift in population to the southern Sunbelt states and to California.

California is now the number one producing state in the USA. So not only can the marketer target this segment using appropriate media, the media can be selected on a geographic or regional basis.

In terms of psychographics, Britain's American visitors tend to enjoy the cultural and traditional aspects of Britain and visit museums and galleries, cathedrals and great heritage sites, as well as patronising the theatre. The leisure traveller can of course be subdivided and segmented infinitesimally, depending on his particular special interest or recreational activity, but generally there are six tourist types:

Elite – invariably high income, who visit very remote places such as the Galapagos Islands or Alaska or alternatively to the 'in' places made fashionable by royals or the 'jet set'. These are the status seekers.

Adventurers – often loners, who are prepared to rough it to an extent in the interests of seeing the new place – Tibet and parts of India are good examples. The explorers.

Quality seekers – perhaps the largest group seeking comfort and security, good quality hotels, guides for excursions and visits to cultural or historic sites. Packaged and independent.

Pursuers – the 'special interest' traveller, who pursues his hobby or avocation even on holiday, ranging from railways buffs to painters and potters.

'Action Man' – who pursues a sport and takes activity holidays – cycling to canoeing, golfing to tennis and, of course, skiing.

Economy seekers – the bargain hunters who will go to wherever is cheapest, invariably packaged.

At least two of these segments – the pursuers and 'Action Man' can be sub-segmented almost infinitely. Special interest packages range from archaeology to Zen and a special interest can also be pursued independently, whether it is birdwatching or getting involved with narrow gauge railways. This whole area of special interest will be examined in more depth in a later chapter.

As the marketer pursues segmentation analysis it becomes clear that while demographic variables are useful in guiding the allocation of marketing resources, they should be used as supplementary bases for determining target groups rather than primary bases. Senior citizens do not represent a homogeneous group. They are heterogeneous, ranging from the sixty-year-old passive entertainment type to the eighty-year-old activist who goes trekking in the Himalayas.

Tourism marketing needs to be selective because no service, indeed no destination is able to satisfy the wants and needs of the total market. Putting this at its simplest, the sun worshipper is hardly likely to visit London, and conversely, the theatre buff is unlikely to visit the Costa Brava in pursuit of his needs and wants. So the appeal must be to those identified groups who are in the right demographic groups, whose motivations and travel behaviour patterns are likely to be met by the destination and the services offered. As a consequence they are likely to be more responsive to the marketing approaches, assuming of course that the marketer has got it right in terms of medium and message. It follows that a global philosophy such as that followed by Coca Cola in its advertising is generally inappropriate for tourism.

The product range offered by a tourist destination or by tour operators is diverse and even when the demographic group is a discrete one there is need to appeal to different segments within that group. Product presentation can be used to differentiate between the segments. Thus Saga Holidays now produces several brochures all aimed at the senior citizen market but differentiating between the sub-segments by age and by travel pattern. Senior citizens as a broad segment can certainly be sub-segmented into quality seekers, pursuers and economy seekers, but there are also elite, adventurers and a few 'Action Men' too.

Differentiated marketing of appropriate products comes into its own in the case of Saga after it has developed the primary demand. This company has identified the target market in broad terms in selecting senior citizens, building up mailing lists and using corporate PR to underline its specialism. It has recognised that the market is a heterogeneous one with many mini-markets enabling it to select products which are appropriate for the sub-segments and these range from luxury cruises to special interest holidays in university accommodation. This is a classic case of a company developing primary demand and then using differentiated marketing as a strategy to reach the sub-segments, which it has identified. Since Saga has developed mailing lists and uses direct mail to sell direct to its potential customers it has been able to estimate the value of operating in each of the sub-segments, while at the same time minimising its marketing costs.

It is, of course, always going to be more expensive to adopt a strategy of differentiated marketing – witness the fact that Saga produces several brochures and not just one to appeal to what on the face of it is one target group – the senior citizen. Certainly it increases the cost of doing business but it creates more sales. The trick is to get the equation right. A company can clearly identify the segments and sub-segments which it plans to sell to, and should then measure profitability of each of these sub-segments in terms of marketing investment. This analysis in depth will lead to refinements in the marketing strategy and techniques and will guide the marketer in the selection of products and product presentation.

The marketer will use segmentation analysis to design advertising appeals and to refine the briefs which he provides to the writers and designers of brochures, highlighting the special benefits which are being sought by the various segments and where the segment is sufficiently big, devoting significant space to it. For example, the British Tourist Authority publishes a number of main guides, each geared to market needs. In the German edition there is a page devoted to walking holidays but there is not a page on walking in the Japanese edition. Japanese motivations and the travel benefits which they pursue are very different from those of the German visiting Britain. Their socio-economic profiles may be very similar but their psychographic profiles are very different.

The tourism marketer must recognise that a market can be subdivided into many parts; one 'orange', but a number of segments. He must select those segments most appropriate to his destination or product and analyse the attractiveness of these segments in terms of profitability *vis-à-vis* the cost of reaching them. Now this would appear to be self-evident but consider the number of resorts (whose market has disappeared to the competition) which have failed to adapt to their new situation and failed to recognise that there are other market segments which offer potential with only a slight change in product but a major change in marketing strategy.

Thus far we have considered segmentation only in the context of leisure travel. The business traveller is also a tourist and the business travel market is also capable of segmentation. There are five main segments:

The independent business traveller;
The conference delegate;
The visitor to a trade fair or exhibition;
The participant in an incentive trip;
Training or study.

Each segment is capable of being measured; each segment is substantial in its own right and each can be reached by the marketer using a variety of marketing tools. It is an important market and is considered separately later in this book.

For those who operate in more than one country, more than a single domestic market, it is still necessary to undertake segmentation analysis, but the first step is to choose markets. It is no accident that Europe, with its developed countries and affluent societies, is at once the largest generator and receiver of traffic. Its geographical position and its cultures and heritage can provide for the majority of segments, no matter how specialist they are. Proximity to markets is an important factor. One has only to look at the USA as a generator and a receiver of tourist traffic.

Several million Canadians cross the border every year and both Canada and Mexico receive a great number of Americans. The fact that Americans do not need a passport to visit these neighbouring countries helps, but the pattern is repeated: New Zealand and Australia, Germany and Austria. Any marketer engaged in international marketing will be aware of this. These are his primary markets which generate the major share of his traffic. Clearly these are the markets on which he should concentrate. What is very often overlooked is that fact that one can become over-reliant on these primary markets. About 90 per cent of the total visits to Spain, Italy and France is intra-European. It is always prudent to develop new markets.

Secondary markets are those which generate a good tourist traffic to the destination but are less important inasmuch as they generate more traffic to alternative destinations, usually because the alternative destinations offer perceived benefits which are unavailable. Germany is a good example of this. The Germans are the biggest international travellers and Germany is an important market for Britain. Britain is not, however, an important destination for Germans. Britain receives less than two per cent of German main holidays, very largely because the mass movements are in pursuit of the sun. These secondary markets have to be researched in some depth in order to discover, through segmentation studies, motivation research and attitude studies, what obstacles there are to further development and more importantly, what opportunities there are which might be exploited through concentrated marketing.

Tertiary markets are those markets which are not currently producing much traffic for the destination but which offer future potential. These markets which offer opportunity for development also need to be researched, but there is a great deal of free information available, a great deal of market intelligence, which can be obtained with a little effort. Invariably the countries concerned will produce travel statistics. Figures on the economy and standard of living will usually be available, and some research into the history of the country, travel and communications links, can provide indicators of future potential for a particular destination.

The Far East is probably the single most important region in the world as a future generator of large volumes of international travellers. The traffic flows at the moment are not great – less than five million out of Japan, but they are growing fast. It is the only region in the world where there has been a net increase in BTA's overseas offices over the past ten years. Britain has a good spread of markets, probably better than any other tourist destination in the world. That fact stood Britain in good stead in 1986 when there was such a massive downturn in American visits to Europe.

It should be one of a national tourist office's principal roles – to develop new markets and new segments. The national tourist office should carry out this essential missionary work in the knowledge that the trade will follow once the potential has been demonstrated.

The marketer must analyse his markets and then segment them in order to assess their relative values and as a basis for determining his marketing strategy and allocation of marketing resources. Not least he should set targets which represent a sensible return on the investment. For a national tourist office or a local destination (resort or region), that investment may well be in the medium or long term, but clearly not at the expense of investment in primary and secondary markets. For the individual company it may well be necessary to seek an immediate return on the investment and tertiary markets would not then feature in his strategy at all.

Recognition of the fact that markets are constituted not as single markets but as a collection of mini-markets will provide the marketer with opportunities for growth, guidance in marketing strategy and techniques as well as allocation of his resources.

Summary

In tourism there are three distinct markets – the domestic, the international and the day visitor. Each needs to be analysed and segmented into meaningful target groups. There are many ways of segmenting: socio-demographic, socio-economic, travel motivations, psychographic groups. One person may belong to several groups. Tourism marketing needs to be selective in terms of target, medium and message. Segmentation leads to differentiated marketing. Each segment is capable of being measured in terms of potential, marketing investment and profitability. Markets on an international level need to be classified into primary, secondary or tertiary markets.

One of the principal roles of a tourist office should be to develop new markets and new segments. Market analysis and segmentation guides the marketer in strategy and techniques as well as allocation of resources.

Reference

1 Kotler, P, *1967 Marketing Management*, Prentice Hall Inc p 45.

7 Market measurement and forecasting

'Would you tell me please, which way I ought to go?' (Alice). Answer, 'That depends a good deal on where you want to get to.'

Market research methods including economic and statistical measures are the tools of the marketer's trade and measuring markets is an essential part of the marketing planning task. Practical application needs operational skills and experience in addition to a knowledge of research techniques. It must be stressed that the marketing managers and not the researchers are in charge and they have the great responsibility, often not fully appreciated, of giving the researchers clear instructions on the objectives of policies, strategies and plans and the objectives and purpose of the research studies.

There are many markets and many market segments, so first define the market to be measured. In most cases this will be related to a destination and its attractions (the true tourist product), or specific services, where the product will involve a combination of means to an end, or the specific service itself (eg a particular hotel which is a component part of the total purchase). Measurement will involve geographic markets for a country or a group of countries, such as Europe, a region within a country, a particular service (air travel), an hotel or an activity or attraction eg historic site, a conference centre or marina.

The geographic market must be complemented by segmentation study where the behaviour groups will need to be identified. Measuring the principal geographic markets is a task for national organisations, the state tourist board, the national airline, railway and major international hotel groups; in other words the broad brush for marketing on a wide canvas. The information will be helpful to many other smaller interests eg regions and resorts as the background to more specific study. For these reasons the geographic studies are usually carried out by governments, or on a cooperative basis between neighbouring countries, and other major interests such as flag carriers.

Principal geographic markets must be measured separately; for example, in the case of Britain, USA and Canada separately, and in Western Europe each of the principal countries or markets; Australia and New Zealand; and in the Far East the key individual markets such as India and Japan should be identified.

Volume and value of traffic; details of trips, such as length of stay, places visited; place of residence; and basic socio-economic data (age, sex, occupation, income), must be explored. Behaviour information is also important: activities pursued, form of travel (package or independent), attitudes, including effect on booking patterns and use of advisers, agents, guide books and other travel counsellors. The following extract from one of the marketing guides produced by the BTA for the trade deals with Canada[1]. These guides are done for each of BTA's markets.

Canada: a market analysis

Two-fifths of the Canadian population (41%) are under 25, 40% are between 25 and 54 and 19% are over 55. As in Britain and the United States, the trend is towards an older population due to a declining birth rate and increasing longevity. The latest census shows that Canadians are marrying later, divorcing more often and having fewer children. They are better educated – twice as many Canadian adults had a university degree (8%) in 1981 as in 1971 (4.8%). Alberta had the highest-education population with 9.6% of its residents possessing degrees.

Canada's population is very varied in terms of birthplace, language and ethnic groupings. According to the 1971 census, 18.3 million Canadians (85%) were born in Canada and 3.3 million (15%) were foreign born. Ontario and British Columbia received the largest influx of immigrants. Countries such as the UK and the USA have been the source of major immigration waves to Canada both in the past and currently. French Canadians, who are concentrated in Quebec, number around six million. The native Indian population living in reserves in the more isolated areas of Canada number around 289,000.

Distribution of population

By Birthplace	%	By Ethnic Group	%
Canada	84.7	British	44.6
Other countries	15.3	French	28.7
UK	4.3	German	6.1
Italy	1.8	Italian	3.4
USA	1.4	Ukrainian	2.7
All others	7.8	All others	14.5

Source: Canada Yearbook.

In the 1981 census 61% of the population reported English as their mother tongue and 26% reported French.

Average incomes

Canadian $

	Canada	Atlant. Prov.	Quebec	Ontario	Prairie Prov.	British Columbia
1982	27,379	23,311	24,774	29,125	28,561	28,844
1985	31,959	29,974	29,435	35,092	31,735	31,163

Source: Statistics Canada.

Travel by Canadian residents outside Canada

	1982		1983		1984	
	000s	%	000s	%	000s	%
Total trips	34,811	100	40,731	100	38,795	100
Day trips to USA	23,056	66	27,163	67	25,982	67
One or more night trips to USA	10,266	29	11,816	29	10,891	28
Trips to other countries	1,489	4	1,752	4	2,012	5

Source: Statistics Canada – Travel Between Canada and other countries.

Residents of Canada spent an average of 21.8 nights on trips abroad excluding the USA in 1984. The average expenditure per trip, excluding fares was around $891 an increase of 3% on 1983. This compares with an average of $285 on a US trip lasting at least one night. The average stay in the USA is much shorter than an abroad trip at eight nights although the average spending per person night is only slightly less on a US trip than an abroad trip, $37 compared with $41.

Around half of Canadian trips to other countries are to Europe. The second major destination is Bermuda and the Caribbean. Europe's share of the abroad market had been decreasing prior to 1981 when it stabilised. In 1984 Europe's share increased – it accounted for 52.6% of Canadian trips abroad. Bermuda and the Caribbean have been losing share since 1981.

Canadian trips to other countries

Total trips to other countries (000s)	1979 1,757 %	1980 1,585 %	1981 1,478 %	1982 1,489 %	1983 1,752 %	1984 2,012 %
Europe	53.2	49.7	50.3	51.1	51.0	52.6
UK only	19.6	17.4	17.0	16.5	16.7	16.7
UK and other Europe	9.3	8.6	7.8	8.5	9.0	9.6
Other Europe	23.0	22.3	24.1	24.8	24.0	25.1
Europe and one other area of destination	1.3	1.4	1.4	1.3	1.2	1.2
Bermuda and Caribbean	25.8	27.1	27.2	25.2	20.3	18.2
Asia	3.8	4.4	4.9	5.2	5.3	5.0
Africa	1.3	1.6	1.6	1.8	1.2	1.6
South America	1.7	1.5	1.8	1.6	1.4	1.8
Central America	0.4	0.5	0.3	0.4	0.4	0.4
Other Areas	9.9	11.3	9.3	9.5	16.4	16.1
Cruises	2.8	3.0	3.5	4.2	4.0	3.4
Combined destinations	1.1	0.9	1.1	1.0	0.4	0.9

Source: Statistics Canada – Travel between Canada and other countries.

Purpose of trip abroad

Trips to Europe and especially the UK are much more likely to be in order to visit friends or relatives than trips to the USA or other countries. The following table compares total trips to other countries of the world and trips to UK only.

	Total trips to other countries 1985 2,300,000 %	Trips to UK only 1985 631,000 %
Business	11	8
Visiting friends and relatives	26	33
Other holiday	54	44
Miscellaneous	9	15

Sources: Statistics Canada
       International Passenger Survey

Expenditure

A total of Canadian $1,004 million were spent in Europe by Canadians in 1984, 23% of which was on trips to Britain only and 27% on trips which included the UK with other European countries. Most of the remainder (47%) was on trips to other European countries excluding Britain. Canadian expenditure in Europe was up by 19% in 1984.

Holiday-taking by Canadians

Canadian paid leave entitlement tends to be shorter than in Europe. Paid vacations are typically of three weeks' duration, while four weeks or more are available for long service employees (ten years). The Canadian Government Office of Tourism in their 1982 Vacation Travel Survey found that over 60% of Canadian adults aged eighteen or over had at least three weeks' vacation time available. Over a third had two weeks' or less vacation time available, 27% three to four weeks and 25% five weeks or more. Another 11% indicated that they could go anytime. Retired people, of course, comprise a sizeable proportion of those with extensive leisure time. The number of public holidays varies according to province but the minimum is ten days.

In 1984, 55% of Canadian adults took at least one vacation trip of one night or more while 3% holidayed at home. The proportion taking a vacation trip away from home has remained around this level since the early 1970s. However, the average number of vacation trips taken by individuals has tended upwards over the years – to 1.8 trips in 1984.

The vast majority of Canadian vacation trips are taken within the North American continent. Canada's share of vacation trips in 1984 marginally decreased from 70% in 1982 to 67% in 1984. The United States' share returned to 25% in 1984 from 23% in 1982. The proportion of off-shore vacation trips increased slightly in 1984 to 13% from 11% in 1982. The UK, which accounts for around half of Canadian vacation trips to Europe remained at 2%.

Vacation destination of Canadians

Base: (Actual trips)	1980 (2,957) %	1982 (3,198) %	1984 (1,682) %
Areas visited overnight or longer			
Canada only	62	66	63
Canada at all	67	70	67
US mainland	26	23	25
Off shore (incl. US Islands)	13	11	13
Europe	5	5	6
(UK)	(2)	(2)	(2)
Caribbean/Bermuda	3	3	1
Hawaii	3	2	2
All other	3	3	4

Source: Vacation travel by Canadians in 1984
Canadian Government Office of Tourism

Reasons for vacation trips

| | Canada | | US mainland | | Offshore* destinations | |
	1982 %	1984 %	1982 %	1984 %	1982 %	1984 %
To visit friends or relatives	52	58	33	36	40	28
To spend some time at a vacation spot	24	22	41	39	42	49
Sightseeing and doing things in cities and towns	15	14	25	26	28	31
Sightseeing and doing things away from cities and towns	12	11	11	14	19	26
Fishing, boating and other outdoor activities	17	14	8	7	14	10
Camping and tenting	11	7	4	4	8	1
Shopping	7	8	15	17	9	13
Combined business/pleasure	7	7	8	11	7	6
Attend festivals sports/special events	6	8	11	9	7	9
Stay at summer place I own	4	4	1	2	3	2
Other	9	5	13	7	10	8

Source: Vacation Travel by Canadians in 1982
*Includes US Islands

Vacation trips in Canada are concentrated in the summer months whereas trips to the USA or offshore destinations are more widely spread throughout the year.

Season of vacation trips

| | Canada | | | US mainland | | | Offshore destinations | | |
	1981 %	1982 %	1984 %	1981 %	1982 %	1984 %	1981 %	1982 %	1984 %
Winter	11	11	13	28	29	28	32	37	46
Spring	20	19	23	23	24	27	27	20	20
Summer	49	51	49	29	26	22	18	26	13
Autumn	20	19	15	22	21	23	23	17	21

Winter = December to March   Spring = April to June
Summer = July to August   Autumn = September to November

Source: Vacation travel by Canadians in 1982

Travel agents are important in planning offshore vacation travel. They were used on 66% of trips in 1982, similar to the previous year.

The average length of a vacation trip was shorter in 1982, 11.5 nights compared with 12.8 nights in 1981. The average length of trip declined in both Canada and the USA but was marginally longer on offshore trips – 23.5 nights compared with 21.4 in 1981.

Most Canadians estimated they spent about the same (45%) or less (27%) on vacation trips in 1982 than they normally spend. A fifth estimated they spent more than usual. The main way in which Canadians curtailed spending was by cancelling or postponing a trip. Others travelled shorter distances or took trips of shorter duration or stayed in less expensive accommodation.

The most common motivation for holidays taken in Canada is to visit friends or relatives. Trips to the USA or offshore are more likely to be motivated by the desire to spend time at a vacation spot or for sightseeing than is the case for Canadian vacations.

Life stage Canadian vacationers (1984)

	Per cent of individuals vacationing in:		
	Canada (1,180) %	US mainland (406) %	Offshore (178) %
Young adults at home	12	11	14
Young singles	6	7	11
Co-op*	9	7	8
Young couples	6	8	4
Pre-teen families	23	17	14
Teen families	4	8	2
Post-teen families	7	7	10
Older working couples	12	16	22
Older working singles	3	4	6
Older retired couples	11	10	9
Older retired singles	7	6	1

* Co-op is defined as single people between the ages of 18–34, two or more in the household.

Principal elements of measurement

1. The profile of Canadian visitors (socio-economic data).
2. The region (place) of residence. This is important in concentrating scarce marketing resources.
3. Details of their visits, or in other words the 'product' they buy. This involves expenditure, length of stay, accommodation, transport, where they went in Britain and what they did (activities), purpose and time of visit.
4. This measurement of what is happening currently (analysis of present traffic), needs to be set in context, firstly, in share of market terms. Travel to Britain compared with total abroad travel from the particular market and to competing areas.
5. Historic trends must be measured. Is the market expanding or

contracting, maturing or demonstrating new growth trends? What is happening to market share? In certain circumstances a reduced level of sales may represent a 'success' story, and further investment for future expansion fully justified.

Market research needs to develop an even wider frame which sets out external factors which might dominate or influence the marketing scene. Factors such as health and safety, political stability, economic stability, exchange rates, public attitudes (fashion and reputation for welcome). There are examples of governments spending considerable sums to restore an unfavourable image of a hostile or unwelcoming people. The residents are the hosts and their perceived attitude towards visitors can be a powerful external factor impinging on the destination's success. This is important in developing a marketing plan (see chapter 10) as are new developments in the market place and the destination.

Product development and supply changes must also be examined, both regarding the current situation and any major change in the foreseeable future likely to affect traffic in the short term. Typical product changes would be the opening of new transport routes, by air or by sea (ferry services and cruises), relief of constraints, removal of visas or exchange controls, expansion of major services such as hotel accommodation.

Regions and resorts

The same methods should be used when the product relates to a smaller destination area. Well developed tourist regions and resorts may have large budgets for key functions in marketing and development. They will need their own strategies for growth, and must take the lead in partnership with the area's tourist services in formulating a marketing plan as the keystone of the development policy. In free market economies this is a vital responsibility since the expansion of tourism will depend on private sector investment, enterprise and management.

National statistics for both international and domestic traffic provide a frame of reference, together with the geographic market analyses. The region, and more particularly the resort, will need records of domestic movement in the country. Generally national organisations, helped by international official bodies, provide a substantial amount of material from regular sample surveys on domestic movement. The 'mega' trends are increasingly identified although orders of magnitude may be imprecise.

It will be essential for the region to identify its share of the national market, and measure it. This will give necessary guidance on variations from the national pattern, point to unique features and highlight strengths and weaknesses. Usually, this information is obtained by surveys of visitors to the locality. Resorts are fortunate if they can secure the cooperation of all local interests, hoteliers, transport concerns, entertainment and attraction managers, including municipal ventures, to check their visitor business. The Retail Audit, used to measure flow of consumer goods indicates the possibilities, recording helpful information on the make-up of resort business. It will not be necessary to carry out expensive in depth surveys each year, as traffic especially holiday movement tends to follow traditional lines. But volume and expenditure will need annual monitoring, and the marketers must be watchful for signs of substantial change or any new trends emerging. Tourists do not have the same loyalty to the product as in earlier years, although some market segments remain very conservative, though not necessarily captive.

Brighton, one of Britain's largest resorts with a record of success in meeting changing market needs and investing substantial amounts of money, from both the public and private sector, has a well developed tourism strategy and a successful marketing programme. This has been helped by a major research exercise based on a number of separate surveys in 1982. The size and characteristics of current visitors were fully explored and described, including the principal market segments. Trends were identified and the main lines of future growth which could be secured were clearly established. This had important implications for product expansion and improvement and helped to establish necessary cooperative action with the inevitably wide range of private sector interests. They have their essential part to play in exploiting the potential trade which had been clearly established.

The following extracts from the Brighton Tourism Study summary will illustrate the scope and value of this market measurement.[2] Study sponsors were Brighton Council; Brighton and Hove Hotels, Guest Houses and Restaurants Association; East Sussex County Council; and the English Tourist Board.

Brighton tourism study background and components

The study comprised eight separate surveys: visitors to Brighton between July and October 1982; short break package buyers; conferences and exhibitions – both organisers and delegates; opinions of Brighton as a holiday resort amongst the British population; tourism trends generally; tourism and leisure resources in Brighton; hotel and guest house use; and the effects of visitor spending in creating local incomes and jobs.

Trends and prospects in tourism generally are described. Some of the main features relevant to Brighton are:

- Continued growth generally in business and conference tourism is expected, but competition will be stiff from new and planned facilities for conferences and exhibitions.
- Short holidays are likely to remain the most buoyant sector of domestic tourism.
- Main holidays by the British – the backbone of most seaside resorts' business – have declined, and future growth is expected to go mainly on holidays abroad.
- Overseas visitors to Britain represent a future growth opportunity.

The characteristics and opinions of the main sorts of visitors in Brighton are described. An estimated £86 million was spent by visitors to Brighton in a year, half by tourists in hotels or guest houses; just over a quarter by day visitors; an eighth by foreign language students; and a tenth by people staying with friends or relatives.

Holidays in Brighton were generally short (seven out of ten being one to three nights in duration) and additional to main annual holidays. Many of the holidaymakers in the town were from the higher (ABC1) social groups and relatively few had children with them. Half of the holidaymakers had been to Brighton before – some many times previously. Visitors were well satisfied with their trips and particularly liked the shops and the lanes, the amenities, the sea, the environment and atmosphere generally. One in five summer holidaymakers was an overseas visitor, and others came as language students or conference delegates.

A similar exercise for Torbay[3], another leading resort in Britain provided this destination with the basis for future marketing and planning. These enquiries need to be repeated from time to time, and in the interim period it is important to monitor traffic flows. Periodically results should be appraised, performance against objectives assessed and measured. Exchange of information between destination areas can be instructive. Unfortunately, the appraisal exercises are often glossed over, especially in the public sector, and sometimes exchange of information is limited for fear of competitive advantage. In truth the benefits of a free exchange usually greatly exceed any possible competitive danger. It has long been the practice in the USA for a relatively free exchange of commercial information, but in Europe a suspicion of disclosure often remains. It is usually the case, where all the destination interests are more interdependent than independent (so far as total business and growth are concerned), that sharing information can only be constructive and helpful.

Tourism services

Market measurement is equally necessary for specific services and businesses. Commercial operators have the advantage of finding out the key characteristics of their existing customers as a first step to comparison with the national and regional markets and trends and so are able to identify unique and competitive features. These, in offering advantages in trade, represent the competitive edge as opposed to the field of cooperative endeavour. Both have their place, but it cannot be expected that this special trading position will be shared with competing businesses. Just as there were differences and additional tasks for the region and resort in looking after its own interests, so also the commercial operators and their separate trades need to supplement the national and regional measurements.

The following table describes in statistical terms the market in the USA for air travel by businessmen, a vital market segment. Clearly, the traffic flows are contained in the total national (and as appropriate

Table 7.1 – A profile of business travellers on airlines

	All Business Fliers	Frequent Domestic* Fliers	Frequent International** Fliers
Sex			
Male	90%	94%	95%
Female	10	6	5
Age			
25–34	23%	21%	14%
35–49	44	47	53
50–54	10	9	11
Median age	43 years	44 years	45 years
Marital status			
Married	80%	84%	80%
Education			
College educated	94%	95%	96%
Graduated from College	76	79	84
Post-graduate degree	31	31	41
Household income			
Under $25,000	9%	4%	4%
$25,000 – $34,999	16	12	7
$35,000 – $49,999	28	29	20
$50,000 – $74,999	26	29	32
$75,000 – $99,999	10	13	14
$100,000 and over	11	13	23
Median income	$48,300	$54,500	$64,400
Job Title			
Top Management	36%	32%	56%
All managers/administrators	72	69	80
Other	28	31	20

*Passengers who have taken twenty or more domestic flights in the past year for business reasons.
**Passengers who have taken ten or more international flights in the past year for business reasons.
Source: 'Business Travelers. The Airline Experience,' *Time Magazine*, Time Marketing Services AA#2268, 1981, pp 4–5.

the international and regional) figures for the country or the local destination. But this large and wealthy segment needs its own targeting, and its own place in the respective destination marketing plans.

Market measurement is easier in theory for the commercial services in tourism since they benefit from face to face contact with their market. Hotels for example have registration records which can easily be supplemented by simple survey methods. Many visitors will be regulars and the management will have an instinctive knowledge of make-up and motivation of their clientele. Many though, do not use the information fully or do not relate to the wider market measurements to watch trends and market shares.

Socio-economic data is important: age, sex, marital status, income, education, occupation, place of residence, family background. But this is not sufficient, and must be supplemented by travel patterns (how do visitors travel, how do they select their service and other purchases). Purpose of visit and frequency of travel are also key factors. While the management will know their regular clients, they need to judge traffic they are missing and which might fill empty rooms, thus increasing occupancy and profitability. Many service trades, transport and accommodation particularly, will have several distinct markets or market segments: business (independent, conference attendance, visiting trade fair, incentive); pleasure (touring, or staying in one centre, specialist travel, visiting friends and relatives, visiting for special events). Each of these segments and sub-segments will need individual treatment. They can be complementary, corporate meetings for example, usually take place outside the main holiday season and so are indispensable for resorts.

The following extracts from *Marketing Hotels in the 90s*[4] by Melvyn Greene illustrates some of the stages in the task of measuring the market for a hotel. The first measurement is on the whole catchment area and related to the hotel's position, facilities and the competition. The catchment area needs to be reviewed in the context of the wider regional and national information, taking into account statistics of visitors to the 'town' and to specific local attractions, statistics of passengers through the airport, road (and motorway information), local bus, coach and rail data.

Information required:

1. Broad background information:
   (a) local community
   (b) local industry, commerce, employment
   (c) communications
   (d) local events and attractions
   (e) catchment area

2. Facilities of the hotel
3. Details of competitive hotels
4. Profile of guests
5. Activity levels
6. Employees – selling ability
7. Specific information on local community, industry, events, communications and catchment area
8. Advantage/limitation list – on own hotel
   – on competitive hotel.

Visitors to specific events (conferences, exhibitions, theatres), historic properties, museums and art galleries, and sporting events can all be measured. BTA and ETB publish annual statistics of visits to historic properties, and other sightseeing or major spectator events. From time to time other surveys amplify the information, giving guidance on market segments, behaviour and principal market characteristics which provides trend information.

Mr Greene suggests a checklist on facilities and competition as well as a checklist on the profile of guests and a careful appraisal of motivations.

Forecasting

Forecasting related to market measurement has a special and key function. It represents target setting, and is a principal objective of market planning. The individual market studies will be compared with the national and as appropriate regional studies. Projection of historic trends will be modified firstly, by reference to product changes and major supply developments, secondly, by taking into account external factors (national economic situation, international market situation, fiscal burdens, inflation and political stability).

Finally, the commercial operator, whether in the public or private sector will seek to maximise revenue and profits in moving towards maximum efficiency in use of resources. His own market measurement will have indicated changes in his market share, new opportunities, the competitive advantages or dangers. Since tourism is essentially a market force requiring a package of services and attractions, the individual operator must take into account his partners' forecasts and plans related to them, and in marketing seek to take advantage of the cooperative task where this supports his own competitive role, as in part it will.

Forecasting methods will follow the national pattern, but must be modified in the light of the specific service or trader's market study, and forward plan remembering that the forecast in this case is the business target or plan.

Measuring market potential

An essential aspect of market measurement relates to market potential. This involves forecasting techniques. Forecasting is not an exact science. Usually estimates of future traffic reflect potential not necessarily targets. The object is to guide, to assist informed judgements in marketing and development. It is not a 'crystal ball' exercise predicting the future but rather giving indications of possibilities, a range of options, orders of magnitude and not precise figures. Costs and benefits, favourable and unfavourable factors, strengths and weaknesses must be considered in assessing likely trends. Furthermore, in the exercise of options account must be taken of proposed action to exploit markets, to use the marketing forces to achieve certain objectives.

The principal methods of forecasting are:

(a)   the projection by extrapolation of historic trends;
(b)   extrapolation, subject to the application of 'weights' or variables.

These may be accompanied by the Delphi method of structured group discussions by experts on changing trends and key factors determining future traffic flows. The 'Delphi' discussion will be used primarily to evaluate weights and variables.

The third method is the use of mathematical models. While this was popular in the earlier periods of growth in mass tourism in the 1950s and 1960s the more sudden and dramatic changes in economic and social backgrounds, and the increasing strength and dynamism of market forces have made the models imprecise and too theoretical for use on their own. Market surveys, identifying trends from listening to the market place have become vital factors in estimations of potential.

In recent years the European Travel Commission has carried out forecasting exercises in cooperation with the principal tourism industry sectors. Methods involved projections, study of industry sector reports, and group discussions. The blend of specialist economic, market research and marketing knowledge and experience resulted in remarkably accurate medium-term forecasting (five to ten years), offering a range of possibilities on a high, medium and low basis. The studies have been repeated. Ideally the potential estimates need to be carried out on a rolling forward basis covering five to ten years, giving ranges of growth indicating the scenarios or likely external and market conditions. Clearly, the studies must take into account not only the longer term changing trends, traffic growth rates but basic 'external' factors such as GNP and personal disposable income, likely tax and other fiscal changes, purchasing power, which might be affected by fluctuating exchange rates, political factors, unrest or restriction. For example, the introduction of visas for Americans and other non-EEC visitors as a security measure by the French had a bad effect on their transatlantic business in late 1986 and in 1987.

The Institut Transport Aerien[5] in Paris carried out the first very detailed forecasting exercise for the European Travel Commission in 1980. Aviation and Tourism International completed a second monitoring exercise for the Commission in 1983.[6] The following chart and table from the latter report indicates the forecasts made, the time scale and looking back how forecasts compared with the results.

Table 7.2 – Comparison of 1990 forecasts

	ITA 'Middle'	ATI 'Most likely'
WORLD TOURIST ARRIVALS		
Annual growth	6.4% (1)	5.1% (2)
1990 forecast	536 M	415 M
ETC EUROPE ARRIVALS		
Annual growth	5.1% (3)	5.1% (2)
1990 forecast	242 M	239 M
MAIN OVERSEAS FLOWS		
USA:		
Annual growth	3.5% (3)	5.0% (2)
1990 forecast:		
European arrivals	16.0 M	14.5 M
US departures	–	6.3 M
Canada:		
Annual growth	4.0% (3)	4.0% (2)
1990 forecast:		
European arrivals	3.7 M	2.9 M
Canadian departures	–	1.1 M
Japan:		
Annual growth	7.6% (3)	6–7% (2)
1990 forecast:		
European arrivals	4.1 M	3.0–3.3 M
Japanese departures	–	0.7–0.75 M

(1) From 1979 base   (2) From 1982 base   (3) From 1978 base

In the first case the economic recession, the oil crises and the end of a long period of continuous growth with slowly emerging changes in life style and behaviour affected the forecasts. The severity of the recession and the speed and scale of other major trends were underestimated – not surprisingly. The second forecast by ATI usefully compared with the earlier forecasts has proved in the longer term remarkably accurate for world travel and for ETC Europe, although not so accurate for Europe, including the countries of eastern Europe.

Both studies were very thorough in their analysis of demand determinants including income elasticity, GDP, price changes and especially exchange rates relative to other competing goods and services. ATI used a 'Delphi' type seminar to evaluate determinants and trends. Generally both groups of experts came to similar conclusions regarding the principal factors affecting future travel movements. This comparison of

Figure 7.1 – International travel trends

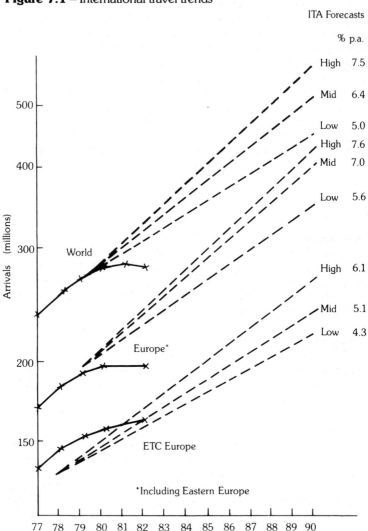

Source: Aviation and Tourism International.

past studies not only vindicates the experts' work and their methods, but provides a valuable case history. Estimates of broad trends need to be on a longer term basis – five to ten years. They should cover a broad field; in this case Europe and the world. They should be seen as indications of potential, and variations from the anticipated trend expected. These changes need careful analysis as they will normally reflect important demand changes or market response to alterations in the key demand determinants. As these were clearly not expected there will be many lessons to be learnt by management and marketers. Variations represent major shifts in demand patterns, not simply changes in one geographic market or one segment, or in one destination area. This can happen for a number of reasons including marketing and price relativity. There is free and fierce competition and the tourist can switch patronage between competing areas while the total market increases.

The international forecasts are necessary checkpoints in national and regional market and development planning. The same principles should be used for national and regional strategies and plans.

Megatrends

The European Travel Commission's member countries' research experts meet periodically to review 'mega' trends (a 'Delphi' exercise). There are other international and regional groups who do this kind of work. Their conclusions are very useful for market planning. ETC researchers' megatrends,[7] published in 1991, identified the following major elements for the longer term scenario.

Megatrends of tourism in Europe 1990–2000

1.   Global travel spending and particularly transport spending in, into and from Europe will increase faster than other budget items due to more frequent, albeit shorter, holidays. However, although daily expenditure will generally be maintained due to higher quality requirements, expenditure per trip may decrease due to shorter duration of holidays.

2.   Long-haul holidays to and from Europe will increase faster than intra-European vacation holidays, to and from practically all the continents, notably America, Asia and Oceania.

3.   Within Europe, city travel will increase faster than summer and beach vacation holidays, due to parallel and steady increases of both 'short breaks' (with cultural or pseudo-cultural motivations) and of 'business travel', including all forms of MIC travel, incentives, conventions, conferences, as well as exhibitions and fairs.

4.   South–north, east–west and west–east travel will increase relatively faster than traditional north–south holidays, although the corresponding figures are still much lower.

5.   Traffic across the present intra-European borders will increase faster than domestic travel in most European countries.

6.   Winter sunshine holidays, cultural winter tours and cruises will

probably increase faster than winter sports holidays for a few years.

7.   Air traffic, both short- and long-haul, will still increase faster than other types of transportation due to various factors including new direct connections – although in Europe crowded airspace and long waiting hours could be a deterrent until these problems are solved. Rail transport will however also show strong growth, in particular owing to new, convenient rail links for short distances.

8.   Given the current trend towards individualisation, packages rather than group travel will become increasingly popular.

9.   Late reservations will increase faster than early bookings as CRS systems and information dissemination systems like Amadeus and Galileo become more and more comprehensive, although at present these benefit the business traveller more than the ordinary tourist.

10. Travel by two age groups will increase faster than others: senior citizens (due *inter alia* to growing numbers and increased means of pensioners) and young people (due to improved education and new travel opportunities).

11. As a consequence, both the demand for cultural visits and cultural holidays and for active summer/winter holidays will grow faster than for other forms of vacation.

12. Groups, including families, will tend to be smaller, and more flexible.

13. Price/quality ratios will play an increasing role in the choice of destinations and accommodation. The quality of the environment will become a determining element in attracting visitors.

The World Tourism Organisation carries out forecasting exercises on the international and European scale. Their seminar on the 'Development of International Tourism in Europe to the year 2000' dealt with demand and supply factors. In the period of study (twelve years) demand rather than supply changes is likely to be the prime factor. Furthermore, with new technology available for building, developing and financing, very rapid reaction and response to demand factors is possible resulting in speedy supply change. This makes professional and cost effective marketing even more compelling than it has been in the past.

Summary

Market research methods and economic and statistical measurement are the tools of the marketer's trade in measuring markets as an essential part of the marketing planning task. There are many markets and many market segments so first define the market to be measured with precision.

Market analysis must embrace volume and value of traffic, trip details, such as length of stay, places visited, residence, and basic socio-economic data. Behaviour information is important, activities undertaken, form of travel, booking patterns and advice services. Principal elements to be covered are profile of visitors, place of residence, details of trip, market share and external factors. National statistics for international and domestic traffic provide a frame of reference.

Share of market needs annual monitoring to detect new trends. Tourists no longer have the strong 'brand' loyalty of earlier years. Exchange of information between destinations can be instructive. Market measurement is important for specific services and businesses. Commercial operators have the advantage of noting key characteristics of their existing business by talking to their customers. Destination marketing plans must be based on key market segments. Researchers' prime task is to ensure that there is a satisfactory inventory of resources and services for the destination needed on a national, regional and resort scale. Charting must be quantified by type and standard and take account of seasonal flows.

Forecasting is not an exact science. Estimates of future traffic reflect potential not necessarily targets. The object is to guide informed judgements in management. Principal methods are:

(a) projection by extrapolation of historic trends;
(b) extrapolation subject to correction by 'weights' or variables, assisted by the results of structured group discussions by experts.

Mathematical models are sometimes used but tend to be too theoretical in view of the increasing strength and dynamism of the market. A number of international organisations publish helpful estimates of future trends periodically, some of which, such as the European Travel Commission studies, have proved reliable.

References

1 *Guide to the Canadian Market*, BTA 1986.
2 *Brighton Tourism Study*, English Tourist Board in cooperation with Brighton Council, East Sussex Council, Brighton and Hove Hotels Association 1982.
3 *Torbay Tourism Study*, English Tourist Board in cooperation with Torbay Borough Council 1981.
4 Greene, M, *Marketing Hotels into the 90's*, Heinemann 1983.
5 *European Tourism Future Prospects 1980–1990*, Institute of Air Transport Paris/European Travel Commission 1980.
6 *European Tourism Future Prospects 1980–1990*, Aviation and Tourism International for ETC 1983.
7 *European Travel Commission*, Paris 1991.

8 Travel and holiday motivations

All motivations are imprecise and evolving but all are within the parameters of social and economic determinants such as affluence, demographics, holiday entitlements, fashion, speed of travel and so on.

The motivations at work in the travel and holiday decision process are extremely complex. There are primary and secondary motivations and sometimes the secondary motivations can be a stronger influence than the primary, insofar as they can affect the choice of holiday destination. There are also what one might call the parameters of possibility, which equally can override the primary motivation. And, of course, wherever there are motivations, there are conversely, deterrents and these too can very often override the primary motivation.

Personality characteristics are vitally important in determining the type of holiday experience and can also be a powerful influence on the primary motivation. Inevitably, there is a blurring of all these influences – they cannot be apportioned an exact value, but a marketer should certainly be aware of them in his planning and if they cannot be evaluated mathematically they almost certainly can be intuitively. Consciously or intuitively, they will be built into product development and product presentation; they will influence the choice of markets and segments within those markets. They will significantly affect the marketer's communications strategy.

Perhaps there is one central feature of any holiday taken away from home – it should provide a change, a relaxation both physically and emotionally, an opportunity to unwind and recharge, a respite, a chance to 'get away from it all'. While this change is generally regarded as beneficial, it can manifest itself, in terms of the holiday experience, in a number of ways: from the wife who wants someone to wait on her, to the husband who claims 'my wife actually does more work on holiday, but it's different', to the view 'the children need a holiday'. This need for a change may at first sight appear to be presumptuous but it is a salutary thought that interviews with respondents in motivation studies have not often elicited the response that holidays should fulfil the wish to have fun or enjoy oneself. It would appear that the primary objective is to have a change: that change is good for you. This apparently simple fact can well influence the relative appeal of different types of holiday. In examining the factors which set the parameters in the holiday decision process we must recognise that in this whole area there is a blurring with primary and secondary motivations and indeed, at the same time, with deterrents. Moreover, these parameters of possibility may very often override both primary and secondary motivations.

Time is a principal parameter. Putting it at its simplest – it is unlikely that someone with two weeks' holiday will opt for a round the world cruise. In the case of the US market, the normal holiday entitlement is usually two weeks, while Japanese businessmen rarely take that much, even if they are entitled to it. Time is a very real constraint in these cases, but it can be more subtle than this. Time is finite and there are competing claims being made on what we might call the discretionary time available.

Someone may wish to devote part of his annual holiday to redecorating his house. Many self-employed people and particularly owners of small businesses may feel that they cannot be away from their place of work for more than a few days, or alternatively, very far away in case they need to be recalled in an emergency. Dependent relatives, who need to be 'farmed out', can prescribe the time available. Whatever the reason, time is a factor which can override all other motivations.

Age and physical ability are vitally important factors over which we have little control. Like Shakespeare's 'ages of man' there are seven distinct age groups in the travel spectrum. First, the child at school, who is subject to parental motivation more than his own. Most foreign children visiting Britain to learn or practise English fall into this category. The first flight from the nest usually takes place during the years of further education – the young Australian on the European tour is but one example. The young singles in work represent the third important group. The social trend to remain unmarried – two upwardly mobile people living together ('yuppies') with two incomes – brings us into a whole new range of primary and secondary motivations relatively unaffected by money (but almost certainly by a time constraint). The fourth is the family group – constrained by lack of disposable income, the age of the children, perhaps a dependent relative. The 'empty nesters', retirees or 'woopies' (wealthier older people), can and should be subdivided into three sub-groups by the marketer. People are retiring earlier and living longer and these three sub-groups are growing as a proportion of the total population in almost all developed countries. The three sub-groups are the young seniors (55 to 65), the seniors (65 to the early 70s) and the old seniors (over 75). Most old seniors will tend to take their holiday in the country of residence, very often staying with friends and relatives in order to avoid the worry of travel, especially travel abroad. However, older people who have had a number of holidays abroad throughout their life are much more likely to see themselves continuing to do so. Indeed, travel to far away places is very often undertaken by rich widows and spinsters. To the young, the first holiday abroad is an exciting prospect, to the very old it can be an alarming one.

At the other end of the age spectrum very young children in the family will tend to discourage that family from going abroad. Costs may of course be an inhibiting factor, but more often than not respondents in discussions on holiday motivation will claim that it is not feasible to take children abroad because it is too hot, or because the food would not be good for them, or quite simply because 'I don't think my children would like it abroad and they are too small. Playing on the sands with a bucket and spade is much more enjoyable for them'. Again, it is very often a question of the parents' experience; if they have been abroad them-selves, myths are exploded and doubts dispelled. It could well be of course, that parents do not interpret holiday preferences accurately. The children recalling the boredom of going back to the same place: the parents claiming that their children loved going back to the same resort.

Weather is a factor which motivates different people in different ways. Some people feel uncomfortable, if not physically ill, in hot weather; for some, chasing the sun is a major determinant, while for others it is of minor importance, and if there is good weather it is regarded as a bonus. The person who wants to return from holiday with a golden tan is unlikely to choose to holiday in Scotland. Overseas visitors to Britain do not come for the weather and consequently Britain has the capability of being a 52-week holiday destination. Weather is well down the motiva-tion charts. On the other hand Californians love Britain's cool weather because it is different, and for Arabs, who need to get away from their long hot summers, Britain's weather is a powerful motivator. Hot wea-ther could increasingly become a deterrent for older people, fearful of skin cancer. There is already evidence of this behavioural change in Florida and Queensland.

Political factors can be most powerful deterrents. Malta, Cyprus, Sri Lanka and Northern Ireland have all been affected. The whole of Europe, and particularly southern Europe, was affected by fears of ter-rorism in 1986. This was especially true of the United States, which accounts for about six million of Europe's visitors annually, but spilled over into Canada and Mexico too. On 9 January 1986 President Reagan remarked in one of his regular press conferences that a number of his fellow Americans had told him that they would not be going over-seas in 1986. This was at a time when the USA was trying to rally Euro-pean support for the imposition of economic sanctions on Libya. The American media was writing about 'spineless Europeans', unprepared to stand shoulder to shoulder with Americans and invoking Americans to impose their own sanctions on Europe, by denying them the Ameri-can tourist dollar. At that time America also had a balance of payments problem and, in early January 1986, it was difficult to know whether the

American administration was taking the line it was, (a) because Europe seemed disinclined to impose economic sanctions on Libya, or (b) because if Americans could be persuaded to stay at home the American economy would benefit, or (c) because if an American travelling overseas did get hijacked it is fairly expensive to try to extricate him.

The cracks in the market were beginning to show in January, for whatever reason but it was only after the Libyan bombing in April 1986 that American traffic to Europe began to decline significantly. Terrorism was never off the front pages and was subject to an enormous amount of media 'hype' in the USA. Consequently, the perceptions that Europe was under siege conditions was real enough and the pictures which appeared in the media seemed to support this contention. Pictures of tanks at Heathrow, British 'bobbies' with guns at London airports appeared to add to the fears. One could well understand parents being concerned about their children in this situation. One could well understand the incentive organiser withdrawing Britain from their programmes. The prospect of a trip to Europe, where they would be a target for terrorists, was hardly calculated to motivate.

The collapse of the American trans-Atlantic traffic to Europe in 1986 effectively reduced the flow by one-third (nearly two million visits) and travel spending by US$2 billion. The incidence of the fall was uneven with the Mediterranean countries taking the brunt. This was understandable as the terrorist scares, including airport shooting, hijacking and then the Libya incident, had a vivid Mediterranean background as portrayed (with full media 'hype') on television in particular. So severe was the effect that political pressures invaded the marketing field. The Greek government spent over a million dollars on television commercials in April. The EC Commissioner of Tourism criticised European state tourist offices and proposed EC action. BTA and the major European countries together with the European Travel Commission did their best with trade relations and PR to mitigate damage. More practically, the ETC mounted a major motivation study in July 1986 with fully industry support to test opinion and attitude and to provide a guide as to when to re-enter the marketplace with major promotional spending and what images or messages would be most effective. This provided a most successful basis and led to a relatively rapid recovery in trans-Atlantic movement.

The return to normality and an American travel movement in 1987 virtually up to the all-time record of 1985 was accomplished even though the US dollar was weakening rapidly. By the end of 1987 the dollar had lost over one-third of its purchasing power in relation to European currencies.

This demonstrates an important aspect of motivations and relative strengths of primary and secondary motivators. A study by the BTA on the effect of exchange rate variations on travel demonstrated that simple correlations do not work. Travel is not simply a function of exchange rates but of a variety of interests and anticipated satisfactions, in short, value for money. There are many destinations that individuals would not visit even if offered free trips. Some people for example will pay to be 'seen' in the right places. Others seek powerful satisfactions in particular activities or places. Often in relatively depressed times travel to far away and exotic places at substantial expense sells well whilst the bargain basement is short of custom.

So here we had a situation where the political factors outweighed all other motivations, both primary and secondary. Or was it the way that it seemed? Certainly terrorism was blamed entirely for the downturn in American traffic, but in March 1985 the exchange rate was US$1.05 to the pound and by the middle of 1986 it was around US$1.50. So was the limiting factor money and the terrorist threat a convenient excuse? The massive and irrational anxiety was the major factor, but there is probably some evidence to suggest there was a monetary concern as well.

Certainly politics can be a powerful factor in the holiday decision process but the most powerful limiting factor in most cases is probably money. A large family is less likely to stay in a luxury hotel than a well-heeled couple. Indeed for many, economics determine their holiday choice. A self-catering holiday or a holiday spent with friends and relatives may well not be from personal preference. Given a free choice, twice as many would stay in licensed hotels than actually do.

Money can affect the choice of holiday in different ways though. Some people are happier with a controlled form of spending and clearly a holiday in their own country is easier to cope with because it is a known environment. There are hazards when the currency is unfamiliar – the unexpectedly large bill in an Austrian cafe for coffee and strudel. There is difficulty too in pre-planning the budget for an overseas holiday because of fluctuating exchange rates. There is a good deal of misinformation too. Someone who says 'it is far too expensive to go abroad with children' may be cloaking the main reason, which could well be more complex. There is, nevertheless, a finality about saying 'I cannot afford it' even though they could well spend the same amount of money at home. So, while money can be a powerful limiting factor, attitudes towards it are very complex. For some the packaged tour provides the necessary budgetary control; for others a holiday is a time for spending more freely than they would normally, and in some cases, money is the excuse given for a more complex reason. Where a specialist satisfaction is involved (education, health, saving face, flattery or affectation) price resistance crumbles.

One must not overlook fashion and social ambitions – the 'yuppies' who go to the smart Swiss ski resorts or those who follow in the footsteps of Royal honeymooners.

These important factors or parameters of possibility – time, age, weather, politics, money and fashion, are perceived by different people in different ways, but personality characteristics colour people's perceptions too. Two women, within the same age bracket and income classification, with the same standard of education and living in the same town, can have remarkably different life styles. Woman A derives her satisfaction from her work as a local councillor, magistrate and committee member; woman B takes a special pride in her role as wife and mother. For woman A, convenience foods are probably just what she wants, whilst woman B would disdain frozen foods and cake mixes.

Life style is made up of attitudes, prejudices, emotions and traditions, and everyone has a life style into which to fit their decisions, including buying choices. There are home-centred people for whom 'abroad' is anathema, and there are travelling people moved by curiosity and wanderlust. In between these extremes we find the majority. Individuals are either gregarious or 'loners' and this will influence the kind of holiday they prefer. A holiday may be seen as a chance to escape from a crowded city life, or it may be seen as an opportunity for more, rather than less, socialising. These variations in attitude will not necessarily affect the choice between a holiday at home or a holiday abroad but the interaction of attitude with other factors will certainly influence choice. Confidence or lack of it will affect the choice of holiday. For the less confident, a holiday in known 'safe' surroundings or a package tour is often the answer.

The wish to have something to do is a powerful need in some people, hence the popularity of the holiday camp in its heyday. For some, the sports enthusiasts, it can mean an activity holiday, for others it is seeing the sights, while increasingly people are developing their hobbies through special interest travel.

The central feature of any holiday taken away from home is that it should provide a change. However, this basic need is hedged around with a variety of factors, some fixed others dynamic, and affected in turn by personality characteristics and life style. Undoubtedly though the need for change is one of the most important primary motivations. The main elements of any holiday away from home are the complete change of scene and the opportunity to see different places, things and people. This interest and stimulation of novelty, however, can be offset by the anxiety and uncertainty of coping with the unfamiliar. The way in which these two opposing needs of novelty on the one hand and security on the other, are balanced by holiday takers is important. It is important in determining whether people are prepared to go abroad or not, the extent to which they are prepared to try new places, especially those further away and different in life style, food, culture, religion and tradition. Some people prefer to take their holiday in an area which is completely unknown to them, but a large minority want a holiday in an area which they know at least a bit about, and some prefer a resort which they know well. The number of Americans with passports has increased very little over the past ten years and even now represents only about nine per cent of the population.

This single basic need for difference can manifest itself also as a secondary motivation. Why do Americans visit Britain? They can find the different ingredients much closer to home in Puerto Rico, Mexico or even in their own vast country. They come to Britain for a different culture, pageantry, history, tradition and a different way of life; they are interested in attractive countryside and the opportunity to meet British people. Ethnic considerations are also extremely important – the 'roots' phenomenon and research into ancestry are still powerful motivators. The fact that a destination is different can have a negative effect too: anxieties about language, foreign currency, sanitation and health, political problems, food. In some of the popular resorts of the Costa Brava they perhaps over-compensate for this anxiety with 'tea like mum makes it' and chips with everything.

Americans holiday in Britain because it is different and foreign but they do not want it to be too different, too frighteningly foreign. Britain, while offering the difference in terms of history, culture, tradition, also offers a common background in terms of antecedents and language. Some research undertaken by the European Travel Commission into the senior citizen potential in the USA showed just how deep are such anxieties as sanitation, communication and availability of medical facilities. Such questions as 'can I drink the water?' or 'will I be able to get good medical attention if I fall ill?' and even 'will I be able to order a meal?' were fairly common. This is a simple illustration of American motivation. American visitors come in many forms. The market is highly segmented, made up of many 'mini' mass markets.

The broadening and educational value of a holiday can be a primary motivation or a secondary one. The grand tour was a form of aristocratic finishing school and clearly motivated by educational aspirations. Young Australians still undertake a kind of grand tour of Europe. Thomas Cook, in his early pioneering days, sold his holidays very largely on their educational value. In fact many of the Victorian pioneers had educational, social, health or other serious specialist and initially, non-profit motives. English language study is a big business. There are holiday courses for all manner of things from archaeology and antiques to yoga and zen. They are all designed to appeal to the primary motivation – that the holiday experience should be broadening and educational. It is often no longer enough to have a holiday and special interest travel, where one learns or at least one appreciates something, is growing in importance.

For others of course, educational values are not a primary motivation but are nevertheless important. On holiday people visit museums and galleries, historic houses and castles, heritage sites. Television programmes and historic films increasingly provide a greater awareness and understanding and a genuine desire to visit such places. Many national tourist offices are turning this secondary motivation to advantage as a device for diverting traffic or extending the season.

Is it the educational aspect or is it perhaps a more complex motivation – a need to demonstrate one's importance? In some developing markets self importance is almost measured in terms of the number of European capitals notched up on the trip. A golden tan is a symbolic way of saying the same thing, and there will always be the 'in' place for the fashion conscious – 'we went to Bali this year'.

Melvyn Greene, in *Marketing Hotels into the Nineties*[7] suggests the following motivational factors that makes people buy or spend money:

Table 8.1 – Motivational factors

1	FEAR	– insurance
2	SECURITY	– burglar alarms, spy holes, new door
3	LONELINESS	– televisions
4	CURIOSITY	– televisions, historical buildings
5	STATUS – 'KEEPING UP WITH THE JONES'	– video tape recorders to a Rolls-Royce
6	EGO	– this seemed to relate to STATUS
7	POSSESSION/ENVY	– this seemed to be related to items under STATUS
8	BASIC NEEDS	– water, salt, bread and a blanket for warmth
9	RELIGION	– money spent on Christenings, etc.
10	MENTAL RELAXATION PHYSICAL HEALTH	– hobbies – sports – relaxation
11	PRICE	– buying something reduced in price
12	VALUE FOR MONEY	– not necessarily related completely to price
13	INVESTMENT	– shares, stocks
14	PERSONAL COMFORT	– central heating, air conditioning
15	GUILT	– present for wife!
16	SHORTAGES	– in some countries with import controls
17	EDUCATIONAL/RESEARCH	– correspondence courses, evening classes
18	SENTIMENT	– photographs

Motivations thus become very blurred and in some cases the motivation is perhaps not even the holiday itself but the post holiday recounting of holiday experiences, the display of purchases, the showing of the holiday movie.

Marketers can change the brand image, those expectations and images which become associated with the product. It is part of the job of any tourism marketer to project a brand image which is calculated to motivate prospective holiday-makers but equally it is incumbent on him to ensure that as far as possible the product reflects the brand image.

The promise offered in the promotion must be delivered and one must never sell a false prospectus.

Promotion needs to be conducted through every psychological level and the marketer ignores motivation at his peril. The large American corporations misinterpreted motivation and produced large motor cars, leaving Volkswagen to clean up. The cigarette manufacturers who tried to market filter cigarettes on the premise that they were less harmful to health in a country where the life expectancy was under thirty years was bound to fail.

Everyone is motivated in a different way. The task of the marketer is to identify the market segments where a number of people have similar wants and needs and are similarly motivated. Marketing is about satisfying the wants and needs of selected groups of consumers at a profit.

Figure. 8.1 – The parameters of possibility, motivations and deterrents

THE PARAMETERS OF POSSIBILITY

Age and Sex
Time and distance
Climate
Affordability/exchange rates
Life style/fashion
Age of children
Personality characteristics

PRIMARY MOTIVATIONS

Need for a change
Study
Special interest/activity
'In' place
Medical treatment
Religions
Business visit – conference
           – trade fair
'Roots'

SECONDARY MOTIVATIONS

Value for money
Leisure add on to business trip
Vicarious pleasure
Security
Culture/heritage
Climate

DETERRENTS

Language
Climate
Hygiene
Political situation
Terrorism
Food
Foreign currency

Summary

Motivations are imprecise and evolving. There are primary and secondary motivations operating within the parameters of possibility which include deterrents (time, affordability, age and physical ability, weather, politics, fashion). Primary motivations extend from a wish to be a conference delegate or to study, a wish to explore one's 'roots' or simply need for a change, while secondary motivations include culture, value for money or vicarious pleasure.

Reference

1 Greene, M, *Marketing Hotels into the 90's*, Heinemann 1983 p 101.

9 External factors

The public or private organisation in tourism, whether concerned with the destination (local, area or national tourist office) or a specific commercial service or product (transport, accommodation packages) has control over policies, strategies, plans and operations within their resource limitations. They decide the 'product' to be promoted and sold and the markets to be targeted, and the extent to which 'cooperative' in contrast to 'competitive' operation is to be selected.

However, in tourism, perhaps more than with most consumer goods, the dictates of the market are often overshadowed by external factors which can set the scene against which promotion and development takes place. These are the principal economic, social and political influences which can condition traffic flows and future development.

Principal external factors influence action directly and indirectly, sometimes individually but more often collectively. They set the scene for operations, for marketing, for sales investment and in most cases need consideration by the marketer in early planning and in tactical plans to meet urgent needs. The BTA marketing plans area by area begin with an analysis of the economic and social background as the basis for operational decisions.

Principal external factors influencing tourist flows
1. Economic growth rates
2. Fiscal regulations
3. Inflation
4. Exchange rates
5. Political stability
6. Price changes (value for money, fares, energy costs)
7. Competition (price but also other features making up the 'value' judgement)
8. Consumerism

Many of these factors are national, some affected by international action, and all subject to government intervention. This can result in difficulties for tourism as public authorities are orientated towards administering for the 'local', native or resident population. Visitors have no vote and no parliamentary representatives. So the collective case needs careful and continuous attention by state and other public tourist bodies acting in cooperation with major interests, earning revenues, foreign currencies and contributing to employment and regional prosperity.

Recitation of tourism's national interest and its contribution to current urgent policies are a necessary task to ensure that the framework for marketing, especially international marketing, is favourable. Cost in lost opportunities, current revenues and future prospects can be very heavy, and take massive efforts in time and money to recapture market share and growth.

An Economist Intelligence Unit report[1] has a chapter called 'The forces at work on holiday-taking in the 1980s' and in this chapter Robert Cleverdon analyses these forces under six major headings:

1. Society's attitudes and expectations
2. Socio-demographic changes
3. Time and money
4. Costs of travel
5. Legal and political developments
6. Technological developments

Robert Cleverdon's conclusion on each of these influences can be summarised briefly as follows:

> The most important feature of society's attitudes and expectations is that holidays are now regarded as a right and a necessity. This attitude will be consolidated in the 1980s by factors like the continuing rise in education levels, the increased awareness of holiday opportunities, the increasing pressure to get away from urban environments, the lower demand for consumer durables and a continuing tendency to emulate the wealthy.

The marketer's role can be the key. In many cases the external problems need collective public and private tourism interests' effort, to concentrate on favourable growth markets, which means ability to read the signs, and not to neglect remedial action, to mitigate damage where necessary. Each factor needs separate consideration, not only at the national level but also at the international level. In the EEC countries the move towards a common or harmonised tax regime can have some very major consequences for tourism.

In the short term imbalances in price, standards and value for money will effect movement, noticeably the shorter impulse trips, made locally or in easily accessible regions. Price and tax changes resulting in bargain basement frontier flows (especially for shopping) is a false and generally unsatisfactory short-lived movement. But, in this case and so with most of the external factors, their effect can be modified and influenced by marketing programmes, sometimes only marginally but sometimes more profoundly. Let us examine each in turn and their connections.

Figure. 9.1 – Tourism and economic growth 1970–1982. World tourist arrivals v GDP of OECD countries

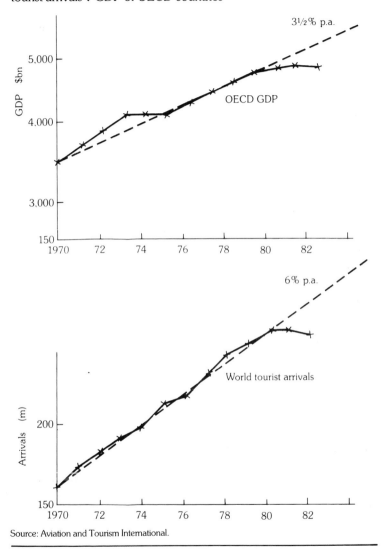

Source: Aviation and Tourism International.

Economic growth rates

There is clear evidence of the long term relationship between economic growth and the demand for tourism, but the link is complex and there are considerable short term variations. Past studies (European Tourism 1980–1990, European Travel Commission) showed that the OECD increase in GDP (1973–82) of 3.5% per annum was related to an annual average increase in travel of six per cent – a multiple of two. Since OECD domestic product (GDP) is expected to continue to rise at about 3% for the remainder of the decade the potential for travel expansion is very great.

The OECD countries, the principal industrialised countries of the world account for eighty per cent of world travel. The chart above shows the relationships.

Experts have not adequately explained the income elasticity effects on travel spending, in other words the extent to which rising personal incomes are increasingly devoted to travel. Clearly for many groups of buyers the richer they become the more they spend, but tastes and fashion and the other external factors have a role to play. In addition, there seems to be low income elasticity in a downturn of economic activity in the short term. For example, the short lived 1974–75 recession following the oil crisis had a very limited effect, although transatlantic travel

Table 9.1 – Travel trends – 1978–1982 – United Kingdom

		1978	1979	1980	1981	1982
HOLIDAY TRAVEL (BNTS)*						
Percent population taking holiday (adults)	(%)	61	63	62	61	59
Total vacation trips	(M)	48.0	48.8	48.5	49.8	46.8
Domestic vacation trips	(M)	39.0	38.5	36.5	36.5	32.5
International vacation trips	(M)	9.0	10.3	12.0	13.3	14.3
Transport mode for international vacations	(%)	18.8	21.1	24.7	26.7	30.6
Air	(%)	69	71	68	68	66
Boat	(%)	27	24	28	28	30
Hovercraft	(%)	3	3	4	3	3
TOTAL VISITS ABROAD (IPS)**	(M)	13.4	15.5	17.5	19.0	20.6
Holiday	(%)	63	64	67	69	70
Business	(%)	17	16	15	14	13
VFR	(%)	15	14	13	12	12
Other	(%)	6	6	5	5	5
ECONOMIC INDICATORS						
Real GDP change	(%)	+2.6	+2.6	−2.4	−2.4	+0.8
Unemployment	(%)		5.1	6.5	10.2	12.0

Sources: Aviation and Tourism International.
*BNTS – British National Travel Survey. British Tourist Authority. Covers stays of 4 nights or more
      away from home which respondents in resident population over 16 consider a holiday.
**IPS – International Passenger Survey. Department of Trade. Covers all UK residents returning from
      visits abroad for all purposes.
(M) – Million.

Table 9.2 – Travel trends, 1978–1982 – Germany

		1978	1979	1980	1981	1982
HOLIDAY TRAVEL						
Percent population taking holiday	(%)	56	57	58	56	55
Total vacation trips	Main* (M)	25.8	26.5	27.1	26.6	26.3
	All** (M)	30.6	32.1	32.8	31.6	32.1
Domestic vacation trips	(M)	10.1	9.6	10.2	9.6	10.2
	DDR (M)	0.4	0.6	0.5	0.6	0.2
International vacation trips	(M)	15.3	16.3	16.3	16.3	16.0
Transport mode for international vacations (Main holidays)						
Air	(%)	14	17	16	16	16
Rail	(%)	17	15	16	16	14
Car	(%)	60	59	59	56	59
Coach	(%)	7	8	8	10	9
Other	(%)	2	2	2	2	2
TRIPS PER PERSON**		1.2	1.2	1.2	1.2	1.2
ECONOMIC INDICATORS						
Real GDP change	(%)		+4.1	+1.9	+0.2	−1.2
Unemployment	(M)		3.8	3.8	5.5	7.5

*Main holiday trips of 5 days or more persons over 14.
**All holiday trips of 5 days or more persons over 14.

Source: Aviation and Tourism International.
Reiseanalyse. Studienkreis fur Tourismus, Starnberg.

Coverage: Stays of 5 days or more away from home for all reasons other than business and vocational. Covers all German citizens over 14 years. Concentrates analysis on main holiday trips of 5 days or more.

(M) – Million.

was temporarily disrupted – largely due to anxieties other than response to income and price changes. In recent years industrial decline and rising unemployment and short term recession or reduction in growth has not been accompanied by any fall-off in travel. Indeed often quite the reverse has happened.

Holiday taking and travel, personal mobility has become part of the way of life in developed countries. So travel continues, even if savings or redundancy payments are used to sustain expenditure. A detailed study of the United Kingdom market is instructive.

The total holiday market was affected by the economic recession but the whole weight of the recession was taken by the domestic market. International holiday trips actually increased by forty per cent between 1979 and 1982. There was a large increase in foreign holidays as a proportion of total holidays 21.1 to 30.6 per cent. Clearly a number of factors were at work. There are serious implications for marketers especially those concerned with the domestic product. Travel trends in Germany over the same period are shown in table 9.2 above.

The holiday market was significantly affected by economic recession. There was little growth over the period and this applied equally to domestic and foreign holidays.

In the Netherlands, the total holiday market ceased to grow but there was trading down especially in the form of a swing from international travel to domestic travel. The latter consumer reaction is what might be expected, but the very different response in different markets is noteworthy. The recession in the early 1980s was accompanied by substantial economic structural changes, declining industries, and unemployment again on a substantial scale. While the travel market is fairly resilient to short term changes in economic growth, the perception of a longer term pattern lessens this resilience. Responses vary considerably and trends need careful study in planning marketing response and the selection of markets and segments for exploitation.

As a general conclusion travel is becoming more resilient to economic recession, and indeed to other deterrents, apart from perceived security and safety. However, the reaction needs careful examination market by market. For example, much travel is business or institutionally controlled, in other words not simply an individual consumer's decision. While the same general conclusions apply business travel may actually increase during a recession to stimulate more trade but marginal activity such as conferences and some incentive movement may decline.

A well diversified tourist trade is even more important in recession. Clearly not all markets will be similarly affected. In Britain's case for example the mid-1970s witnessed an enormous growth in Middle East markets of visitors from Arab countries to Britain and London in particular, following the rapid increase in wealth from rising oil prices. This new source of tourism revenues was not shared equally by Britain's European neighbours for a number of good marketing reasons. Once again the case history of this new and rapidly emerging traffic flow was complex and not a simple response to vastly inflated incomes.

The main conclusion must be that there is a relationship between travel and economic growth especially in the longer term. Economic growth is a determinant of demand. It can play an important role but the relationship is complex and varies considerably from market to market in the short term.

Fiscal and other statutory regulations

In general the western and industrialised countries have pursued a policy of liberalising travel removing or easing frontier formalities (passports, visas, customs and currency control). However, freedom cannot be taken for granted. For example, France introduced a visa requirement in the interests of security, which had a drastic effect in reducing

American and other foreign travel. Similarly in 1983, France introduced a severe curtailment of foreign holiday spend for its residents' travel abroad, which had the effect in the short term of a heavy reduction in outward movement. But again effects cannot be estimated accurately, reaction is often uncertain and the administration complex.

The most common and potentially serious regulation is the limitation or withdrawal of foreign currency. This effectively creates a false and restricted market. Freedom to travel (granted by governments to ensure its citizens of free conditions for mobility) is written in the principal international agreements affecting travel. But governments usually reserve the right to suspend or vary these conditions or freedoms in times of crisis or emergency. Generally speaking, currency restrictions do not work well; evasion is common and often easy. Black markets can be operated efficiently. In a mobile world with easy communication and growing personal links through business, family and friends, currency restriction is never wholly effective. Moreover it distorts movement and the imperfect market place may often call for a special marketing response. In most developed countries freedom to travel is an established fact but there is much intercontinental movement which flourishes in spite of currency limitations. In many cases travellers will use international currencies such as the US dollar, Sterling or Swiss francs.

Controls on passports, visa requirements and travel taxes can prove more serious obstacles because they are often impossible to evade and can be punitive. Departure taxes, generally condemned in international agreements can present problems but usually their effect is to delay frontier control procedures and to annoy visitors, rather than to limit travel. However, charter taxes in Scandinavia tend to penalise short haul destinations such as Britain. The departure tax for Israeli residents travelling abroad in 1988 was US$168 but outward movement continued to grow.

In conclusion, apart from short term effects following the introduction of new restrictions, regulations by themselves may prove less effective in restricting movement than is generally supposed. An outright ban of course, rarely practised or admitted, could distort market reaction and limit or stop traffic flows. More usually, a combination of factors, unfavourable exchange rates, restrictions on transport and other essential travel services, are more likely reasons for market decline. There are many other forms of regulation affecting visitors: internal taxes (VAT, charges on liquor, tobacco), social legislation limiting drinking hours, gambling and shopping hours. The effects can be important in terms of competition: VAT rates in the EC countries on tourist services vary from zero to twenty-two per cent according to country. The effect is similar to an internal tariff, but unless corrected by exchange rate variation there can be price differentials distorting a free and competitive market region. Social regulations (liquor, gambling and other restrictions) contribute to the general competitive situation. Although no single control may influence tourism greatly, taken together they may affect the image and visitors' attitudes, and favour a more relaxed neighbour country. In Britain the state tourist organisations have pressed government to liberalise some of these controls (licensing and shopping hours and gaming, for example) partly on the grounds that the competition from European neighbours was stronger because of their more relaxed conditions for visitors' enjoyment.

Inflation and exchange rates

These factors, setting important price conditions, should go hand in hand. Rapid inflation should be corrected by alterations in the exchange rate to give a degree of visitor purchasing power parity. In the long run this will happen, the problem is often in the time lag and in the controls which governments introduce to protect the currency and control black markets – which are very susceptible to tourist influence. Controls may limit repatriation of profits or earnings affecting international traders (tour operators and airlines) as well as investors. The distortions can be serious and will generally result in loss of traffic and switching of travel to more competitive substitute areas. Tour operators may withdraw from the market. Loss of international trading partners can result in heavy loss which may take some years to overcome and to achieve restoration of traffic. A true cost benefit appraisal of such a situation, including heavy marketing costs to relaunch the 'product', can demonstrate the seriousness and the non-productive nature of attempting to cure basic economic weakness by controls on a free international market such as tourism.

It is often supposed that exchange rates are the principal determinant of international tourism. Nothing could be further from the truth. Some forms of travel are less price sensitive and very resilient to adverse factors. Where the satisfaction is high, the preferred destination regarded as unique or where the journey is verging on the essential (visits for business, or to friends and relatives), for a special and unique satisfaction often with specialist purpose (health, education, a unique cultural or religious experience), the will to travel is far stronger than the exchange rate. It is of course partly a matter of degree. Tourism is increasingly resilient. Where there is a similar and competitive product such as a hot sunny beach, price will be a key determinant, not in the decision to take a holiday but in the decision regarding the destination. There are many examples in recent years of individual Mediterranean countries (Spain, Italy, Greece, Malta) losing market share drastically and rapidly when marked price differentials often manifest in exchange rate variations occurred. But on the other hand in 1987 when the US dollar weakened dramatically losing twenty per cent of its value against Sterling and most European currencies, American travel to Europe recovered beyond all expectations from the 1986 low to new record levels. Part of the reason was limitation of cost increase since transatlantic air fares are quoted in dollars. Thus half the cost of the trip was not affected by exchange rate variation. Hotel and other service providers, tour operators with their efficient purchasing ability, could also temper the rate increases. But perhaps most important the European product was greatly desired and unique – there were no substitutes.

The conclusion must be that the marketer cannot take the inflation or exchange rate influence for granted. Each principal market must be considered, and preference given to the more secure, unique or specialist segments which are more resilient to price and other pressures and deterrents.

An in depth study for the British Tourist Authority[2] on exchange rate effects concluded that exchange rates are an important factor, but only one of many factors which influence the patterns of demand for tourism. Many market changes cannot be explained solely by reference to price factors. On the other hand, there have been some market changes in the past decade in which the influence of exchange rates on 'perceived price' in the originating country seems to have been particularly important.

Political factors

In our age of insecurity and violence political stability is one of the most important external factors. Travellers, especially tourists on holiday, leave home for pleasure and relaxation. Expectations of something better than every day life must be assured. Anxieties should be left behind. To paraphrase St Paul, every tourist going on holiday must be assured of his prize. Danger, disorder, threats to safety or health are compelling deterrents. Governments must assure the visitors invited to their countries of peace and tranquillity. If this cannot be assured and equally damaging, if the potential visitor thinks it cannot be assured, then traffic will collapse and it may take many months or even years (and heavy promotional spending) to restore the position.

Tourism in crisis

A feature of recent years has been the sudden eruption of great political instability, which can have disastrous short-term effects on international and sometimes domestic travel. Threats to safety and security due mainly to terrorism have become a new hazard to travel.

Unfortunately there have been a number of major crises in recent years, so that it is possible to study effects and results of action taken by governments and the trade. In an insecure world travellers are prepared to face a degree of risk not contemplated previously, for example travel to Ireland continues to develop even in disturbed areas, although in some cases at a lower level of movement.

The first major crisis of this kind occurred in 1986 following the US–Libya conflict. US citizen departures to Europe and the Mediterranean fell by twenty per cent in 1986 compared with 1985, from 6.5 million to 5.12 million visits. Although traffic recovered towards the end of 1986, total arrivals for 1987 were still four per cent less than in 1985 at a time of steady annual increase in foreign travel by US residents. Losses varied considerably from country to country according to perceived image of terrorism and dangers, US travel to Egypt fell by sixty per cent, to Israel by forty-eight per cent, and to Austria, Switzerland and France by forty per cent. The UK held traffic better than most with a decrease of twenty-eight per cent. In the case of Britain the high proportion of independent movement, ethnic and trade connections helped to contain losses.

Dr Raymond Bar-On of the Israel Ministry of Tourism in a special study on tourism and terrorism[3] estimated that tourist receipts in Europe and the Mediterranean from US travel decreased by US$2.8 billion in 1986, and taking the loss at the end of 1985, and the halt in growth in 1987, the total fall in revenues over the years 1985–87 was nearly US$5 billion.

The industry was not well geared to deal with the crisis. Marketing efforts in the face of damaging mass media coverage of travel dangers effectively stopped non-essential movement for a time. Recovery was slow. By the autumn of 1986 national and collective promotion through the European Travel Commission succeeded in reassuring the trade and the tourist. Attitude research and public relations work proved effective.

Much business, specialist and independent traffic and travel to meet friends and relatives returned relatively quickly – within months. But package travel and traffic dependent on tour operators who changed plans and diverted business was lost for a year or more.

International travel to China from industrialised countries collapsed in 1989 following the disorders in Beijing. This was a major disaster as China had made massive investment in hotels and tourist plant. The danger to visitors' safety and comfort was short lived. But the massive media coverage, especially through television, dramatised events to a compelling degree. The image of China was fatally flawed. It took nearly a year before effective action could be taken to restore the image, and regain traffic worth US$2 billion.

Promotion cannot be effective until the market is prepared to listen to the sales invitations. Mistakes are made in continuing expensive consumer promotion. In such circumstances it is better to adopt low visibility, and maintain trade and information links. Market research to test attitudes and changing tides of opinion is advisable, followed by public relations activity stressing cultural and specialist appeals where interest tends to be strong. Price cutting alone is a dangerous formula. Action by some of China's hotels to reduce prices to a major extent (US$20 per room) had doubtful results. Tours from Europe were on sale for as little as £600, and US$350 from the West coast of the USA for ten days inclusive. The inevitable return to normal trading and pricing can then give the country a poor value for money reputation.

The Gulf war in early 1991 had a very sudden and serious impact on world tourism. Middle East airlines and European hoteliers were particularly affected. There were blanket bans on executive travel by some corporations and many governments issued advisories to its nationals which resulted in some cases of markets almost drying up completely. The US market was already suffering from recession and a weak dollar against some currencies so the Gulf war and fears of terrorism were simply superimposed on an already serious situation. The industry was caught in a double squeeze. Fortunately the Gulf war was in January and February, traditionally low months for Northern destinations, and the effects of the war, if not the recession, were fairly short lived. On the other hand destinations like Israel and Egypt suffered disproportionately and will take very much longer to recover. Airlines, which were particularly hard hit, were quick to respond with slashed fares in an attempt to get the leisure traveller to fly again. The independent business traveller responded more quickly when hostilities ended. Political situations can, and do sometimes, have an immediate impact on traffic flows but the effect may not necessarily be the same in every market; some remain relatively unaffected, some are decimated, while others can even provide increased business because of a switch in holiday destinations.

Airlines were said to be making losses at an alarming rate. Airline traffic in Europe dropped by twenty to twenty-five per cent. Hotels in city centres saw occupancy decrease by fifty per cent. Incentive traffic collapsed and much conference trade was lost. There were some areas which benefited. Winter sports resorts did well. The Eastern Mediterranean lost most of its trade, but Western areas picked up business. Some domestic tourist flows increased.

Independent and much specialist travel returned almost as soon as the short war ended. Package tour bookings which had fallen by seventy per cent in the UK returned strongly, but not to troubled regions in the Mediterranean.

The reaction of the trade was largely uncoordinated and there was no official support from the European Community. Some countries (UK, Belgium and Holland) increased national budgets for promotion. The European Travel Commission with the support of the European Tourism Action Group withheld consumer promotion but maintained trade and information services, and research including monitoring traffic flows.

A major promotion was undertaken for Europe with full trade support in the USA and Japan, featuring special attractions – for example cultural events, and special offers, including price advantages – which the trade and most countries encouraged successfully.

The 1991 results were difficult to interpret at the time because a number of separate market forces were operating together, for example recession in the UK and USA, falling dollar exchange rates, value for money and even fashion changes in some Mediterranean regions.

The effects of the war while it lasted were more widespread than in previous incidents, and massive losses, including business failures were a real threat. There is a growing realisation that collective action is necessary, and that some precautionary planning including action by governments is necessary.

The experience of the transatlantic traffic recession in 1986 is a classic case. After attacks at European airports, hijacks on a cruise ship as well as on planes, the threats of continuing violence after the Libyan attack, American travellers lost confidence in Europe's stability. Travel to some of the Mediterranean countries (Greece and Italy) stopped almost completely.

Total US travel to Europe in 1986 fell by thirty per cent from a record six million visits in 1985 to four million in 1986, with a loss of travel income to Europe of US$2,000 million.

Marketing had a key role, to mitigate damage and to restore business. By and large this was well done by the state organisations and industry. Traffic was regained in 1987 more rapidly than expected. Some of the reasons and the consequent enormous economic and financial benefits are explained in this assessment of key external factors. Again the conclusion must be that international travel is increasingly resilient, responsive to favourable factors, and influenced by marketing, product presentation and pricing initiatives.

Price changes, competition

Although these factors can operate separately they have a common influence. The compelling result is the tourist perception of value for money. This is not simply a question of dear or cheap but whether the foreign traveller is satisfied with his 'bargain'. Sometimes, paradoxically, a service or attraction may be too cheap. Value for money has a strong element of competition.

Is the service more expensive than at home or in competing destinations in a neighbouring country? Tourists generally are not well briefed about places they visit. They are strangers and therefore, ignorant, so competitive shocks in terms of price can be keenly felt and loudly reported on return home. The relative price situation is influenced by government fiscal policies. Drinks may be expensive, fuel costs high, taxes applied to luxury items and hotels and airports. It is important not to get out of line if the competitive position is to be held.

Governments need to be sensitive to the visitors' attitude and perception of price, particularly in regard to taxes. Sometimes efforts are made to relieve visitors from indirect taxes. Most countries offer tax free shopping facilities, Italy offers reduced price petrol coupons. But these are palliatives and rarely work well. The marketer has a vital task in market research to judge value for money perceptions and to do this in detail covering the major elements in the visitor purchases. Good information with the help of the travel trade, price initiatives, special offers (rail passes) can all play their part, together with action by government to take visitors' needs into account in their fiscal measures. It is estimated that in Britain tourism expenditure on indirect taxes, which are in effect direct taxes on visitors VAT, liquor and fuel, amounted to £800 million in 1988.

Consumerism

In recent years public interest and subsequent government action in industrialised countries has resulted in a range of consumer 'protection' measures constraining the free interplay of market forces. The reasons are complex; the increasing technical changes often on a massive scale, the influence of modern marketing and communication techniques, the scale of big business operation sometimes verging on monopoly situations, are held to put the consumers at a disadvantage. The old adage of *caveat emptor* cannot apply if lack of knowledge or experience limits the consumers' ability to choose and judge adequately in purchasing situations. Furthermore, the growing wealth and credit revolution has meant that individual purchases have become that much larger.

Consumer protection accordingly takes the form of regulations setting conditions of trading and marketing within which the marketing and sales operation must work. So the marketer must study carefully the new rules of the game which will vary from country to country. Furthermore, the industry must consider in its relations with governments and intergovernmental bodies such as the EC representation to ensure that legislation is practical and does not work paradoxically to the consumers' disadvantage stifling enterprise and initiation of new services. There are broadly two kinds of consumer protection or state intervention:

1.   Regulation of trading in general, firstly, to prevent the establishment of monopolies, or the introduction of restrictive practices such as price fixing agreements, which are thought to limit competition and keep prices artificially high. There may be state price fixing machinery (hotel prices) or legislation to secure proper information and guidance for the purchaser. In Britain hoteliers, for example, must display or tell travellers (by notice or in writing) room prices before booking.

2. The second form of protection relates to information and promotion. In Britain, for example, the Trade Descriptions Act makes it mandatory to present a truthful image of the product and service. Although this may try the tourist marketer's conscience claims and standards which cannot be delivered are subject to legal redress.

There can be no objection to the application of general consumer protection rules to tourist services. In many cases they are justified and necessary. Indeed by relieving anxiety and improving consumer advice they may increase and certainly not dimish a competitive market.

The situation is more debatable where consumer protection rules are applied specifically to tourist services only. In some countries there have been attempts to limit or control promotional claims or to give tourists rights to seek redress if satisfaction was limited. But in an industry as theatrical as tourism this comes close to allowing theatre goers to sue as well as boo. Controls for more measurable and practical reasons – safety, security or financial guarantees – are of course, a different matter. In most cases essential guarantees of this kind, including the control or bonding of tour operators to protect the traveller, are common and widely applied. In many cases the protection schemes are operated in cooperation or directly by the industry itself (eg the National Travel Agents Association) and this is probably the most practical solution.

Although government intervention may lead to difficult or impractical regulation with diminished benefit or security for the traveller, there is a place for consumer protection in travel. Historically, governments intervened with legislation for innkeepers. The licensing of guides, travel agents and bureaux de change is common, especially in the remoter and poorer countries. Action to guarantee standards is needed and indeed is an important part of marketing. But much can be done by the industry itself on a self-regulating basis. By protecting goodwill and re-moving anxieties or making it easier to buy and to choose, tourism and tourist markets will grow.

Unlike the purchase of consumer goods where guarantees offer to replace defective or unsatisfactory purchases, there can be no 'physical' guarantee of that kind in tourism. But the acceptance and maintenance of standards and especially in the case of tour operators, financial guarantees to ensure holidays and return journeys are protected, are important. In most European countries and in developing countries the government intervenes directly or indirectly through state agencies to establish control systems of this kind. But standards need establishing in cooperation with the doers, the trade which provides the service and not simply on a bureaucratic basis. The EC which is developing an important tourism policy and programme has been working on a common system of information and signs and symbols for tourist services, a system of information not classification, grading and price control.

The food and accommodation industries offer examples of the complexity and often confusion of principles in the approach to setting of standards and controls. Countries vary in their systems of classification and control. Some have government systems enforced by law, some have voluntary systems or depend heavily on commercial or unofficial guides. In cases of public health and safety the government must act. Indeed without such assurance of minimum standards tourism will not grow. Apart from health and safety, there is a need for effective information of the services offered. This is not an aspect of control or government administration but marketing, part of the informing selling (reservation) task. Governments may enter the field of grading but historically this was on a basis of price and fiscal control. In a number of countries today tax varies according to the standard of hotel, de luxe hotels paying a higher rate. Generally speaking, governments are not the best judges of quality or presentation of quality information to the market place. The well known Michelin Guide is of course a private venture by a leading commercial company. There are differing needs by type or standard of service, by market and differing requirements in distribution and information according to market and product. First class hotels and their standards are well known. The international travel trade have their own information systems often linked to airline reservation networks. The large international hotel chains offer a standard and known product worldwide. Most countries have a public or private generally accepted star system (the motoring organisations do this throughout Britain). But classified information and some guarantee of standard is most needed for the more modest priced accommodation, inns, guest houses, bed and breakfast. Much of this stock is demanded locally and at short notice. The regional tourist boards in Britain introduced a valuable service for the visitor on a book a bed ahead basis, especially for one night stays by the touring holidaymaker.

There is no one right way to deal with standard setting and information 'guarantees'. For some specialist services checks on quality may be necessary. The British Council for example, with BTA support, introduced a system of inspection for English Language Schools, paid for by the establishments themselves. They appreciated that dealing with young people in particular some assurance of standard and care was needed, and a recognised school benefited from this guarantee in promotion. Systems for health establishments, individual sporting facilities eg horse riding and sailing may be necessary and in certain cases safety will be a consideration. But generally the purpose is basically a marketing need, to make it easy to buy, to remove anxiety, to assist in presenting a range of products and in the task of advising and choosing. Both the trade (the retailers, organisers and advisers) and the potential traveller need this information service. Standard setting and information provision can be very expensive, but benefits in new business can be great.

New information technology makes the task less daunting but no less difficult to get right.

The purpose of standard setting and classification or control must be very clear. Is it for social reasons (health and safety)? If so, assuming the need is established it is a government task. Is it for consumer information, to make it easy to buy? If so it is a normal but essential part of marketing and unless the government wishes to control for fiscal or other reasons (tax, price controls) it should be left to the industry or the private sector.

Generally speaking all standard systems should be worked out with the trade, and self policing practised. Since where there is a proven need such action increases trade and profitability, the industry should have the will and skill to do the job. Assistance from destination interests, notably through regional and local tourist boards or agencies may be necessary and they and the state bodies will have an important task in distribution of the information.

There will be special cases either in undeveloped countries or in rural areas or for small and moderate priced units of accommodation, where the trade cannot or will not provide the necessary service. In such cases the local or central state bodies will need to act to ensure the desired flow of traffic to destinations which will be difficult to sell. This should be the state priority to encourage the development of good standards, consumer 'guarantees' and the provision of an efficient information service to trade and public at home and abroad, which will embrace commercial, voluntary as well as official systems, in the best possible information service for the potential visitor. To do this requires many willing cooperators, and is more likely to be achieved in the wide ranging tourism trades by concentrating on the end product, the information needed by the potential traveller at the different stages of planning and making the trip, according to market and type of service.

Summary

In tourism more than in most consumer trades the dictates of the market are often overshadowed by external factors which set the scene for promotion and development. The principal external factors influencing tourist flows are:

1. Economic growth rates
2. Fiscal regulations
3. Inflation
4. Exchange rates
5. Political stability
6. Price changes (value for money)

7.   Competition (including a number of features making up value judgements)

8.   Consumerism

The factors are subject to government intervention and the tourist case must be presented to governments accordingly. Effects can be modified or influenced by marketing activity. Factors' influence varies from market to market. Recession is not inevitably a constraint. Currency restrictions can prove less effective than planned. Fiscal changes can influence the competitive position. Exchange rates are not the principal determinants of international tourism. Their effects vary considerably according to differing market situations. Political stability, peace and safety, are in these modern times of violence and insecurity one of the most serious external factors.

References

1 Cleverdon, R, *The USA and the UK on Holiday*, EIU Special Report 1983.
2 *Exchange Rates and Tourism Demand – A Study for the British Tourist Authority* by Aviation Tourism International 1984.
3 Bar-On, R, *The Effects of Terrorism on International Tourism*. Proceedings of the first International Seminar on Aviation Security (ISAS), Jerusalem, 1990.

10 Marketing planning

The 'Marketing Plan' is the communications plan of the organisation. It is a tactical plan for the year ahead and is consequently about 'now', the constraints which exist currently, the new developments likely to affect traffic flows in the period under review, the opportunities and the challenges for the year ahead. It is also set in the context of the marketing strategy and plan, which is longer term – five or perhaps ten years. It is a written document with specific tasks and targets and as such it must be regularly monitored and reviewed.

The Marketing Plan is not a document which is produced in an ivory tower by an elite group of marketers. Clearly, the marketers will be the prime movers, the initiators and the writers, but if the Marketing Plan is to have any credibility at all it has to involve the people who are charged with implementing it. It is essential for success that colleagues are taken along at every stage of development. The key people, who are responsible for the successful operation of the business, must subscribe to and agree what the objectives are, both for the organisation and the marketing operation. The marketing objectives will stem from the organisation's objectives. Any conflicts, any disputes about objectives must be resolved before the detailed Marketing Plan is started. This does not mean finding out what the boss wants and then developing the Plan from that starting point. Any good marketer will have carefully analysed his markets, supported where necessary by research; he will have diagnosed the situation, taking account of external factors which are likely to impinge on marketing activities and affect success. He will be on firm ground and will have the courage of his convictions. He must, if he is going to make any sort of contribution to the organisation's success.

There are many stages in the development of the Marketing Plan, some have been considered in earlier chapters. Desk research and formal market research in turn have led to product and market analysis, market segmentation, market measurement and forecasting. Then a careful analysis of external factors is needed grouped as follows:

Political – wars, unrest, strikes either in the market place or at the destination;
Fiscal – governmental controls or restrictions, eg taxes, limit on spend abroad;
Currency exchange – weak or strong position of the destination currency relative to that of the source market;

Economic – the state of the economy in source markets which affects
the amount of discretionary and disposable income available;
Inflation – this can affect disposable income in the source market or
purchasing power at the destination;
Unemployment – can affect the size of the target market;
Consumerism – legislation concerned with consumer protection.

In an international marketing situation these are key factors which can
very easily be presented in the form of a simple table thus:

Australia:

Economy	Unemployment	Inflation	Currency	Fiscal controls
Strengthening	4.5%	6.0%	stable	A$25 airport tax

External factors will also embrace competition and include an
analysis of competitors' spend where this is available, eg on advertising.
Has there been any loss in 'share of voice' in the market place? This will
have implications for the allocation of marketing resources by market
and for the marketing mix. Is it the policy of the organisation to concentrate on a few markets or defend market share in all established markets?
In 1988 the French National Tourist Office announced that it would concentrate on expanding only eleven major markets. The BTA on the
other hand in its Marketing Plan stated that it intended to defend market
share in all established markets and develop a number of new markets.
Clearly such policy decisions will determine not only the allocation of
marketing resources on advertising, print and other marketing tools but
on the disposition of overseas offices too.

These analyses, while forming part of the final document called the
Marketing Plan, will have been completed before the planning process
starts. The policy will have been established and agreed by the key decision makers and in the case of a national tourist office it is always desirable to get the endorsement of relevant trade committees or advisory
groups as well.

Marketing is a comprehensive concept which demands total involvement of the whole operation, its activities and relationship to the market.
It follows then, that those people in the organisation who are going to
be responsible for implementing the Plan, both generalists and specialists, need to be involved. They must understand where the organisation
is going, its objectives, how their own efforts fit into the overall scheme
of things. They must subscribe to the objectives and the methods
whereby these objectives, supported by targets where appropriate, will
be achieved.

This is itself a very good reason for developing a Marketing Plan but it is not the only reason. In order to discover how to get to where one wants to go it is first necessary to know where one is now. Diagnosis followed by prognosis is essential to impart a sense of direction for the organisation. It is vital for any organisation to know where it is going. The Marketing Plan is the coordinating machinery for everyone in the organisation and provides a very necessary sense of cohesion. The *dramatis personnae* of the organisation need to know what part they each have to play in the annual operation and how they relate one with another, how their contributions dovetail and most essentially the timing of their performance. If an exhibition or trade show is scheduled for January in a particular market, print is required on territory ahead of this. So the editorial staff, designers, printers and distributors are all required to perform their tasks to ensure delivery at the right time. The Plan takes account of lead times and requirements on individuals to meet deadlines. Above all it is an action plan, systematically developed from the initial diagnosis, with an end goal always in view. It is a reconciliation of the organisation's objectives with their resources and the allocation and disposition of those resources. The alternative is that the organisation will simply react to emergencies, crises and the activity of competition with everyone pushing in different directions, which in turn leads to confusion and demoralisation.

At the end of the period covered by the Marketing Plan and at intermediate stages as appropriate, there should be a review of performance against objectives. But the end is the beginning of a new period and the review is also beneficial in guiding thoughts for the future. What succeeded or failed over the past year, what remained undone and why, what could have been done better, what more could have been done? Time spent on this review and assessment is not simply a control mechanism, a measure of whether a company is succeeding or not: it is a useful guide to future activity. So the planning process while starting with the diagnostic activity (where are we now?) also looks back at what has been achieved in detail over the past year. This evaluation or audit will be dealt with more fully in a later chapter.

Past performance will also assist in the prognosis stage and in the establishment of the organisation's marketing objectives which stem in turn from the overall objectives.

Marketing objectives

In tourism marketing there are two objectives which are invariably common to operators – regional spread and seasonal spread. Both objectives are geared to maximising the economic benefits of tourism over as wide an area as possible and over as long a season as possible. Conquering the seasonality challenge brings many rewards. Ideally, objectives should be measurable. This is not always possible but they should always be meaningful. In the case of an hotel where peaks and troughs in occupancy are known, it is possible to set objectives and precise targets for dealing with the situation. On the other hand it is more difficult in the case of a country where off-peak means different things to different sectors.

Marketing objectives will differ from one organisation to another and will be very different for regions, resorts, local authorities, countries or even groups of countries. There may be some commonality but much will depend on whether or not the objectives are capable of being measured. For a destination tourist office, the marketing objectives will almost certainly include some or all of the following:

(1)   total visits and per cent increase over the previous year;
(2)   visits from key markets;
(3)   expenditure in the country overall;
(4)   expenditure/earnings from key markets;
(5)   benefit to specific regions of the country measured in terms of bed nights, spending (these regions will normally have special needs in terms of fragile economies, high unemployment);
(6)   seasonality, which may be measured by quarterly or monthly visit figures if these are available, hotel occupancy surveys;
(7)   brand share (in terms of earnings) in main markets *vis* spending by residents of that country in the destination country as a percentage of total spend by residents of that country on foreign travel. Source of the latter is OECD or WTO.

For an attraction, objectives could include visits, spending in shops, spend on refreshments, seasonal targets, coach traffic. For an hotel, there will be yet another set of objectives and targets which might include bed nights, split between rack rate and group rate, banqueting, sales of food and beverages plus targets for markets and segments. Those hotels with many of their eggs in the American group market suffered badly in 1986. Those with a good spread of markets were able to mitigate damage. For a transport service, load factors and revenue achieved will be major considerations. This will involve flattening peak demand and securing adequate fare levels. Competition will also have a bearing on added value offers, eg free drinks, free headsets.

The marketing task

These objectives will translate into a number of key tasks, which in turn will devolve onto certain areas and executives in the organisation. The objectives will also be translated into the identification of key segments to be addressed, for example, the senior citizen segment and the special interest traveller in the case of seasonality. The regional spread objective will translate into specific target areas and identified markets appropriate to these areas. Some objectives will translate into generic tasks and others into very specific tasks, while yet others will embrace both the generic and the specific. These set the scene for the year ahead and concentrate attention on the half-dozen or so key tasks which the organisation needs to address in the coming year.

Product/market fit

Having analysed products and markets and segments within those markets as part of the diagnostic phase of planning, the important next stage is to match the right product against the right market and the right segment within that market. Market research and analysis will have helped to identify the appropriate segments and the sub-segments. Business travel can be sub-segmented into incentive groups, convention business, visits to trade fairs and exhibitions, management study as well as the independent business traveller and perhaps accompanying spouse. Leisure travel can similarly be sub-segmented into well defined consumer groups which may be demographic or by type of travel or specialist interest. For attractions, segments will include day visitors; for an hotel, banqueting and functions for the local population, ranging from hobby groups to club dinners, wedding receptions to birthday parties.

BTA's Marketing Plan finds it most useful to broadly segment markets into three main groups: touring holidays, centred holidays and business travel. These are then sub-segmented into a number of sub-groups, each capable of being addressed separately and specifically. Each sub-group, having its own wants and needs, will need to have a separate approach while recognising at the same time that some activity will be generic and provide a backcloth for the specifically targeted message which will hopefully fall on receptive ears and eyes. For example, advertising and public relations activities will appear in media, which will be seen by leisure traveller and business traveller alike and while specifically targeted at the leisure traveller, it could also influence the conference organiser in the choice of a destination and conference venue. Similarly, the English language student considering a destination (the USA, Malta, Cyprus and Ireland also offer English language courses) could well be influenced by an effective public relations campaign with generic appeal.

The independent motoring visitor from Europe is a very different touring visitor from the Australian who takes an extended coach tour or even a European taking a coach tour to a part of Britain. One needs to be reached direct or perhaps through a ferry company, given suggested itineraries which include places to visit, things to see and reassured about places to stay and how to book, where to eat, and so on. The visitor on a coach tour will have his accommodation and meals pre-booked and he will have been reached through the coach operator, who in turn will need information and advice on accommodation, lunch stops and places to visit, perhaps from a 'coach operators' manual' or perhaps through attendance at a workshop. A touring visitor with his own caravan will need to have advice on caravan sites, charges and road conditions. But all of these sub-segments will need to have been convinced that Britain is an attractive place to visit and offers good value for money.

Having segmented the market into meaningful target groups it is then necessary to match the product with them appropriately. In the case of BTA's Marketing Plan this is done on a geographical basis. For example, in meeting the regional spread objective it is possible to persuade the motoring visitor to go to those parts of the country which are most in need of the economic benefits which tourism can bring. People may not know where they want to go. Invariably they know where they do not want to go. It is for BTA to persuade the potential visitor to go to those parts of Britain in line with marketing objectives, by presenting them as attractive, appealing, exciting places to visit.

Sometimes the product dictates the geographical area featured in the Product/Market Fit tables. For example, English language schools are very largely concentrated in the southern part of England and most especially on the south coast; farmhouse holidays on working farms are mainly available in Wales, narrow boat holidays can only be taken where canals exist and so on. The discipline of the Product/Market Fit tables, which in the case of a national tourist office should be constructed in cooperation with regional tourist offices, ensures that the marketer will be specific in directing the right message to the right target group. It is the launch pad for the Marketing Plan and an integral part of it, since the marketing activity is designed to communicate the right product to the right market and the right segment within that market.

An example of BTA's Product/Market Fit table illustrates how it is developed and how it can be adapted to an individual organisation's or resort's needs.

Although the examples in tables 10.1 and 10.2 show the task of a state marketing agency for their national destination, the same principles apply to a region, resort or a specific product – transport, accommodation or attraction.

New developments

A catalogue of new developments is a useful exercise in listing developments which have occurred since the last Marketing Plan or where developments are known to be planned to come into effect or operation during the life of the Plan. Again these will variously impact on different organisations but wherever possible it should be a catalogue which is developed by the individual operator, whether that be a group hotel manager, the manager of an individual attraction within a group of attractions, or the manager of an overseas office. In the case of the latter, new developments would typically include new air or sea services, increased capacity, changes in the structure of the travel trade, representation in the market place, including general sales agents or changes in legislation or fiscal controls. For an hotel it could include a new factory development in the area, a new office development, a new or expanded visitor attraction or a new motorway or major road.

Constraints

Conversely, there should be a catalogue of constraints which would include cessation or reduction of carrier services, fiscal controls, political uncertainty, perceived lack of value for money – reduction in group allocations by hotels in key locations. While new developments can very often point up opportunities, constraints present challenges and problems to be addressed and if possible overcome.

Marketing opportunities

A list of marketing opportunities should then be prepared some of which will derive from new developments, some the result of research, some the result of reviewing the previous year's activities.

Marketing initiatives

What new initiatives are planned for the year ahead? These result in part directly from the catalogue of marketing opportunities capable of being developed through specifically targeted marketing activity or perhaps in addressing a problem identified in the catalogue of constraints. For example, a perception that a destination is expensive can be corrected with a publication which shows good value offers in accommodation, fixed price menus, how to 'live like the natives' (and thus benefit from the experience of the locals who have sought out good value offers), pointing up discount offers for travel or entertainment and so on. When France introduced a limit on foreign holiday spending, a few years ago, BTA mounted a campaign which demonstrated that a visit to Britain was still affordable within the spending limits. The initiative may derive from the analysis of product (a new conference venue or a new coaching

Table 10.1 – 1979–1980 Product/market fit table – Northern Europe

		SCANDINAVIA				BENELUX		CENTRAL EUROPE			EIRE
1979–80 Product/market Fit tables / Northern Europe markets / Visit categories		DENMARK	NORWAY	SWEDEN	FINLAND	BELGIUM/ LUXEMBOURG	NETHERLANDS	GERMANY	SWITZERLAND	AUSTRIA	EIRE
TOURING HOLIDAYS	Serviced accommodation using own/hire car	WAL SCO NOR EMD EAN HOE (SE)	SCO esp. H&I NOR (EMI) EAN (SE) HOE WAL	SCO esp. H&I NOR (EMI) EAN HOE (SE) WAL	BRI esp. SCO EST	BRI	BRI	BRI	BRI esp. WAL SCO NOR	BRI esp. WAL SCO	WAL SCO WES NW CUM
	Camping and caravanning using own car or motor-homes	(WAL) SBC NOR EAN (HOE)	(WAL) SBC NOR EAN (HOE)	(WAL) SBC NOR EAN (HOE)		WAL) SBC NOR EST (HOE)	(WAL) SBC NOR EST (HOE)	(WAL) SBC NOR EST (HOE)	SBC	(WAL)	SBC NOR
	Independent travel by public transport, including Britrail pass, Travelpass and Coachmaster	BRI	BRI	BRI	BRI	BRI	BRI	BRI	BRI	BRI	BRI
	Inclusive travel – coach tours originating overseas or in the UK	BRI	BRI	BRI	BRI	BRI	BRI	BRI	BRI	BRI	BRI
	Serviced accommodation for centred holidays	WAL NES H&I CES NOR EST	WAL NES H&I CES NOR EST	WAL NES CES H&I NOR EST WCT STH		WAL CES NOR EST HOE WCT STH	WAL CES NOR EST HOE WCT STH NES	WAL SCO NOR EST HOE WCT STH	CES	CES	WAL SCO CUM NW WCT STH SE
	Serviced Farmhouse accommodation	WAL NOR HOE	WAL NOR HOE	WAL NOR HOE WCT		WAL NOR HOE WCT	WAL NOR HOE WCT	WAL NOR HOE WCT	HOE WCT WAL		HOE WCT
	Self catering in cottages, chalets and flats	WAL SCO WES EAN	WAL SCO WES EAN	WAL SCO WES EAN		WAL SCO NW WES	WAL SCO NW WES EST*	WAL SCO NW WES	WAL WES EST		WAL SCO NW WCT TAC

Group	Segment	(H&I) HOE EST	(H&I) HOE EST	(H&I) HOE EST		(TAC) (H&I) (EMD) HOE (SE) NW EAN	H&I NW	H&I HOE EST	HOE EST	EST	NW
CENTRED HOLIDAYS	Waterways										
	Static caravans (Wales: Dragon sites only)					(WAL) (NW)	WAL NES WCT STH NW	WAL WCT STH			WAL WCT
	Senior citizens – tailored holidays	EAN NW				SE YOR EAN	WAL SCO NW EAN SE STH YOR EAN	(NW) (YOR) STH SE			WAL WCT
	Language studies	WCT STH SE LON EAN	WCT STH SE LON EAN	WCT STH SE LON EAN	WCT STH SE LON EAN LON	(WCT) STH SE EAN CON TAC		WCT HOE STH CUM SE EMD LON TAC	WCT STH SE LON TAC (SCO)	WCT STH SE LON TAC	
	Port of entry: short stay	CES NW NTB EAN SE HOE	NES CES NW NTB SE EAN	CES NW NTB EAN SE		YOR SE EAN	WAL NES YOR CES NTB EMD SE EAN	YOR HOE TAC NTB SE EAN	NW CUM SE		WAL NW
BUSINESS TRAVEL	London – using serviced accommodation – independent or inclusive visits with day-trips from London	LON EAN WES SE TAC	LON EAN WES SE TAC	LON EAN WES SE TAC	LON EAN WES SE TAC	LON EAN WES SE TAC	LON EAN WES SE TAC	LON EAN WES SE TAC	LON EAN WES SE TAC	LON EAN WES SE TAC	LON
	Including: Conference / Trade Fair/Exhibition / Incentive and study tour traffic	Britain in all N. European markets – but selling specific destinations appropriate to sub-segments									

Table 10.2 – 1979–80 Product/market fit table – Intercontinental markets.

1979–80 Product/market Fit table Visit categories		Major English speaking markets			
		United States	Canada	Australia and N.Z.	South Africa
TOURING HOLIDAYS	Serviced accommodation using hire car (or own car purchased in Britain)	BRI	BRI	BRI	BRI
	Camping and Caravanning using hired vehicles, especially motor-homes	(WAL) SCO	(WAL) SCO	(WAL) SCO (NTB)	(BRI)
	Independent travel by public transport, including Britrail pass, Travelpass and Coachmaster	BRI	BRI	BRI	BRI
	Inclusive travel – coach tours originating in the UK	BRI	BRI	BRI	BRI
CENTRED HOLIDAYS	Serviced accommodation for centre holidays	CES WCT SE HOE STH	CES WCT HOE STH SE		
	Serviced farmhouse accommodation			WAL	
	Self catering in cottages, chalets and flats	WCT HOE LON	WCT HOE LON	HOE	
	Waterways – self catering	HOE (H&I) EST (NW)	HOE (H&I) EST (NW)		
	– serviced 'floatels'	NW HOE TAC EMD	NW HOE TAC EMD	NW HOE TAC	TAC HOE
	Language studies				
	London – using serviced accommodation – independent or inclusive visits with day-trips from London	LON EAN SE TAC WES	LON EAN SE TAC WES	LON EAN SE TAC WES	LON EAN SE TAC WES
BUSINESS TRAVEL	Including: Conference Trade Fair/ Exhibition Incentive and study tour traffic	Britain in all intercontinental markets –			

REGIONAL CODES:

BRI Britain

NOR North of England
NTB Northumbria
YOR Yorkshire and Humberside
CUM Cumbria/English Lakes
NW North West

WES West of England
HOE Heart of England
STH Southern
WCT West Country

EST East of England
EMD East Midlands
EAN East Anglia
SE South East
TAC Thames and Chilterns
NB EST* Low priority for three regions except East
　　　　　Anglia where greater emphasis is required.

Other principal long haul markets					
Latin America	Japan	Rest of the Far East	Iran	Rest of the Middle East & N. Africa	Africa (excl. N. and S. Africa)
BRI	BRI	BRI	BRI	BRI	BRI
(BRI)					
BRI	BRI	BRI	BRI	BRI	BRI
BRI	BRI	BRI			
LON		LON	LON	LON	
SCO (EAN) LON SE T&C WES NOR HOE	LON SE STH	LON SE STH	LON SE STH T&C	LON SE STH T&C	
LON EAN SE TAC WES	LON EAN SE TAC WES	LON EAN SE TAC WES	LON EAN SE TAC WES	LON EAN SE TAC WES	LON EAN SE TAC WES

but selling specific destinations appropriate to sub-segments

LON London

SCO Scotland
H & I Highlands and Islands (including Highlands, Western Isles, Shetland and Orkney).
NES North East Scotland (including Fife, Tayside and Grampian).
SBC Scottish Borders (including Dumfries and Galloway and Borders).
CES Central Scotland (including Strathclyde, Lothian and Central).

WAL Wales
Low priority.

hotel) or market (a newly identified special interest segment); it can derive from a significant anniversary or even a new promotional technique. Alternatively, new initiatives can be the result of having identified a new partner with a common interest, for example, an airline with a new service.

The ongoing marketing programme

But marketing is not just about taking new initiatives. They are vitally important in helping to stay ahead of the game and the competition but there is an ongoing programme to be planned, a continuation of the tested and tried techniques. The ongoing programme even so is capable of further refinement and improvement, higher targets may be agreed, a more ambitious activity planned on the strength of the previous year's experience.

Again it is essential that the new initiatives section and the ongoing marketing programme are agreed with those who will be responsible for executing the programme. They must believe that they are realistic and realisable goals. The Plan should never be imposed but mutually agreed with the doers. In developing the ongoing programme, objectives should always be firmly in view and wherever possible targets mutually agreed between the Marketing Director and the executive responsible for carrying out the activity and thus meeting the targets.

Targets

These will naturally differ greatly, depending on the type of operation but they would typically include sales calls on the travel trade, participants in exhibitions workshops, familiarisation trips, roadshows, sales missions and inspection visits. Advertising (coupon response generated), direct mail (bookings through the partner plus response), advertising revenue to support the print programme, journalists' visits and television crew visits can all have a target and be capable of measurement.

Targets also need to be established for the specialist departments where they exist in terms of press stories planned to be issued, print programme, research programme, product marketing activity, as well as the amount of cooperative marketing revenue to be raised.

Targets cascade down through all the strata of an organisation; each person has a part to play in carrying out the agreed programme and in reaching the targets set. The Marketing Plan is the coordinating machinery which formally records the task and the goals. A wide range of activities and tasks have to be carried out. They have to be coordinated and properly timed along their critical paths and it all depends on people knowing where they and the organisation is going, giving a sense of direction and motivation to carry out their part of the grand plan efficiently and effectively.

The Marketing Plan for the destination is also the source of the catalogue or 'shopping list' of cooperative marketing opportunities which can be offered and sold to potential partners, tourist boards, resorts and marketing agencies, especially in the case of cooperative marketing activity. These offers will include line entry and advertising in publications, participation in exhibitions and trade shows, workshops and sales missions, opportunities for cooperative advertising or direct mail, as well as jointly funded print, films, research or even full scale marketing campaigns. It makes a lot of sense for partners with similar objectives to work together in jointly funded activity – activity which has been carefully planned following thorough analysis.

Summary

The Marketing Plan is the tactical communications plan for the year ahead. It is a formal written document developed and agreed with those generalists and specialists in the organisation responsible for its execution. Building the Plan entails analysis of markets and products, matching them, selecting the marketing tools and developing the marketing mix to communicate product to market cost effectively, taking account of competition and external factors where appropriate. The establishment of targets and regular review of progress are fundamental to all marketing planning.

11 Marketing tools and techniques

Advertising is a marketing tool, so is promotion and public relations, print and exhibitions, radio and film. There are many more. They are the media that carry the messages, the communications machinery, the ambassadors.

Each individual medium or tool has its special advantages and cost benefits. Advertising gives the marketer complete control over timing, message and target: public relations activity may be more powerful, cheaper and effective in sales terms, but control is much more limited. PR has a special value in changing attitude, reassurance, mitigating damage and, over a period, helping to create a fashion or special appeal.

No medium can be effective on its own so the mix or combination is important. They must all be dovetailed into the marketing mix, or the total marketing programme of the organisation embracing product price, promotion and market place. The marketer does not ask 'shall I use advertising or not?' without considering all the other marketing tools and how they inter-relate one with the other.

There are as many definitions of individual marketing tools, such as advertising, as there are of the marketing concept itself and it would be wrong to state categorically that any one is more correct than another. However, one must attempt to establish a generally accepted definition to provide some grounds for common understanding.

Advertising

The American Marketing Association defines advertising as 'any paid form of non-personal presentation of goods, ideas or services by an identified sponsor'. An alternative definition is non-personal persuasive communication in media which is not managed by the company, eg press, magazines, radio, television, posters, cinema. Advertising can be precise in terms of message and timing and can be more specifically targeted at the right audience than some other marketing tools. It is part of the total marketing effort and must always be very clearly aligned with, and indeed governed by, the objectives of the organisation.

Many research techniques are available to help guide the advertising decisions in terms of media, message and timing, but even with the benefit of research the marketer needs to make a number of basic decisions.

1. What is the objective?
2. Over what time scale are the objectives to be achieved?
3. What is the target audience?
4. Should it be a national, international or regional campaign?
5. If international, should it be global or separate campaigns each geared to individual markets?
6. What is the part which is planned for advertising in the marketing mix?
7. How much money is needed to achieve the objectives?
8. What is the copy theme and image to be?
9. What is the optimum timing?
10. Whether to advertise or not.

Advertising, even though it can be fairly precisely targeted, uses mass media to talk directly to the potential buyers of the product. So it must persuade these potential buyers that the product will satisfy their wants and needs in a unique way. It becomes generally more cost efficient as a medium when the number of consumers needed to be reached is large. Furthermore, unlike most products, a tourist destination cannot be taken to the market place, the consumer has to travel to the product and that product must be presented in an appealing and attractive way through the advertising and other vehicles too.

The marketer must be very clear about the objectives to be achieved. Is it coupon response? Is it to increase brand share, to increase the total market, to change image, to reassure? All these are relevant objectives for tourism advertising and the time scales can be quite different. The time scale in which a given set of objectives are achieved is very often, though not always, directly proportional to the money spent. It may take several years, even with reasonable budgets, to effect changes in traffic flows, for example, to unknown parts of a country. The Spanish National Tourist Office is undoubtedly aware of this in trying to move traffic from the seaside resorts to the inland towns. On the other hand the reassurance campaign which BTA mounted in the USA in July 1986 following the bombing of Libya and fears of terrorism, had to work in a relatively short time scale. The timing had to be right and it had to work quickly.

Research can give useful guidance on the holiday decision process, the gestation period of decision, planning and buying. It can also help to determine the target audience. The marketer must clearly define the consumer who is likely to buy his product in terms of age, sex, socio-economic group, standard of education, purchasing power, region of residence and the size and nature of the target audience has a bearing on the size of the advertising appropriation. This is particularly true of socio-economic group and region of residence.

To run a national or regional campaign can be one of the more important strategic decisions. Research will show that one region outperforms another in terms of buyers or, alternatively, it can demonstrate where the potential is higher. There has been a shift in Britain's target market in the USA to California and the Sunbelt states and the advertising plans have needed to keep pace with these population shifts. Never put advertising money into a weak area in preference to a strong area. There are more effective tools for carrying out the missionary work.

How does the marketer decide how much to spend? The organisation's top management will need to calculate how much it can afford to spend on its marketing and the marketer will then need to define the job to be done and cost it, taking account of competitive spend, objectives to be attained and promotional message. He will then need to reconcile the two figures and accept a compromise if necessary but taking care not to waste money in trying to make too small a budget work miracles. Far better to consider alternative marketing tools, such as public relations or direct mail. It is easier to determine how much to spend on advertising a manufactured product where unit costs and fixed costs are known, selling and distribution expenses and other overheads can be determined, sales value and revenue forecast. It is then possible to calculate a sum which can be divided between profit and advertising and promotion.

Working with an advertising agency is rather like working with a computer. If the input is good and clear, the output will be too. It is the marketer's job to ensure that the agency has all the information needed to formulate the campaign. That means the marketing plan and the research data which led up to it. The marketer must also suggest the copy theme or platform; he must suggest the image that he wants to create, the target audience and, finally, guidance on consumer rationalisation. In other words, 'I want to buy this product because . . . ' Remember it is advertising which draws the consumer to the product. Remember too that advertising is a substitute for personal selling. It follows that the advertising agency is as important as a sales manager running a sales force and should be regarded as an integral part of the marketing organisation.

It is the agency's job to produce advertising ideas but it is the marketer's job to produce the right brief, to have a clear picture of what image the organisation wishes to project for the product and to agree the copy theme. The guidance needed to fulfil these tasks should come from research and from the Marketing Plan; then more research to check that the advertising is working.

Advertising is that part of the marketing process which communicates effectively and economically to a chosen group of consumers. It exists as a substitute for personal selling and it should be designed to do the best selling job possible. It is more effective when it is precisely focused and projected on a backcloth of receptivity created through good public relations.

Public relations

This is a vitally important part of the communications strategy of an organisation and generally operates on three levels:

(1) The corporate level – creating the best climate and reputation for the organisation in terms of receptivity and favourable public opinion.
(2) The consumer level – creating the right backcloth onto which the organisation can project more precisely focused messages.
(3) The trade level – who in turn can influence the consumer either directly or indirectly and for destination public authorities guiding and influencing standards (award schemes).

Public relations however is different from advertising. While its purpose, like that of advertising, is communication it is different inasmuch as it does not use paid media space, may well not identify the sponsor, and does not target the message as precisely as advertising does in terms of timing, media or message. The marketer can get lucky of course and have an independent journalist write things which he may well think twice about claiming in the advertising. Public relations activity is vital in tourism as it is the most powerful medium in the task of guarding the image.

In tourism, public relations can be the most cost-effective of all the weapons in the marketer's armoury and it is capable of working effectively not only at the three levels identified above, but multi-dimensionally in communicating the messages which the marketer wishes to get across to particular audiences. A marketer in tourism, and especially one in an official tourist organisation, must never forget that there are several audiences.

At the corporate level, there is a need to seek to influence the shareholders. In the case of a resort tourist officer this may well be the elected members on the local authority and the commercial interests in the resort who benefit from the tourist spend. At the regional level it will be a number of local authorities and commercial operators in the region, who may well subscribe funds on a membership basis to the regional tourist board. At the national level, almost certainly the shareholders are the tax-payers, who in turn are represented by the civil servants, ministers and elected members. At these levels there is a need to create a favourable climate and a positive image of the organisation and what it is achieving in terms of economic benefit, job creation, conservation or general public good. The principle applies to commercial interests or the local, regional and national level, according to the scale of operation.

There are a number of tools and techniques available to the PR department which are used to communicate to these audiences. Press releases to newspapers and magazines, feature stories, press interviews, press conferences, newsletters and magazines are all effective in their various ways. Newsletters and magazines should be published regularly and mailed to a prescribed audience. Press conferences should normally be used sparingly. In the case of an organisation whose marketing work is conducted principally overseas, it is important to ensure that the influencers and decision-makers are aware of what it does and how effective its work is in terms of expected benefits.

Depending on the size of the organisation, the corporate PR function may well be separate from marketing but in smaller organisations it will necessarily be a task for the tourist officer. Whether it is or not, it is part of the essential work of marketing the organisation. The organisation can consciously seek to improve its reputation or neglect it. There are always those who can damage an organisation's reputation. Public relations has been defined as 'the deliberate, planned and sustained effort to establish and maintain mutual understanding between an organisation and its public'.

Public relations, like marketing, should be an attitude of mind at every level of the organisation from the Chairman to the receptionist and telephone operator; especially the receptionist and the telephone operator, when one is mounting a corporate PR campaign.

At the consumer level the public relations programme must be closely geared to the Marketing Plan and in line with marketing policy and objectives. Essentially, it should be designed to create and maintain an image for the destination which is at once appetising and appealing. It must make the consumer think 'I would like to go or be there'. The objective of the PR campaign will differ from market to market. Where a currency is weak against that of the destination it will be necessary to make the consumer aware of best buys, how to make his budget go further, where to find value for money. Reassure him with actual examples that the destination is affordable. On the other hand, in an area of special interest travel, it will be necessary to communicate the unique appeals of the destination *vis-à-vis* the consumer's hobby or avocation. The PR machine will be used to communicate new developments – hotels, events, facilities, to promote themes or anniversaries, and to provide reassurance, and it uses a number of techniques to achieve the desired results.

The main tools at the disposal of the PR staff are press releases, press news bulletins, picture stories, feature articles, photographs and visual material, press facility visits for the media, radio and film producers and, of course, the press conference. There is also a range of special events such as receptions and 'theatrical' shows or promotions, including personality visits to the market place, seminars, surveys and audio visual presentations.

There is no point in preparing a press release, writing a feature or developing news bulletins unless there is a mailing list of appropriate media. The media must be carefully selected to match target groups of consumers and vigilantly refined and kept up to date. In maintaining the media list it will be necessary to make enquiries of recipients, asking if they still want the material, whether it is of value to them, whether they would like to see any changes. Press releases should be straightforward statements which are newsworthy together with the name of the organisation issuing the release, its status (for immediate release or not) and the name of a contact in the organisation for further information. Specially printed press release forms are often developed where the volume is sufficient to justify it. Picture stories are similar to press releases, where the picture tells the story, and are a cost efficient way of securing editorial coverage.

In the case of a national tourist office where there are hundreds of potentially good stories – new products and packages, events and exhibitions, theatre productions and festivals, new attractions and facilities – it is a good idea to have a regular newsletter with fifty or sixty items of news from which editors or journalists can select those which they consider to be of interest to their readers.

Familiarisation visits for the media are expensive and difficult to organise well. They are designed to take advantage of a journalist's special interest, eg theatre or fishing; to provide an opportunity for the journalist to see new developments in the destination, eg a specialist writer in the business travel field may be shown a new conference facility; to point up a promotional theme or anniversary, or simply to provide an opportunity for showing the visiting journalist a part of the country. Success in this field is determined by careful selection of those invited on press facility trips (beware the freeloaders), attention to detail in preparing the itinerary and in booking the accommodation, travel arrangements and entertainment.

A tourist officer will need to work closely with the carriers in facilitating media visits and every effort should be made to secure as much 'in kind' support from the potential beneficiaries as possible in terms of free or discounted accommodation, travel, meals and entertainment. Journalists tend to be individualists and consequently prefer to travel independently rather than as members of a group, though group trips are normally arranged and acceptable in the case of inaugurals arranged to publicise new routes or new aircraft on existing routes.

Television companies can sometimes be persuaded to make documentary films and will need a great deal of assistance in carrying out the 'recce'. In particular the tourist office will need to ensure that the film crew will be facilitated and welcomed at places they wish to film. There are many examples of owners wanting to charge a fee to the film production team, who are not unnaturally angered by this, since the film or documentary will provide a great deal of free publicity for the product. Production teams have cancelled film projects when this unwelcome treatment has been meted out. So it is essential to find out the situation before the visit is arranged.

The larger national tourist offices will sometimes have their own radio department and just as the staff journalists will produce features and news stories for distribution to the media, the radio officer will be producing tapes comprising interviews, news and regular features for distribution to radio stations on a carefully developed mailing list.

Departmental store promotions and hotel promotions can also be effective public relations vehicles but they should be very carefully assessed for cost effectiveness in terms of the promotion offered. All too often they are designed to fill a trough, or fallow period in the store or hotel calendar at someone else's expense.

As with marketing generally, setting objectives is indispensable for each of the marketing tools, including public relations. They should be drawn up in a specific and detailed way and they will vary from market to market and by segment. They should be supportive of the objectives and targets set for advertising. Since public relations uses a variety of techniques, some will be more relevant and effective than others. In Japan for example store promotions can well be more cost effective than feature stories, which would get limited pick-up by the media. So priorities need to be established for techniques as well as markets in ensuring that the budget is allocated as effectively as possible.

The results achieved by the PR programme can be determined in a number of ways:

(1)　The amount picked up by the media and the resultant editorial coverage, which can be measured from the press clipping obtained. This can be very expensive and in some cases difficult to achieve. Furthermore, it is too simplistic to measure column inches: a piece in the 'New York Times' travel section is worth infinitely more than the same piece in the 'Hicksville Herald'.

(2)　By asking recipients of features and newsletters whether or not they find them of value, though there will never be a 100 per cent response to such a mailing.

(3)　By encouraging the beneficiaries of the editorial to advise the estimated volume of business resulting. One effective way of achieving this is by ensuring that clippings are sent to the beneficiaries on a regular basis, demonstrating the coverage which has been obtained.

Dissemination of information is one of the *raisons d'êtres* of a tourist office and will feature prominently in PR activity. But PR staff cannot make bricks without straw and the marketer must take every opportunity to remind the trade and the producers that information is the life blood of the PR machine. Channels for the dissemination of information can be set up; it is equally important that good channels are established for receiving the information.

Direct mail

A marketing technique once used almost exclusively by book clubs and record clubs, it is being used increasingly by marketers from blue chip corporations to charities. In the USA, direct marketing now accounts for one in seven consumer transactions. It is now the third largest advertising medium in Britain and the fastest growing. Tourist offices too are embracing this technique and discovering that it is a very cost effective way of reaching that all important target audience. At one end of the spectrum is the television commercial, reaching a wide audience at high cost and at the other the direct mail shot, precisely targeted and addressed to one potential customer – accurate, cheap and measurable.

The most important key to success in any direct mail campaign is the mailing list. To reach the right market you need the right mailing list. Lists can be rented from a list broker and the number and variety of lists is almost infinite, from income levels to members of social clubs, affinity groups to members of learned societies or professions. There is a high level of wastage for 'junk mail', yet the technique with generally a two to five per cent response rate is highly profitable. Success in getting the mailing shot accepted by the consumer is in the real or perceived value of the product. The offer must be right and also the way the price is positioned and presented. The direct mail shot is in effect a sales presentation for both high and low cost items and its success is determined by the format and the creative treatment.

Tourist organisations and operators can develop their own mailing lists. Hoteliers can maintain records of guests. Tourist offices receive enquiries by letter, by telephone and in person. Advertising should carry a coupon, which is not just used to mail literature but is added to the mailing list for a future sales pitch. These are a few ways of building up consumer mailing lists and they can be further categorised by interest, region of residence and even age. BTA built up a mailing list of senior citizens by offering a free publication written for seniors and featured in editorial. In the case of the trade, business cards can be collected at trade shows or names and addresses culled from association handbooks.

The mailing list is a perishable product and must be constantly replenished and updated. The new technology in the form of micro computers and word processors makes it increasingly easy to maintain lists on machines which will print out labels. As costs of conventional methods of promotion increase it is a technique well worth study.

Literature

Brochure production is expensive and considerable thought should be given to the print programme before rushing into production. In the case of international marketing, translation of copy into a number of languages will be required and these can pose quite a problem.

Objectives, purpose and target audience must be carefully researched, agreed and planned. All too often resorts will produce a poster without any real thought as to where, how or who will see it. In the case of print, the medium is the product and the target audience must be firmly in the marketer's mind when he produces the pagination and design brief. There is a trade audience and a consumer audience and each have their specific needs.

Print can very broadly be subdivided into three stages. First, the promotional print or 'come on', where the marketer must try and persuade the reader to select a particular destination. Second, is the guide on how to buy, the publication which makes it easy to buy. Stage three is the how to travel, what to see and do guide, designed to ensure that the visitor gains the maximum satisfaction from his trip. Great guide books fall into this third category. In practice however, stages one and two or stages two and three are often combined. While stage one publications should always be free, stage three publications can and should be sold. They have potentially a great and profitable importance. Baedeker, it was said, was not a guide book but a way of life. In recent years they have lost some of their original status and quality. The more talented writer may prefer writing armchair travel books while the practical vade-mecum is sometimes downgraded and trivialised.

Print is one of the essential weapons in the tourism marketer's armoury. It was suggested earlier that, unlike consumer goods which can be taken to the market place, in the case of a tourist destination or facility the market must be brought to the product. The brochure is the representation of that product containing as it does illustrations, descriptions, information and prices. In the case of the tourist office it must inform the prospective customer about the facilities and attractions available at the destination, including how to get there.

The marketer is not and indeed cannot be, an expert in print production. He is a coordinator of expertise, the initiator and the arbiter. Like advertising, like public relations, like direct mail, clear objectives must be drawn up for the print programme and for each individual title in that print programme. What is the rationale? What is the target audience?

The answers to these two questions will invariably provide the necessary guidance in terms of content, quality, quantity and, in the case of international marketing, language.

The marketer must provide the pagination brief to the editorial and design team. The brief should reflect the product/market fit (see chapter 10), motivation analysis (see chapter 8), carefully researched information needs and overall it should reflect the established and agreed marketing objectives. The marketer must then satisfy himself that the finished copy does indeed measure up in these terms and is exciting to the reader. He must also ensure that design is exciting and pleasing to the eye, not forgetting that the age profile of the audience can dictate the type face. Older people dislike having to read small print. There are two key tasks – first, ordering of information so that it can be absorbed easily and there are many graphics tricks to aid this rapid absorption; secondly, the balance between pictures and copy, or the lay-out must be pleasing. The designer will differentiate between editorial pages and advertising by ensuring there is a consistency of style. Readers of tourist literature, especially destination print, do not read it from cover to cover like a novel. They will usually scan the headlines, look at the pictures, read the captions to the pictures and then read the copy. It is generally the copy which is meticulously approved by the marketer when he should be approaching approval from a consumer point of view. It can never be said often enough – the job of the marketer is to try and see things through the consumer's eyes.

Once the page lay-outs are available, it is possible to check headlines and position of illustrations – usually the first chance that a non-expert can really judge what it is going to look like. Once the page film is made it becomes very expensive to start making corrections and once the four colour proof has been submitted nothing should be corrected unless it is critical, like mis-spelling the name of the destination. There are a few useful rules:

(1)   always use international sizes, preferably A4, A5 or one-third A4;
(2)   it is preferable to use one good picture on the cover unless there are compelling reasons for a multi-picture approach;
(3)   include a map or maps showing the location of the facility or resort in relation to the town or in relation to other major tourist centres;
(4)   feature your address and telephone number (including the international dialling code);
(5)   if appropriate, the address of your overseas office or representative;
(6)   maintain a good editorial : advertising balance so that the publication is not swamped by the advertising.

National tourist offices are usually helpful in recommending designers, writers, translation agencies and very often have excellent photo libraries which can be accessed.

Information data collection and presentation is an increasingly complex area. Computer data banks and desk top publishing, electronic transmission of data from collection agency to printer, have made enormous strides in the past few years. Again, it is not the marketer's job to be a skilled professional in this area. It is his job to provide the brief and to set the budgets; to ensure that the right information is available in the market place at the right time. It must not be forgotten that there are distribution costs too.

Distribution is difficult and expensive, but literature is but a means to an end. In order to reach travel prospects effective distribution is required. This may seem obvious but it happens surprisingly frequently that promoters, especially if product-orientated, see the printed matter as the final product and sometimes judge it according to their own criteria and not the prospective visitor's needs. Posters in particular, which can represent an art form, are not infrequently distributed almost at random and with little planning and appraisal and sometimes not in relation to the marketing mix designed to implement the marketing plan.

Promotion costs to reach the audience may well equal or exceed literature production cost, so effective control of distribution is imperative. To an extent, the distribution network of tourist information centres, transport and travel agency networks help to ensure this but it does not happen automatically.

For the state and destination tourist organisation there are ways of improving cost effectiveness. Staging of print will require the prospect to make a second request for more detailed information, having received a first stage print in answer to an advertising coupon, which is itself a selection device. The more detailed the print the more likely the respondent will be to pay postage or purchase the booklet. Destination print should carry advertising, which provides the essential commercial and price information needed to make it easy to buy the product. Sales of literature and advertising support for publications are to an extent self-regulating factors, directing the literature to those who want to buy on the one hand and guiding the marketer to the most effective targets on the other. Research into commercial advertising response will provide this valuable guidance.

Exhibitions

There are consumer exhibitions and trade exhibitions. An exhibition, provided it is the right exhibition, can be an excellent showcase for products, services or destination. It can also be a very cost effective way of generating sales leads and names and addresses for mailing lists. All too often the opportunities afforded are thrown away, either because of poor location, bad stand design, weak publicity or because of untrained staff on the stand. The marketer must assess the exhibition like other sales media in terms of the marketing objectives and in the context of the marketing mix. He must then seek the best possible location, having evaluated traffic flows, stand shape, position *vis-à-vis* competition and cost.

For a destination tourist office, participation in exhibitions presents opportunities for coordination and cooperation, as well as providing a focal point for transport and destination interests to pool resources.

Exhibition space is usually sold as 'space' or 'shell', that is to say the organiser of the exhibition will rent the floor space to the exhibitor who then has to brief a stand designer and stand fitter, who will construct the stand. The 'shell' scheme is sold by the organiser as space plus a simple stand. Do check precisely what is included in the 'shell' price. Does it include lighting, and if so what? Does it include floor covering, and if so what? Often it is lino or carpet tiles. The shell price usually includes the fascia but excludes such things as electric points, plants, furniture and cleaning. Most exhibition organisers will provide attendance figures for previous shows and number of exhibitors, making it possible to evaluate the show.

It is important to budget for all the 'extras' including travel, accommodation and subsistence, photography and entertainment, and to check with the organiser's rules as well as the regulations, eg fire regulations, imposed on the organiser. The biggest mistake is in assuming that once the stand is built and the exhibition open the job is finished. It is in fact only the beginning. Staff must be adequately briefed and properly trained. Let the stand be inviting for the visitors and the staff keenly aware of the visitors' needs and anxious to sell. It is difficult to provide any guidance on budgets, which are dependent on objectives, the type and size of exhibition and venue. Generally, a good rule of thumb is to reckon on a quarter of the budget going on space, another quarter on stand-fitting and decoration, and the balance on staffing and associated costs, photography, entertainment, security and insurance. Where a national tourist office takes space they will usually coordinate a national presence selling modular stands to participants which they can decorate individually. The national tourist office will usually provide a lounge area, perhaps a bar, stand cleaning, telephone and additional promotion. These 'extras' should not be overlooked when comparing the cost of a shell stand with a modular stand offered by the national tourist office. Not least the coordinated national presence will have much more impact than a solo position with a shell scheme.

Store promotions and hotel promotions

A departmental store or an hotel will very often decide to mount a special week or two devoted to a country and will invite the destination tourist office to provide display, entertainment, perhaps a chef or craftsmen. It can be very expensive and the objectives must be clearly thought through and costed. The store or hotel will be motivated for non-altruistic reasons such as a fallow period when business needs to be boosted. The tourism marketer must be careful to ensure that he is not being invited to pay for that boost. It can be a good opportunity but it can equally be a drain on precious resources without a great deal of benefit, except to the store or hotel.

Films and video

Making a film or video is increasingly attractive. The widespread avail-ability of video equipment makes it an attractive new medium and if it is done well, it is a very effective marketing tool for the tourism marketer. It can be more effective in taking the product to the market place, yet production is complex and costly and there are many pitfalls on the way. The brochure can be read and a passage can be reread if need be; the video is necessarily more impressionistic. The cost will be determined by the number of locations, travel costs between locations, hotel accom-modation, hire of actors perhaps, complicated lighting set-ups. All this apart from the basic cost of film and duplication. If there is music, clear-ance can be expensive and it may well be cheaper to commission a score and record specially. It will almost certainly be necessary to hire a professional narrator. So the costs mount. In any video production there are three processes – shooting, editing and post-production, mastering and duplication. Add to this the fact that there are different systems in overseas markets if it is intended to use it internationally. The marketer should have a clear idea of why he wants to make a film or video, where and to whom it will be shown. It is a complex subject and mistakes can be costly. So the best advice is to hire a good production company and provide them with a clear brief. Just as important, there must be ade-quate 'control' of the audience through plans which ensure that the film is shown to potential travellers.

The travel trade

Finally, there are some marketing techniques which are of particular relevance to the tourism industry, though not uniquely so.

The trade show is very similar to the public exhibition. Fundamental differences are the audience, the staff on the stand (who need different skills and knowledge), the level of hospitality, promotional techniques and literature.

Familiarisation trips are very similar to journalists' visits and the same criteria apply in terms of selection of participants and attention to detail in planning the itinerary. Many tourist offices feel it is sufficient to issue invitations to travel agents, ship them to the destination, put them in a coach and then transport them around showing them the maximum possible in between lavish meals and plentiful drink at no cost to the participant. The result can be a tired, over-fed travel agent with a kaleidoscopic impression of the country or resort he is passing through. Once again, clear objectives and targets should be set.

Tourist offices are beginning to make a charge to participants on educational visits and finding that the calibre of the participants is improving. It is a good idea to make them work. The British Tourist Authority is increasingly organising do-it-yourself educational visits, sometimes in the form of a treasure hunt whereby the participants are despatched in car-loads to find their own way, make their own purchases and book their own accommodation. At the end of each day, or second day, the whole group is brought together to compare notes and to be debriefed. The result is that they enjoy it more, they learn more, they are better equipped to provide travel counselling to their clients, having experienced the product at first hand and, not least, the competitive spirit which is introduced ensures that the sub-groups learn from each other at the debriefing sessions.

Roadshows and sales missions can be organised for the producer of services (transport, hotels, attractions) to meet with the potential buyer (tour operator or travel agent) in the market place. The sales mission is usually to one or two places whereas a roadshow can cover maybe twenty cities over a three week period. Producers can make short presentations to specially invited groups of agents or a mini-workshop can be organised at each stop on the tour.

The workshop was invented and developed specifically for the travel trade and is a forum where buyers meet sellers. The potential buyers can either be brought to the destination or the producers or sellers taken to the market place. Workshops can be for the general travel trade or specifically targeted at a specialist area, such as coach operators, language schools or incentive travel specialists. Interviews are scheduled, largely on the basis of the potential buyer's requests against the list of producers which has been submitted to him. The interview is normally twenty or twenty-five minutes before a bell signifies the end of the period and the signal to move on to the next interview. Targets should be set for numbers of buyers and sellers, costs, total income and expenditure and the aim should be to make the exercise self-financing. Of course the potential buyers do not expect to invest more than their time in the workshop. As a measure of a workshop's success, targets should be set for business negotiated and participants surveyed at a reasonable time after the end to allow for business to come to fruition, to establish whether or not targets have been met.

The travel trade's retail outlets provide strategic sites for posters and other display material. The poster's message must be essentially simple but attractive. Stunning pictues are an excellent way of gaining prestige publicity at the point of sale. Of course posters and display material can also be used in store promotions, at seminars, roadshows and workshops.

The tour operator and the retail travel agent are the core of the tourism distribution system. They need special care and this includes sales aids, especially literature designed to guide them and to hand out to the travelling public. Literature designed to guide them will include agents' sales guide, hotel directories, operators' manuals and shell folders (destination literature which travel operators can overprint with their own sales offers).

Computerised reservation systems (CRS)

The tourism product is an amalgam of many fragmented products, each independent yet inter-dependent. Increasingly, the need is to make it easy for the consumer to buy, taking full account of flexibility of packaging, pricing and value-added components. It follows that the producers need to have rapid access through the channels of distribution to the ultimate consumer, to gain the maximum possible exposure for their products. Every sale made by international air carriers is made through CRS, largely through the travel trade. Most of the bookings are made off the first screen so it is clearly essential to be in charge of the distribution chain. A number of systems are in operation. The American Airlines SABRE system is in about 10,000 agency outlets in the USA. They have about forty per cent of the market with United Airline's APOLLO accounting for about thirty per cent. European carriers are developing competitive systems. On the one hand British Airways, Air Lingus, Swissair, KLM, Alitalia and others with GALILEO, and Lufthansa, Air France and SAS with others developing AMADEUS. Since airlines are carrying both business and leisure travellers and since the vast majority of bookings are made through the travel trade, it is important the accommodation, car hire and other tourism products should be available on the CRS. There is increasingly a need for a 'switch' to link the central reservation offices of the major vendors, such as hotel groups and consortia, with the main international distribution systems such as SABRE or AMADEUS or GALILEO. The need essentially is to provide a single interface between one industry reservation system and a number of CRS's and one CRS and many industry reservation systems. The owners of the CRS typically make a charge of US$2–5 in addition to any agent's selling commission.

Some National Tourist Offices are already coordinating information data for distribution through CRS; BTA is working with SABRE in the USA and RESERVAC in Canada. BRAVO, initiated by BTA and developed in the industry, links vendors to consumers by being able to pass information in both directions from vendors' databanks to CRS and value added networks. From the agent's point of view BRAVO is designed to work with existing technology. From the vendor's point of view he will be linked directly or via a representative to distribution sytems. BRAVO Communications Systems Ltd is owned by British Airways, Cable and Wireless and Finite, with a User Representation structure representing accommodation, public sector, non-accommodation and technology groups. It is planned to have BRAVO fully operational by 30 June 1991.

These marketing tools are some of the most popular used in tourism promotion. There are many others – sales promotion, pricing, packaging, tour operators' evenings and personal selling – and some of these will be covered in succeeding chapters.

Summary

The weapons in the tourism marketer's armoury are many and varied. They differ in the degree of precision in reaching the target audience and they vary enormously in cost, and consequently cost-efficiency. They are increasing in number and some of the latest entrants – direct mail and CRS (Central Reservation Systems) – are increasing in importance. The most important marketing ingredients are advertising, public relations, film, radio, direct mail, literature, exhibitions, promotions, workshops, trade educationals, posters, display, videotex and CRS. Very few marketers will want to use them all. He will select and mix his ingredients appropriate to his marketing strategy and tactics.

12 The marketing mix and cooperative marketing

In developing a marketing plan and building a marketing programme one starts with an analysis of markets and segments within those markets; this is followed by further analysis of consumers' wants and needs and methods of communicating to these consumers. The marketer then selects from the marketing tools at his disposal commensurate with the allocation of budget available. He needs to decide too whether it is more appropriate to employ PULL or PUSH tactics. That is to say, he has the option of operating through distributive channels and through them pushing the product to the consumer (PUSH), or alternatively the appeal can be direct to the consumer, who will ask for the product (PULL).

Figure 12.1 – The push/pull principle

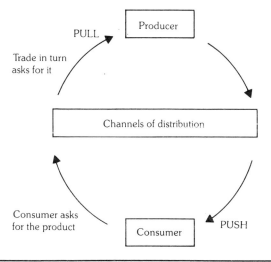

So the first question must be 'what is my marketing strategy?' and the second 'what combination of marketing tools at my disposal are appropriate for reaching the consumer in order that the product may be sold profitably?' Part of the marketing allocation may well be used for trade activity but this is a means to an end. The consumer is king and the aim is to secure a sale to the consumer.

It was Neil H. Borden, Professor at the Harvard Business School, who first started using the phrase 'marketing mix' though he attributes the concept to Professor James Culliton, who described the marketing executive as 'a mixer of ingredients', someone who selects from the ingredients at his disposal the mix he feels is right to secure sales of the product profitably. This would embrace pricing, promotion and distribution.

It would be tremendously helpful to the marketer if there was some magic recipe which would provide him with the right formula in any given set of circumstances, or at least for a particular type of product. Alas there is not, as Harvard Business School researchers found as far back as 1929 when they tried to determine commonality for various marketing programmes among food manufacturing companies. They found that the ratios of sales devoted to the various components of the marketing mix – selling, advertising, packaging, public relations and so on – were widely divergent. Professor Culliton, using a bigger sample, tried again almost twenty years later but the answer was the same.

There is no single right answer to any marketing challenge or problem; there is no secret formula for determining the marketing mix. There are no clearly defined laws which will help the marketer to build his marketing programmes. Scientific techniques have helped him on the way in identifying markets, targeting segments and measuring previous results. But when it comes to deciding what the marketing mix should be, he is on his own, drawing on experience and intuition. Marketing at this stage is an art.

Not all the marketing tools are appropriate for any one organisation, or indeed for any one marketing programme. The ingredients of the marketing mix will vary in usage and weighting and while many hoteliers and national tourist offices would not necessarily agree, the table below lists and shows notional weights for both.

Theoretically the marketer has all the marketing tools at his disposal but he may not need to use all the tools available to him; he may be confined to a narrower range because they are not available to him (for example pricing, in the case of a national tourist office) or he may not be able to afford to use them all (television advertising is prohibitively expensive for national tourist offices in Japan). Whatever the mix selected though, they are all inter-related one with the other within a single marketing programme and furthermore the choice of tools to address one consumer group may constrain him in addressing other

Table 12.1 – Relative weighting of marketing tools

Hotel		NTO
= 3	New product policy	
= 1	Pricing and margins	
= 2	Branding	3
= 2	Promotions/themes	= 4
4	Channels of distribution	= 3
= 1	Personal selling	= 6
= 6	Public relations	= 3
5	Advertising	= 2
= 3	Packaging/product marketing	5
= 5	Exhibitions	= 3
	Display and posters	= 6
	Information servicing	1
= 6	Print	= 2
7	Films and video	= 4

consumer groups. For a national tourist office marketing in the USA and Japan the cost of consumer advertising, whether TV, magazines or newspapers, is very high. The marketer's budget may not be enough to run advertising campaigns at an effective level in both markets. So the choices open to him are to run one good campaign in one market, to run two ineffective campaigns one in each market, or to run none. The sensible marketer would opt for running an effective campaign in his primary market and use more cost effective, though less precisely targeted tools such as public relations, in the other.

A study of 'marketing mixes' used by different types of producers would reveal a tremendous variety of combinations and patterns.

Destination promoters (national or resort tourist offices) will usually spend less than one per cent of their visitor revenue: commercial concerns rarely more than five per cent. This compares with ten per cent or even more for leading branded consumer goods.

In some cases advertising is used to pull the product through the channels of distribution – the consumer is persuaded to ask for the product and so little effort is made to secure selling support at the retail end of the selling chain. In other cases, the manufacturer of aeroplanes, for example, will rely heavily on personal selling or the push technique. Similarly the use of price as a marketing tool will vary enormously. In some cases margins will be set deliberately low, while in other prices will be calculated, to provide wide margins which in turn support a heavy promotional programme. Typically, the cosmetic and perfumery industry will devote a high percentage of gross profits to packaging and promotion, using expensive advertising, packaging and point-of-sale display. Price can also be used as a marketing tool in addressing a particular problem such as seasonality. This is perhaps most prevalent in the tourism industry with transporters using off-peak or off-season fares, hoteliers offering bargain breaks and facility operators charging differentially at different times of the year or even days of the week. Tour operators in pricing their packages in turn feature high season and low season offers.

So the 'marketing mix' used in different fields varies enormously and even in the same industry one will find competing companies adopting different mixes.

Price

Pricing is of fundamental importance to the marketer. It is through pricing that the marketer in industry recovers the costs of his marketing (the separate ingredients of the marketing mix), plus the cost of creating the product and of course profit for the organisation.

Pricing is an important aspect of marketing and often a key marketing tool in tourism. Historically the transport and resort interests, notably the hotels, developed the use of pricing as a fine art. The railways invented the class system and excursions, and later a whole variety or tariff of fares. This discrimination in the market to achieve maximum load factors led to sophisticated promotion, the growth of the distribution system and of creative travel agents or tour operators such as Thomas Cook. There are two important aspects of pricing: the open market rate (door price or rack rate), and the discounted price to which conditions are attached (eg available only to groups or at low peak periods). But it is a complex subject compounded by legislation which may ensure competition, or alternatively restrict maximum and sometimes even minimum prices.

Tourism is made up of many segments; the tourist population is heterogeneous; response varies. A low price may erode revenues and create no extra business. This is especially true of off-season travel. Bargain basements do not always work. Value for money is key and this means ensuring satisfaction at the destination. Price incentives vary considerably according to the nature of the market. Mass travel to hot beaches will be very price sensitive, since the product will be assumed not to vary with the special offer. Essential travel will be less responsive. A classic example of the limitations of pricing can be found in the post-war transatlantic travel history. Cheaper winter fares to Europe were offered by the airlines without much result until they introduced the eight day ticket (GIT). Then almost immediately traffic took off on short visits to European cultural capitals. Time was a key element. Short breaks subsequently revolutionised winter business in many resort destinations.

In determining prices the marketer will need to take into account the competition and thus the parameters of pricing discretion. The new invention can command a premium price for a time but when patents prove to be ineffective and other manufacturers come in with 'me too' product plagiarism then prices will fall dramatically. An excellent example of this was the ball point pen, which when it was first introduced was thirty or forty times more expensive than it is now, even without taking account of inflation. The marketer should estimate the likely demand for the product, and determine channels of distribution, discount structure and his promotional strategy. He must analyse and reconcile these factors in determining price and this in turn will dictate the marketing mix. The product innovator must always remember that he has to create a market and his initial outlays on promotion will not be recovered until he has established a market for the new product. The imitators will benefit from his investment. Consequently the innovator will have to set his prices with this factor very much in mind and his strategy must seek to recover this initial outlay and, in determining the right price and promotion mix, maximise long term profits.

The innovator has a period when there is no competition but this is a unique case. Generally the competitive structure of an industry is a vitally important factor in determining price. In an industry where there are a great many organisations selling essentially the same product, competition will be fierce and the marketer will have very little pricing discretion. At the other end of the spectrum organisations with a monopoly position can determine their own prices. In the travel industry in Britain, tour operators who are going after the mass market are fiercely price competitive. The British market has clearly demonstrated the theory of price sensitivity of the total market demand. Prices have been lowered to a point where demand has been massively increased at the expense of profit margins, though not at the expense of promotion.

If, on the other hand, the product has 'up-market' appeal to a travelling elite this will lead to a totally different pricing and promotion policy.

Clearly price is a fundamental element in marketing. Victor Middleton cites the four 'P's' – Product, Price, Promotion and Place (market place) as the determining factors.[1]

But, as already explained, pricing is an art as much as a science and depends on many factors, some of which are external to the marketing organisation. It is sometimes claimed that the destination marketer – the tourist board or resort authority – has no control over price. While in market economies price controls have no place, the destination marketers can have a very powerful influence on pricing, and this must be part of their marketing strategy.

The following factors should be taken into account in commercial sales direct to the customer or indirectly through agents, as they will influence price setting and the response to prices selected:

1. Economic criteria

It is usual in selling tourist services to estimate sales by market segment, and accordingly to offer the same item at a variety of prices and discounts. For example an airline seat or an hotel bed will be on offer at the same time for different prices. The rack rate (the hoteliers published room price), or the 'standard' air fare may in fact only be achieved in a minority of cases. IATA report that ninety per cent of scheduled service fares are discounted to a greater or lesser degree. The rule is to charge 'what the traffic will bear', but this is modified by the supply situation and the need to sell current production to the maximum possible occupancy, as the production cannot be stored for future use. The marketer's task is made more difficult by the need to avoid diverting higher rate traffic to the lower prices, which are introduced evidently to create extra trade.

2. Competition and current prices in the market

Unless the service has some monopoly value or is in short supply, the marketer will be constrained in choice by the competition. This can be limited in tourism, by the establishment of a premium position because of better quality, reputation or loyalty. Fashion plays its part. A theatrical hit will leave the competition standing.

Making it 'easy to buy' with an assurance of quality and personal service can be a major factor. In the down turn in package travel in Britain in the 1990–91 recession some tour operators in the right market segments increased trade while others suffered seriously.

Repeat business for many destinations and their services may also ensure a degree of stability, and resilience to depression.

3. Marketing strategy and segmentation

The trader must know which market to select. He cannot be all things to all tourists who are of mankind. Behaviour varies in most respects according to the segment, for example old or young, first class or budget travel, business or pleasure, group or individual clientele, gregarious and noisy or independent and reserved. There are many 'mini mass markets' each exhibiting its own blend of behaviour patterns and preferences.

Segmentation can hardly be taken too far. It is important and practical. Market research and experience in the market place will offer good guidance, but it is hard work which cannot safely be left undone. To ensure high use (occupancy and loads) the operator will need to be in a number of markets at the same time. This diversification will give some added protection against market failure, recession for example in any one area. In recent years the growth of business travel, notably conference traffic, and short breaks has transformed the off season. For most city hotels pleasure tourism is now a minority trade in year round business. Furthermore as trends change more rapidly there will be new product developments at least as important in the near future.

Segmentation is characterised by behaviour and price, and is the basis of price variation. In the short break trade attractive price offers demonstrate value for money and create new business in off-peak periods. But the value must be there.

All the above factors (1–3) are to a large extent within the traders control. But there are external factors outside the operators control, and more difficult to deal with.

1. The economy (national and international)

There are booms and recessions, which not only affect the market but alter the conditions of trade. The trade cycle will be accompanied by inflation, interest rate and taxation changes by government. Furthermore if the trade is in the international market there will be the added complications of originating countries economic situations, exchange rates, and from time to time government constraint and taxation of travel.

Effects on price and pricing can influence the business and the destination to a major extent. Safeguarding trade and mitigating damage is a key collective marketing task for all the destination interests, but often ignored at great loss in revenues.

2. Security and political crises

Security has become a major and unfortunately continuing issue. Travellers away from home are inevitably anxious, and their families often more so. There are pressures to avoid these anxieties and limit risks. This is particularly true for pleasure travel where 'getting away from it all' is a powerful appeal. From time to time crises escalate and have disastrous effect on international movement, as for example in 1986 following the Libya incident when US travel to Europe stopped suddenly. Travel to China ceased from Western countries after the Beijing disorders in 1989. The Gulf war in 1991 again halted much international movement. Crisis tourism is examined in detail in chapter 9. There are important marketing implications and price can play an important role which is often misunderstood.

It is important to distinguish short-term or temporary external influences and long term and substantive changes. Travel has proved amazingly resilient. The political crises mentioned were short lived, and traffic reduction limited in most cases to little more than a year or less. Traffic tends to return to the long term forecast level, although massive loss during the period of difficulty, often serious enough to cause business collapse, may not be recovered.

Aviation and Tourism International in a study for the BTA[2] identified six factors other than price, which in international tourism is expressed through the exchange rate, that operate powerfully in the long run.

1. Supply factors, which comprise product change. For example the introduction of wide bodied jets and consequent lower fares from airline productivity gains.
2. Unusual happenings (or perturbations). In addition to political crises these would include pollution scares – a new phenomenon.
3. Marketing effectiveness. The short break innovation has had a dramatic effect on off-peak travel throughout Europe.

These three supply factors are matched by three long term demand influences.

4. Socio-economic change. The increase in senior citizen travel potential in the industrialised countries has had a major effect on off-peak and long distance travel, not yet fully recognised.
5. Time lags. Although travel is becoming more volatile in many segments, reaction to price change, destination services and even quality deterioration is relatively slow. Much packaging is on a one year time scale and some, conferences and international events for example may be much longer – up to four years.

Tourism requires massive long term infrastructure investment. Tourism behaviour tends to be traditional in choice of resort and holiday activity, although this is changing.

6. Fashion. This is potentially the most powerful longer term factor. The appeal of 'in' places, activities and even hobbies (golf) or clothes can dictate in the market place. Success in image creation is like finding oil, and once the right approach is discovered success may follow for a generation or more. However there is a danger that the time scale of success can be shortened if value for money, an expression of price, is eroded. The recent history of severe decline in travel to some of the Mediterranean's cheaper and congested resort areas where quality and satisfaction became suspect is an example of reversal in fortune. Significantly the decline has been in the bargain basement and not in 'the carriage trade'. The up market and even the more expensive travel services have proved more resilient to depression and some, for example long distance travel, have increased market share.

The pricing element in marketing travel is complex at the best of times, but even more so for the destination authority and marketer. Although their control of pricing is a remote one, they have a vital interest, and are not without considerable influence and responsibility. The destination marketer as the guardian of the image has a key task to ensure that the image is not tarnished by the wrong price tag, whether too cheap or too dear.

The Greek government introduced minimum prices in a system of licensed accommodation and a ban on seat only charters in an effort to preserve quality in clientele and services. Countries faced with exchange rate or recession threats can urge traders to hold prices, guarantee exchange rates at the time of booking or beginning of the season and encourage operators to introduce special 'offers'.

The National Tourist Office or tourist board through persuasion and cooperative marketing can help steady prices. The special offers or packages for specific or limited purposes (off-peak travel and regional or geographical spread, post crisis traffic restoration for example) can be very effective in mitigating damage.

It may sometimes be the task of the marketer to hold prices. A panic price cut in response to a crisis may have little immediate effect but can create problems for longer term packaging when traffic promises to return to 'normal' as there will be an apparent substantial price rise, and an 'expensive' reputation hard to live with. After the Beijing problems some of the new international hotels in China were offering accommodation at US$20 per night. Packages were available in Europe for little more than £600, a fifty per cent reduction, and US$1,399 for an inclusive ten day trip from San Francisco.

Britain's mass package tour operators suffered major loss of traffic to the Mediterranean of more than twenty-five per cent or 3 million trips in the 1989–90 period, mostly in the cheaper price category. The average package tour price on the British market increased from £300 in 1990 to £350 in 1991, a rise far above the inflation rate, in a wise attempt by the tour operators to restore their profit margins, dangerously low in recession, and their product quality responding to clear signs from the market place.

Attempts to deal with seasonality by price reduction alone have rarely been successful. Such reductions may simply dilute inadequate revenue. The 'off season' package whether trade organised or a 'do it yourself' arrangement must include all the basic components (eg accommodation and transport). The appeal and attractions of the destination must be in place. This may seem evident, yet there is a long history of failure because of lack of coordination, fare reductions at different times by accommodation, transport and other suppliers, and often absence of key attractions. Many of Britain's historic houses are closed in the off season. Yet winter short breaks in the countryside are increasingly popular. Thus the destination marketer has a vital role to play through stimulating collective action.

The apparent lack of logic in airline fares results from the variation in price according to the response of each identifiable market segment. Terms such as cheap, dear, bargain or even budget rates have subjective meanings. The tourist class fare London–Brussels return in 1991 was £269, for a journey of less than 200 miles and 45 minutes flying time, and included limitations on flexibility of flights and cancellation penalties. At the same time the London travel trade was offering flights to Tenerife return for as little as £129, a journey of 2,000 miles and four hours flight. Complete packages to Turkey for seven nights (2,000 miles), started from £199.

Pricing and destination marketing

The commercial marketer will be looking for diversification through a number of segments, and thus offering services for a number of travel purposes (ie business and pleasure) to achieve the highest possible loading or sale of his total capacity. The outlook may be very short term and in a competitive situation he may have little loyalty or concern for the total destination success, especially if he is able to transfer his productive resources to alternative destinations. The tour operator is free to do this, but much transport and resort accommodation and infrastructure services cannot move. It is important that competitive pricing does not damage the destination image or goodwill, an important part of its capital.

The destination marketer has this principle concern and responsibility. The longer term view must be taken, and a marketing strategy evolved according to the competitive position selecting specific segments as targets suited to the image of the place (ie mass or selective traffic, young or older clientele, first class or budget trade).

Pricing will play an important part in the marketing approach, since the infrastructure will have been and continue to be developed for the markets selected. This requires a consistent and continuing long term marketing plan and programme which will shape, clarify and safeguard the image, in which quality, whatever product is chosen, is more important than the bargain basement.

The destination marketer has a special responsibility in forecasts as a basic for public and private sector development and investment. It has been generally held in the past that tourism has a high income elasticity, and that for international travel in the industrialised countries demand will grow at twice the rate of increase in GDP (gross domestic product) or disposable incomes. This optimistic scenario can lead to complacency in the public sector. Even if in the long run disposable incomes rise, world competition increases, fashions change, traffic can become more volatile. So there will be losers as well as winners amongst the tourist countries. In the USA in recent years total spend on recreational activities declined from 6.6 per cent of total consumption in 1970 to 6.36 per cent in 1982. The macro approach may be difficult to relate to specific destinations or products because it covers such an enormous sector or personal spending. But it demonstrates that some of the old and comfortable rules of thumb may no longer apply.

The destination authority as the government has the ultimate option of direct intervention through price or exchange rate control. The Greek minimum price may be unusual. But setting maximum prices for accommodation is common, often as a tax base where statutory classification is in force for administrative control as much as for consumer protection and marketing convenience. The systems often fall expensively between stools. Governments may introduce a tourist rate of exchange, although the practice is condemned by the IMF (International Monetary Fund). In such cases the object is often to protect foreign currency revenues from the black market. In fact in China there is a tourism currency operating alongside the national currency. The Italian government introduced petrol coupons for foreign visitors travelling in their own cars, offering substantial discounts on the price of fuel.

Most countries allow duty free shopping for export. The threat of the European Community to remove duty free concessions has been strongly opposed by carriers who claim that loss of revenue will lead to fare increases of ten per cent or more which will gravely distort some traffic flows, and competition between member countries.

Tax holidays and investment subsidies, are quite common for tourism investment, but not normally applicable to operations, except through local authority trading, and social subsidies in transport for example. Nevertheless price changes through government intervention are substantial in tourism. The introduction of the Single Market carries some threats in this respect through increase in Value Added Tax and major changes in excise duties which will alter relative tourism prices substantially in the member countries.

The marketer, both the provider of services and the destination authority have a considerable influence and choice in pricing. But competition and external factors limit their choice. In a highly segmented market the price structure will be complex with prices set for each segment. Quality is important. A price reduction by itself may not prove effective. There are dangers in unprofitable price cutting, as there are in subsidised operations. The state must ensure a competitive situation free from constraint, with a tax regime favourable for tourism development in a competitive world market place.

The state can and does intervene for a variety of reasons, to shape and channel tourism flows according to national policy, but market forces will prevail. The state's role described in chapter 23 is essential but limited to creating conditions for tourism prosperity as a major national resource and benefit, including conditions for effective marketing by the destination authority.

Pricing is only one factor in the equation. Personal selling, public relations, packaging, channels of distribution, advertising, print, exhibitions, films and others are all ingredients of the mix which the marketer has available to him in developing his marketing programme or plan. The marketing plan is concerned with communications – communicating the right product to the right market and the right segment within that market cost effectively and profitably.

Product and purchase

The product must be available and easy to buy. Even though tourism is perhaps unique in that the product is not taken to the market but rather the market place comes to the product, it is nevertheless 'distributed' and there are channels of distribution. In the case of tourism there are a number of product elements and some or all may be available through channels of distribution. Some elements may be purchased at the point of origin or residence, while others are bought at the destination. The basic elements of any travel package are transport and accommodation. To that can be added insurance, entertainment, eating out, shopping, excursions from the destination or travelling around in a region, country, or even several countries.

The motoring visitor to Mexico from the USA may purchase nothing before he leaves; the overseas visitor to Britain on the other hand will need to purchase at least an airline ticket or a ferry ticket, and generally any traveller to another country is well advised to purchase travellers' cheques and to take out insurance to cover illness, injury, loss or damage.

Those travellers who want the security of the fully inclusive package can pre-purchase travel, transfers, accommodation and meals and in some cases excursions and theatre tickets, as well as insurance.

The marketer will have analysed his source markets and know how his markets segment into fully inclusive, independent, business travellers, etc. Indeed he may, as an hotelier for instance, have determined his optimum mix in terms of group and independent and fixed his allocations accordingly. In almost all cases it will be a mix of inclusive and independent and thus it will be necessary for the marketer to allocate marketing resources for reaching the consumer direct and through the tour operator and retail chain as well. The stage of market development, proximity, language, culture all have a bearing on the balance between inclusive and independent. In the case of Britain, about 80% of all leisure visitors are independent, or to put it another way, only 20% are fully inclusive. Some 'independent' travellers may in fact have purchased 'Go as you please' vouchers and arranged for car hire in the country of residence. While almost 80% of American visitors to Britain do not buy a fully inclusive package, over 70% make a visit to a retail agent in order to purchase an airline ticket and some will also arrange accommodation at least for the first night.

Ingredients of the marketing mix

Clearly, in the case of Britain, the need is to reach the consumer direct, which has implications for the amount of marketing spend allocated to advertising, public relations and, not least, print.

Further analysis will show that the consumer profile of visitors to Britain is ABC1, highly educated professional or managerial status, with English as a first language or a good second language and a high level of repeaters (almost 80% have visited Britain before, some several times). So they are confident and adventurous. They are also demanding in terms of information needs. They are prepared to travel around the country, book their own accommodation, buy their own pub lunches, arrange their own visits to historic houses, museums, theatre or event. This presents the marketer with a great opportunity as well as a great challenge. The print programme needs to be complex and provide a great deal of information. But the promotional print can be designed to meet the objectives of regional and seasonal spread because the consumer is generally confident and adventurous. Indeed in the case of BTA, more of the marketing budget is allocated to consumer print than any other single item.

The trade must not be forgotten. Agents' sales guides, hotel directories, events lists, maps, shell folders, posters and display material have to be built into the marketing mix as well.

The travel trade also need to be influenced through educational tours or familiarisation trips, seminars and product missions, as well as through workshops, trade shows, sales missions and road shows. The hotel at the destination may be ready to receive guests, the theatre ready with the show, but very often it is the counter clerk in an agency many thousands of miles away who is at the point of sale. If he has experienced the product at first hand as a result of a 'fam trip' and enjoyed the experience he is much more likely to effect a sale.

It is the aim of advertising and public relations to ensure that the product or destination is seen in a favourable way and thus lead to purchase. The destination must be seen as a nice place to visit, the hotel as a nice place to stay. It is designed to heighten the appeal but it is essential that the promise offered in the promotion is delivered. If not, the PR backlash could be considerable, long-lived and very expensive to correct. The advertising and the print can be tailored and targeted, they must create awareness and make the product appealing against the clamour of competing claims and ultimately create a predisposition on the part of the potential visitor to buy. It has often been said that tourism promotion is selling a dream, a dream where images are important.

Where there is a high level of repeat business potential direct mail is increasingly being used as a very cost effective way of reaching the target group. The mailing list can be derived from coupon response to previous advertising campaigns, enquiries received direct, previous visitors or clients, special interest groups or purchased from mailing houses. Direct mail must feature in the marketing mix and be designed to reach both trade and consumer.

Holiday exhibitions are more important tools in Europe than in most other parts of the world. Nevertheless, any tourism marketer who is interested in developing the European market should certainly consider participating in the most important holiday exhibitions. It is unlikely that he will be able to take space in all of them. Indeed it is unnecessary. The national tourist office can usually provide guidance.

Films and radio, and increasingly video, are important media in tourism marketing. They can very effectively 'take' the product to the market place and sell the dream. All too often though films and videos can become creative indulgences. They are costly to make but they are useless unless they can be effectively distributed to the right target audience. Before any travel film is made, the marketer should determine its purpose and its reach. Certainly film and radio have the potential of a place in the marketing mix but only if the two key questions of effectiveness and cost can be adequately answered.

Posters and very often display are either the poor relations or top of the pops for the marketer. They can be very effective in projecting images. Spain, Italy and Ireland have all produced some notable posters at once appealing and evocative. The good poster has many outlets – in retail agents' windows, in store promotions, at airports, seaports and railway stations. They have their place in the mix as cost effective stimuli in a wide variety of situations. The Victorian marketers certainly knew their worth. The poster and the brochure were developed in the railway age and remain as practical and powerful as ever.

Determining the mix

The promotional media of advertising, PR, direct mail, print, posters, films and radio are all vital elements in the marketing mix and their relative importance and how each interacts with the other will differ with each situation and with each marketer. Each is a selling tool but the best of tools and the best of channels are substitutes for personal selling. Transporters, hoteliers, tour operators and, where possible, tourist offices and agencies should have their sales force keeping up the pressure on the channels of distribution, the influencers and the decision-makers. The marketer needs to address the question of the place of the sales force in the marketing mix. Some tasks are heavily reliant on personal selling, for example selling a conference venue to an organiser or organising committee, while others can be effectively sold via ambassadors such as direct mail and print.

More salesmen or more advertising and promotion can only be determined by the marketer following careful analysis of his markets, his situation and not least by the amount of marketing budget at his disposal. Each of the main ingredients must be finely mixed, each compared for cost effectiveness one with the other, but remembering that they are often inter-related and inter-dependent. There is no point in producing print if no money is allocated for distribution of that print to the right markets. When developing his marketing programme the marketer has to juggle the marketing ingredients in his mix with a knowledge of the behavioural forces of his consumers in terms of motivation, buying habits and purchasing power. He must do this within the resources available to him and an eye to the competition.

The mix will also represent the marketing programme which has naturally evolved from years of experience in a dynamic market situation. Part theoretical, part empirical, part strategic and part tactical. Short term forces can very often play a large part in determining the mix Terrorist fears in North American markets in 1986, the introduction of controls on foreign holiday spend or the relaxation of such controls by governments, are but two examples which can influence and fashion the mix. But the overall strategy employed is the result of experience on the one hand and long range plans on the other. The marketer always needs to keep his sights on future potential if he is to keep his organisation in the vanguard of the industry. He must have the foresight to devise a mix which is capable of evolving over the next five to ten years to meet the needs of tomorrow's markets as well as responding to today's situation. There will be a need for tactical manoeuvres in response to external factors or a competitor's activities but underlying the tactics there must be a golden thread of strategy, and all within the resources available.

Cooperative marketing

Resources may not be limited to those which an organisation allocates to its marketing operation. In addition to national and regional tourist organisations, the tourism industry is supported by carriers and hoteliers, car hire operators and other beneficiaries of the tourist spend. The chart demonstrates the synergistic potential offered by different organisations cooperating in various marketing activities. There are many more examples of cooperative marketing, and while table 12.2 has been produced from the national tourist office viewpoint, it can be developed for any organisation and in many cases the national tourist office would feature in the potential cooperator box.

Sometimes financial support can be negotiated on an 'in kind' basis, that is to say the operator will provide a car, rail ticket, accommodation, etc. Conversely many hotels, attractions and destination services cannot afford to reach overseas or even national markets. For them a cooperative support platform is essential. So in developing the marketing mix the marketer engaged in tourism should be aware of his potential partners and take into account the amount which he can realistically expect to raise from them in his budget forecasts.

Table 12.2 – Opportunities for cooperative marketing

Marketing Tool	Potential Cooperators	Comments
Advertising	air/sea carriers, hotel groups, car hire companies, large stores, smaller operators	TV, magazines and newspapers classified
Direct mail	regions, carriers, specialist operators, car hire companies	ideally with specific product offers
Print: informational and promotional,	all operators, large operators, regional/resort, tourist boards, tour operators	line entry, advertising sponsorship, jointly funded print
Exhibitions and trade fairs	regions, resorts, major operators	modular stand sold off to participants
Workshops	all producers/operators, specialist, eg language schools	general workshops specialist workshops
Films and video	regions, resorts, local authorities, car hire companies, railways, manufacturers, hotel groups, etc	footage of product
Posters and display	carriers	jointly funded or sold with carrier's own message
Trade educationals	carriers, regions, resorts, local authorities, hotels, railways, coach operators	sometimes cooperation takes the form of 'in kind' support
Journalists' visits, other media visits	carriers, hotels, railways, car hire companies	usually takes the form of 'in kind' support

Summary

There is no single right answer to any marketing challenge, no secret formula for determining the right level of investment in marketing or the right marketing mix. The marketer selects from the marketing tools or ingredients available and within the budget available to him and then develops the optimum mix needed to reach the consumer and sell him the product. The marketing mix includes pricing, advertising, public relations, print, exhibitions, promotions, direct mail, films and radio, posters and display, personal selling and trade activities such as workshops, trade shows, sales missions, and familiarisation trips.

References

1 Middleton, V, *Marketing in Travel and Tourism*. Heinnemann, 1988.
2 Aviation and Tourism International, *Exchange rates and Tourism Demand*. Report for the British Tourist Authority, 1984.

13 Budgets and allocations

While this chapter is primarily concerned with the destination tourist office and its promotion, the principles apply to the marketing budgets of all destination interests and the essential cooperative action between the public and private sectors.

Generally speaking a country's tourism development will be commensurate with the amount of its marketing spend. Those small countries which are heavily reliant on tourism, such as Jamaica and Bermuda, will outspend many large countries. While it is very difficult to demonstrate a correlation between spend on marketing and earnings from tourism in the case of a national or regional tourist office, there is evidence to suggest that where marketing spend has been cut back there is a consequential loss of brand share.

During the 1970s the American government cut the budget of its tourism agency. Clearly the feeling was that the visitors would come anyway and the USA was top of the league table for foreign currency earnings from tourism. In 1976 America had a 13% share but ten years later it had dropped to just over ten per cent. It seems remarkable that this was allowed to happen in a country which has about five million directly employed in tourism and a further two million plus indirectly employed; a country whose biggest export earner in the service field is tourism.

While external factors – economic and political especially – are very potent influences on travel patterns, national government promotional spend is a very significant factor. The Australian government has substantially increased the tourism budget over the past few years and Australia has substantially increased its visitors too. The world average tourism promotion spend is just under $4 per capita: the Bahamas spends almost $120 per capita while the USA spends less than 4 cents per capita through its own tourism agency, USTTA. The theory that the industry in the form of the private sector should be doing the job of promoting tourism was clearly in the minds of the US legislators. The effect has been a significant loss of share for the USA. The carriers and the hoteliers are fighting brand share battles and an analysis of the marketing spend of the national carriers would clearly demonstrate that in fact very little of their promotional budgets is devoted to the destination.

Government agencies have a vitally important role to play as guardians of the image, catalysts and coordinators of all the disparate interests – regions, areas, resorts, cities, and the producers themselves. Individual organisations in the travel industry are concerned to maximise their share of the existing market. They are not interested in increasing share of the world market for their country. Neither are they concerned particularly to develop new markets and new segments, which is one of the principal roles of a national tourist office.

It is difficult to obtain comparable figures of spend by governments on tourist agencies. In some cases development funds are included and in others not. In some cases several government agencies will be funding tourism development and marketing. In a smaller country all tourism funding may well repose in a single agency. It is incumbent on the national tourist office, whether a government department or an agency of government, to apprise its paymasters of the strength of competition and any loss of share of voice in the market place; to set out clearly what it plans to achieve with a given level of funding and what would need to be aborted if that level of funding was not forthcoming. In the final analysis the level of funding granted will rarely be what was requested and the marketing director will have to make his case against competing claims of colleagues and adapt his programmes accordingly.

Even in a single organisation it is virtually impossible to assess the sales resulting from a given investment in marketing activity. Input-output models for a national tourist office to simulate return on investment would involve multiple correlations of an extremely complex character. The variables are infinite even in one market and almost impossible to estimate. How does one measure the impact of a picture of an armed policeman at Heathrow Airport on the target audience in California? How does one measure the effect of a good piece of travel writing in 'Gourmet' magazine on a particular region of the destination (the subject of the article)? Furthermore, the period of pay-off from an advertising campaign or even a piece of print, may well extend over a long time and the investment is cumulative, particularly in a situation where the national tourist office is developing a new market or a new segment.

Ideally the budget should be developed in tandem with the marketing plan, but this may well not prove to be possible in the case of a national tourist office, or indeed a local authority or resort tourist office. The plan may well have to be adapted in the light of the budget. Yet the budget, or at least that part of the budget devoted to marketing, is the translation of the marketing plan into financial expenditures. It is the investment which the marketer believes is needed to carry on his planned programmes and thus achieve targeted results and meet marketing objectives.

In preparing a marketing budget it is not a question of simply dividing the total amount available among the various markets in line with forecast visits or earnings from those markets. There is no question of simply guessing at the amounts which are to be allocated across the marketing mix for individual markets. The budget must be carefully constructed, it must be detailed and it must be flexible (it may be necessary to respond to an unknown situation which could develop suddenly in a key market).

Allocation of the budget by market

The first stage in determining the allocation for individual markets is to assess the forecast performance of each market in terms of the organisation's marketing objectives. The main objective may be visits or it may be spend but in any event the marketer will need to have a base from which to develop the model. Secondary objectives will almost certainly be regional and seasonal spread and again there should be a forecast of how each market is likely to perform. Thus it is possible to determine weighting factors for each of the secondary objectives and so modify the basic figures. Is it an established market or a new market? In the case of the latter there will almost certainly need to be a disproportionate amount of marketing investment in order to create an awareness of the destination. Does the appeal have to be direct to the consumer or through the trade? What is the nature of the market in terms of media availability? Is it controlled or even censored? Some of these factors will of course have been taken into account in determining the hierarchical ordering of target markets and in the determination of the marketing mix appropriate for each market.

The budget allocation should be a rational process made on a factual basis. It is too simplistic to think in terms of established markets or developing markets since all markets are evolving and there can be new markets and new segments identified within existing markets. For example, the movement of target markets from the eastern seaboard of the United States to the 'Sunbelt' and California, the main holiday market in Germany as opposed to the secondary holiday market, a new segment to be targeted such as senior citizens in the Netherlands. All these factors should be taken into account in determining allocations. Not least the marketer must realistically assess just how the market may be influenced. Finally there is the missionary work which needs to be done in new markets, where a disproportionate amount of investment is needed in the early years to realise future potential five or even ten years hence.

Allocation across the marketing mix

There is a wide divergence between organisations, even in the same industry, in the allocation of budget across activities. Numerous studies have been undertaken mainly in the consumer goods industries, but alas there is no magic formula to help the marketer to do this. There is, however, a practical way of judging budget allocations and rationalising the proposed promotion investment.

The Operational Marketing Plan will set targets related to each geographic market and market segment, but marketing spend will depend on the type of trade – traditional business where basically reminders and good information is the requirement, to new markets where creation of traffic will require much persuasion and guidance. In the latter case there will need to be a practical campaign to communicate, to reach and 'talk' to prospective travellers directly or through intermediaries such as travel agents. The cost of reaching the prospects through advertising, literature or in other ways can be estimated fairly accurately. It is also possible to get good professional advice on method of approach, timing, and frequency (in other words how often should you repeat your message or advertisement). In this way the expense of buying the necessary promotional services can be calculated. Similarly, reasonably good estimates can be made of likely response levels (the cash return on the promotion investment) and ultimately the results achieved can be monitored.

The exercise is by no means perfect, but it is a good discipline and helps to avoid expensive mistakes. It is too easy to waste money by errors in targeting, failure to reach the right prospects or failure to follow up. Certainly it should be possible for the marketers to advise management that targets cannot be reached if marketing resources are too limited, and that scarce means must be devoted to correspondingly reduced ends.

The individual budget heads are likely to be as follows:

Advertising – consumer magazines, newspapers, TV, radio, direct mail

Advertising – trade press

Public Relations – features, press bulletins, photo stories, etc.

Press facilities – journalist and media visits

Literature – promotional

Literature – informational and trade

Distribution – literature, display and merchandising

Travel trade – familiarisation trips, receptions, etc.

Travel trade – workshops, road shows, trade fairs

Travel trade – sales missions

Exhibitions

Posters and display

Films and video

Product marketing – product presentation, theme development, award schemes, etc.

Research

Additionally there may well be the need for separate budgets for specialist departments, eg business travel, which will invariably spend against many of the above budget heads but where the specialist department needs to control the spending. It will be desirable to allocate a promotional budget for free spend by individual overseas offices.

The cost of operating the overseas offices – salaries and associated expenses, overheads, etc – will be allocated separately since control will be the responsibility of the individual office manager. Salaries and associated expenses of specialist staff in head office may well be allocated against the appropriate budget heads. For example, the advertising budget will include the salaries and associated costs of the staff of the advertising department. While the specialists can be accommodated in this way it is not always easy to accommodate the generalists. Each budget head should be supported by a detailed plan for the budgetary period. For example the print programme should be detailed in terms of titles, quantities, languages, etc. Indeed the budget should be built up from the territorial requirements for print, which in turn had been rationalised in terms of objectives and targets.

Having established the allocation by budget head, the national tourist office, regional or resort marketer must then estimate how much of the budget can be raised from partners in the form of cooperative marketing activity, how much from sales of advertising in publications, how much revenue from line entry fees, bulk sales of shell folders, maps, etc to the trade, how much from joint research programmes, film ventures, and so on. BTA typically raises about two-thirds of its total marketing spend in the form of non-government funding. It is essential that the revenue or non-government funding targets set are realistic, since very often the expenditure needs to be committed ahead of receiving the income – for example with print. BTA also operates a joint marketing schemes budget which funds cooperative ventures which may be single partner or multi-partner and can utilise one, some or all of the marketing tools. These joint schemes are undertaken with regions, local authorities, resorts, and British and foreign trade partners.

When all the estimates and analyses have been done it will almost certainly be necessary to make adjustments to the ideal plan of spend in the light of the likely budget available. This may mean opting for low cost PR against high cost (though low reach cost) advertising, aborting a print title or posters, a research project or a film production. Experience and intuition will be necessary in arriving at the final plan of spend and there will inevitably be changes made to the marketing plan itself in the light of budgetary constraints.

The budget is a part of the marketing plan.

How much should be allocated to each of the ingredients in the marketing mix? There is no general rule but typically a tourist office will spend about a quarter of its marketing budget (excluding the cost of overseas offices) on advertising, and another quarter on print and distribution. These are the two largest budgets for a national tourist office.

Budgetary control

The budget is a control device and budgetary control must be carefully exercised throughout the year. Budgetary control demonstrates how policy and plans are developing throughout the year and at the same time allows the organisation to establish responsibilities for the administration of functional budgets. Any deviation from the plan of budgeted spend will be highlighted through a regular reporting mechanism. Clearly control of budgets is best done at the point where costs are incurred. Thus the advertising manager will be responsible for the control of the advertising budgets and for achieving targets set for cooperative funds from partners. The control periods for regular reporting would be a month typically, or four/five week periods which build into thirteen-week quarters.

The principles of management accountancy are far beyond the scope of this book. It is a vast subject and preparation of budgets and methods of budgetary control will differ from one organisation to another, depending on the size and nature of the business. But no matter how small the business is, budgetary control is essential because it measures performance against plans, which in turn have been developed out of agreed policy. It is a vital aid to management, indicating the way in which the organisation is going and pointing up the need to change plans if necessary.

The budget, like the marketing plan, is primarily a tool of management and like the marketing plan should be developed in consultation with executives who will be charged with carrying out their particular part of it. Targets set for cooperative marketing revenue for example must be agreed with the executives concerned. If they have subscribed to it they will invariably do their utmost to live up to the target figures agreed. The monthly reporting will show how they are performing against forecast, planned spend and target. By agreeing to the budget the departmental head is agreeing to the plan and the targets set in that plan. In preparing monthly out-turn statements actual performance is being compared on a regular basis against targeted performance. Budgets are used for planning: they are also used for control.

The marketing budget in commercial organisations

While it is generally agreed that there is a great deal of intuitive judgement involved in allocating marketing budgets across budget heads, pre-determining the total marketing budget and budgetary control are nevertheless essential. There are a number of methods available for determining the marketing budget, including a percentage of total sales value, the amount which it is estimated competition is spending, a fixed amount per unit based on the selling price. All have their shortcomings. The percentage of forecast total sales value assumes that the conditions pertaining in previous years (since the percentage would normally be based on historical precedent) will apply in the forthcoming year. In fact competition may well be much more intense, the organisation may be introducing a number of new products, external factors could be markedly different. Fixing on an amount geared to what the competition is estimated to be spending assumes that competition is spending as effectively. Moreover it is only possible to really know what the competition is spending after the event. There is no obligation to spend as much as the competition if it can be spent more effectively by exercising more skill in allocating resources by market, by segment and by devising a more cost effective marketing mix. The shortcoming of fixing a marketing allocation as a percentage of the unit selling price is the assumption that the sales mix *vis-à-vis* the number of products of each type as well as the total sales will be precisely as forecast. Moreover it takes no account of the tactics of competition, such as a substantial increase in selling effort in support of a particular product line or a reduction in price or a special promotion.

In theory marketing spend should be incurred so long as there is an increase in gross profits arising from increased sales. In fact it is impossible to determine at which point the marketing effort becomes unproductive. By its very nature marketing produces some short term benefits but it also produces long term benefits, building cumulatively on previous efforts.

Summary

Generally marketing success is commensurate with marketing spend, though there is no precise measure for determining this accurately. Marketing budgets must be carefully constructed, detailed and flexible. The first stage is allocation by market in terms of the estimated performance of that market against marketing objectives and targets. The second stage is allocation across budget heads to support the marketing mix selected. Budgetary control is an essential tool of management which measures performance against plans and involves executives charged with carrying out agreed tasks.

14 Marketing organisation and structure

The marketer in any organisation is totally involved in the operation and primarily has a coordinating function at whatever level he operates. But whether he is the marketing director, with both specialist executives and generalists reporting to him, or whether he is a brand manager or product manager, he will be coordinating and seeking to get the best out of the departments and executives whose work he coordinates. It follows that there must be effective working arrangements and relationships. Roles and relationships need to be clearly defined. The specialist skills may be available in-house or they may have to be bought in. The expertise of the advertising agency will be bought in from an outside organisation, but equally there may be a PR consultant, printing house, merchandising specialist, all reporting to the marketer. Indeed, in the case of the local tourist officer, very often he is at once marketing director, personnel manager, entertainment manager and chief accountant.

Whatever the size of the organisation, whatever the proportion of skills provided in-house or out-house, there is a need for a structure of authority to ensure proper coordination and direction. With authority goes responsibility. Responsibility for the achievement of results clearly is only possible if the executive has authority over the staff whose task it is to achieve those results and typically the organisation structure is pyramid shaped.

Top management share in the determination of policy, marketing objectives and the division of budgets into broad groupings: purchasing, production, marketing. It is for the marketing director to allocate the budget, to develop the marketing plan and he is responsible for the execution of that plan, and the translation of the plan into activity within the budgetary limits set. Major decisions such as a reorganisation of the sales force, establishment of overseas offices, development of new channels of distribution or change in the advertising agency, would almost certainly be shared decisions among the top management team.

The marketing director then is responsible for managing a complex organisation of specialists and generalists and the size of the marketing department will clearly depend on the size of the organisation. The specialists will include advertising, print production, personal selling, research, sales promotion and planning. Furthermore there may be specialists in particular geographical territories or product lines (brand managers) who report to the marketing chief. Additionally there are the generalists and it is obviously impossible for him to manage all of them. Management cascades through an organisational structure and the size and shape of the marketing organisation will depend very much on the type of operation. Generally the organisation will be geared in the main to the specialist functions, the number of people reporting at each level being determined by the philosophy and culture of the organisation. Close supervision under a narrow span of control or loose supervision and greater delegation of authority – each have their merits. There are fundamental differences in operating in one domestic market or operating internationally in a variety of markets, which again will be reflected in the organisation of the marketing department.

In tourism marketing the structure of the industry is such that there are numerous small enterprises which do not have the expertise or the marketing resources to promote their products in all the markets on which they are dependent. In the hotel industry, independently owned hotels have grouped themselves into marketing cooperatives. In other cases and at a local level a number of attractions may well group themselves into a marketing cooperative and benefit from joint marketing and referral business. Most tourism enterprises, while independent, are in fact interdependent and rely on the complementary services provided by other tourism enterprises. It is therefore in the interests of such enterprises to cooperate with and participate in activities which are coordinated by the regional or national tourist boards. Government sponsored national tourist offices are in fact the coordinators of marketing cooperatives, the catalysts of the industry as well as guardians of the image.

The consortium

An excellent way for an independent hotel or attraction to make their marketing spend go further is through the consortium, which is a type of marketing cooperative. The benefits which derive are:

(1)   awareness of the brand nationally and perhaps internationally;
(2)   more cost effective use of resources through joint promotion;
(3)   sometimes a reservation agency or office in key overseas markets;
(4)   sales activity by consortium staff, including attendance at workshops, trade shows and exhibitions;
(5)   enhanced product appeal and referral business from other members.

Consortia can be international such as the Best Western hotel consortium with about 200 members or local, where up to a dozen attractions in an area form themselves into a marketing cooperative. There is cost benefit in both. In the case of the national consortium there is usually a team of marketing specialists which it would be unusual to find in a consortium of tourist attractions at local level. Nevertheless whether the grouping is a variety of attractions in a geographical area or a group of similar attractions, such as historic houses, it is certainly desirable that a coordinator should be appointed by mutual agreement. This could be on a revolving basis with each property taking it in turn to provide the coordinator.

Structure of a marketing orientated destination tourist organisation

The detail is set out for the national body, which will normally have a larger task, budget and staff. Although the region or resort will be smaller, usually depending on functions, the main tasks and principles of operation will be the same. Clearly it is not possible to suggest a structure for every destination tourist organisation. In the case of a national tourist office it will depend very much on the size of the country, the size of the budget (which in turn is determined by the importance which government attaches to tourism), whether the national tourist office is responsible for both overseas and domestic marketing, the form of government (central or federal), the statutory responsibilities of the national tourist office and, not least, the availability of marketing specialists. All these factors would need to be taken into account in preparing a blue print for the organisation of a national tourist office marketing organisation. Indeed it may well be necessary to develop a five-year plan and start in an embryonic way if staff have to be trained into their jobs.

Whatever the level, national, regional or local, relationships between the marketers and others in the organisation should be clearly defined at the outset. The roles of the key players must be clearly set, budgetary responsibilities assigned and a culture agreed. If it is an organisation which accepts that marketing is a management philosophy, then it follows that marketing will be the coordinator and driving force and this will be evidenced in the marketing plan, which moves the whole organisation in a particular direction aimed at the achievement of organisational, departmental and territorial goals.

A marketing oriented tourist organisation will not permit personal interests to dominate company interests. This may result from a chief executive's particular interest in a sector or segment, resulting in turn in over-promotion or incorrectly targeted promotion. If an organisation does permit such interests to dominate it is a recipe for it to become a collection of independent entrepreneurs rather than an organisation.

Sales is part of marketing. The key functional areas of the organisation, which are marketing oriented, are manufacturing, finance and marketing. Customer logic reposes in the marketing department and permeates other departments in the organisation.

A destination tourist office operating in a dynamic marketing environment without the ability to manufacture the product or determine channels or pricing policies is clearly in a very different position from the manufacturer of consumer goods. The tourist office should be the coordinator of marketing cooperatives, the catalyst of the industry as well as the guardian of the image. The tourism marketing machinery devised for the operation must reflect this. In an organisation of several hundred people various 'organisational' functions are essential:

Administration – offices, equipment, maintenance, etc
Personnel – people, training, etc
Finance – budgets, accounts, etc

If the national tourist office has an advisory role to government and if a statutory registration scheme for accommodation is in position in the country these will be reflected in the organisation too:

Policy – advisory
Registration – classification and grading of tourism products related to standard setting and monitoring if needed
Corporate PR – should be directly responsible to the chief executive

This leaves a number of areas of activity:

Planning – strategic and tactical
Marketing –
     generalist
     specialists, eg advertising, research, PR etc
     personal selling
     territorial offices
     information data collection and dissemination which could
     include tourist information centres
Training – industry and academic as opposed to own staff training.

In many countries, especially in developing countries in the third world, the development task and supervisory activity may be an important role for the state tourist organisation. This however should not obscure the principal role of the destination marketing force as coordinator and focal point for industry and supplier cooperation. Governments may require the national tourist office to implement development schemes, to regulate (price fixing), to supervise standards in public health and safety. All these functions – regional economic development, safety, hygiene – are broad community responsibilities not exclusive to tourism and will be better carried out by government departments and agencies specialising in the function. The destination tourist office should advise and guide as well as coordinate but its unique function is in the marketing field, which includes tourism strategies and policies, standard setting monitoring and training.

A tourist office for a small country or region responsible for both domestic and overseas marketing would probably find it sufficient to have a structure for the organisation which was geared to a triumvirate reporting to the Chief Executive as follows:

Table 14.1 – Organisation structure

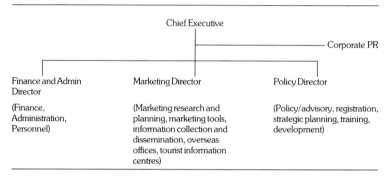

This group of key executives would share in the determination of policy, marketing objectives and budget allocations but each director would have separate responsibility within his own area. The group will need to meet regularly, at least weekly, to monitor progress and discuss key issues as a collective. The directors should in turn communicate downwards to departmental heads as appropriate.

The marketing division organisation in such a national tourist office could look something like the following:

Table 14.2 – Marketing organisation structure

In BTA 'desk' executives have responsibility for a particular group of markets. Generally they are the 'fount of knowledge' on all aspects of their markets.

Product marketing executives similarly have responsibility for coordinating particular product ranges, eg sailing and boating, equestrian and pony trekking, farmhouse accommodation, camping and caravanning, etc.

Clearly the allocation of 'desk' responsibilities for both marketing and product marketing executives will stem from the disposition and importance of regional and overseas markets on the one hand and product sectors on the other. These in turn will have stemmed from the continuing work in the fields of market and product analysis.

The further sub-division of responsibilities will be dependent on the relative importance of functional areas. Thus the travel trade may be much more important if the majority of visits from overseas are for leisure purposes and the majority of those trips are sold as fully inclusive packages. Business travel on the other hand may be much less important as a market segment. In such a situation there may be only one business travel specialist but the travel trade manager could well have a department which looked like this:

Table 14.3 – Travel trade department

Trade Liaison Executive	Workshops Organiser	Tours and Visits Organiser	Print Co-ordinator
Buying trips and product missions	Home and overseas workshops, sales missions out	Familiarisation trips for agency staff	Agents and coach operators' manuals, newsletters, shell folders, posters etc

In a converse situation, where business travel is more important than the travel trade, the department structure may well be as follows:

Table 14.4 – Business travel department

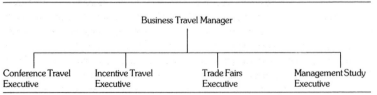

Conference Travel Executive	Incentive Travel Executive	Trade Fairs Executive	Management Study Executive

These broad functions and structure apply to all international travel marketing in principle. Clearly resources, task and staffing must reflect the scale of the operation. Smaller organisations with limited resources can benefit from specialist and sophisticated marketing practices by contracting out to specialists or specialist agencies. But this requires skilled supervision and coordination of the agency activities, especially if they are working internationally.

Thus the organisational structure will stem from the marketing and segmentation studies on the one hand and the marketing mix on the other. Since tourism is dynamic there will be a need for constant re-definition of tasks and adaptation to the changing marketing environment.

The organisation's requirements

The organisational structure should be the subject of major review every five years or so, since in the intervening years new opportunities or new techniques will have resulted in an imposition of additional tasks on certain executives. It is important that individual members of staff have their jobs clearly defined in terms of responsibility, reporting and accountability. This is best achieved by providing job descriptions for each member of staff. This should only be done after the structure has been examined and, if necessary, reorganised to achieve the one which is best suited to achieve its purpose.

The system should also ensure that the potential is being developed taking into account the ages of the organisation's key personnel, wastage rate of the current human resources and future needs in terms of possible expansion. The marketing organisation, as we have seen, consists of generalists and specialists. Typically future overseas managers should be developed through the generalist stream.

The individual's requirements

Each member of staff needs a framework of standards and responsibilities within which he can operate and against which he can be judged. He also will need training, both in day-to-day contact with his manager and more formalised out of house training in specific techniques. This may be a public speaking course or one in management skills. He will expect the opportunity to keep abreast of developments in the field of marketing too. The job specification should provide the framework in which he will operate, define responsibilities and reporting and list the main areas of activity. The annual appraisal should be the means of reviewing performance against goals set, establishing new goals for the following year and identifying training needs and constraints in carrying out the job. For his manager it provides a formal opportunity for assessing the individual's readiness for promotion and how he might be best developed for future positions within the organisation.

The appraisal system plays a major part in management development and this too should stem from the marketing plan. While the plan should be developed on a territorial or market basis and new initiatives and ongoing marketing activity catalogued by market, it is nevertheless for individuals to realise the activity; their part in the plans must be played out effectively, at the right time and within budget. The people in the organisation with responsibility for implementing the plan were consulted at the planning stage, they subscribed to the plan.

The marketing plan is the formal written document which sets out the great variety of tasks necessary for its execution. These tasks cascade down through the whole organisation and it is vital that each person knows the part which he is expected to play, how his efforts fit into the overall scheme of things. The marketing manager has responsibility for carrying out a programme of activities which are geared to the achievement of the marketing objectives. He will devolve that area of work with the travel trade to the travel trade manager, who may well have, among other things, the task of ensuring over the course of the year that ten workshops are organised in various places both at home and overseas.

The appraisal system is not a substitute for day to day management and counselling of subordinates. It is a formal means of ensuring that staff know what is expected of them, a means of appraising performance against objectives and targets, and plays a key part in the organisation's management development programme.

Liaison committees and working parties

No organisation operates in a vacuum and this is especially true of a tourist organisation, whether local, regional or national. If one accepts that one of the principal roles of a national tourist office or destination tourist office is as a coordinator of cooperative marketing activity, if one accepts that individual operators in the tourism industry are at once independent yet at the same time interdependent, then it follows that there must be some sort of machinery established to ensure that they work together. This working together may be in the area of product presentation, such as themes or cooperative marketing activity, and exhibitions or trade shows. It also provides a platform for the industry to discern market needs and help ensure that products are being developed which are appropriate to those needs.

The structure of these committees and working parties, their composition of membership and terms of reference will depend on the size of the organisation. In a large national tourist office it will be rewarding to develop committees in major markets where operators have representation either direct or through general sales agents. These committees will develop cooperative marketing programmes in their mutual interests, and exchange market intelligence and perhaps sales figures. A similar consultative and cooperative machinery with the industry has a vital role at local level as well as nationally or internationally.

If an organisation is developing a theme year, then it will be invaluable to have a working party which is representative of the various sectors of the industry to develop it. Typically it will start its work three years ahead and finish one year after the theme year when it monitors and appraises the effectiveness of the promotion.

It may be necessary to have a publicity committee or a training committee, a membership committee or a committee of regions. Whatever their number or scope they can be invaluable to the marketer in helping him to do his job more effectively. They are capable of providing market intelligence, act as a sounding board for new initiatives and provide feed-back on the organisation's cooperative marketing activities. Members can be evangelists as well as critics, supporters of the cooperative movement while taking a partisan stand. Above all they must be given a purpose if they are to survive and be of value.

Summary

Marketing's coordinating function must be recognised by the organisation and the marketing department organisation must reflect this. The organisational structure must clearly define responsibilities and relationships: it will have among its members generalists and specialists. Each must be clear about his role and responsibilities. In part this is fulfilled by the job description and in part through formal appraisal which also provides for performance measurement. For the organisation the marketing structure must be geared to objectives and tasks but it should also recognise future management needs.

For small organisations the consortium provides a marketing service for individual members. For the tourist organisation (local, regional, or national), committees and working parties have an important part to play in developing cooperative marketing as well as helping to develop effective marketing, from product development and presentation to market intelligence and appraisal of marketing techniques and activities.

15 Marketing strategy

Philip Kotler defines marketing strategy as 'a set of principles for adjusting the marketing programme to changing conditions. Marketing strategy acts as an overall plan that comprehends various possible developments and states the principles for meeting them.'[1]

The marketing programme follows, involving allocation of promotional resources, and the marketing mix of media (print, advertising etc) aimed specifically at selected market segments to achieve agreed objectives and economic and business targets.

The strategy must be related to agreed policy and objectives for the destination or the specific product. In the case of national destination (the country) there will be Government Tourism Policy implicit or explicit. Although this directly concerns the national marketing activity it is clearly of importance to the trade and their marketing operations. It is also important for the industry in its widest sense (the suppliers) to take part in the discussions and consultations leading to the formulation of the national policy or plan.

The following check list of possible key objectives in the national plan will illustrate the close relationship, and explain why the plan must be the basis for a detailed tourism policy, plan and marketing strategy. Marketing will be a dominant element in implementing any tourism plan. In fact product orientated plans will certainly fail. The policy must be market orientated, and in the elaboration of the action plan the time scale for marketing and market development will be as long as the physical build up of the tourism infrastructure.

National plan (check list)

1. Purpose
2. Objectives
Maximise foreign exchange (note leakage but also free trade)
Increase national income
Stimulate regional prosperity (selective options)
Increase employment
Maximise social benefits for residents
Enhance amenities for leisure and recreation (quality of life)
(note domestic tourism)
Culture (conservation and enhancement)

Commercial and transport (communications), infrastructure support
Other (including non-economic benefits e.g. international links)
3.   Government policy (statement)
4.   Tourism plan (policy/strategy)
(a)   purpose
(b)   objectives (see as for national plan but linked to tourism)
(c)   options
(d)   organisation/machinery
(e)   time scale
(f)   market assessments and product market fit (match)
(g)   development plan
(h)   marketing plan
(i)   appraisals and reviews

Governments and tourist organisations, public and private, will choose their priorities taking into account national or the organisation's (or company) policy. They will also have to take into account the current situation. It will be rare that tourism in any given destination is starting from scratch. There will be some existing infrastructure and current development plans. There will be some history or tradition of travel and so some goodwill. But there will also be competition and the pressures of the external factors notably in international tourism. These will limit options.

Application of national policies to tourism is well illustrated in the extract from a lecture by Dr T. O'Driscoll,[2] formerly Executive Director ETC, relating to the Seychelles:

Planning and development of specific regions
As one who has studied the organising for tourism and seen the machinery as a consultant in countries as far apart as the United States of America and India, Iran, Jordan and the Bahamas and of course in European countries, I am quite clear that the principles of organisation and the resulting machinery are fundamentally the same for all national authorities promoting tourism regardless of the particular products. The scale of operations of the national tourism administrations will vary of course in line with national priorities and resources provided. The basic requirements is to have stated a national policy with respect to tourism. I quote as a typical example of developing areas the statement of tourism policy of the Seychelles set out in the National Development Plan. They are:

(1)   to maximise the economic benefits derived from touristic expenditure particularly tourism from overseas and to increase foreign exchange earnings from tourism;
(2)   to spread tourist traffic and the derived social and economic

benefits more evenly throughout the islands of the Seychelles;

(3)   to promote and generate all year round tourism and in particular to increase off-season traffic to the Seychelles;

(4)   to encourage investment by commercial and public sector interests in tourism facilities within the Seychelles;

(5)   to maintain a steady orderly and controlled growth in tourism development in the Seychelles;

(6)   to protect and enhance the natural attraction, scenic beauty and cultural heritage of the islands;

(7)   to encourage participation by the people of the Seychelles in tourism developments and services;

(8)   to encourage the training and education of the Seychelles people in tourism skills and expertise.

> To support these policy statements three objectives were articulated. The first objective is concerned with the level of visitor expenditure and the objective is to achieve the maximum revenue per head from visitors. The net contribution from tourism is the difference between revenue earned and the cost in imports to service those earnings. The second objective of tourism from this point of view of the balance of payments should be to maximise the net contribution to the economy. Finally export tourism should be concerned with regional development. This is helped as an objective by setting targets for tourism bednights in at least the main regions.
>
> There you have the ingredients of any tourism policy. The generation of foreign exchange, year round custom, regional spread, protection of the human and natural environment, employment and participation by local people. The major problem is having enunciated a tourism policy or plan, to implement it.
>
> (Lecture to the Tourism Policy and Development Course, London 1987, Royal Institute of Public Administration.)

Although there must be long term plans and consistency in the marketing strategy, there may be an urgent need to maintain or defend markets as well as the more speculative exploitation of new ground. It can take three years or more of constant and effective work to create new streams of movement. Of course the reward is great; almost like striking oil. If the development is sound the new traffic movement will grow rapidly and may continue, with reducing marketing investment, for some years. The selection of options will also be influenced by available marketing resources, and the difficult task, particularly on a world-wide basis, of applying scarce means to a selected few objectives. Consider some examples. Some governments have decided from time to time to leave tourism marketing, including the national destination marketing, to the tourist interests themselves, on the grounds that as a commercial trade, marketing investment is a commercial decision. The US Tourism Administration has been starved of funds for years, and worked with a reducing budget in real terms for some time. Of course tourism to the USA has continued, but unevenly, much affected by the tides of inflation and exchange rates, subject to the ebb and flow of volatile traffic, helpful in filling surplus capacity but no basis for building a profitable national industry. More importantly US share of world tourism, and the USA has the biggest national share of world (incoming) travel of any country, has fallen steadily.

Some countries may decide that the cost benefits, in social, cultural and economic terms, of international tourism growth do not justify a tourism programme. Burma took this view for some years and even today takes a low profile in international tourism. The French government when the socialist party took control in 1981 gave priority to social tourism, and plans to assist the underprivileged or poorer sections of the community to take holidays. This was accompanied by severe restrictions on foreign currency for travel abroad by French residents. The effect on the industry was serious. But as explained in other chapters currency restrictions, in developed countries particularly, do not work well and often in the longer term have unfortunate economic effects and do not save foreign currency. Britain's experience in introducing restrictions on currency for foreign travel also showed this result.

A comparison of a number of countries' Tourism Policies and related plans can illustrate the selection of options:

British Tourist Authority[3]

Statutory responsibilties

Mission

In accordance with the Development of Tourism Act 1969, the BTA works to strengthen the performance of Britain's tourist industry in international markets by encouraging people to visit Britain and by encouraging the improvement and provision of tourist amenities and facilities in Britain.

BTA's aims

1.   To advise government and public bodies on all matters concerning inward tourism to Britain.
2.   To assist the industry in areas where it most needs support; to promote to overseas consumers tourism opportunities in Britain.
3.   To make available to overseas consumers the information which will enable them to make informed choices about destinations and

facilities in Britain, where this is inadequate and where intervention will be effective.

4.   To improve deficiencies in the flow of information to private and public sector bodies, where this is necessary to assist them in identifying opportunities and in rectifying shortcomings in overseas marketing and product development.

The board will carry out aims 2–4 by seeking to improve the operation of overseas markets for inward tourism to Britain, and by addressing problems in the operation of those markets, making cost-effective use of public funds to support the industry to overcome obstacles caused by, for example, its fragmented nature. It will intervene only where the industry cannot do so itself and where intervention is likely to be effective. It will seek to ensure that its policies take account of the need to conserve and enhance our built heritage, landscape and environment, sporting, cultural and artistic strengths.

Standing objectives

The aims set out areas of action to guide BTA operations and will be pursued by means of the following output orientated standing objectives.

●   To ensure that overseas markets with significant potential are identified and exploited by the British tourist industry, where necessary spearheading and coordinating marketing effort and guarding against over-dependence on any one market.

●   In partnership with national and regional boards, other bodies and the industry, to ensure that the needs of visitors to Britain are taken into account in the planning and development of facilities and infrastructure.

●   In the interests of gaining and distributing the economic benefits of tourism and of safeguarding the environment, to extend the geographical and seasonal spread of tourism in Britain.

●   Too meet the needs of overseas visitors for information where there are significant gaps left unfilled by the market.

●   To advise Government and public bodies on all issues relating to inward tourism.

●   To sustain a continuing improvement in BTA's effectiveness and efficiency.

Irish Tourist Board 1979[4]

National objective

The national objective is to optimise the economic and social benefits to

Ireland gained by the promotion and development of tourism both to and within the country taking account of:

1. the balance of payments;
2. the quality of life and the development of the community;
3. the enhancement and preservation of the nation's cultural heritage;
4. the conservation of the physical resources of the country;
5. tourism's contribution to the progress of regional development.

This was the stated policy in 1979. By 1987–88 the marketing strategy had become sophisticated and well targeted both and to geographic markets and market segments, as the following extracts from the Board's reports covering promotion in Great Britain and North America demonstrates.

Great Britain

Marketing Objectives
- Primarily to increase revenue with emphasis on holidaymakers with close Irish ties.
- To increase the specialist segments, particularly anglers and golf.
- To increase VFR traffic.

Marketing Strategy
The Marketing objectives will be achieved by:

- A projection of Ireland as a desirable, different and affordable holiday destination, through advertising, publicity and literature.
- Greater emphasis will be placed on promoting activity holidays.
- Further efforts will be made to increase the short break holiday segment and improve the early/late shoulder season business.
- Emphasis is being placed on the promotion of value for money holiday offers in order to offset the high cost perception of Ireland. The lower access fares and product costs will greatly enhance this direction.

Target Audience
- Pure holidaymakers with particular emphasis on: ABC1s, with significant coverage of C2s; the 25–45 year age group; the affluent London/South East regions, and the North West of England.
- Specialist activity market segments and conference group travel. VFR segment.

North America

Marketing Objectives
- To maximise tourism revenue with a projected growth in volume of 4 per cent in 1988.
- To increase Ireland's share of US–Europe traffic.
- To generate off season business.

Marketing Strategy
- To position Ireland as a unique, desirable and different holiday destination, with a broad European context.
- To use all the elements of the marketing mix to explain the aspects of an Irish holiday that are important to European vacation travellers and, importantly that are currently unknown.
These include:

- Ireland's castles, manor houses;
- Ireland's history, music and cultural events;
- Ireland's first class accommodation, sporting events, and facilities;
- Ireland's varied landscape;
- Ireland's major 'European' cities.

- To exploit the ancestral link with 40 million Americans of Irish heritage, which offers an immediate prospect for Ireland, and this segment will receive extra attention.
- To develop the growing importance of specialist products and considerable promotion of golf will occur, together with campaigns geared to exploit the opportunities created by cycling, walking, angling and equestrian activities.
- To consolidate air services to Ireland with youth programmes being undertaken with the carriers and it is hoped to broaden Ireland's trade base by bringing on stream additional tour wholesalers.

Target Audience
Broadly defined, the target audience for travel to Ireland is:

- Adults 25–64 years of age, with previous travel experience of Europe.
- Special emphasis on adults 50–64 age grouping, with incomes of $50,000 or more, and the 25–34 age category, with minimum incomes of $35,000.

France

A summary follows of the French Government's tourism marketing agency's (Maison de la France) strategy.[5]

The analysis of foreign markets has shown clearly three positive and three negative characteristics.

Positive:
France is a very well-known country, universally in demand and sought after, and one which everybody wants to visit.

The range of products offered in France is exceptionally varied, and provides an advantage over other competing European countries. France has a reputation as top of the scale, and this image is universal. This emphasises the importance of quality and welcome.

Negative:
Welcome is considered generally to be inadequate.

This strong unfortunate image exists in many markets and needs correcting.

France is considered as expensive.

Strategy is based on these findings. The aim is to catch up with Spain and to reach the number two or number three position in the world market. This is achievable because the product is there. France has the necessary attractions to do much better in foreign markets. Furthermore the attractions match exactly international tourism trends; more frequent trips, the search for activity and demand for quality. More than any other European country France can respond to tourist expectations towards the end of the century, thanks to the diversity of the regions of the country and the rich heritage.

To catch up with Spain it is not a case of selling one region or one theme, but by promoting the infinite diversity of the countryside, activities and attractions which the country offers in all seasons.

The strategy has three objectives:

1.   To avoid dispersing effort by concentrating resources on markets of high potential and products in demand so that there is a product market match.
2.   To end ad hoc policies by fixing medium term objectives. This stable policy will lead to effective action.
3.   Open up all activity to partners and provide a focal point for initiatives.

The Maison de la France has selected options: efforts will be concentrated on eleven countries considered essential. Ninety per cent of resources will be devoted to them over several years. Of the 11, seven are European constituting the commercial base for French tourism – Germany, Britain, Netherlands, Belgium, Italy, Switzerland and Spain. Four distant countries – USA, Japan, Australia and Canada – are developing markets and complement in clientele, products and seasonality the neighbouring countries. The present level of activity will be maintained in Scandinavia, Africa, Hong Kong and Mexico.

1.   To sell destination France in its regional diversity with the partners concerned.
2.   To concentrate on products in demand. In this way the interests of the regions and those of the producers will be linked in the product market match.

Special efforts will be made for seven products considered to be leaders:

1   Winter sports
2   Inland waterways
3   Business travel
4   Cycling holidays
5   Short trips
6   Tourism in French overseas territories
7   Cultural tourism

Canada[6]

Growth in Canada's international and domestic markets has occurred since 1984. 1986 was the best year for the tourism industry since 1972. Share of global market has rebounded from a low of 2.4% to 2.9%; the deficit in the travel account dropped dramatically from a high of $2.1 billion to an estimated $1.1 billion; international visits of at least one night were up some 18% in 1986 over 1985. The growth, while not uniform, has occurred in almost every part of the country.

The recent recovery encouraged Tourism Canada to set a new target: a nil balance in the travel account by 1990. If a 28% increase in one or more night person-visits over four years occurred a nil balance would be achieved.

To achieve that difficult goal, much must be done. Canada's $22 billion a year tourism industry (preliminary estimates for 1986) has a product line that appeals to consumers, foreign and domestic. According to research, Canada is seen in all markets as an outstanding outdoors and touring vacation destination that offers unique cultural and heritage products. At the same time, our city product is not well known although the majority of visits to Canada by all modes of transportation involve cities, either as a gateway, a destination, or a segment of a touring trip.

1987/88 Plan

Goals

● To increase person-visits from Canada's top five international markets (USA, Japan, West Germany, France, and the United Kingdom) by 28% over 1985 by 1990.

● To identify, develop and market specific internationally competitive regional products in cooperation with major public and private sector partners.

● To address the seasonality issue by examining the market potential of Canada's winter product line.

● To integrate/coordinate export market activities of the federal government with private and public sector partners, resulting in an increased 'Canada' impact in the market place and increasing effectiveness and efficiency of resource utilisation levering $7.5 million in jointly targeted or incremental resources.

● To examine the efficiency/effectiveness of market development expenditures in secondary markets.

Strategy

Driving off the 'Medium-Term Marketing Strategy for Marketing Canada's Products – The Federal Government's Game Plan' which was tabled at the May 1987 Tourism Marketing Council meeting, Tourism Canada will:

● Concentrate and focus our efforts and resources in Canada's primary international markets: the United States, the United Kingdom, France, West Germany and Japan. Based on our recent research, it would appear that opportunities are being missed to significantly increase the number of visitors to Canada from those markets. Tourism Canada is therefore developing Market Business Plans to set out our four year strategic direction and identify partnership opportunities.

● Continue, in cooperation with USTTA (USA) to research geographic markets to establish their potential for long-haul international pleasure travel (1987/88 – Hong Kong, Singapore, Switzerland).

● Develop and, in cooperation with industry partners, test new or underdeveloped product lines and market segments (i.e. culture, native products, winter season).

● Expand our programming in cooperation with public and private sector partners and lever resources from both traditional and non-traditional partners. Relationships will continue to be managed both on a project basis (such as on individual advertising campaigns and post-related activities) and under Joint Marketing Accords/Agreements.

● Develop a year round advertising presence in the US market under the theme 'Canada. The World Next Door.' This will include an expansion of our successful spring/summer, fall and ski campaigns and, beginning in 1988/89, including an entirely new winter-orientated campaign probably keyed to regional product offerings.

● Review/evaluate the federal tourism marketing program delivered by DEA (Dept. of External Affairs) posts to assess the most effective and efficient use of federal resources.

● Ensure that the fulfilment of our advertising, especially in the United States, is handled effectively: a client servicing review is underway.

● Examine the federal role and the level of resources devoted to the promotion of meetings and conventions with a view to maximising the effectiveness of the program.

Elements of the strategy

The final agreed national tourism policy and plan, hopefully worked out in consultation with the major sectors of industry (including regional and key resort destinations), will be the basis for the marketing strategy. Whether this is the state, region, resort or major operators (a flag carrier for example) it must reflect destination and commercial objectives and priorities. It will take into account:

1.   The current supply situation, occupancy/load factor, and the combination of existing attractions. The inventory will highlight peaks and troughs, strengths and weaknesses in the national and key sector provision.

2.   The competitive situation, noting strengths and weaknesses, any monopoly positions or unique advantages.

3.   International and domestic market situations, some markets may be temporarily depressed or in decline as a result of political or economic pressures.

4.   The external factors, exchange rates, inflation and prices, government restrictions (or incentives).

5.   Marketing resources.

A first broad selection of priorities and objectives will begin to emerge, and can be checked in some preliminary product market match tests. This broad selection is most important, since it is the beginning of the difficult tasks of selecting objectives for the application (and rationing) of scarce resources. It will ultimately also be the basis for appraisals and policy and plan revision, on which the marketers and their principals will be judged. Some of the broad objectives will concern allocations between maintenance of existing key markets, and the longer term and more difficult task of investment in new business. The need for speedy return on investment will be a key factor. A priority might be given to improving viability (for example by investing heavily in programmes to spread travel seasonally and geographically, evening out peaks and troughs in existing business).

Marketing must be a strong feature in the discussion and consultation leading to policy formulation and objective and target setting. Identification of product life cycles is important at this stage as there will be declining areas. Perception of new trends must be the basis for future product development. Changes in competition will follow new trends and these must be anticipated.

In addition to national strategies and trade sector or large organisation policies there may also be important regional and local destination strategies. Birmingham, Britain's second largest city, is encouraging expansion of inner city areas needing regeneration and developing a large and profitable visitor movement based on business related travel, conferences, trade fairs and major events. This can be a successful formula for a high spending year round travel movement. But investment and promotion implications are substantial. In addition to the country's largest exhibition complex (The National Exhibition Centre), which is still expanding, the country's largest conference and event centre is being built in the heart of the city at a cost of over £130 million, helped by European Community funding. This major state and local 'destination' funding will need supporting investment (hotel accommodation) and the guarantee of expanding and high standard support services, such as transport, entertainment etc. In addition all the interests must plan marketing cooperatively and independently on almost as long a time scale. It may take several years to attract a major international conference, or to secure and build up a major international trade show or spectator event.

There are also internationally agreed intergovernmental policies. In Europe the twelve countries of the European Community (EC) are increasingly introducing common policies. Many of these affect tourism directly. Some including liberalisation measures (air transport for example) should have positive results. But there are also others which are based on broad economic or social objectives and the side effects on tourism good, bad or indifferent must be taken into account. Two examples will suffice as indication of this further area of interest to tourism traders in formulating policies and marketing strategies. The food surpluses and the need for radical reform of agriculture must have a serious effect on the economies of marginal or poorer farming regions. But many of these have good natural resources and unspoilt environments very suitable for the right kind of leisure development.

Thus the EC has in its tourism policy given priority to the growth of rural tourism, bringing a new source of wealth to farmers and rural areas where traditional agriculture must change or decrease. A strong social policy embraces leisure and tourism. While some of the ideas may prove controversial, member countries' interest in leisure services as an area for state intervention, even if usually at the local level, will need attention. Sometimes the state intervenes directly in the form of subsidies. Industry has generally accepted such initiatives, provided the subsidy is given to the needy individual not to the basic services provided by the trading sectors. There is more argument when the state subsidises specific operations or sets up its own agencies in competition with the tax paying trading sector.

Thus international and national government policies may directly affect traders for better or worse, with a mixture of constraints and incentives altering the terms and conditions of trade and the operation of a free and competitive market. But the basic fact remains that the market will dictate. Product orientated schemes to use tourism for social or other state purposes can only work if they fit in with market trends, and even then there may be a cost – lost opportunities elsewhere. Some years ago an important tourism region in Britain announced through its state representatives that they would accept and develop tourism as a tool of regional development, almost as though this vital trade was a last resource. Success was certainly not assured. Tourism is a business of mankind; it cannot be taken for granted and deserves essential priorities in development as any other major industry. When tourism flourishes it is true that many beneficial side effects result from the prosperity traffic brings to the visitor receiving areas.

Tourism policies, plans and the related market strategies must take a long term view. There is a considerable range of interests and destinations: some operating partly in competition. There must be harmonious development. Growth of travel to a destination needs transport and related accommodation: facilities and attractions. With the best of technical liaison between them, and usually this is lacking, the sectors will not develop together at the same rate. Key factors must operate, first a market trend or demand (the destination must be in fashion) and transport must exist. There will be shortages and bottlenecks but in the technological age they can be overcome quickly if market pressure is maintained. Too often over-investment occurs. Historically the expansion of Britain's resorts resulted relatively quickly with transport developments once the health interest and fashion were created. Fishermen's cottages provided accommodation long before grand hotels were built. But the stream of movement had been created, the oil well, as it were, discovered.

The marketing strategy for the destination or service should be prepared after close consultation with the government or management in setting policy and plans. These must be clear and consistent, taking into account the likelihood that time scales for growth will be relatively long – three to five years. The policy may have social and economic elements. Where possible targets should be set partly to provide reference points for appraisals and at least annual reviews of plan and strategies. Judgement will not be perfect and the marketing operation will contain errors. Although marketers and market research experts have an inbuilt optimism and a belief that all promotion is successful, at least in part, this is far from the truth. Objective assessments are vital as strategies are implemented.

Having considered all the elements which contribute to strategy formulation the task of constructing the strategy can begin. The organisation (destination, national or local, the specific service or business) will have agreed the main policy lines. They will vary according to the public or private sector interest but will have a number of common elements. Since the destination and its services are interdependent there must be a considerable area of common objectives. These are likely to include the improvement of seasonal flows, and thus prosperity and profitability, leading in turn to improvements in quality and new investment.

All interests will seek to maximise use of resources, and this will include geographic as well as seasonal spread of traffic. Seasonality and area spread should not be considered problems in this age of leisure and mobility but rather as challenges and opportunities. A further common objective is likely to be the increase in visitor spending per capita or per diem. This will involve trading up, extra attractions, special events such as festivals, shopping incentives etc. Government may have social, political or broad economic aims which may not be shared, and many even conflict with local destinations and traders. These may include help for poorer regions, support for declining agriculture and may divert traffic at some cost to commercial success. The state may go for maximum foreign currency as a first priority. These national objectives use tourism for benefits other than those that will flow from normal and profitable development of the trade. There can be cost and lost opportunity in consequence, so that the implications need careful and objective expert study.

The marketing strategy seeking to implement the national tourism plan based on agreed objectives must take into account the current situation. Existing resources and their products will include some well advanced in the product life cycle, some declining fast, some needing restructuring or major regeneration. Similarly there will be declining markets, changes in fashion and emerging new trends. Competition and new entrants in the national and international market place must be noted. One of the most difficult tasks will be the allocation of priorities and thus resources between existing major markets where business must be maintained, and the exploitation of new markets.

Consideration must be given to time factors. Is a quick return vital? Long term investment in marketing will also be necessary depending on the particular stage of tourism development. There will be a capital investment situation. The strategy must take into account major new developments in transport, accommodation, attractions and facilities (conference halls, exhibition centres, marinas and major sports facilities, leisure centre and resort development), and apart from the physical infrastructure new products and product presentation, for example a major festival or event. Sometimes with attractions such as World Fairs, Olympic Games or other major sporting events, or an International Garden Festival, the infrastructure cost is relatively high and the time scale extends over several years. Yet the provision for marketing planning may be totally inadequate and short term.

Following decisions on major objective and market options, the strategy must reflect the 'External Factors' set out in some detail in chapter 9. There will be advantages and disadvantages, favourable exchange rates for example, or worsening political situations. The American setback in 1986 has already been described, when Europe's dollar tourism income fell almost without warning in a few months. Thus there will always be a place for tactical marketing to seize immediate opportunity or to mitigate damage. Failure to deal with external factors in marketing terms could be very costly and have long term implications.

The allocation of resources in total and then by market and market segment and finally in the marketing mix is the most difficult part of the strategy. Some markets will respond quickly to marketing treatment, some may need massive intervention and investment. So there must be conscious and stated choice, otherwise appraisals and reviews are inefficient or impossible. Markets will be growing at differing rates. There must be consistency in the marketing investment. It takes at least three years to grow new business. Seeds are slow to germinate, but the longer term rewards can be massive.

At this stage the product market match exercise must be carried out in some depth, relating the objectives, the physical resources to the tourist products that can be made and offered (the product being an attraction or required activity at a selected or desired destination).

Some examples of the selection process will illustrate the range and scale of options going into the strategy.

If seasonality is a major problem the growth of the senior citizen segment offers great opportunities. The Woopies (wealthier older people) have money, mobility and need for travel and leisure services. They are often bored and lonely. Organisation of their interests and time can fill, indeed is filling, many out of season empty facilities.

The poorer, remote and rugged rural areas, perhaps deficient in creature comforts, are a magnet for wilderness and adventure trips and for many active pursuits needed by young people.

The greater the growth in technology and canned communication the bigger the need for face to face communication, so conferences and trade fairs have an ever increasing appeal. This is important for inner cities and their regeneration programmes.

Special events, festivals and exhibitions in cultural as well as economic fields can be important elements in creating new streams of movement; of bolstering main or even declining traffic movement.

There will be specialist situations capable of major exploitation in education, training, sport, cultural areas and religious appeals (pilgrimages are still the source of major travel). Thus the markets and the segments in the product market fit exercise offer almost endless permutations and combinations. But one must remember life cycles and emerging trends. There are ebbs and flows in fashion and behaviour. Time scales of change are much shorter, and modern technology capable of massive expansion of capacity very rapidly. But markets will rule. The marketing strategy, although time scales may be brief enough, must demonstrate a longer vision than the infrastructure development plan. In the end the tourist (the demand factor) will decide in a competitive world with choices for leisure growing apace.

Summary

Marketing strategy is defined by Kotler as 'a set of principles for adjusting the marketing programme to changing conditions. Marketing strategy acts as an overall plan that comprehends various possible developments and states the principles for meeting them'.

The strategy must be related to agreed policy and tourism objectives for the destination of the specific tourist product. Marketing must be a dominant element if implementing any tourism plan, the policy itself must be market orientated, and the time scale for market development must be as long as the infrastructure and physical build up operation. It can take three years or more of consistent effort to create new streams of movement.

A national tourism plan agreed in consultation with the major industry sectors will be the basis for marketing strategy. It will take into account:

1. The supply situation and the mix of existing attractions, peaks and troughs, strengths and weaknesses.
2. The competitive situation.
3. International and domestic marketing situations.
4. External factors.
5. Marketing resources.

A selection of priorities and objectives will emerge as a basis for application of scarce resources to selected objectives, including maintenance of existing markets and investment in new markets. Targets should be set and will be reference points. Although much tourism marketing is long term there will always be allocation of resources by market and market segment and the related marketing mix is the most difficult part of the strategy. The product market match exercise must be carried out in depth, relating objectives, resources and products.

References

1 Kotler, P, *1967 Marketing Management.* Prentice Hall Inc p 281.
2 Lecture by Dr T. O'Driscoll for the Royal Institute of Public Administration. London 1987.
3 *British Tourist Authority Strategy 1991.*
4 Irish Tourist Board (Bord Failte) *Tourism Plan.*
5 *Maison de la France Marketing Plan.* Paris 1988.
6 *International Tourism Development Plan.* Tourism Canada 1987/88.

16　After sales service

This is always an important part of marketing and often overlooked or given little priority. It is a vital concern in tourism because in most cases the product only becomes available after the sale. Welcome, reception, information and personal servicing in a people trade are fundamental to success.

A large proportion of the clientele will be repeat visitors or regular customers, for the country as well as for the individual service or business. Over 60% of Britain's overseas visitors have been before, and the trend is to more frequent visiting by the 'regulars'. Furthermore first time travellers and repeat visitors alike are influenced by the experience and one must never forget that it is also the source of travellers' tales, the most powerful form of counsel, recommendation and promotion in international travel.

It is vital therefore to give priority to visitor servicing (in areas of key after sales service), not only to safeguard future business, but to increase satisfaction, and thus length of stay and expenditure in the country.

Visitor satisfaction must be regularly researched. The national and local tourist organisations (tourist boards) in cooperation with industry must monitor visitor progress. BTA carries out an annual Overseas Visitor Survey sampling visitors in a number of centres throughout the country and throughout the year. This not only provides useful market research information on behaviour, ie where the visitors go, where they stay, how they travel, what they do, but gives an indication of satisfaction and attitudes to price (the all important value for money).

In addition a London Visitor Survey checks the huge visitor influx to London in the summer months, as the capital is not only the principal destination for overseas visitors but is the principal place of entry and departure, and the base from which visitors plan trips to other parts of the country.

Apart from regular checks by sample surveys, more technical examination of key services in cooperation with the industries concerned can be valuable to the country, the resort and the traders. Visitors should be followed through all stages of their itinerary.

After sales service in tourism must be planned service by service, and be assured after each principal stage of the visit. The promise of the promotion must be delivered, quality assured and satisfaction given. Tourism is after all a trade in people, a human experience and to an extent a theatrical and cultural performance. The first arrival in a foreign country is a memorable experience, even if all goes according to plan.

In 1985 BTA in cooperation with government departments, customs and immigration, sea and air ports and the carriers, examined visitor reception at ports and transport terminals. As an island the majority of overseas visitors entered and left through some twelve sea and air ports. Thus reception and welcome, information and passenger handling arrangements, can colour tourists' attitude to the country and, if satisfactory, contribute substantially to satisfaction and goodwill.

Regular study and monitoring of the information and reception service is a necessary prelude to effective after sales service, since the official information services provide at considerable expense an essential advisory service to enhance value for money, visitor satisfaction and, in consequence, increase length of stay and visitor spend. The appendix 1 summarises a useful survey of five important Tourist Information Centres in London, carried out between July and October 1987. The survey provided an important guide not only to improving service but sharpening some important aspects of marketing.

The USA, which some years ago compared unfavourably in the image of personal services compared with skilled European international visitor services, now leads the world in training and attention to visitors. Staff are courteous, smart, often in uniform, which can greatly assist international visitors who need reassurance and advice in foreign and thus strange places. Signposting, symbols, literature, information points, new technology for information and reservations, all help to ensure standards, making it easy to choose and thus to buy.

Good advice and counselling, in other words good tourist information, implies standard setting, and clear action to report on standards. This in turn will lead to good standard monitoring by national, local and trade organisations. The standard setting and reporting activity, and related standard enhancement, with its essential value for money implication, is not necessarily a matter for state control. Indeed as explained in chapter 9 (hotel classification), the most effective systems are marketing systems operated by the trade or trade related bodies. From the visitors' point of view they must be efficient and clearly understood.

After sales service should follow the visitor through the journey. While a substantial proportion of traffic, dependent on the destination, may be packaged and thus controlled by the travel trade and their suppliers, the majority will make individual and independent arrangements. Thus there will be a combination of advisers and suppliers in the distribution or retail chain. It is important to examine who caters for the visitor at the destination, and whether adequate information and advice to make it easy to choose is forthcoming. The visitor will depend on a number of guides: the hotel porters, the local official information centre, the local travel agent or friends and acquaintances.

It is surprising how often the services which provide information on what to do, where to go and how to buy, are inefficient and difficult. Hotel porters are important providers of certain services, theatre tickets, car hire etc, although the skilled professional retail travel agent should be easily in contact. Information centres may be badly signposted, poorly staffed and unable to make reservations or sales (except necessary maps and literature which are sold irrespective of the value of certain give away material). Visitors arrive at ports, terminals (railway stations), car parks, as well as at a range of accommodation establishments. But at least at the main transport termini (including major central car parks) location of information centres should be clearly indicated.

Languages are important, as well as training in handling visitors, phone calls and giving advice. It may seem strange to many Europeans that American service staff regularly greet their clients with a cheerful 'Have a nice day' (even if it is approaching midnight), but the personal interest stimulates friendship and appreciation.

In 1991 BTA got together with Thomas Cook to launch a new tourism awards campaign. 'Winning Words' is designed to recognise and encourage foreign language initiatives in the UK tourism industry and a report provides detailed advice to tourism employers on ways in which they can enhance their welcome of non-English speaking visitors. Examples include: the development of company language policies; language audits; making the most of existing skills; recruitment, language and cultural awareness training; provision of information in a foreign language. The report also includes examples of good practice and sources for further information. A series of awards was developed to encourage language learning, to recognise those organisations who have taken action to enhance the service provided for non-English speaking visitors and to encourage others to make progress in this area.

Another example of an advisory publication designed to enhance the visitor's experience – in this case the Japanese – was published by BTA in 1990. *Caring for the Japanese Visitor* gives advice on developing and presenting the product to ensure the maximum appeal for Japanese visitors. Sections cover accommodation, catering, golf, information provision, language schools, shopping, attractions, transportation and guiding. Advice is given on a whole range of topics from Japanese superstitions to tipping, food likes and dislikes, portion size, as well as doing business with Japanese in the market place.

The BTA opened next to Piccadilly in London the British Travel Centre, a specially built large information centre with industry support in the form of transport, accommodation and other travel reservation services. It has staff capable of dealing with most foreign language speaking visitors. One of the principal objectives was to encourage visitors to travel out of London by making it easy for them, especially the large number of independent travellers, to plan their trip. Comprehensive services are important. With the development of information technology and reservation systems it should be possible for a greater number of smaller retail travel agents and the local tourist information centres to provide a greater range of services, and a much improved system of counselling to make it easy to buy. Many local centres provide an effective service locally, which cannot be offered at entry points or nationally for local services (sightseeing, bookings for entertainments etc). This is clearly of the utmost importance in the case of special events (festivals and anniversaries), but often it is not well done. Yet the local centre is the focal point and the cooperative base for all the local services. Bed and Breakfast accommodation, which is one of Britain's tourist success stories (now copied in North America and Europe), is best handled at the local level. The centre's system of 'Book A Bed Ahead', for the next stage of a motoring itinerary, can be especially rewarding.

A system of linking service points, the network of information, is important, related to information material (literature, telephone or computer), signs, symbols and maps, and standards are an important part of visitor servicing. In Britain and many European countries the *i* sign is now an accepted symbol for the officially recognised visitor information point. Not everything can be centralised. The servicing must follow the visitor, and the information and services provided must be planned according to the changing demand, on the one hand for advance information, on the other for immediate guidance. It is essential that all the interests in the chain are an active and conscious part of the network, and that the visitor knows how to get information and service as his journey progresses. In some European countries, especially those in their earlier stages of development, a tourist police service was established with great success. The London bobby for years was regarded as the most reliable guide to finding the way about town. This in fact placed a burden on the police which they accepted willingly, generating much good will. But it indicated the lack of attention the trade and the tourist organisations were paying to this essential servicing. It was, and is, their responsibility to ensure satisfaction and maximise sales.

Standard setting in some cases will need public sector intervention, sometimes by control or regulation, sometimes by encouragement and example and sometimes by direct action. As already explained, the public sector is not simply the community guardian, the regulator and legislator, the umpire, but also the operator, especially at the municipal level. Many tourist attractions are publicly owned and sometimes publicly operated as well; for example, theatres, conference centres, museums and art galleries, entertainment centres, historic properties, sports centres, health spas. The list is almost endless, sometimes extending to service operation in transport and accommodation. But it is in the regulatory, example giving and leadership role that the key lies in the industrialised countries. Hygiene, health and safety, cleanliness and welcome are all aspects of official duties even if action requires, as it usually does, a cooperative effort with the commercial interests. The destination authority must take the lead. Signposting and official symbols and guiding services depend on positive and nationwide action by public authorities.

There are many services which may need a degree of control, or where standard setting is a governmental or trade professional job (a form of self policing). Bureaux de change, taxis and other public transport fares, travel agent and guide services, and in certain cases accommodation charges (especially in the cheaper categories) are examples. Visitor servicing requires considerable effort to ensure that the tourist is informed about these controls or guarantees of standards. In a number of cases little is done to ensure that visitors understand the system, their rights, which might have a legal base, and obligations. Failure by tourist interests to ensure this will give rise to an increasing interest in consumerism and government intervention. This may not be the cure though and indeed can aggravate problems. In the end those servicing visitors, usually the service trades, are in contact with individual travellers and in the best position to explain the rules and regulations for their protection and satisfaction. Good marketing, which is concerned with maximising satisfaction and sales, requires a high priority to visitor servicing during their stay. The after sales service alone can ensure satisfaction and repeat business.

The travel industry is making great strides in information technology, supplementing, rather than supplanting, the long established travel brochure and manned information points. The systems must be linked, and furthermore the new systems will be capable of an international compatible basis, to exchange information rapidly, and on a vast scale, between all the major destinations. This will be an important factor in competition. Information linked to reservations will be the new leap forward in extending the range of choice and making it easy to buy. This means making it easy to go. But the servicing will be continuous, greatly improving the flow of traffic to the less well known destinations, and for a greater range of specialist products. For many smaller service providers, who are able, if organised, to expand capacity and handle a large number of independent travellers, the new technology can be especially important. But the network and the chain must be in place, either with people or machines, the traditional or the new information technology. There is today little difficulty in arranging the big purchase, making the big decision (eg to cross the Atlantic) but the service infrastructure especially for the independent traveller, to enable easy travel at the destination, is not in place.

Greater development of component packaging (rail or bus passes, pre-booked theatre, concerts and other events, mini packages, internal transport) is needed and will be increasingly important. The large car hire companies have done an expert marketing job for the individual with information, maps, insurance etc. In 1984 Avis introduced 'Personally Yours' in Britain and this provides bespoke tailored, computerised and personalised itineraries geared to special interests, such as gardens, religious heritage, castles, antiques etc. It has subsequently been extended to several other countries following its successful launch in Britain as part of the theme 'Heritage '84'.

Visitor research can be carried out after departure but this is likely to be less effective than sampling during the stay. Mailed questionnaire response may be low, especially if foreign language problems arise. Personal interviews on an international basis are expensive.

It is worthwhile offering to keep in touch with visitors if they would like a continuing link. They can be invited before departure to ask for future information on special events or general destination news. Some of the State Tourist Organisations publish and often sell successfully attractive general destination publications of a very high standard. BTA's 'In Britain', the Irish Tourist Board's 'Ireland of the Welcomes', prestigious and well produced annuals from Greece and Turkey are good examples. Response will provide a valuable mailing list, which however must be used with discretion and skill. The sample responding will be 'skewed' or not representative of the whole, likely to reflect one or two specific market segments, for example ethnic groups and cultural roots groups. There is a special marketing value in these segments derived from the massive migrant flows over the past 100 years. The majority are faced with long and relatively expensive journeys (Australians and New Zealand residents for example). Reminders will encourage more frequent journeys, and avoid postponements or 'putting off' decisions. In this way more journeys are achieved in the individual lifetime.

Summary

The after sales service begins with careful and periodic research to identify problems and in particular lack of information and deficiencies in purchasing facilities, which will reduce satisfaction and expenditure. Research should indicate necessary improvement in welcome and reception services, including staff training, current standard setting and standard 'signing' which should make it easy to choose and to buy, particularly services and attractions wanted during the visit. There is much impulse buying during the trip, but a great deal more is thwarted or results in unsatisfactory purchases for which there may be little or no redress.

Regular checks are essential for information services, location, signposting and accessibility (including hours of opening). Shop or office hours may not be suited to the visitors' advisory service or reservation needs. Many information offices are closed on Sundays, now a principal leisure and travel day. Staff training, foreign language facilities, information materials, brochures, signs, symbols, maps, telephone, audio visual and computer systems all feature in the good after sales service. This is the age of communication but the services which can add so much satisfaction and revenue are rarely adequate. Yet it can be too expensive in terms of lost trade to fail.

Appendix 1

A Survey of Users of Major Tourist Information Centres in London (ETB/BTA 1988)

• Of the five TICs surveyed here, users largely found them by accident – particularly those at Heathrow Terminal 2/ Gatwick – or by 'instinct' ('expected it to be there'). Only the British Travel Centre (BTC), Piccadilly, appears to have benefited from publicity in the form of guide books/advertising overseas etc. There are also indications that the London Heathrow Underground TIC, in view of its location, would benefit from more publicity/sign posting within the airport.

• Users of the TICs were mostly first time users of them although the BTC and Victoria TIC have relatively high proportions of 'repeat' users (33% and 26% respectively).

• The vast majority of people who came into the TICs were looking for information, help and advice on:

• Accommodation – especially at Heathrow Underground TIC

• Travel/directions/booking information
. . . for London (the airport TICs)
. . . for Britain (BTC)

• Events/places to visit/things to do – BTC and Victoria TIC

• Maps/guides etc – all five TICs

• Most overseas users of the TICs had not booked any accommodation before arriving in Britain and of those that had, relatively high proportions (33% to 54%) had only booked for part or the first night of their trip.

- Over a half or more of those who were visiting or had planned to visit London had booked accommodation mostly before they came to Britain, whereas on average only a third of those who were visiting or had planned to visit regions outside London had booked such accommodation (again, mostly before they came to Britain).

- In general, less than half of those who had visited or were planning to visit London had made travel arrangements for getting about the Capital.

- For travel outside London, again less than half who had visited or planned to visit other regions had made arrangements.

Appendix 2

London Visitors Survey (1990)

Summary of results

1. In the summer of 1990 just under a half of those interviewed were from Western Europe, a third from North America and a quarter from other countries. Visitors from the United States formed the largest group with a quarter of the total with West Germany and Australia/New Zealand coming next with a tenth each. A third were in the 16–24 age group and a further quarter in the 25–34 age group.
2. Two thirds of those questioned were in London for holiday purposes with just under a half being in London on a repeat visit. Nearly a fifth of those on repeat visits had been in London during 1989 and just under a tenth had been before in 1990. A fifth had not been since 1980 or before.
3. The average length of stay was 11 nights. Those having rented flats or staying as paying guests tended to stay twice as long.
4. Three quarters had made their own arrangements for coming to London with the remainder coming in organised groups of which just over a fifth were on a package tour. Youth groups made up the rest of those questioned.
5. A third stayed in licensed hotels and a quarter stayed with friends or

relatives. Over two thirds of those in London for business stayed in a hotel and three quarters of those on a package holiday also used a hotel. The older the visitor the more likely they were to be staying in a hotel. At least a fifth of those visiting friends or relations did not actually stay with them.

6.   Just under a half had arrived at Heathrow with just under a quarter at Gatwick. Dover was the most important seaport of arrival. The underground was used by two fifths of those travelling into London from Heathrow with taxis being next most important with a fifth. From Gatwick nearly three fifths used rail and two fifths from Dover. Other important modes of transport were coach services and being picked up by private car.

7. The London Underground remains the most used form of transport by visitors with nine tenths having used this service. Over a half used regular bus services and a third used taxis at various times during their stay. Nearly a fifth had been on a sightseeing bus/coach by the time they were interviewed. Over two thirds used a Travelcard during their stay with nearly a tenth having bought it before arrival in this country. On average just over 2 1/2 trips per day were taken on the Underground and a taxi journey every third day.

London Transport leaflets remain an important source of information. Two fifths had obtained or been given their *Travelling in London* leaflet but rather fewer had the more specific leaflet *Linking London's Airports and Hotels*. These were obtained from a variety of sources including the point of arrival, information centres and at their place of accommodation.

8.   Just under two fifths had visited an information centre by the time they were interviewed. The longer the time in London, the greater the use of a centre showing that they are not only used on arrival in London. Nevertheless, Victoria with its London Tourist Board Centre and London Transport Centre is used by over two fifths of those who visited a centre for information.

9.   Three quarters of those questioned felt London had a lot of things for them to do with the majority of others having quite a lot to do. There were a wide variety of responses to the question of which attraction they had enjoyed most. A fifth had enjoyed most some form of paid attraction. Also popular were museum/exhibitions, art galleries and palaces/stately homes. The Tower of London was the most popular mentioned by a tenth, followed by Madame Tussauds.

The attraction likely to be visited most was the Tower of London (three fifths) followed by Madame Tussauds with just under a half and the British Museum just over a third. The recently opened Museum of the Moving Image attracted just over a tenth.

Hampton Court was the most popular non-central site which was likely to be visited with just over a fifth saying they had or were intending to visit. Both Kew Gardens and Greenwich also were expected to be visited by a fifth. An important factor in determining the extent to which visits are made outside central London is the length of stay and to a lesser extent whether on a repeat visit. Nearly three quarters staying only between 1–3 nights had not or did not think they would visit any of the areas listed compared to only a third for those staying 15+ nights.

10.   Two thirds had purchased souvenirs or postcards by the time they were interviewed with clothing/footwear being the next most important with nearly two fifths having made purchases of this kind. It seems that although shopping is not given as a main reason for their visit, nearly all spend some money on shopping during their trip.

11.   Visitors to London use the Underground and buses frequently and, as a result, are exposed to many advertisements displayed there. The level of recall varies depending partly on the length of stay but at least a fifth remembered most of the advertisements shown and McDonalds and British Telecom on average were remembered by half.

12.   Just over four fifths had arranged all their accommodation in advance with the remainder making all or some of their arrangements after arrival. Of the latter, two fifths went direct to a hotel or place of accommodation with a quarter phoning to make a booking. Friends or relations were also used by over a tenth to find accommodation. Victoria Tourist Information Centre was used by a tenth.

13.   Over four fifths were satisfied with their hotel with only a small number being very dissatisfied. The main reasons for dissatisfaction were price, standards generally, cleanliness and service.

14.   London was generally seen as being no more expensive than in 1989 although rather more thought that the range of services listed were more expensive than cheap. Buses and the Underground were perceived as giving the best value with hotels being seen as expensive by three quarters of those who expressed an opinion.

15.   A third considered that London generally did not have a litter problem with just under a fifth considering it a big problem. Compared to 1989, the opinions this year were much more favourable. Over a quarter felt that London streets had no problem with those saying it was a big problem down from a half to just over a quarter. Similar improvements were seen for the Underground trains and stations.

16.   London remains a friendly city with over three quarters expressing the view that Londoners were either fairly or very friendly.

17 Product development

The tourist product needs clear definition. It is a satisfying activity at a desired destination. This applies to all reasons for travel – business and pleasure. 'The quality of the experience is the product itself.'[1] Components of the product 'manufactured' by separate and often competing industries are the means to the end, principally transport, accommodation and catering. The chapter on the product dealt with the primary and support trades and services in some detail. It was clear that these trades although independently operated have close links; a degree of interdependence, which requires distributive and cooperative services and organisation. The key task of official tourist boards is to provide the destination cooperative marketing base, and as part of this role the focal point for consultation and technical liaison as the basis for product development.

Product development in tourism must be marketing orientated, since tourism is itself a demand or market force. The product market fit analysis and the task of formulating the market strategy provides the base for product development plans covering destination infrastructure and industry operation. But the marketers have a further function. Their activity should not only be the guiding force for the developing and investing interests. The marketers themselves can shape development. They can alter the product, and innovate and initiate new services and attractions. To an extent in tourism the package, and the brochure which describes it, is the product. So promotion itself can be the product. Certainly the task of product presentation is a vital marketing skill.

The marketing strategy embracing present needs and future growth should be formulated together with product development plans. Both will reflect the agreed policy, its selection of options and targets. In the case of most destinations, national and local, much infrastructure investment, in transport for example, will be planned either for general economic and industrial expansion or for other reasons (even social ones) not directly related to tourism. New transport investment, notably in roads, seaports and airports, are examples. But all new transport investment and new transport routes offer opportunities and create new traffic. Admittedly there may be traffic diversion from existing facilities.

The investment may not pay. But while the facility exists there is a new opportunity for marketers to exploit.

Plans must look at the existing situation, the present stock, the capacity and usage (occupancy rates and load factors), the known and realistically planned programme of expansion. There will be gaps and bottlenecks. In competitive industrialised countries it is unlikely that all trade sectors and service providers (public and private) will have planned simultaneous and linked expansion. Most tourism infrastructure investment requiring massive long term capital is made unevenly, and in large chunks. There is a tendency for massive over investment when some types of service or attraction become fashionable.

Investment decisions are not only uncoordinated in a competitive free trade economy but at times unrelated to a tourism market assessment. The problem is aggravated by the intervention of state monopolies (in transport, railways, and ports) where necessary expansion is held back for political reasons, and pressures on the national economy as a whole. Much investment will be for purposes other than the prosperity of the tourist business. Transport routes (sea ferries) may depend for half or more of their revenue on freight and manufacturing industry.

In this complex situation the marketer's role can be crucial. Marketing strategy will lead to marketing plans to secure agreed targets. The time scale should be adequate (three years or more) and the appraisal and annual review of performance against objectives will offer a continuing monitoring service for the planners.

Product market match analysis as the key to this continuing exercise must embrace a very detailed study and classification of resources – for all destinations and the service trades that support them.

Key features of the destination's resources, as we have seen in chapter 5, can be described as either natural or man made, the latter clearly capable of relatively easier and quicker alteration. On this foundation the destination will have a range of facilities and services. The third element most directly under the marketer's control lies in product innovation and presentation.

There will be an existing infrastructure and supply of services. There will also be opportunities for new investment, or indeed the creation of a new destination. The French in their vast Languedoc Rousillon Scheme, and the Mexicans at Cancun deliberately planned the creation of new resorts in undeveloped coastal areas, with a number of physical handicaps. The Mediterranean coast especially in Spain has seen massive resort development turning coastal regions and islands into built-up resort areas.

More usually, and now of course for these built-up Mediterranean areas, the planners and marketers start from an inherited infrastructure and existing capacity. Once built the infrastructure has a relatively long life and the options for change or redevelopment may be limited. In contrast traffic may be volatile; travel and leisure trends can alter rapidly. The old traditional nature of travel is vanishing. Furthermore the scale of the movement is enormous. International travel has grown by 300% in two decades; Europe's international tourism movement by 500% to 300 million visits annually. Thus speed is more for marketing initiatives than for capital investment. Build in a hurry and certainly repent at leisure, to paraphrase the adage. One must be certain that trends have been correctly identified and with them the outline of product development needs.

Speed of change in behaviour and currently accepted ways of social behaviour have come with such a revolutionary force that market research although itself a new profession is changing. And not before time. Developed in the immediate post war years when western society still demonstrated traditional traits, it became conservative, focusing on income groups as social groups, a technique which does not adequately reflect behaviour groups that are fundamentally important in tourism.

Until the 1960s security, the importance of saving, putting down roots, the home, were guiding objectives for most people in western societies. Tradition in morality and social behaviour was strong. The permissive society had not arrived to alter consumer behaviour. Change came quickly. Increase in wealth, in leisure time, communications, the falling away of economic and social constraints to behaviour had profound effects. Credit in all its forms altered thresholds of consumption and attitudes to price. Tourism and travel previously regarded as a luxury or non-essential, foreign travel formerly regarded as difficult, exclusive and expensive suddenly presented new, attractive and accessible images. These changes had much to contribute to the revolutionary growth in travel and leisure spending.

Eating out, frequent trips away from home, a willingness in business and the professions to travel and meet, put an end to the old concept, much promoted in the war, 'Is your journey really necessary?'. From a relatively locally based society whole communities became mobile, trips and outings escalated. As the GDP research indicates this mobility would seem to have no end as personal disposable incomes increase. New market segments of great potential purchasing power are emerging, notably senior citizens. One in four of western populations will be over sixty years of age by the end of the decade. They are healthier, wealthier and more mobile. The marketing control of product development for such fast growing segments will be fundamental.

In many ways the permissive society as a brand name is misleading. As one door opens another closes. The reality is that as social constraints and taboos change the old guard is replaced by the new. Old fears and anxieties disappear just as old needs are replaced by new desires. The end of the twentieth century, albeit free from war, is subject to urban violence, lack of courtesy, coarse behaviour and untidiness. There are racist movements which are themselves inconsiderate of those not following their dictates. Some of these changes can have an effect on tourism. Reception and welcome, even of what may be regarded as an old-fashioned kind, is important. Qualities in cultural presentation, in conservation, in presentation of the heritage are matters of great human importance. Tourism is of course theatrical in nature but it is also of mankind and a trade in people. Thus these considerations represent vital ingredients of the total product. Generally speaking technology and physical and economic resources are far ahead of the product and market development. There is a vast potential market with money and time looking for something to see and do. There may in fact be no new technological revolution to come for some time. But many discoveries remain to be developed. The lead must come from marketing and its guidance in product development and specific product manufacture. By and large the distribution and creative system is poor. In the domestic market, where there has been little success in Britain in recent years, less than 10% of total travel and tourism spend is directed through the retail travel trade. The major tour operators or wholesalers are almost totally engrossed in one domestic market, sending British people to the Mediterranean beaches.

The history of tourism expansion was very different. Thomas Cook started with his temperance train from Derby to Leicester, and developed a highly sophisticated world travel service, with its own new technology. This included manufacture not only of the package product but infrastructure services, Nile steamers, and in later years the link with Wagon Lits grew into a major transport service.

Polytechnic Travel and Sir Henry Lunn (linked to the Church of Scotland) had evident social and educational aims. The Workers Travel Association, sprang from the Workers Educational Association. Although the workers who responded were white-collar and with an intellectual bent, the venture, established as a cooperative, was very successful. Eventually, in addition to a chain of holiday centres in Britain, some large country mansions, and a fleet of motor coaches, the Association developed as a skilled European package tour operator.

The Holiday Fellowship was another social cooperative which established holiday centres throughout Britain at the end of the nineteenth century, continues with changing clientele and objectives to the present day. Tourism's early expansion owes much to the vigour of the voluntary organisations.

This cannot be said for many of the tourism and leisure groups, notably in what came to be called the social tourism field. There was in fact an association of social tourism organisations throughout Europe like the Workers Travel Association (the Reso in Sweden for example), many of which no longer exist because they did not adapt to changing needs and behaviour. But their existence and life history is instructive. A few examples only have been given. But there were many more: the touring clubs, at first bicycle-dominated, which became the motoring organisations, and revolutionised the provision of information guide books, signs and symbols (the AA star system classification). Their contribution to product innovation and impact on the distribution system (making it easy to buy or do) was profound. The Youth Hostels Association, the National Trust, the Ramblers Association, Boy Scouts and Girl Guides' organisations were all to the forefront of leisure travel. They responded to growing demand. They catered for their chosen segment and although the term was unknown, they acted as highly expert marketers, inventing and controlling products, in the brand name game, and where necessary manufacturing the product, not only packages, but investing in tourism infrastructure (accommodation and transport).

There are other important examples of market led product development. The most important is in the local government field. Long before nationalisation of industry was heard of, municipalisation or local government enterprise helped build the amazingly successful seaside and inland (spa) resorts. Britain and its railways led the way internationally in this massive expansion. The largest resorts in Europe were originally developed in Britain (Blackpool, Scarborough, Brighton, Hastings, etc). Piers, theatres, assembly rooms, spa and sporting facilities, promenades and festivals, entertainment and special events, were more often than not the enterprise of the municipality, and directly related to the publicity and entertainments officer, who was in fact the resort director and marketer. They were great people with outstanding skills. Apart from perfecting marketing tools such as the poster and brochure, still used today, they invented theatrical shows, festivals and special events, such as beauty competitions. The product was successfully controlled by the marketers on a fiercely competitive basis.

So much of the basic tourism marketing skills were developed in this first grand age of tourism, and some unfortunately forgotten. There are even earlier examples. The inland resorts grew up before the railways. Bath, which remains one of Britain's most famous and renowned historic towns, was built for tourism in the eighteenth century, and created by the country's first tourist director Beau Nash, in concert with a builder and property developer. But he made the expansion possible, by correctly identifying the market and designing the product for it. He was employed by private enterprise as manager of the Assembly Rooms, the centre of the resort's society, where he laid down a code of behaviour, mixed social classes in ways which made the new community possible, designed the entertainment and the provision of facilities to make it easy to buy, easy to enjoy and highly desirable to visit. He was one of the first marketers to introduce an accommodation classification system, again to assist the traveller in making his arrangements, and all on a highly efficient business basis.

In addition to the considerable range of public or voluntary organisations the classic free enterprise organisation, especially the transport organisations, were full of enterprise. Railways invented excursions and short holidays. The Dutch bulb field tours were pioneered by the LNER to improve occupancy of its Harwich–Hook service. London Transport organised a whole series of days out, and with the railways, walking trips with professional guides or leaders. Many of the bus companies built up successful touring companies operating in Britain and abroad.

There were many examples of product development from a marketing base when a demand or segment had been identified. Transport was often the originator or product innovator with its long history of profitable action to even out peaks and troughs and to improve load factors. This initiative continues today but generally on a lower scale.

There are many examples and monuments to product-orientated failure. In the changes of the 1960s and 1970s patronage of many traditional attractions changed or declined. Race course and cinema attendance declined drastically, many spectator sports, and other recreations altered. Traditional seaside resorts and their Victorian hotels and infrastructure declined, losing heart and confidence in their ability to adapt the product. Yet in most cases the decline did not reflect an absolute change in the market. An even greater potential existed. Resorts are meeting places and the need for personal and more frequent communication, and for new forms of entertainment, relaxation, health and pleasure is growing on an almost unimagined scale. But to exploit potential the old skills of identifying demands and market segments, and organisation of the marketing forces have been lacking.

There was a revolution in the pubs in England. The number and usage declined dramatically in the late 1950s and 1960s. Then there was a transformation in comfort and facilities with a general provision of attractive catering. Pub lunches became an appealing product across social classes. This too was a reflection of social change, patronage by women, higher income and higher standards. In tourism and leisure generally the widespread use of cars and car ownership and the effect of television in presenting consumers with a wide range of choice, never before so efficiently presented, has contributed to a revolution in demand. But production has lagged, mainly because of product orientation. Some examples have been given. The potential is almost unlimited, and certainly occupancy rates and load factors, off peaks and off season are now a reflection of marketing incapacity or failure to adapt product rather than lack of demand over a period of time.

The destination will have mature products and declining products. Market analysis will have highlighted emerging trends, and the plant or business structure needed to satisfy wants and needs. There will be peaks but more likely extensive and damaging off-peak troughs with little business offering.

Yet transport, accommodation and catering can service large numbers of people seeking many different benefits from the destination and drawn from a variety of markets. A diversified market is a strength and important in evening out peaks and troughs. The resort (the destination) has this special characteristic – that it can play host to a large visiting population, far greater than its resident population, and coming from a number of market segments and for many different reasons: business and pleasure, health, relaxation, education, sport or cultural pursuits. Few visitors to Britain choose the country's seaside resorts for hot sunny beaches. But this is no disadvantage. It has lessened the dependence on good weather. A majority of Britain's attractions and most services are indoor. Travel is increasingly a year round business and the marketers are exploiting new markets (notably senior citizens) with dramatic effect on their off-peak occupancies.

The destination and its component product partners have a series of options and a number of vital choices to make. They will or should have a plan and a longer term marketing strategy. They will have an existing infrastructure of services and products, a number of markets: some main markets, some in decline, some mature and stable and, most important of all, some emerging.

Much coastal development in Britain was unplanned (caravans and poorly built chalets). The short season and poor income generating power have been legacies for a number of resort areas. Change will be difficult and expensive. The attack on seasonality must be a priority and here the attraction of conferences and meetings of all kinds (face to face communication), trade fairs, sporting and cultural events can afford a basis for success. Specialist traffic and sporting and cultural attraction must be carefully planned and promoted, though each specialist appeal must be catered for separately. One man's addiction is another man's hate. Golfers may not mix with bird watchers. But resorts and resort areas are expert at making separate provision, while at the same time maintaining many components which are shared in common.

The attraction must be packaged or presented. Here the marketers are designing the product for current sales. Weekend breaks are often linked to a particular sport (tennis) or interest (music); a festival of music and the arts, an historic anniversary, a sporting event with competitions. This does not have to be on an international scale and can just as easily be among amateur teams from nearby counties. Senior citizen groups and many others look for an excuse to go away – for a change, for relaxation, for company, to 'live it up'. This segment is often undemanding in product terms – sightseeing, rest, service, welcome company, entertainment (bingo and old time dancing).

Business travel is capable of substantial traffic creation – for meetings, for training, for trade shows and special promotions, product launches or incentive travel. In this case however, there may be a substantial infrastructure cost. The destination must provide the plant and equipment, the meeting halls and show places, accommodation and services of a satisfactory standard. But once made the investment will be capable of creating business for many years to come.

It may be possible to find a double use for existing plants. In Britain the vast stock of university and education accommodation finds a ready if specialist market during the summer vacation months which in many areas is a peak demand period. Race courses little used over the year make good camping and caravan sites. The scale of such operations (the British Universities Accommodation Consortium handles a stock of 76,000 beds) makes a considerable impact on tourism movement in certain areas.

All destinations have some tourist potential, even if only visits to friends and relatives, and usually the traffic and revenues are larger than is recognised. Whatever traffic there may be is capable of responding to promotion and product development if the will is there to seek new business.

There are at least three main types of tourist destination from the point of view of tourism planning and marketing strategy. First, the destination where tourism is and always will be a by-product or a minority interest, for example the industrial town, the rural or natural area where the main business is agriculture or forestry.

In the second category destinations have substantial tourism potential but the visitor movement represents a junior economic partner, and even though profitable and important in scale it is not the main business of the place. Such destinations are often very prosperous centres and their diversified economy gives strength, stability and year round employment. Examples are large cities, historic towns, country towns and areas with a clear identity as tourist regions. Regions will offer scenic and heritage values, ethnic appeal including the cuisine, rest, relaxation and the pursuit of special hobbies, and can build up a powerful tourism following and revenues.

The third group, and in many ways the most challenging of the three, embraces the classic resort destination centre or region, where tourism is the main business of the place, notably seaside towns, inland centres and resort areas. In some cases destinations in the second group grow fast as visitor centres and effectively expand to the point where tourism is the main business of the place. Then the local and municipal role changes. The local authority representing the host has a special responsibility for inviting and receiving the guests, and planning and marketing the major asset which will determine future prosperity and the residents' livelihood.

There is no simple formula for classification. Most resorts at peak times find the visiting population far outnumbers the residents. It is a matter of degree and scale. The incidence of tourism or the density of proportion of visitors to residents identifies the development of the destination as a tourism resort. Resorts are extraordinary towns, and must be seen as such. They may decline and become ordinary, everyday, industrial or commercial centres with quite different marketing needs.

It is essential in policy making, marketing and related development to be clear about the status of any tourism centre and its objectives. Some destinations will not find market growth, some are in decline and can only be saved by substantial investment in product development and product relaunch. Some have a good future, but face the difficult task of identifying appropriate growth trends, selecting new traffic to be created, and then planning the new infrastructure, with its relatively long life, accordingly. This is a difficult and expert task.

The destination's growth will be determined through the marketing strategy to exploit selected markets and secure the new demand. A country area in the first or second category with a declining agriculture, may be able to sustain its population and increase per capita income through tourism, often a natural complement to rural economies. There is a historic link. Summer visitors were traditionally an important secondary resource in years gone by. The railways produced admirable guides to holiday accommodation, both serviced and self service, with the local station master an infallible source of expert information. New leisure centres, camping and caravan parks, forest and national parks with special visitor provision, self catering cottages, sporting and recreational facilities, and the scenery and heritage making up the local environment can lead to a build up of tourism revenues over a relatively long season far exceeding agricultural incomes.

Pony trekking is a now well developed and popular tourist product in Britain, especially in the remoter hill farming areas. This was first developed in the Scottish Highlands after the war. Ponies used for stag shooting parties over a very short season were not earning their keep in spring and early summer. Good market research and the identification of an important new trend led to rapid and successful product development creating new streams of profitable business.

Activity holidays, and participatory and spectator sports offer a year round range of holiday and leisure appeals in Britain and many other temperate climate countries. But the destination must have suitable natural resources, and be accessible. It will need to ensure adequate development of basic services and facilities for the selected activities and markets. It should have a clear identity. Visitors must be aware of its attractions (to anticipate the satisfaction) and find the total product easy to buy. So promotion and reservation services must be effective. Dr Johnson's famous tourism remark should be a warning. When asked if certain famous European sights were desirable (such as Paris) he said they were certainly worth seeing but not worth going to see. Villages and small towns can expand visitor services in rural areas when the visitor movement is exploited with many attendant benefits in transport services and amenities. The countryside and its cultural wealth in architecture and historic treasures will be conserved. But to achieve these benefits a destination marketing programme and the selection of appropriate markets is essential. Tourism is not homogeneous. There are country lovers and marketers must find them. There are gregarious people for whom the larger urban recreational centre is suited. Much of the recent Mediterranean coastal development offers a town environment by the sea suited to Europe's northern industrial city dwellers.

Large cities and industrial towns in industrialised countries are often in need of replacement trades. Old industries decline or die. City centre docklands become redundant. Inner city decay can be arrested and centres regenerated with help from tourism. But policies and plans and related marketing strategy must be clear, objectives assessed and expertly implemented.

It is easy to point the way ahead, but so often policies are linked to national and local politics, short term in nature and too rarely professionally targeted and appraised. Tourism is a trade, a vast confederation of business and commerce. Enormous investment, both public and private, is at stake. So clear objectives and target setting, and appraisals to check performance against objectives are essential for success. Many of Britain's resorts and much of the country's main holiday trade would not be in decline if such precepts had been followed in past years. Many industrial cities and towns will never become resorts. Their visitor potential is limited, and the product development for their markets highly specialised. The word tourism can be misleading, it denotes main summer holidays and above all foreign travel and package tours. These towns will not be in the main summer holiday market. However to an extent main summer holidays, in terms of one holiday away from home in the year in high summer, are becoming anachronistic. There are main holidays and secondary or shorter holidays. Business, specialist and social journeys are made increasingly all the year round.

Many industrial city centres in Britain and in other European countries have developed a successful tourism business which gives strong support to the economy. Business, conference and trade fair visitors are complemented by pleasure or specialist visitors using the city as a touring base, or attracted by the wealth of cultural (museums and art galleries for example) and sporting facilities. Many industrial towns have an attractive hinterland with scenic and heritage appeal. After a day's touring the sophisticated pleasures of a large city with shopping and other personal services can be appealing. One cannot after all eat the scenery. Sheffield with superb scenery, heritage properties and other facilities in the surrounding countryside (the Peak District and the Yorkshire Moors and Dales), was one of the first large cities to appreciate the potential in the 1960s. More recently Bradford has surprised the public by its successful efforts to attract visitors. But again this is due to the misunderstanding of the word 'tourism'. Bradford is in a specialist visitor field, with mainly short stays or day visits, and is not a summer main holiday resort in any way.

Tourism can have a powerful effect on inner city regeneration. Many of the decayed inner city dock areas in a number of countries have restored their visiting and residential population with a mixture of hotels, restaurants, shops and entertainment. Good examples can be seen in London, Bristol, Liverpool, in Copenhagen in Denmark, and in Baltimore and Boston in the USA. London's Covent Garden centre rejuvenated a disused vegetable market with its attractive architecture and is a fine case history.

Thus the larger city and many urban areas have good potential for visitor services. But their markets are several and specialist, and need both promotion and the creation of products suited to the specialist demands. Conferences and exhibitions have a great potential, for pleasure visitors as well as business. The vast range of specialist interests and hobbies offers great opportunity for marketing and product expansion. Furthermore pleasure meetings' traffic can complement business group trade which tends to die away in the summer when cities need visitors. The meetings and communication traffic, business and pleasure, needs a highly skilled form of marketing more akin to capital goods selling in manufacturing trade.

There is a growing serious side to specialist travel, making journeys and attending events to learn, to improve skills or knowledge. Market segmentation is intense, and the identification of demand and product not easy. But there is a special value in this form of traffic, which is often resilient to climate, price change or recession. Furthermore it has a strong brand loyalty, above average spending and enormous potential. Pleasures once found in one's own back yard are now sought in far distant places. City tourism is well suited to large resorts if they have or can adapt their infrastructure and product (meeting facilities). In Britain and northern Europe the cold water resorts and inland centres need product refurbishment and relaunch. Their main holiday appeal for families and activity holidays can be extended.

Most British resorts have good sporting facilities. They are natural centres for special events, festivals. They are in danger of losing confidence. The founding fathers and resort directors were brilliant impresarios, inventing appeals (products) such as baby shows, dog shows and beauty competitions. These can still be big business. Most resorts have an attactive hinterland of scenery, historic and cultural appeal. Sports can be the subject of competitions with amateur teams from nearby countries. Some sports are simple to organise but neglected. Walking for example was a traffic creating feature of London Transport and the railways before the war. Education and training for all ages are well suited to resort facilities. Many English south coast resorts have built up an important visitor movement of this kind. For many the English language is more magnetic than Spanish sunshine.

Harrogate is an example of resort regeneration after the war, and restoration of a most successful visitor movement from unpromising beginnings. Hotels had been requisitioned in the war. The Spa trade had finished. There was a lack of confidence in the dictum that it was the duty of the doctor to entertain the patient while nature effected the cure. Thanks to a small group of leaders and an active and consistent municipal authority, hotels and attractions were restored. Harrogate's appeal as a garden town set in scenically attractive countryside was strongly promoted. But the key to success was accurate identification of markets and product. There were three, business conventions and trade fairs, large meetings, and in the summer the establishment of the town as a touring base especially for private cars which were to grow fast, and an overnight coach stop for round Britain and other sightseeing tours. There were many doubts at the beginning and indeed some northern resorts never recovered as their traditional traffic moved south to the sun.

It must be emphasised that the cooler resorts can be highly competitive. Although things are changing thanks to good marketing research and planning, most sun resorts have a short season, a relatively primitive segmented and volatile traffic, and a trend to low spending. Bournemouth has a longer season and a more profitable business than Benidorm. Fifty per cent of British residents travelling abroad do not go to hot sunny beaches. But resorts need new investment, new product creation for new business, if fortunes are to be restored. This needs leadership not least at the local level.

The ETB reports an annual level of new investment in tourist facilities and attractions of over £1,000 million a year. This includes developments such as climate controlled leisure centres, theme parks, museums, speciality shopping, heritage and sporting attractions. However, much of this new development is not in the resort areas.

These examples deal with strategy and longer term growth. But marketing and product creation has a shorter term and practical role over a wide field. It is the business of the marketer to increase revenue, to improve length of stay, to look for marginal traffic to increase occupancy and load factors. There is an immense field of opportunity for product creation and presentation. It is often forgotten that the greater part of tourism including international tourism in Europe is not packaged. But the individual traveller needs DIY services especially in component packaging, to make it easy to plan, easy to go and hopefully with some of the price benefits of group purchase. There have been some outstanding successes. The BritRail Pass, the American Greyhound bus ticket (launched as a famous $90 for 90 days unlimited travel across the USA), the Eurail Pass, but Britain's bus services never captured the foreign market in the same way.

BTA introduced an Open To View ticket, a season ticket to visit historic properties covering both state and private ownership. Hotel groups successfully offered short and weekend breaks, some linked mini packages to rail or coach travel. The half price theatre ticket booth in Leicester Square has contributed much in marketing tickets unsold for the day of the performance, the Book A Bed Ahead service through local tourist information centres has put smaller establishments and Bed and Breakfast on the market.

There are many other examples but not enough. The field is wide open. Too often this innovative packaging and product creation is undertaken only when there is some surplus of service to be sold off. The approach should be more to exploit new markets and create new streams of traffic for future growth as a basic marketing endeavour.

Summary

The tourist product is a satisfying activity at a desired destination. Product development in tourism must be marketing orientated since tourism is itself a demand force. Marketers themselves can shape development.

Investment decisions are not only uncoordinated in a free trade economy but may be unrelated to a tourism market assessment. Much development, for example in transport, will be for purposes other than the prosperity of the tourist business. The marketer's role can be crucial. Product market match analysis is the key to market planning.

Change comes quickly now in consumer behaviour. This has contributed much to the revolutionary growth in travel and leisure spending.

Technology and the ability to develop economic resources rapidly and massively are far ahead of product and market development in tourism, although there may not be new technological revolution for some time to come. The lead must come from marketing and its influence on product development. Currently the distributive and creative system is inadequate.

Historically municipalities, transport and a range of institutions played a leading role in market led product expansion. The need for enterprise remains.

But there are many examples of product orientated failure. The destination and its product partners should have a tourism plan. There will be a number of options. There are declining markets, mature markets, growth and emerging markets. Seasonality is a priority. There are many segments and special appeals, eg business travel and double use of existing 'plant'. All destinations have some tourism prospects, but for some as a minor interest, some where tourism is a flourishing but junior partner in the local economy and some where tourism is the main business of the place.

Tourism can have a powerful effect on inner city regeneration. In addition to the search for longer term growth, marketing and product creation has a shorter term and practical role to increase revenues by raising load factors and occupancy of existing services.

Too often innovative packaging and product creation is undertaken only when there is some surplus of services. The approach should be more to exploit new markets for future growth.

Reference

1 Sir Peter Parker. *British Tourism – The Next 50 Years*. BTA 1979.

18 Product presentation

Product analysis enables the marketer to assess the strengths and weaknesses of the product. Market analysis, segmentation and research have identified consumer wants and needs. In order to sell the product it may well be necessary to make it easier for the consumer to buy. The product as it exists may well have consumer appeal but may not be marketable or it may not be cost effective to market it. The product may have limited appeal but needs to be represented, perhaps in association with similar products to make it more appealing, to give it more PR appeal or 'a better position on the supermarket shelf'. The tourism product is notoriously fragmented and individual units may find it impossible to market themselves effectively.

The travel trade – wholesalers and retailers – play an important role in marketing travel but generally have no allegiance to any one destination. A very few do specialise in a particular destination but they are nevertheless not responsible for promoting the destination. Most travel destination marketing is undertaken by government or semi-governmental bodies at national, regional and local levels. It may be a national statutory agency or a marketing bureau at local level; it may be that the organisation's only responsibility is marketing tourism or tourism may be just one of the functions which it carries out. For example, a director of marketing in a local authority may well be responsible for attracting industry to the area as well as tourists. It is these bodies which have responsibility for marketing the destination and this necessarily extends to product presentation which can take a number of forms. The extent to which the organisation needs to get involved in product presentation is very much linked to the sort of visitor which it attracts. An organisation responsible for marketing a destination which is heavily reliant on mass movement of packaged travellers, for example most Mediterranean resorts, will work with the tour operators. On the other hand if the destination is largely visited by independent travellers making their own purchases it will be much more essential for that organisation to engage in product presentation. Product presentation can mean:

(1) creating a marketing cooperative with central booking facility for independently owned products;
(2) presenting a collection of similar products to selected audiences for a specific purpose;

(3)   creating a range of packaging components so that the independent travellers can do it themselves, plan the trip benefiting from price advantages;
(4)   cooperating with similar attractions in the development of a thematic approach at local level;
(5)   translating consumer wishes into a bespoke tailored product based on a particular theme;
(6)   encouraging the creation of events, exhibitions, trails, to mark a particular anniversary;
(7)   developing theme years at national level;
(8)   literally presenting the product and enhancing interpretation.

Marketing cooperatives

A farmhouse in Jutland, France or Wales does not have the turnover necessary to provide a meaningful budget for marketing itself in overseas markets and may be limited to the local guide and 'word of mouth' in the home market. Moreover the farmer's wife would almost certainly not be able to deal in foreign currencies or carry on a correspondence in foreign languages. Similarly an operator of a canal narrow boat or a few cruisers on the river would not be in a position to undertake international marketing. Owners of bed and breakfast establishments have neither the budget nor the expertise. They have two alternatives – they can either put their product in the hands of an operator who will need allocations and commission and may not sell anyway, or they can join a marketing cooperative, which is usually (though not always) set up by the destination tourism organisation. The tourism organisation, having created the cooperative, may then with the members' consent hand over the selling to appointed general sales agents in various markets. The Scottish Tourist Board's 'Roamin' Holidays' was created for the independent motoring segment and offered to various specialist operators in key markets throughout the world. On the other hand, the Wales Tourist Board, having helped in the development of the farmhouse product with a grant scheme, having then trained farmers' wives, who attended specially designed courses at local polytechnic colleges in financial management and other techniques, then needed to set up a marketing cooperative and provide a central booking facility in one of the regional offices.

The Federation National de Gites Ruraux de France was established in 1955 under the joint patronage of the Secretary of State for Tourism and the Minister of Agriculture, together with the presidents of the Regional General Councils Assembly, the Association of 'Mairies' and chambers of agriculture and industry. Unlike the Welsh product it is self-catering accommodation as opposed to serviced accommodation, and living with the family in a Welsh farmhouse. Establishments are classified, members pay a joining fee and an annual membership fee and the regional offices of the organisation undertake the marketing and letting of the accommodation. 'Gites de France' fulfils three principal roles: as a development and advisory service at local level, a national network coordinating role and a letting agency. 'Gites de France' apart from its regional offices in France has offices in four major markets outside France – Denmark, The Netherlands, West Germany and the United Kingdom. Central booking facilities are provided for gites and some were computerised in 1987.

In Britain, UK Waterways Holidays was established by the British Waterways Board as a marketing organisation for selling holidays on narrow boats which operate on Britain's vast network of canals. These narrow boats are mainly independently owned. UK Waterways Holidays represents these individual operators as a collective at workshops, trade shows and the like and markets the product through overseas operators. In Spain there are the paradores, the government organised national chain.

The initiative in all these cases was taken by the destination tourism organisation or a statutory organisation, but this need not be so. Bed and breakfast is a uniquely British institution which has great appeal in overseas markets since it represents excellent value for money and affords an opportunity to meet with British people. Clearly it is not possible for these Bed and Breakfast establishments to market themselves effectively overseas as individual units and often difficult to reach the national market effectively. As a result of a clearly identified demand for the product, commercial organisations have taken on the marketing and letting of the properties. Wolsey Lodges is a consortium of 'up market' bed and breakfast establishments mainly in the south of England, while B&B (GB) has on its books bed and breakfast establishments throughout Britain. The latter offers a computerised booking service. All establishments are inspected and pay commission. Both organisations, and indeed UK Waterways Holidays too, have enjoyed BTA joint marketing scheme support.

Presenting similar products to selected audiences

In the case of marketing cooperatives, booking is channeled through the operator but in some cases it is simply a case of presenting similar products and encouraging referral business. BTA's 'Commended Country Hotels, Restaurants and Guesthouses' scheme falls into this category. Each property is anonymously inspected and assessed against stringent criteria. Most are privately owned, all are attractively furnished, immaculately maintained, serve food of the highest quality, and provide excellent service. They are judged to be excellent of their type and very largely appeal to the motoring visitor. They are, of course, uniquely British, many being old country houses of architectural and historical interest. BTA undertakes the marketing of Commended establishments through PR, print, exhibitions and at the British Travel Centre in London. Establishments are encouraged to work together with the travel trade, to undertake referral business among members and work with BTA in PR activity. In this case the 'Commendeds' as a group are targeted at the independent motorist, but the target audience may be the trade itself through familiarisation trips.

This is certainly the case with BTA's publication 'Historic Houses Open October through March'. The Operation Off Peak Campaign is designed to fill troughs whenever and wherever they occur and this is especially true of the period October to March. While hotels in many parts of the country stay open during these months, many of the facilities and attractions were closed. BTA suggested to the historic house owners that if they were prepared to open for groups by prior arrangement, specifying the days, size of group, minimum charge and so on, then BTA would be prepared to present the opportunity to hoteliers, coach operators and incoming handling agents who were developing off-season packages. This form of product presentation was designed in response to the seasonality challenge. The number prepared to open on this basis is now increasing.

Consumer building blocks

The leisure traveller increasingly is making independent arrangements geared to satisfying wants and needs in a fairly precise way. Motivation may well be self fulfilment but it may also be concerned with cost when the mini packages are attractively priced, such as off-peak products. Travel passes and bargain breaks are the bricks and mortar of the bespoke tailored package. This will undoubtedly become increasingly attractive to the sophisticated international traveller and the marketer will need to be skilled in presenting the package components in an attractive and easy to use way which allows the consumer to 'mix and match'.

Cooperating with similar attractions

The benefits of cooperating at a local level are twofold: the cost of marketing is shared between all the cooperating members and each member establishment promotes other establishments and provides referral business. The basis for cooperation can be geographical and attractions as diverse as an historic house and a butterfly farm can market together. It is preferable however for the attractions to be themed in some way. This is the case, for example, with 'The Defence of the Realm' campaign where over thirty heritage attractions in the south of England have cooperated in marketing themselves under a particular banner. The properties include ships such as HMS Victory, the Mary Rose and the Warrior, castles such as Carisbrooke, Porchester and Calshot, military and maritime museums, forts and fortifications, all dedicated to 'The Defence of the Realm'.

There are many other examples of cooperative marketing by similar attractions as a collective – The Grand Tour of Scotland and the Magnificent Seven, both of which are relatively small groups of historic houses, are but two examples.

Themed tours

Product presentation is designed to make individual products more appealing and to make it easy for the consumer to buy. This will usually need a fair amount of research into the particular theme, which may take the form of a literary heritage trail or an architectural heritage trail, a religious pilgrimage or simply an itinerary based on similar products – gardens, castles or historic houses. Thus they may be specific – The Robert Burns heritage trail or romanesque architecture, or general – gardens of Scotland, festival of Welsh castles. These trails are itineraries which pick up key sites associated with a famous person, a style or attraction.

Avis, with their computerised personalised itineraries for their car rental clients, have taken this a stage further inasmuch as they have identified key special interests and developed a number of geographical itineraries for each special interest. Thus a visitor from Nevada can book his car before departure and pick it up at London's Heathrow together with his personalised itinerary. This itinerary was prescribed by the visitor at the time of booking and he may for example have asked for a tour based on the gardens of south and south-west England. Generally the national tourist office or regional tourist board will have identified key interests and developed a specific piece of literature designed to appeal to a particular special interest group.

Theme years and anniversaries

These may be specific, eg the novocentenary of the Tower of London or the tercentenary of William and Mary, the Australian bicentennial of 1988 or the American bicentennial of 1976. In the case of the latter,

BTA's research resulted in a gazetteer of places with American associations in Britain, itineraries, a list of famous Americans of British extraction, as well as a list of events to mark the anniversary.

In deciding on a theme year it is very important to decide on a theme which will have wide appeal. The William and Mary anniversary was only relevant in the Benelux markets, the Australian bicentennial in Australia. Christian heritage, while taking in a much wider diaspora, nevertheless is irrelevant in certain markets. Britain's theme year for 1984 – 'Heritage '84' – was designed to have maximum worldwide appeal, drew on the three major appeals for overseas visitors, viz. countryside, history and culture, the British people. It was multifaceted and benefited from a rich crop of anniversaries that year.

Themes and anniversaries are the subject of the next chapter but there is another dimension to product presentation which is becoming increasingly popular – the wide selection of attractions which now offer living heritage and visitor interpretation facilities.

Enhancing interpretation of the product

At Kentwell Hall in England, Mr and Mrs Phillips decided to set up an historical recreation, and to research everything down to the last detail. The Hall now has all the domestic areas working, the hierarchy within the household, all the outbuildings working, as well as the grounds. They now have almost 400 people taking part in the recreation over a period of three weeks. There are hay-makers, carpenters and forge workers. The bakery is working and the dairy produces butter and cheese. They also recreate Tudor banquets, putting on authentic meals set out correctly with the correct courses.

The North of England Open Air Museum at Beamish shows northern life at the turn of the century with period shops, a Victorian pub with stables, a printer's workshop and tea rooms plus an electric tramway and home farm. Wigan Pier in Lancashire, England, features live interpretation of local life and industry circa 1900, with Victorian schoolroom, bereavement in a miner's cottage and a suffragette.

At the Jorvik Centre in York the visitor steps aboard a time car and is whisked back through the centuries on a journey to real life Viking Britain with a market, wharf and dark smoky houses – all recreated in accurate detail featuring sounds and smells too.

At Chatterley Whitfield Mining Museum the visitor can experience the miner's life, just as he can at the Big Pit, Blaenavon, Wales, where he can go down a mine in an original cage.

These are important developments in showing off the basic permanent attractions of environment, heritage or culture. But some are capital intensive and many in Britain and abroad have substantial state financing, partly for tourism benefits but also for cultural, conservation or other national purposes.

The Jorvik Viking presentation in York is a case in point where substantial government funds were supplemented by city and other institutional support. There is an almost unlimited field for experiment and investment in finding new ways of presenting basic visitor attractions. The basic idea of interpretation, an American concept designed to show off tourist assets in a realistic and entertaining way, has a long way to go. The inventor of the interpretation principles, much distorted in practice in other countries including Britain, was 'to make people happy'. Interpretation centres should be cheerful places dispensing information and education with entertainment. There are still too many which feature stuffed owls and static displays of flora and fauna of the locality. Yet, this is an age of communication with new techniques that make presentation a highly popular art, with audio visual capabilities which make reality look inferior. Disney World has shown what can be done in theme parks where the artificial has to recreate history. In Britain and Europe generally there is no need to 'make believe'. The reality is the appeal in all its rich attraction.

Nearly 80% of Britain's overseas visitors visit historic buildings of one sort or another, but visitors are becoming more discerning. It is often no longer enough to have a holiday. One must learn something or at least appreciate something when on holiday. One of the most recondite cultural vacations available in the USA recently was a 27-day Plantagenet tour of medieval England and France.

For most visitors to historic houses the most important single reason for visiting is the human aspects of the house, seeing how people live or lived. This, for visitors, is as fascinating, if not more fascinating, than the physical aspects. The attention to detail at the Paul Revere House in Boston and at Mount Vernon suggests that the occupants have just left the room – in the dining-room there is food left on the plate, glasses of unfinished drinks, dying log fires in the grates. The US National Trust presents the rooms at Woodlawn in a similar way and there is no doubt that such touches bring the room to life.

Warwick Castle in England and the Royalty and Railways exhibition in Windsor, both devised by Tussaud's, demonstrate their own special skills in the recreation of tableaux of things as they well might have been. At Warwick Castle there is a group in the music room, another in the library, the Countess of Warwick being dressed for dinner, a valet drawing a bath. At Windsor it is even more ambitious – a royal train, horses and carriages, a guard of honour, and the attention to detail is remarkable – the royal children being restrained, the tail of a coat caught up, the groups of royal personages, the baggage being unloaded. It is a frozen moment of history, brilliantly executed by Tussaud's craftsmen. Taking interpretation to these extremes should be left to the craftsmen, but the lived-in feeling can be achieved without the wax-works. At Chartwell the brushes and the palette, the unfinished painting on the easel, suggest that Winston Churchill has just slipped out for a moment. The tennis museum at Wimbledon uses background noises – the unmistakable sounds of racket meeting ball and a match in progress. The sound of a croquet mallet hitting a ball overhead through the open French windows of a drawing-room enhances the experience, explains the place and makes it relevant to the visitor. The first requirement is visitor orientation and this can be achieved in a variety of ways – maps, print, graphic displays, audio visual programmes and increasingly time cars which whisk the visitor back through time – a technique used at Jorvik and at Oxford. Orientation ensures that the visitor does not proceed to the next stage cold. Travel and tourism is theatre and like theatre the attractions need to be stage managed. Marketing is basically about seeing things through the eyes of the consumer. Houses and attractions too must be market orientated rather than product orientated. As Sir Peter Parker said in the 'Come to Britain' Golden Jubilee lecture on 26 November 1979, 'more people are discovering the art of the new possible'. That is certainly true of the exciting new skills in the field of interpretation. Yet in many ways the market is ahead of the trade.

New ventures that demonstrate product presentation at its best are capable of almost immediate and often mass support. There is much to be done though – music and drama, pageants at historic properties for example. The National Trust in Britain in recent years has shown great entrepreneurial skill in mounting pageants, concerts and *fêtes champêtres* in appropriate properties. Bath has presented Roman nights (and banquets) in their famous hot water Roman baths. Increasingly visitors want more than just sightseeing, they must be involved.

Summary

Product presentation takes a variety of forms but all stemming from the creativity of the marketer of the special skills which he can call on and coordinate. At one end of the spectrum product presentation is concerned with making it easy for the consumer to buy through marketing cooperatives and central booking facilities, or creating a range of components which the purchaser can build into a bespoke tailored package. At the other end of the spectrum it is concerned with enhancing the visitor experience through interpretation, which is becoming increasingly exciting and benefiting from the leaps in technological advancement. In this whole field the market is ahead of the trade.

19 Themes and anniversaries

Festivals, commemorations, anniversaries and special events are all basic material for tourism. They provide the essential attraction at the destination, the activity and the desired satisfaction which makes the visit worthwhile, or indeed provides the reason for the choice of the destination and often an excuse for making the trip.

Mr George Camacho in a special study and report for the BTA in 1978/79[1] wrote: 'the celebration of anniversaries would seem to be almost instinctive in mankind. There is no community even at a low level of civilisation, which does not or has not done so; all that is necessary is a calendar. Incas and Aztecs, Burmese and Indonesians, Arabs and Europeans – in fact every nation and people in the world salute the past, honour the great and glory in doing so.' Mr Camacho studied also some special events such as the International Gathering of the Clans in Scotland in 1977, the Malvern Festival with its links with Shaw and Elgar and the Edinburgh Military Tattoo. These events are not linked directly to an anniversary but many are or have become annual happenings of significance, and the same considerations apply to them as to the celebration of an anniversary.

The distinguishing features of these kind of events and tourism attractions are that they are special, limited in time, requiring professional treatment in planning, promotion, organising and operating.

Special occasions can attract large numbers of visitors. The town or resort must play host in a special way calling on all its resources, talents and reserves. Special provision and investment may be needed for major occasions such as national exhibitions or international 'expositions', the Olympic Games or unique presentations of cultural artistic or religious occasions (festivals of the arts and music: for example Salzburg, Edinburgh or the passion plays of Oberammergau).

An interesting study in 'Tourism Management'[2] examined the Summer Olympic Tourism Market. The authors' purpose was to diagnose 'why the recent Olympic Host cities were not successful in generating the expected number of tourists during the games, and to recommend possible alternative strategies for attracting a larger number of tourists'.

The following table in the report indicates the order of magnitude of the visitor traffic.

Olympic tourists for the last six summer games

Year	City	Expected	Actual
1964	Tokyo	130,000	70,000
1968	Mexico	200,000	not found
1972	Munich	1,800,00	not found
1976	Montreal	1,500,000	not found
1980	Moscow	30,000–300,000	30,000
1984	Los Angeles	625,000	400,000

Sources: The Organising Committees for the Games and others.

The effect of the 1976 Montreal Olympic Games upon tourism spending was assessed to be between $77 and $135 million. The value added out of town tourist expenditure during the Los Angeles Games was $417 million or 38.1% of the total of such spending.

The authors point out that 'two kinds of tourist visited Olympic Games host cities. One was the usual tourist, primarily interested in the host country and its culture, or in business not directly related to the Olympic events. The other was the sports enthusiast with great interest in the Olympic events. The sports enthusiasts were less affluent than the usual tourists and not big spenders.' In 1964, the year of the Tokyo Olympics, visitors to Japan actually decreased compared with the previous year.

Special Events

The authors conclude that the Olympic Games should be recognised as an investment for the future and an image building event rather than a profit generating opportunity.

In spite of their great importance for the town or resort, and for the creation of tourism income and goodwill, special events are often badly managed, poorly promoted and inadequately presented with a resultant loss of tourism impact and revenue. Loss is compounded since in many cases the benefits are greater in the long term than during the relatively brief period of the event itself. Infrastructure (roads, parks, gardens, sporting and meeting and cultural facilities) may remain, reputation and goodwill too, which can be the basis for great expansion in future traffic and revenues. These substantial gains can be jeopardised by mismanagement though, and revenues much reduced and inadequate to fund future events.

Mr Camacho referred to some of the reasons for disappointment:

Not a few of those involved in the commemoration of anniversaries were primarily interested in cultural aspects, archaeological and historical, literary and aesthetic, or alternatively had as their only purpose the honouring of the memory of a great man or woman . . . Those active in such commemorations mainly for cultural or pietistic reasons might overlook the stimulus to tourism and the practical benefits which a town or city, locality or country, or indeed the nation as a whole, might derive from their activities. Almost . . . it might be thought unworthy to commercialise the event, consciously to attract tourists from at home and abroad, and purposefully to seek the means of recouping the money expended, by charging for admission to performances and gatherings and by the sales of souvenirs, books and programmes.[3]

Times have changed, but necessary improvement and the adoption of a professional tourist approach is still often lacking. Amateurism, intervention of political influences, especially if public funding is needed, and on the cultural side a lack of management and tourism marketing skills can prove very damaging. Of course the artistic director has a key role, but so also has the professional (Festival) manager and the tourism marketers, who will need the active support of the destination marketing agencies (the national and local tourist boards). The most common mistake is to leave marketing plans to the last, and inadequate time will mean poor returns. Marketing time scales are as long as the production cycle.

There is a wide range of specialist attractions, some very large, organised for limited periods, and thus concentrating on adding quality and appeal which highlight the destinations' resources, amenities and appeal. They are the very stuff of tourism. Shakespeare's words 'All the world's a stage and all the men and women merely players' apply particularly, for tourism is essentially theatrical. So much of the appeal of international travel is to see strange and new and foreign places, which through talented and artistic product presentation have a romance and even glamour reaching far beyond the reality of ordinary everyday places.

Principal specialist attractions come within the following categories:

Festivals

These are special celebrations for a limited period, usually featuring music and the arts, but may cover almost any aspect of leisure, for example food and drink. Recently international and national garden festivals have become popular. Many of these are major developments requiring years of planning, substantial investment and normally public support. The International Garden Festival in Liverpool in 1984 required a public financed investment of over £20 million, a fully staffed organisation working for two years prior to the event, and attracted over 3.3 million visitors and a revenue of £6.1 million (not including admission costs).

Anniversaries and events

These may be annual but are more often planned on a single and unique event basis. There are however a number of annual commemorations, and these can have a special value for the destination's promotion.

Special events take many forms, including expositions and major nationally organised events, such as the Vancouver Expo in 1986 or the Brisbane Expo in 1988.

HM the Queen's Silver Jubilee in 1977 provided an occasion for tourism promotion in a number of new fields. In practice the great interest overseas, especially in English speaking countries, and the need to provide information and guidance on 'what's on' provided a much needed focal point for information and visitor reception. The tourist organisations were in fact the first to produce a national calendar of events, whereas the organisers in government departments were concerned with security, official events, leaving the celebrations on the ground to local initiative. But there must be a coordinator, a focal point if tourism and marketing is to play a constructive role. Furthermore, where there is a massive public interest and demand it cannot be ignored or uncatered for without limiting or indeed reducing the significance of the event.

1991 marked the 500th anniversary of the birth of Henry VIII, one of England's most colourful monarchs, best known for his six marriages and his break with the Church of Rome. He was also, however, a wise and able ruler and father of Queen Elizabeth I. There are many places and existing properties in England associated with Henry VIII and a number of events were created to mark the anniversary. These included a river pageant; special exhibitions at the National Maritime Museum, Greenwich (where Henry was born) and at Hampton Court Palace (which Henry acquired from Cardinal Wolsey); themed events during the annual Greenwich Festival, and Tudor banquets. BTA undertook research into Henry's reign as well as into places associated with him throughout the country and produced a Fact Sheet in September 1990 to provide guidance for staff at home and overseas. The Overseas Press office wrote features which got wide distribution and publication in the world's media and BTA persuaded Tudor Photographic to sponsor a publication to mark the anniversary

International anniversaries and events are more difficult to organise, present and sell, unless they are regular occurrences such as the Olympics, or the World Cup and other leading sporting events. Some have been worthy, but generally the unique occasions, the 'one offs', could have been, and indeed often deserved to be, more successful. Two examples can be instructively examined, European Architectural Heritage Year 1976 and European Music Year 1985, both Council of Europe sponsored. The architectural event, closely connected with the cultural heritage, also enjoyed EEC help. Britain played a very active part, Countess Spencer leading a distinguished team for the architectural event, and the Duke of Kent chairing the Music Year committee. Both 'years' were instructive for their weaknesses and successes. They had impact and encouraged substantial initiatives and provided some continuing benefits not least in the tourism field. Architectural Heritage Year saw the publication of a unique study by experts on redevelopment of Britain's seaside resorts and spa towns, badly needing a restoration of confidence, and a reminder of their architectural and environmental heritage and treasures. Buxton, one of the case towns, took the message seriously and embarked upon a major programme of restoration and improvements, including the rebuilding of their famous opera house, and from this an annual festival was developed. A minor exercise – the Festival of Villages – had much significance in encouraging villages, which in the English countryside in particular have outstanding heritage attractions, to organise 'at home' weeks for visitors, embracing fetes, handicrafts, signposting, pageants, flower festivals, mini music festivals, open house (and teas). Surprisingly many new ways of greeting visitors were discovered or rediscovered, funds were raised for local charities, and for the visitor a unique welcome and something to see and do in the countryside. The ideas have developed, and although there is a long way to go the invention has been successfully launched.

European Music Year, celebrating the Bicentenary of Handel, Bach and Scarlatti, led to the introduction of a number of outstanding concerts, the creation of a baroque orchestra, the stimulation of youth orchestras and players, and substantial publicity for music events at the national level, and with the help of the European Travel Commission at the international level.

Both events, and notably European Music Year, suffered from inadequate planning time, relatively late incursion of the tourism interest, very limited international and national sponsoring finance, but above all at the international level, weak leadership and coordination, and the assumption that action and responsibility could be left basically to the national or local levels. This cannot work in tourism without strong central leadership and encouragement, and an active focal point for the stimulation of cooperative marketing. The ideas were good and important, but the professional approach in management and marketing was too often lacking in the case of many unique events.

The American Bicentennial Celebrations in 1976 stimulated much interest in the USA in 'roots', heritage institutions and properties, but had little effect on international tourism. The results in traffic terms were very localised.

Exhibitions

These are common in the field of culture and the arts. They can be large and create a major tourism impact, for example the Tutankhamun Exhibition in London in 1972 was open for six months and was visited by 1½ million people from Britain and all over the world. They include military tattoos or displays, pageants (usually depicting local or national history), religious events (passion plays) and sporting events, marathon races in large cities attract thousands of spectators and participants; the Oxford and Cambridge boat race on the Thames; the London to Brighton veteran car rally, which was invented by an hotel company (Gordon Hotels) as an off season promotion following the successful launch of the Monte Carlo car rally, where the company had major hotel investment also; the Blackpool Illuminations creating a large off season visitor movement each autumn estimated at eight million visits over just nine weeks.

It can be seen from this short list that the opportunities are limitless. The skills of the marketer and tourist impresarios can always find new traffic sources, but the investment needs a cooperative destination, trade investment and enthusiastic backing.

Themes

They represent a story line or framework to highlight a particular attraction at a destination, or more often in connection with a festival or anniversary. They can be launched on a regional or national basis to embrace a number of attractions or events, to pull together the appeals of many separate tourism assets, but this is more difficult. BTA's Heritage Year 1984 or 'Heritage '84' is a good example of how to do it, avoiding a common error of treating the theme as a purely promotional device and ignoring the essential need to present a product which is accessible and easy to buy. Promoters need to bear in mind that the promotion must be, or embrace, the product. A campaign without it stops at the point where nothing remains to be done except to do it. The prospective visitor must be able to envisage the product and to buy it (reservations at Festivals and clear information as to what is on, what there is to see). The promise offered in the promotion must be delivered.

Themes can be modest. Hotels create theme events, such as an Italian week, with food, decor and entertainment given a particular Italian slant. In past years with government support British weeks and events were organised abroad (in the USA and European countries in particular) to promote trade. Tourism often contributed the major part of the background, the scene setting, posters, entertainers (folk music and dance) and even the setting up of a temporary British pub. BTA sent the first red London buses to the USA for such an event. They were a great success.

Often anniversaries themselves provided the theme. Examples of this were the tercentenary of the sailing of the Mayflower which gave a 'roots' basis for the year's American visitor promotion and reception arrangements. The American Bicentennial in 1976 was successful in providing a theme of 'roots' and heritage. An American Heritage trail was organised in Britain, one of the first of the new forms of historic and cultural itineraries with supporting information and reception arrangements. The Novocentenary of the Tower of London in 1978 provided an important theme as a basis for promotion and product presentation, including the introduction of a Norman heritage trail as a feature of the general Norman heritage theme. As a by-product the anniversary provided an opportunity for the Tower authorities to introduce a wider and more imaginative range of souvenirs, including articles of a superior quality. This indicates the lasting benefits that can come from professionally planned events.

The special forms of tourist attraction will usually have lasting benefits, often much greater than the immediate return. Many represent substantial investment and aim to attract large numbers of people and correspondingly high revenue. They are undoubtedly in most cases prime tourist attractions offering major marketing benefits short and long term for the destination. But most do not live up to the expectations of success. As a general rule they attract local residents, domestic visitors mainly from the neighbourhood. They may divert tourist traffic and substitute short-stay low-spending visits for higher revenue trade. The reasons for this, generally management failures, are many, usually inadequate planning and too short a lead time for marketing. Mr Camacho suggests that the John Bunyan tercentenary celebrations (Pilgrim's Progress) at Bedford 1978 could have had its potential more fully exploited especially overseas if planning had started earlier. The Anniversary Committee was not set up until 1977, the previous year. For major unique events, which have not been held before, two years at least and preferably three should be the time scale, and marketing in the broadest sense the base for planning and preparation. This is another common cause of weakness in results. The organisers are often totally product orientated. They wish to create the perfect event, pleasing to the experts and specialists, letting the visitors in somewhat reluctantly for their money. But tourists are 'ignorant' in the nicest possible way, often of the event, the history, the background and even the geography of the destination. There is an elaborate process of communication with far away populations, quite apart from foreign languages. Prospective visitors have different time scales. They need professional help, travel agents, counsellors and tour packages.

The following extracts are based on extensive experience. The first provides some points to bear in mind in preparing a practical guide or plan for organising an anniversary, festival or special event, included in Mr Camacho's report 'Festivals, Commemorations and Anniversaries', BTA 1979.

The second is from a paper given by Alan Jefferson to the Heritage Conference at Oxford in 1983, attended by the principal owners and guardians of Britain's and Europe's historic properties, and explains the anatomy of the major national campaign, 'Heritage '84', led by BTA, the tourist boards in Britain and the key local authority and trade interests (the Travel Association's Consultative Council).

Mr Camacho wrote

> It may be helpful to attempt a summary of all the aspects of festivals and commemorative celebrations I have tried to cover in the foregoing sections. I will try to make this summary in such a way as to constitute a memorandum of points to bear in mind, which may serve as a practical guide. Not all the items will be applicable to all festivals and this memorandum should not be regarded as a comprehensive compendium or as definitive and mandatory instructions..For my part I shall be satisfied if it serves to alert people as to possibilities and warn them as to dangers.

(a) Form small initial group for early discussion and making provisional outline of project

(b) Consult local Regional Tourist Board and Local Authorities

(c) Form official Management Committee and ensure membership includes necessary skills in law, finance and insurance and representatives of appropriate sections of community. Consider possibility superior Council to determine policy and/or patrons of substantial local or national stature. Consider how work can be divided and decision-making efficiency improved by formation of sub-committees.

(d) Consider possible sources of funds from private donations, grants or guarantees from commercial and industrial communities, Local Authorities, official tourist bodies, Arts Council of Great Britain etc. In the light of plans made estimate total expenditure and sum to be recouped, ie nett cost.

(e) Make plans for nature, scale and length of celebrations which may have to be modified in the light of financial and other support which can be reasonably expected. Relate plans to availability of halls, theatres, weather expectation, hotel accommodation, catering and transport facilities, etc.

(f) Consider whether project justifies or needs engagement of professionals for artistic direction, management, performances, publicity, public relations, etc.

(g) Consider whether the cultural and artistic element of the celebration justifies applying for financial support from the Arts Council of Great Britain, or, alternatively, from the Scottish, Welsh or Northern Ireland Arts Councils, or one of the regional Arts Associations.

(h) Consider whether the benefit to the public justifies application for registration as a charity with consequent tax advantages particularly when continuing existence envisaged.

(i) Consider whether scale and nature of operations contemplated suggest formation of company incorporated with limited liability.

(j) Make certain there is adequate insurance against accident and other risks.

(k) Begin promotional publicity early: leaflets, posters, brochures, etc., and ensure their useful and appropriate distribution. Seek publicity from media. Consult official tourist bodies. Is any area at home or abroad likely to have special interest? Bear in mind that foreign tourists alone will not guarantee success; visits from within a country will form the basis of success and financial support. Consider advisability of allocation of block bookings to travel agents, coach operators etc., and encouragement of package tours. Leaflet to contain information re hotels, restaurants, transport facilities, etc. Adopt symbol or emblem.

(l) Consider advisability of attracting associated events.

(m) Explore all means of recouping expenses, including sale of brochures and programmes and advertising space, admission charges, bar and catering and souvenirs.

(n) Consultation with police and motoring organisations.

This is a formidable and almost forbidding list of things to be borne in mind and carried out. But all over the country, every year, many people are doing just that; and in the main they achieve considerable success.[4]

For 'Heritage '84' an industry working party was established two years in advance, chaired by Alan Jefferson, BTA's Director of Marketing, to suggest a theme for 1984:

> The first point of reference was to look at the major appeals of Britain as a destination for overseas visitors. They are basically three: the British countryside; the opportunity to meet with the British people, and the history, culture and traditions of Britain. Ideally, we needed to come up with a theme which embraced all three. We then looked back at our history and especially at the anniversaries which were due to fall in 1984, and we found to our delight that '84 seems to have been a vintage year over the centuries.
> 'Heritage '84', if we could develop it into a great celebration, was something which could potentially embrace all three appeals. We have been extravagantly endowed with heritage product, and the heritage product is spread throughout the country, so it would also help our regional spread objectives. The natural beauty of the countryside is enhanced by the wealth of historical places within it, the castles and stately homes, the gardens, the cathedrals and abbeys, places associated with great men and women down the ages.
> In many of our overseas markets, Britain has influenced social values, struc-

tures and institutions. Parliamentary democracy, the legal and educational systems, the industrial revolution, language and literature, international sport – all have their roots in Britain. Of course, we have been promoting these appeals over the years – we would have been fools not to, but 'Heritage '84' provided several new dimensions. First, and foremost, it provided us with an opportunity for a representation of the appeals, a sharper focusing of the many facets of British heritage.

The product is the foundation of the marketing programme, and product development and product presentation, in an exciting and appealing way, are essential ingredients in the marketing mix.

Secondly, it provided an opportunity for all those organisations concerned with the incoming business to cooperate in marketing the theme. The synergistic potential of such a marketing cooperative would be formidable indeed.

'Heritage '84' seems to have grabbed the imagination, it has been seized as an opportunity up and down the country and the new products and the represented products which are coming on stream are legion: the Trinity Trust is developing Christian Heritage which will run from May; the RIBA is organising a Festival of Architecture. The Institute of Building, the Structural Engineers and Civil Engineers, celebrating anniversaries in 1984, will play their part too, in polishing and presenting the architectural facet. The Wales Tourist Board is embracing industrial archaeology and castles, and has decided to adopt heritage as the theme for domestic marketing too, the Northern Ireland Tourist Board similarly and they will concentrate on Christian heritage, the musical heritage and the Ulster American Connections. The Scottish Tourist Board is concentrating on literary and sporting heritage but will develop other themes such as a fishing heritage trail. The English Tourist Board will be promoting 'A Celebration of English Gardens' and Maritime England. But it's not just the national tourist boards who are involving themselves. Regions, areas, cities, towns and resorts have enthusiastically taken up the challenge.

The benefits of this great promotion will only accrue to those who are prepared to work at providing something special. We have produced guidelines and checklists to help in product planning and marketing, we have a PR coordinator who is bursting with ideas. We can help, we can advise and we can promote, but the promise offered in the promotion must be fulfilled with product on the ground when the overseas visitors arrive. A special exhibition, jousting, soirees, fetes, recitals, poetry readings, trails, restorations – all commend themselves.

But no matter how good the product is, unless it is communicated in the marketplace, it will fail. BTA's marketing programmes for 1984 are totally committed to the heritage theme. British Airways, British Rail, the British Incoming Tour Operators' Association, the hoteliers and the travel trade will all be marketing 'Heritage '84'. In our advertising, our print and public relations activities, it will be paramount. A great deal is already underway – editorial is appearing now in the marketplace, television films are being made for showing overseas this winter. Plans are being developed for merchandising – souvenirs and gifts, banners and balloons, T-shirts and tea-trays.

From the point of arrival our overseas visitors will be aware – both British Airports Authority and Sealink will have 'Heritage '84' banners in the baggage arrival halls. When they leave they will find souvenirs in the airport shops and special promotions in the duty free shops. We have been extravagantly endowed and we should be proud to celebrate our heritage, to share our heritage with our overseas guests.

The need for a theme was advanced in 1982 when Britain was experiencing a down turn in incoming visits and a significant increase in outgoing. In the event 1984 visits at 13.6 million were over nine per cent higher than 1983, and this growth continued into 1985 when the heritage theme was extended into a second year. Many of the events created for 1984 have become handy arrivals, trails have continued to flourish, 'heritage' has almost become a word in the German vocabulary and in 1985 Canada had 'Heritage 1985'. A good illustration of the oak from acorn is a television series made by Saarlandischer Rundfunk. In 1984 BTA's PR manager in Frankfurt persuaded this TV company to make a film on the heritage theme. That one film has become a series 'Reisewege zur Kunst' and to date over 30 such films have been made. Avis launched 'Personally Yours' in support of 'Heritage '84'. These computerised personalised itineraries still flourish in Britain and the concept has been extended by them to many other countries.

European Tourism Year

This was a classic example of how not to do it. It was in December 1988 that Tourism Ministers of the twelve EC countries designated 1990 European Tourism Year. In international tourism marketing one is working at least twelve months ahead in developing and distributing the print programme, which has to be published in many languages, so even if events could have been created in the short time scale the opportunities for promoting these events were extremely limited. So far as the Ministers were concerned, the objectives of the year were: to encourage greater understanding of the lifestyle and culture of other EC countries as a way of preparing residents for the changes that will come after 1992, when the Community becomes 'one large space without frontiers' and to demonstrate the importance of tourism to the economy of Europe. Several specific objectives were set, including seasonality, regionality, economic, educational and co-operation. A special European Tourism Year (ETY) logo was commissioned. In the event the final version of this logo was not available until half way through 1989.

It was decided to launch Britain's contribution to ETY in May 1989 at a ceremony in London. Fortunately a number of 1990 events were at an advanced stage of planning. When ETY was announced, Glasgow had a coup on its hands inasmuch as it had already been selected by the EC as 'European City of Culture 1990'. It had a two year start in planning a mammoth arts and entertainment festival with over 1,500 events. A new international concert hall was being built and negotiations were well advanced with a wide variety of orchestras, opera, ballet and drama companies. A National Garden Festival was planned for Gateshead in the North of England, which would run from May through October. 1990 marked the centenary of the birth of Agatha Christie and BTA had already been in discussion with Torbay, where she lived, to mark the anniversary with a festival designated 'Mystery on the English Riviera'. Highlights of the festival included a series of plays and films based on thrillers by Agatha Christie, the world Cluedo championships, the Crime Writers' Convention, the arrival of the Orient Express filled with celebrities who would participate in a gala night, murder and mystery weekends. In short the Agatha Christie centenary was simply the peg for a festival encompassing the whole genre of mystery and detective stories. 1990 was also the centenary of the Forth Bridge, the 150th anniversary of the birth of the novelist Thomas Hardy, and a few less important events. The EC announced that grants of up to forty per cent would be available for ETY activities approved by the European Commission, but applications had to be made through member states and the procedure was protracted. So while a few major events were at an advanced stage of planning and some funding was available, for other events there really was insufficient time to mark such a potentially important theme year.

BTA decided to mark European Tourism Year by seeking to improve standards and visitor welcome and a challenge was given to every sector of the industry urging them to take more care of customers. Staff motivation schemes and awards, customer care training programmes, 'at home' events, language training were soon being put in place. The Education and Training Unit of the British Tourist Authority and English Tourist Board produced an induction training manual and other guidance on staff training programmes. The British Hotels Restaurants and Caterers Association picked up the challenge and its Chairman urged all members to endorse the BTA's two key objectives. Other trade associations, regional tourist boards and local authorities also responded and by the end of the year over two thousand events and campaigns had been staged throughout Britain. The planning time had been much too short but it was remarkable just how many companies, councils, agencies and individuals did respond. Some of the most impressive results came from the smallest operators and ETY encouraged hundreds of suppliers to see that they could be effective in improving the tourism product. The year had been turned around and many of the initiatives taken will be ongoing. With more lead time though, ETY could have been so much better and especially in the area of international operation.

Summary

Festivals, commemorations, anniversaries and special events provide the essential attraction at the destination.

Distinguishing features of these tourist attractions are that they are special, limited in time, requiring professional treatment in planning, promotion and operation.

Despite their great importance for the resort and for the creation of traffic the events are often poorly promoted and badly managed, particularly if they are a 'one-off'. A lack of management and marketing skills can be very damaging. A common mistake is to leave marketing plans with inadequate time and resources. Marketing time scales are as long as the production cycle.

Specialist attractions come within the following categories:

- Festivals
- Anniversaries
- Special events (exhibitions, pageants and historical presentations, religious events, sports events, such as the Olympic Games and marathons)

Themes have an important role in promotion, representing a story line or framework to highlight a particular attraction or destination. Promotion must be or must embrace the product. The prospective visitor must be able to visualise and demand the attraction and be able to buy it.

These special forms of tourism attraction can offer substantial short and long term benefits (a major festival of the arts, such as Edinburgh). But as a general rule they do not live up to the expectations and tend to attract, in the main, local residents.

International anniversaries and events are difficult to organise and sell, unless they are regular events such as the Olympic Games where great prestige accumulates over the years, much heightened by mass media such as television, but the rewards can be great and often lasting.

There must be strong leadership centrally and an active focal point for the stimulation of cooperative and coordinated action and marketing.

References

1 Camacho, G, *Festivals Commemorations and Anniversaries*. BTA London 1979, p 4.
2 *Tourism Management*, Volume 9, No. 2. Butterworths, June 1988. Summer Olympic Tourist Market – learning from the past, Pyo S, Cook R, Howell R L.
3 Camacho, G, *ibid.*
4 Camacho, G, *ibid* p 29.

20 Seasonality

There is one major and fundamental factor which is at once a problem and an opportunity. It faces most operators in the field of tourism. Certainly national tourist offices grapple with it and so do resorts, cities and regions. Hoteliers and transporters, attractions and facility operators all face the problem. It means different things to different operators but it remains the single biggest challenge facing the tourism industry today. Seasonality or how to level out the demand.

Ski resorts suffer the problem in the summer while seaside resorts suffer it in the winter. City centre hotels face it every weekend and certainly on Bank Holiday weekends, when they are not accommodating the business traveller. University accommodation is available during the summer (long) vacation when the students are down. The challenge is great but the rewards are enormous. More visits, a better spread of visits, full employment, higher profits and with increased profitability re-investment in the product and a raising of standards. Full employment as opposed to part-time employment, laying off staff and subsequent re-training is not only more cost effective it ensures higher standards of service and more commitment from staff. Re-investment in the product not only ensures higher standards it means higher prices and profits.

It is very important to define what is meant by off-peak or off-season in any given situation or for any operator. For Brighton hoteliers in England August is off-season because this is the month when conferences are at their least popular; it is the month when most families with children are on vacation and the traditional holiday period when government and business leaders 'get away'. On the other hand the Edinburgh Festival is in full swing, so for Edinburgh's hoteliers August is high season. But it need not be a month, it may be a week, or even part of a week. It may for transporters be a part of the day. For railways and metro systems serving the needs of commuters, for airlines providing day trips for businessmen, the middle of the day represents a trough when the equipment is not being fully utilised. For theatres it is usually Mondays but historic houses, museums and galleries, restaurants all have their peaks and troughs when the plant is idle and staff less than fully occupied.

Can anything be done about it?

It took a long time to realise that the crown jewels sparkle as brightly in January as in June and it took years to realise that this and many other glittering pleasures and satisfactions were indoor and not weather dependent.

The European Travel Commission (ETC) with industry support carried out a basic study into seasonality in the USA in 1983. The results were perhaps surprising. It indicated in fact that a substantial proportion of the leisure market could be diverted from the peak season months provided that their perception of the activities and attractions offered by the destination were sufficiently appealing. To describe winter months in Europe as off-season as the trade did publicly for many years was 'off-putting' for the traveller. ETC changed its theme to describe winter in the cultural capitals of Europe as 'the lively months'. The whole concept of traditional vacations had to be overturned, the perceptions that it always rains or 'there's nothing to do' had to be dispelled. Potential travellers in the off-peak periods need this sort of re-assurance in that they will find something to see or do.

But the need for good value re-assurance is also vitally important. Hoteliers and transporters alike use price as a marketing tool in developing off-peak traffic. There are discounted fares on the ferries from Europe to Britain November through March and some hoteliers offer bargain break weekends throughout the year. London invented the city winter weekend break (shops, sport, culture, entertainment, city lights) and it worked from the start. Other cities followed.

In Britain there has been a decline in the long holiday market (long holidays taken by the British in Britain) to some extent the result of ineffective marketing and a growth in the second or short holiday market. This is a direct result of increasing affluence and higher disposable incomes among the working population and a higher proportion of senior citizens or retirees in the total population. These factors together with increased mobility and an increase in leisure time has led to this increase in short break holidays. The peak for short breaks in Britain is April and May with a secondary peak in September, though Christmas is coming up fast. Near European markets increasingly see Britain as a second holiday destination and can very often be persuaded to come in the off-peak periods. Since the length of stay is short those regions with European gateways tend to benefit most from this business.

Hotel accommodation is used by the majority of people taking short break holidays but in order to attract this additional business hotels must be prepared to introduce flexible pricing and create a special reason for going, such as a special interest weekend, hobby or activity breaks, romantic weekends or a break tied to a special event.

Blackpool was among the first to recognise the seasonality problem and responded to the challenge as far back as 1912 when it started the illuminations in a very modest and experimental way. It was not until 1925 that the first major show was organised and Blackpool has managed to stay ahead of the competition ever since, though there have been many imitators. Indeed room occupancy in Blackpool during the period of the illuminations is now higher than the summer months very often. While curing one off-peak problem they have created another inasmuch as weekend traffic during the nine-week period of the illuminations is at capacity, but there is space mid-week. So now the task is to fill that mid-week trough. There is a spin off for the coach operators who benefit from an extended season.

The Blackpool Illuminations is not the only off-season event which can be promoted by the coach operators though. Firework displays, theatre outings, shopping trips (both pre-Christmas and during the January sales), race meetings, factory visits all offer potential for developing business in what was the off-season. Above all they must be imaginative, well presented and offer good value.

Specialist tour operators are offering mini-holidays to city centre hotels; not just London but places like Bradford for Brontë Country or Washington New Town in the North of England for Catherine Cookson Country.

They all have two things in common – they are imaginative and price is used as a marketing tool or alternatively the package offers added value.

These few examples serve to illustrate the vast potential market which undoubtedly exists for the individual resort or operator in developing off-peak holidays. But how to go about it? It really is a question of research again, a question of market analysis, segmentation and product analysis. These techniques hold the key to all marketing success stories.

First it is necessary to define the problem and the challenge. Off-peak means different things to different people. Every marketer must ask himself 'when is my off-peak?' It is not difficult to carry out the desk research to establish this. For the hotelier there are booking patterns and occupancy figures; for the attraction there are admission figures; the coach operator knows when his coaches are standing idle; the airline or ferry operator certainly knows when he has spare capacity.

Secondly, examine competitors' activities. What are they doing to respond to the off-peak challenge? Which of their offers is proving to be successful? Again, it is neither difficult nor costly to acquire this market intelligence. This stage of analysis should also extend to identifying those products which it is felt would have a year round appeal and a listing of events in the area, which can usually be obtained from the local Tourist Information Centre. It may well be that competitors have missed an event, which can be turned into a mini-break. The marketer should also develop some unusual, imaginative, yet inexpensive ideas. Keep it simple, price it attractively or highlight added value and avoid any hidden extras.

The challenge of seasonality is one which engages the national and regional boards, resorts and local authorities and most of them are actively engaged in tackling the problem. Much of the research which the national tourist offices have carried out into the market potential for the off-peak is available in their publications or newsletters.

A number of key segments have been identified which can be persuaded to take a holiday at any time of the year. In the British domestic market senior citizens aged 65 or more represent an important segment. But people are retiring earlier so there are the retirees of lesser years and the 'empty nesters' – those people, usually over 45, whose children have left home and the mortgage is probably paid. Add to this the youth segment. Up to 16 they are in full-time education but between 16 and 25 a large number are in some form of full-time education as well. There are special interest groups and business travellers. In overseas markets the same key segments exist overall but they differ in importance from market to market and the incidence of both school and public holidays differs from the domestic market too.

Senior citizens

Without doubt the senior citizen segment presents a viable solution to the seasonality problem. In 2025, according to a recent study for the International Monetary Fund nearly 20% of the total population of the top seven OECD countries, which are the big traffic generators, will be 65 or over. This is twice the share which they account for today. A recent survey by the Bank of Japan reported that people of 60 or more owned more financial assets than any other age group. In America 72% of those aged 65 plus own their own homes compared with 65% for the population as a whole. By the end of this century there will be 35 million people over 65 in the USA. The pattern is repeated in Europe and Australia. This demographic data serves to demonstrate the vast potential which the mature traveller offers and can be the answer to every tourism marketer's seasonality challenge. Yet it is a comparatively short time ago that the tourism and travel industry has recognised this potential. The demographic facts were known. The increasing proportion of senior citizens is a result of the trend for retiring earlier and living longer.

The potential of this market segment was demonstrated in a study commissioned by the European Travel Commission[1] in 1986. The ETC and the International Hotel Association launched seasonality pilot programmes in Malta, Cyprus and Rhodes particularly aimed at the senior citizen traveller which proved to be successful. Then in 1985 ETC and IHA jointly organised a conference in Cannes with the title 'The Senior Tourist: The Solution to Seasonality'.

The Plan of Action following the ETC/IHA/ETAG Mediterranean islands experiment is set out in the appendix to this chapter. The plan was put into action through a collective effort and showed some successful results particularly in Cyprus. The recommendations are broadly valid for more general application, indicating the essential need for cooperative work in seasonality programmes.

De Haan had recognised the potential when he established Saga Holidays in Britain immediately after the war. Cruise lines in the 1960s drew their market almost entirely from the seniors.

Let us look at the potential more closely. Europe has an older population profile than any other continent though Japan as a single country has the most rapidly ageing population in the world. The proportion of people over 55 approaches 30% in both Germany and Italy. The teenagers of the 1960s will be approaching senior citizenship by the end of the century. By then one in four of all Europeans will be over the age of 55. When one looks at this group by sex though we find that over 60% at the moment are women – the result of the war years and its impact on the male population. But the question is – do they travel and will they travel internationally? It would seem that about half of the over 55s do though the propensity to travel differs from one market to another. However, the trend is up, there is a growing proportion who are travelling. Niko de Rooij, Secretary General of the Dutch foundation Tourism of Senior Citizens, showed a table at the ETC/IHA Seminar in Cannes[2] which demonstrates this very graphically.

Holiday participation by the 55 to 64 age group in key countries:

Country	Years	Holiday Participation %
Netherlands	1975–83	27–33
West Germany	1973–83	38–45
United Kingdom	1974–81	38–51
Belgium	1976–82	24–26
Spain	1979	36
France	1974–81	29–37

The wide variation is interesting. While over half of the British population in this large group take a holiday only a quarter of Belgians do. Britain's elderly seem to want to travel abroad too. In 1987 Saga handled about 150,000 clients but other operators such as Intasun (Golden Days), Thomson (Young at Heart), Yugotours (Golden Age), Lancaster (Good Companions), Global (Golden Circle), Golden Rail and carriers' tour operating divisions all sold packages to the senior segment. Increasingly the tour operators are setting up subsidiary companies, which specialise in travel for the mature market. Increasingly the trend to earlier retirement has resulted in a reduction in the qualifying age to 55 and in some cases 50. Olau, the Channel ferry operator for example, offers bargain breaks for the over 50s. The elderly in the Netherlands and in the Nordic countries have a high propensity to travel abroad. Nevertheless about one third of Europe's elderly seldom take a holiday of four nights or more away from home according to an EC European Omnibus Survey conducted in 1986. This will change as the teenagers of the Swinging Sixties move up the age scale.

If we look at the American market the situation is slightly different. There is no official retirement age but the model retirement age is 65. Already there are 28.6 million of them representing 12% of the total population. By the end of the century it is forecast that there will be 35 million and there is also a trend to early retirement. Already there are about two million of them with a household income of $20,000 or more. So there is even now a large potential market for international travel. Indeed one in eight of American visitors to Europe are 65 plus, half of them travelling in the spring and the autumn. They are already travelling off-peak! They are not geriatric but active, intelligent people with the will, the means and, very often, the need to travel. Specialists in the field of senior citizen travel have found that low activity itineraries do not sell.

The senior citizen segment is not a homogeneous market though. In Europe the number of women is greater than the number of men. This is no less true in the USA where about 80% of the occupants of single householders are women. Nick Tarsh, Managing Director of Insight International Tours Ltd, speaking at the Senior Citizen seminar organised by the Council for Travel and Tourism in 1986 suggested that you have to look at three distinct markets:

– The 50 to 65 years group: The 'new olds' or junior seniors.
– The 65 to 75 years group: The Old.
– The 75 plus group: The 'Old Olds'.

The 'new olds' are generally at the peak of their earning capability if they are still working but as 'empty nesters' they are able to take several short breaks. The 65 to 75 year group offers potential for the longer stay off-peak holiday while the 'old olds' will, generally speaking, tend to stay in their own country more often than not with friends or relatives. Saga Holidays, the market leader in the field of senior citizen travel, produces seven different brochures for seven specific segments all within the senior citizen age group.

The ETC/IHA Conference in Cannes produced a number of resolutions, the most important of which were:

(a)   the senior citizen market should be regarded as a multi-segment market;
(b)   the travel trade must recognise the older traveller's special needs;
(c)   off season opportunities should be emphasised;
(d)   tourist boards should co-ordinate senior citizen (and especially off-peak) travel promotion;

(e)   off-peak travel should not mean a reduction in service quality but should maintain full value for money standards.

Special interests travel

A second, and perhaps equally important, key segment for attacking the seasonality problem is in the fast growing field of special interest travel.

Self fulfilment and self expression are increasingly powerful motivators in travel and this segment can be encouraged to come at times of the year, or indeed times of the week when troughs need to be filled. Price is less important than the degree of personal satisfaction derived. In some cases special interest packages can be developed which are based on a product which already exists, for example Egypt's pyramids and temples. In other cases it will be necessary to present the existing product in an appealing and structured way; examples of this include wildlife trips around the Scottish islands or literary heritage tours. Yet other special interest packages can be developed without recourse to an existing product base – music appreciation, antiques collecting, flower arranging, painting, jewellery making and so many more. Finally special interest product can be developed with some investment – tennis clinics, equestrian centres and golf courses and other types of activity holidays or a festival geared to a particular person or theme.

Opportunities for developing special interest travel depend to a large extent then, though not exclusively, on the availability of indigenous product and the time invested in careful and thorough product analysis will repay the marketer by pointing up these opportunities in his own area. For the special interest traveller there is a high degree of commitment to product, particularly if that product is a unique one. Hindu temples and the Aztec inheritance but also Brontë country or places featured in Jane Austen's novels for the literary afficionados are surely unique products. In Britain we have been extravagantly endowed with product; the heart of a once great empire, a place where great minds have pushed out the frontiers of human learning. But in every country and every area it is possible to find product which will have potential appeal to a mini-market. Heritage can be developed into a themed product, and towns which were inconceivable as tourist destinations are discovering how yesterday's history can be presented as a present day attraction. 1988 marks the 250th anniversary of the enlightenment of John Wesley and 1991 is the 200th anniversary of his death. Since he travelled extensively throughout Britain for almost 50 years preaching in towns and villages there must be many places which can lay claim to a visit: many can form themselves into a heritage trail which will prove attractive to Wesleyans around the world, who can be persuaded to make the pilgrimage in one of the anniversary years.

There are many examples of successful marketing campaigns geared to special interest travel and offering year round travel potential. The Portuguese Tourist Office, taking advantage of its good winter weather, developed golf courses and tennis clinics on the Algarve and marketed off-peak travel under the brand name Sportugal. Torbay with its Riviera Breaks similarly used activities as the special interest – canoeing, golf, cycling, walking as well as the less active like painting. The Riviera Breaks brochure generated £100,000 worth of business for Torbay in its first five months. In 1987 Southampton booked more than 2,000 visitors on 'Howard's Way' weekends, based on a TV series. For Southampton every weekend in the year is off-peak. Cultural appeals are strong – London has had great success with theatre trips. The range of offers is wide – from Gilbert and Sullivan weekends to old time dancing, silver-smithing holidays and Herriot holidays in Yorkshire, birdwatching breaks in Northumbria, Coinnoisseur's Cornwall or Cornish Gardens in the West Country. Trusthouse Forte Hotels (THF) have successfully mar-keted 'Country Pursuits' which includes country sports such as clay pigeon shooting, art and antiques, wine appreciation and painting. THF identified 3 distinct sub-segments – the experimentalist who wants to try out a new sport, the hobbyist or keen enthusiast and the culturalist. Archery and clay pigeon shooting, water colour painting, arts and anti-ques and garden appreciation, music at leisure and wine appreciation, are just a few examples. They discovered too that their customers were looking for value for money, rather than a cheap package and indeed were prepared to pay a premium, if necessary, to enjoy a well-organised and packaged break.

At the other end of the price spectrum the Youth Hostels Association has developed a whole range of special interest and activity packages to fill their off-peak troughs and have found that their repeat business on such breaks throughout the year is a staggering 60%. Countrywide Holi-days Association has successfully launched Winter Walking activities to a 50-plus market.

In 1983 Earthwatch, an American non-profit scientific research organisation, sent 625 special interest travellers on expeditions which included a probe of HMS Coronation which sank off Plymouth in 1697 and a dig for Bronze Age artefacts in the Scottish Borders. Special interest travel will develop even faster over the next decade as travellers seek more rewarding and enriching holiday experiences. They can be persuaded to visit at the time of the year when they are wanted, pro-vided the product offer is sufficiently appealing.

Special events

There must be a reason for going, to pursue an activity or hobby or to learn something new. A special event can equally well create this need.

Almost 80% visit Aldeburgh in June from outside Suffolk, specifically for the Aldeburgh Festival. Visitors to the Bath Festival in May 1986 spent more than £12 million in the city excluding ticket sales and it was estimated from research that about quarter of a million were from outside the area.

The British Arts Festival Association (BAFA) represents over 30 of Britain's major festivals and they flourish throughout the year not just in the peak summer months. Brighton's festival is in May as is the Sheffield Chamber Music Festival, Bath and Aldeburgh in June while Belfast and Cardiff stage theirs in November.

It need not be an Arts Festival. Off-peak business can be generated around significant sporting events, or major exhibitions. Edinburgh promoted off-peak travel around the exhibition of Egyptian treasures from February to April 1988. Events can be created around a literary figure, a religious figure, a musician or an artist and especially if it marks an important anniversary.

Product development

For the afficionados of special interest weather is not vitally important; for the senior citizen lying on beaches is not as appealing as it was 20 years ago. Many of Britain's attractions – the theatres and concert halls, the museums and galleries, the castles and historic houses are not weather dependent. Even if climate is an important consideration it need not be a deterrent. Consider the number of hotels which have developed indoor leisure complexes over the past decade. The Rhyl Sun Centre and Blackpool's Sandcastle are not weather dependent. These are not just new facilities, they are controlled climates.

The tourism marketer must be sensitive to the needs of a swiftly changing market and provide visitors with what they want at a price they are prepared to pay. Most European countries and certainly Britain have the capability of being a year round every day of the week destination, but it requires imaginative development and it requires flair, innovation and creative marketing.

'Operation Off-Peak'

Following an initiative by Britain's Council for Travel and Tourism (CTT), it was decided in 1985 to launch 'Operation Off-Peak', a major cooperative tourism campaign, and it turned out to be a major strategic offensive. All sectors of the travel and tourism trades rose to the challenge of seasonality. A newsletter was launched by BTA and distributed extensively. The CTT organised an 'Operation Off-Peak' seminar in the autumn of 1986 and this was followed by others on the themes of senior citizens, special interest travel, creative marketing, special events and sponsorship. A series of award schemes was also launched by CTT. BTA used the theme 'Britain for All Seasons' in its world-wide marketing in 1986 and in successive years. A consultant was appointed who offered advice and suggestions – 'dial-an-idea' service. BTA published check-lists and guides to off-peak marketing. Six years on it was still going from strength to strength; the phrase 'off-peak' was firmly established among tourism interests. In 1985 it had been necessary to explain the concept and why the 'operation' was important. Today it is widely understood and there are countless operators and producers, right across the spec-trum of tourism interests in Britain, who have accepted the challenge and devised marketing methods to meet it. The challenge remains for all travel and tourism interests though – off-peak is any time when the hotel, the aeroplane, the ship, the train, the restaurant, the theatre or the attention is less than 100% full. Most tourism destinations have the capa-bility of being 52 weeks of the year destinations.

Summary

Seasonality is a perennial problem facing tourism marketers. Filling the troughs is a major challenge. Off peak means different things to different people and organisations. It must be properly researched, including product and market analysis. Two key segments in the leisure field can provide the answer, both growing fast – senior citizens and the special interest traveller. They have their special needs. Price is a useful market-ing tool but value for money is more important. Special events can be successfully exploited to fill the troughs. Better utilisation of the product over the whole year means full employment, increased profitability and consequent re-investment in the product for future expansion.

References

1   *The Older American Traveller to Europe.* ETC October 1985.
2   The Senior Tourist: Solution to Seasonality. IHA ETC Cannes Seminar, 20–22 November 1985.

Appendix

Recommendations and plan of action decided during the 1st IHA/ETC Meeting on Seasonality in Malta (25/26 November 1982)

A standard plan of action was established for each sector of the travel industry in the destination concerned, requesting each of the three countries to adjust plans more specifically to its respective conditions as a next step.

Action by National Tourism Organisations

Individual National Tourism Organisations of Malta, Rhodes and Cyprus will take the responsibility for the coordination and implementation of the plans of action for the various sectors of the travel industry in their country, the industry promising its full support.

NTOs will act as communication channels for the industry with the relevant national authorities, making representations to ensure that services and facilities connected with tourism are kept fully available during the low season even at a reduced cost.

Part of the overall budget of NTOs will be set aside to fight against seasonality problems. NTOs will finance special research on seasonality and stimulate innovation and product development. They will support image building in traffic generating countries, eg by use of audio-visual shows and by contacts with the press – concentrating on the low season product. NTOs will also support initiatives of off-season events (festivals, exhibitions, and offer special facilities for important trade fairs (ITB, WTM, etc).

Action by airlines

Airlines will continue to develop lower promotional fares to cater for the low season months, provided that they generate a wider traffic base, that the dilution of revenue can be checked, and that the losses of airlines are not increased.

Fares discounts in shoulder months will also be offered by airlines, so as to move away from the peak months' travel which can disrupt the 'back-to-back' pattern. Optimum use of capacity will thus be made in shoulder months without having to programme additional capacity in the peak months.

Airlines, in coordination with hotels and other suppliers, will further break down seasons in their pricing structure, if possible with different promotional price discounts, to bring them in line with those of tour operators and other middlemen.

Special fares will be granted by airlines to families (especially during school holidays), to senior citizens and to spouses (particularly honeymooners).

Airlines will endeavour to facilitate interconnections between domestic flights in traffic generating countries and flights to the destinations concerned. Incentives will be offered on domestic flights to people travelling to these resorts.

Regular consideration of the policy towards charter carriers will be undertaken by airlines, in conjunction with relevant bodies, and the release of seats (charter and schedule) will be more flexible during the low season.

Action by hotels

Hotels, in cooperation with other suppliers, will endeavour to keep all their summer season facilities and services fully available during the off-season and even to add other facilities to compensate for the lack of sun.

Short stay holidays and week-ends will be encouraged by hotels through special promotional rates.

Hotels will also analyse the conference market as a diversification of their winter product (not as an extension to the holiday market) and a great potential to temper seasonal problems, bearing in mind the high competitiveness in the conference market and the need for long term investment in specific infrastructure, equipment, facilities and staff.

As far as labour is concerned, hotels will encourage the freedom of movement of trained personnel between countries where the low season does not correspond to the same period of the year. They will favour flexibility, within reasonable limits, in working hours and holiday periods, as well as in the allocation of duties and responsibilities.

Action by tour operators

Tour operators will reflect fully the lower prices given by hoteliers and airlines in their price lists to customers: they will not absorb the concessions for themselves and will reduce their mark-ups in proportion.

Winter brochures will portray the destinations concerned as a winter product – not as an abridged version of the summer product – emphasising for example the cultural and archaeological aspects.

Tour operators will endeavour to improve communications with hoteliers and other suppliers on the progress of advance bookings in the context of their allotment contracts.

They will also assist National Tourism Organisations in their promotional activities.

21   Business travel

When the Gulf region in the Middle East was under-hoteled and the business opportunities great, the business traveller was prepared to make do. If a major news story breaks the world's press will descend on a place, no matter what the under-capacity in terms of transport, accommodation or communication. If, however, one is designing structured marketing programmes to attract the business traveller, the right product at the right price is just as important to him as it is to the leisure traveller.

The four cornerstones of service essential for the international business traveller are transportation, accommodation, entertainment and communication. So once again one starts with product analysis. What does the destination have to offer? The business traveller will need air services to suit his needs, frequency, efficiency and convenience, plus speedy processing through immigration and customs and good onward transport facilities at the airport – train or metro, taxis and car hire. For example, a German businessman wanting to visit a trade fair in Birmingham, England may well want to fly in and out in a day. He will find the airport adjacent to the National Exhibition Centre. The Palexpo complex in Geneva similarly enables visitors to walk from the airport terminal into the exhibition hall. Conversely, a British businessman may want to make a two-day trip to a trade fair in Hanover, where he will expect good overnight accommodation in addition to air services and onward transportation to the exhibition hall and from there to the hotel. He could well be looking for restaurants and night spots for entertaining in addition to the transport and accommodation needs. International business visits must not be constrained by limitations at gateways or transport links. Generally speaking, international business travellers demand first class accommodation with full business facilities but all business travellers do not. Some are looking for budget accommodation. Not all business travellers can afford to stay in the high price properties. French companies such as Accor are exploiting this potential in their development programmes. Academics and other professional bodies may well be very happy with university accommodation.

Twenty years or more ago, teleconferencing was claimed to sound the death knell for conventions. Yet they are still alive and healthy today. People still want face to face meetings, especially international associations. Increasingly though, these international associations are recognising their purchasing power and demanding more in the way of hospitality from the host city or even country, free meeting facilities, discounted accommodation, transportation deals and secretariat support. Product analysis will take account of conference halls, hotel and banqueting facilities, lecture theatres and university accommodation, exhibition centres and, of course, the exhibition and trade fair calendar.

Product analysis will lead to the identification of gaps in the product range when the second stage of analysis has been completed – market analysis. Business travel is a segment of the market with many sub-segments. It can broadly be sub-segmented as follows:

(1)   Incentive traveller – invariably with spouse
(2)   Convention delegate – association or corporate meetings
(3)   Visitor to trade fair or exhibition
(4)   Vocational training – business or management course, business or specialist English
(5)   Independent business traveller with or without spouse
(6)   Study tours of an educational or vocational nature, eg farm tours.

Analysis of these sub-segments in terms of size and needs will undoubtedly throw up product gaps. Not enough accommodation in the right price category for the independent business traveller; lack of incentive style hotels where all members of the group can be accommodated in the same type of room. It may well be that if there is a shortage of the latter, added to inadequate banqueting facilities, the marketer will have to look to markets where group sizes are small and accommodation needs more flexible. Information on the trade fairs planned in terms of type of exhibitor, names of exhibitors or visitor packages may not be available far enough ahead. It is remarkable that for the most part development of conference centres has concentrated on the 2,000 plus delegate convention, which only represents about 20% of the market. There is need for a bespoke tailored facility for up to 250 delegates which represents the major part of the market. They may have to settle for function rooms in larger hotels with flat floors, Vienna cafe chairs and sometimes less than adequate audio visual facilities. This size of conference moreover is usually less demanding in terms of hospitality, less disruptive of hotel bookings and offers a much better seasonal spread. It seems remarkable that market analysis and product analysis, which clearly demonstrates the need, has not yet resulted in development of the right product. Plans for the new £120 million International Convention Centre in Birmingham, England, comprise eleven halls for audiences of 30 to 3,000 delegates – a skilled approach to the market. However, too many large centres owe their existence more to the aspirations of local politicians rather than market analysis.

Incentive travel

Motivational travel would be an equally good description of incentive travel. The distinguishing characteristic of incentive travel is the 'award', the recognition of merit. Instead of medals or mention in dispatches, a journey to exotic or famous places in luxurious conditions is the prize. The return for the parent company or organisation can be great. There can be other objectives, for example improving morale and motivating the work force generally. Strangely the first incentives were developed many years ago in communist Russia, when the Stakanovites, or workers who exceeded production targets, were rewarded by holidays (generally in Russia, typically at a Black Sea resort, not abroad). Government tourist offices and industry groups which have in the past accepted a sometimes hostile attitude on the part of tax authorities are beginning to question tax treatment. There are important economic and social values to the community as well as to the firm and the individual. Many incentive trips include training or educational sessions and seminars, especially if the company or organisation is multinational. But in some countries incentive travel remains under suspicion in the belief that such leisure trips or 'jollies' have no intrinsic corporate or social value. Yet the winners are often leaders in their community or organisation and international travel in a professionally arranged vocational sense can benefit both originating and receiving countries. Greater efforts will be needed by tourist organisations to demonstrate these values if the movement is to develop the great potential which undoubtedly exists in Europe, without tax restraints.

It represents the glittering prize offered to the sales force or the dealer network or perhaps the work force in order to motivate them to achieve exceptional sales goals or production targets. Usually the objective of offering the star trip is to increase sales. It follows that the destination must be attractive, glamorous, appealing, and ideally relatively unattainable by those who are working to win. It can be a very effective motivator inasmuch as the anticipation of the trip goads the salesman or dealer to greater efforts. The secret is to sustain the anticipation in a variety of ways over a period, which could well be up to a year before the prize trip is actually taken. Unlike manufactured goods which can be taken to the market place, in travel and tourism markets have to be brought to the product. This fundamental difference works in favour of this need for sustained motivation over a long period. Imagination, imagery, teasers must all be used to present the award in an exciting and appealing way.

Using great expectations to motivate great achievers must be fulfilled with a prize of exceptional quality in terms of travel and experience at the destination. It must be bespoke tailored and deluxe. Yet so many make the mistake of believing that a standard package with a few extra frills – a champagne reception on arrival and a final evening's banquet, is enough. Nothing could be further from the truth. The incentive trip has to be special, different, unique, memorable. That means attention to detail, and pre-planning to the nth degree. It is increasingly the practice for the specialist operator to charge a fee in addition to the normal commissions which he would expect to earn from suppliers. This fee is charged for creating the programme. The programme itself will be charged separately and invariably the components will include first class or deluxe charter travel, pre-check in arrangements at the airport, limousine transfers, pre-check in at the hotel, planned menus, flowers in the rooms, official receptions, banquets in unique venues – a castle or historic house, a livery hall, on a boat – superb entertainment, surprise heaped on surprise. There can be no mistakes; everything about the trip must run like clockwork. This sub-segment, however, is perhaps the highest yield of all in terms of expenditure at the destination and since a number of the participants are unlikely to have visited the destination before it is possible that they will become repeat visitors.

It cannot be stressed enough that the trip must be faultless and memorable. The memory of a disastrous holiday stays for many years; a disastrous incentive trip can be much more harmful to motivation than no incentive at all. It is important therefore that the tax implications of the trip are fully understood by the potential participants.

The tax authorities in a number of countries regard the incentive trip as a fringe benefit and consequently subject to tax in the same way as a company motor car. This tax bill has to be paid, either by the company or the employee or dealer. In some countries because of 'grossing up' or value added this could result in payment of a final amount in excess of the rate which the employee would normally pay. It is preferable then to draw the tax implications to the attention of participants.

An undesirable or unknown destination is equally unlikely to motivate. The ideal destination will be perceived as glamorous and exciting and ideally just unattainable, which makes it all the more desirable. If the destination is perceived to be unappealing and has a negative image, it will not encourage greater effort. A trip to London by dealers from the mid-west in the USA would be appealing, though Bermuda or Bangkok would be more appealing as a destination to a Dutch sales force, since London is easily attainable for them. The incentive trip must be a status symbol and enhance the sense of achievement.

Since incentive travel sets out to provide a unique travel experience and is dependent on meticulous planning, it has become increasingly the preserve of specialist companies – the ITS or incentive travel specialists – who generally are knowledgeable about their clients' needs. They in turn will very often use a destination management company to make the ground arrangements.

Incentive travel can have its drawbacks. For airlines it can mean with advanced booking the need to give heavily discounted rates and then the operator only confirming numbers at the last minute. For hotels, incentive groups can be disruptive in terms of allocations (a group series may be lost because of an incentive group which has been booked in much earlier) and in terms of the 'invasion' by the large group, which will tend to take over. The marketer in a national tourist office or in a region or resort must be honest with himself. He must ask 'Can I deliver the product which is expected by the incentive group?' If he believes that he has fully understood the needs of this important sub-segment and can fulfil its expectations then it will be necessary to work with the specialist operators in the field and those suppliers (hoteliers, transporters and facility operators) in the business. In the USA, the Society of Incentive Travel Executives (SITE) has been providing an invaluable training and educational service for clients and suppliers alike. In the United Kingdom there is the Incentive Travel Association of the United Kingdom (ITA:UK). There are similar associations and consortia in Europe. However, the trade is only in its infancy in Europe, but is likely to grow fast.

There are specialist shows such as IT and ME in Chicago or EIBTM in Geneva, and large specialist operators such as E F MacDonald Incentive Company, which determines preferred destinations. This will almost certainly have been preceded by a day put on by the national tourist office designed to sell the destination to E F MacDonald. The marketer in the national tourist office will also need to advise on (and in some cases supply) gimmicks and teasers from postcards to local products which can be used to sustain the motivation in the long lead up to the trip. Destinations need to promote themselves to the decision makers and the influencers, promote the high quality of the product and follow up with education visits which should ideally be modelled on an actual incentive trip.

There is still a great deal of confusion about incentive travel. In part this is due to the practice in the USA of the achievers also being delegates to a national convention or the trip being billed as a convention for administrative purposes. These 'conventions' have very little in common with the professional or association conferences which attract paying delegates. Nevertheless, educational or vocational elements in the programme are increasing and the setting of the visit enhances their effectiveness.

Conferences, meetings and conventions

Nothing can really replace the face to face contact of delegates at a conference with its plenary sessions, break-out seminars and especially in the social programme. There are broadly two types of meetings: the corporate, which is usually designed to effectively disseminate a corporate strategy or sales message throughout the organisation in a compelling way, and the association, which is much more concerned with the exchange of ideas and techniques in a particular field. The corporate meeting can take a wide ranging form from a few key senior executives who gather together to evolve a strategy, to a major get-together of a company's sales force, dealers and distributors to disseminate the sales message and perhaps launch a new product. Product launches can be a major feature of the convention.

For the tourism marketer or the marketing executive of a conference venue the need is to promote to conference organisers. This is more difficult than selling to potential buyers in other industries. It is similar to selling capital goods and quite different from the mass travel market. The first problem is in identifying the buyer or perhaps the influencer. He could be the chief executive, marketing director, marketing manager, personnel manager, training manager or even conference organiser for the corporate meeting, and the secretary general or more usually an organising committee in the case of the association meeting. Then there is the great variety in number, type and frequency of meetings as well as practice. For example a trade association may have a policy of one meeting in the home country and one overseas in alternative years. The number of venues available to the conference organiser increases almost daily and consequently the competition is great. Segmentation of the conference market essentially falls into three main groups but these can be subdivided further:

(1) Association meetings (i) national
                          (ii) international
(2) Corporate meetings (i) national
                          (ii) international
(3) Sponsored meetings, usually by government departments or agencies, newspapers, professional bodies.

Associations which can be trade, professional or educational usually meet at least once a year at national or international level though regional meetings may be more frequent. Normally such associations have a permanent secretary who is a useful contact and can advise an policy and practice. They vary in size but about 80% are for less than 500 people.

The corporate meetings market is more complex and varies enormously in size from the small strategy group or Board meeting to product launches or meetings of shareholders. It is difficult to identify the conference organiser or decision maker which could be at corporate level or departmental level. Just as in the incentive travel business there are specialist operators, in the conference field there are professional conference organisers (PCOs) as well as associations – Association of British

Professional Conference Organisers and the Association of Conference Executives in Great Britain. These associations and their members are influential and knowledgeable and well worth contacting. The sponsored meetings segment is equally difficult inasmuch as it is not easy to identify the key person in Government departments or agencies with responsibility for organising conferences. Additionally there are training courses organised throughout the year.

In the field of marketing to conference organisers the most effective tool is undoubtedly personal selling, though public relations, direct mail and facility visits are also important. Print is essential in providing information such as plans, details of facilities available including technical equipment, prices, location maps, accommodation available etc as well as attractive pictures of the venue. The effectiveness of advertising in this field is questionable.

A number of conference databanks are available at national and international level through commercial bureaux or associations such as the International Congress and Convention Association (ICCA). These are sometimes supplemented by databanks maintained by national tourist offices. The national tourist office and the town convention bureau needs to build a database of contacts including educational and training bodies, government and private. They should exchange information since there is often no competitive loss. These computer based services together with directories can produce the contact names in associations and companies who are the potential buyers.

Having researched the company or association contact it is then necessary to research their needs. Personal calls on contacts researched in this way can produce business. It can also be very rewarding to follow up those who have recently organised a conference in the resort or centre in order to secure repeat business. If the potential buyer has not used the facility before it will almost certainly be necessary to arrange an inspection visit to the site.

The direct mail shot is a sales presentation, a substitute for personal selling but clearly not nearly so effective. The aim should be to get a response from the potential customer, which can be followed up with a personal call. It is less costly to mail an attractive flyer leaflet than the main brochure; that can come later at the time of the sales call. Telephone selling can also be effective, not only in selling the site to conference organisers, but increasingly on behalf of organisers in selling the conference itself to delegates.

Bidding for an international conference is expensive and difficult, involving research, lobbying, promoting to association officers, preparation of the bid document, perhaps a video, reception and certainly a facility visit before any decision is taken.

Follow up of the conference organiser after the conference is over is something which is easily overlooked. A follow up letter asking for comments and inviting a return visit accompanied by a small gift can be very rewarding.

The marketing campaign needs to be timed carefully and the marketing mix carefully thought through. Like any marketing campaign it starts with product analysis, market analysis, segmentation and research. This is followed by budget allocation and selection of the marketing tools. Finally the campaign should be assessed against the performance indicators established for the campaign, which should include: conversion to business resulting from sales calls, personal calls resulting from direct mail activity, facility visits arranged, enquiries resulting from PR or advertising, results or telephone selling, repeat business resulting from follow up.

The convention bureau at national level, in the town or resort, has a key role to play. Meetings are very big business. Conference travel is a specific market segment needing professional and specialist selling. It needs its own pre-, during and post-meeting servicing including purpose designed literature and information.

The convention trade is highly competitive but there is an element of profitable cooperation. Meetings are often peripatetic, changing location each time, and unwilling to return to a convention city for some time. So, for example, the London Tourist Board can afford to alert Paris regarding future prospects for a meeting finishing in London and unlikely to return for some years in return for similar 'leads' from Paris. Convention bureaux can afford to swap information with 'rivals'.

In recent years there has been a growing practice of adding exhibitions or trade shows to conventions and vice versa. This trend is highly susceptible to promotion and can greatly enhance values, appeals and profitability of the event.

Conventions and exhibitions are year round attractions; indeed they are often concentrated in the 'tourist' off season. They deserve top priority as important revenue generators in visitor destinations.

It is estimated that there are about 100,000 corporate and association meetings in Britain each year, with a total spend exceeding £700 million.

Trade fairs and exhibitions

This is a long-established activity generating mass travel movement and a high spending type of business tourism with profound effects on the destination. In recent years growth has been very substantial, rivalling the convention segment, but still has a very large potential. The trade fair and exhibition medium, like conferences, offers face to face communication and trading and needs a very specialised form of marketing. Mass promotion through TV or the consumer press can motivate and arouse interest and thus create a demand, but the final act of purchase more usually needs a direct, personal contact. Marketing techniques will vary. Some events attract mass movement. Attendances at the great international expositions are numbered in millions.

The Exhibition Industry Federation's continuing survey of British exhibitions reported substantial growth of 39% in the numbers of exhibitions and trade shows over the period 1984–88 and a further 8.6% in 1989 to a total of over 700 events in centres of more than 2,000 square metres capacity. Total expenditure by visitors and exhibitors was estimated at £1,337 million in 1989, when 0.6 million visitors attended exhibitions, an increase of 11% on the previous year.

Overseas visits, still a small proportion of the total at about 250,000, have been rising steadily.

The organiser of trade fairs, business or technical exhibitions will identify his markets from the products or services being offered at the show. This will include, where appropriate, overseas markets. The Association of Exhibition Organisers in Britain states that an international exhibition should have a minimum of 20% of exhibits from outside Britain, or at least 20% of promotional expenditure directed towards overseas visitors. The Union des Foires Internationales states that an international exhibition should have a minimum of 30% of foreign exhibitors (stand holders) and a minimum of 20% of stand space allotted to foreign exhibitors.

If the exhibition is designated international it is important that the access and communications are excellent. It must be easy to get to for exhibitor and visitor alike. In order to make it even easier to buy, operators should be invited to package travel and accommodation for both the domestic and overseas markets. These packages can be offered to exhibitors and visitors and can be simple or provide more comprehensive packages including entry, catalogue, meals, entertainment and even post-exhibition study tours.

The specialist exhibition should have the sponsorship of the relevant trade associations and the specialist journals ideally in all the target markets. This will provide the show with credibility. One should always be wary of giving an exclusive deal to one trade journal since it could limit the appeal of the exhibition for the media generally. Literature needs to be available in the languages appropriate to the markets selected and at the event itself it is desirable to have multi-lingual staff available and an overseas visitors' lounge with refreshments, telephone and telex facilities. The press office must have a good supply of news stories, literature on products displayed and photographs, as well as telephone, telex, facsimile, typewriter and refreshment services.

Promotion of the exhibition before the event will use advertising, public relations and direct mail. The organiser should also ensure that the exhibition is listed in the appropriate lists and directories available in the domestic and overseas markets. Press releases and features on the show and major exhibitors will be distributed to the industry trade journals and to relevant business and financial media plus government agencies and the various trade and industry associations as well as chambers of commerce. Advertising in the right media will almost certainly be through an advertising agency. The advertising should carry a coupon or address for further information and the name of the travel agent appointed to package the exhibition for a particular market. Direct mail is particularly effective in promoting to potential visitors, particularly if the direct mail letters can be personalised.

If time and the budget allows, presentations in key markets to the potential influencers – media, trade associations, official bodies and leading companies in the field – can be very effective.

There are usually a number of influential government departments or agencies with an interest in promoting exhibitions, especially abroad, and their support is well worth seeking. In Britain, these include the British Overseas Trade Board, the Central Office of Information, British Posts Overseas, British Broadcasting Corporation, British Tourist Authority and the carriers.

Just as there is sometimes a blurred boundary between the incentive traveller and the conference delegate, there is increasingly a blurring between the conference delegate and the trade show visitor. There is a trend towards trade shows being an integral part of the convention and consequently increasingly a need for the venue to provide a convention centre with space for audiences and exhibitors.

Vocational training

English is the language of international communications and consequently there is a need for schools to teach specialist English, whether in the field of navigation or banking and insurance. As more countries are added to the European Community there is increased demand for courses in English by businessmen and women. Quite apart from this important field, there are opportunities for a great variety of courses from business studies to hairdressing. All are capable of filling troughs in occupancy. Business studies courses can use accommodation and teaching facilities available at universities and polytechnics. Advertising in the trade press, direct mail and PR are effective media in this field as well as sales missions organised by national tourist offices to the market place.

Independent business travellers

In terms of size, this sub-segment is much the most important. In terms of influence, perhaps the least susceptible to promotion. Nevertheless, while acknowledging that the independent business traveller visits the destination because his customer is there or his office is there, there are opportunities to influence the pattern and style of visit. The business traveller can be persuaded to bring a spouse if there is an attractive fare or accommodation deal. Alternatively, the business visitor can be encouraged to extend length of stay to embrace a leisure weekend playing golf, shopping or visiting the theatre.

Study tours

As the world shrinks in communication terms the need grows for global links in government, trade and the professions. This stimulates much individual and group travel for meeting and contact. Travel to learn, to witness and experience other countries' practices and to make personal contacts in occupational groups, grows in importance and value. In the travel industry the practice of familiarisation trips is widespread. It is now extending to many other fields and is likely to develop rapidly. Examples are to be found in study tours to farms to see practices in other countries, to museums to study presentational and marketing techniques, or even to study policing or fire fighting.

Summary

Business travel is an important segment. It is higher spending generally than the leisure travel segment. It is also more demanding in terms of product needs. There are a number of sub-segments, most of which can be influenced. The most important of these are incentive travel, conference business, visits to trade fairs and exhibitions and professional study. The independent business traveller can also be influenced. Each sub-segment has different wants and needs. Each should be addressed with a specific marketing mix, and for each sub-segment specialist operators have emerged over the last two or three decades.

22   The marketing audit

This is a subject of great importance but often neglected with a resultant loss of efficiency. In commercial and trading organisations, public or private, the discipline of profit and loss provides, through financial reports and audit, indicators of success and failure. These may be taken to considerable lengths, with analysis of return on capital, measurement of cost and profit centres. This is more difficult in the public sector when non-commercial considerations must be taken into account, and generally speaking the destination's progress (one of the key elements in the tourism product) is difficult to measure.

Marketing spend for commercial and public interests alike is difficult to evaluate. The marketing audit in tourism has a wide as well as a narrow function. It starts with the strategy or policy, the objectives and the plan to achieve those objectives. Progress will be influenced by the external factors analysed in chapter 9. Often unexpected and major consequences of sudden change will affect short term results. Some cannot be anticipated, but some should be expected and action taken accordingly, for example by diversification and securing a good spread of markets and segments. Trends must be identified, and the annual review of strategy and plans modified accordingly. The audit must take this reaction to change into account.

Clearly such activity has a fundamental importance. Monitoring operations and appraising progress is the basis for reviewing strategies, operational plans, investment and marketing. Yet in the public sector generally, relatively little effort or research is devoted to the audit function. One rarely hears an admission that marketing campaigns were wrongly directed, that market research gave incorrect indications, that strategies were faulty. But such objective assessment is essential if mistakes are to be avoided and the marketing effort profitably directed. Kotler defines the marketing audit as follows:

> A marketing audit is an independent examination of the entire marketing effort of a company, or some specific marketing activity, covering objectives, programme, implementation and organisation, for the triple purpose of determining what is being done, appraising what is being done and recommending what should be done in the future.[1]

Kotler refers to a comprehensive concept of the marketing audit covering the company's (or organisation's) entire marketing operation, which is: 'Periodic rather than used only during a crisis; concerned with evaluating the basic framework for marketing action as well as performance within the framework; interested in appraising all the elements of the marketing operation not just the problem-ridden ones'.[2]

Bearing in mind that the essential characteristic of tourism is its nature as a market or demand force, and that the product is a compound of destination and activity at that destination, the audit for public and commercial organisations alike must embrace two basic tasks, first the appraisal of the strategy and objectives; secondly the appraisal of the marketing operation or the implementation of the marketing plan through specific campaigns and the use of a mix of marketing media.

Performance against objectives

In the first case the destination interest will be measuring the visitor flow, numbers and expenditure, seasonal spread and in the case of the larger destination the geographic spread of traffic throughout the destination area. Share of market must be examined particularly where there is direct and strong competition. There may be special elements in the strategy and specific objectives to diversity in geographic markets and market segments to ensure against external factors (eg political/ economic crises in major originating countries which may take them out of the market for some time). The plan may call for product relaunches, for trading up, to go for value or spend rather than increased volume.

Performance against objectives needs to be assessed in each case separately. The appraisal will assess the impact of external factors, seek to identify emerging trends and measure or estimate speed of change.

Effectiveness of the audit will depend very much on the clarity of the objectives and adequate target setting. Furthermore proper allowance must be made for time scales. Many strategic marketing decisions will be made on the basis of a three year or longer consistent operational plan modified annually in detail, but not in basic concepts. Variation from targets will be significant and must be carefully analysed.

The example of BTA's test marketing operations in 1973–4 is perhaps the best example of a major marketing experiment financed by government. Although external factors in the form of major economic problems changed the market situation dramatically, it was still possible to evaluate results and benefits.

The BTA invited Mr Victor Middleton to carry out a study on the results and an extract is given in the appendix to this chapter. Mr Middleton examined other studies on promotion effectiveness. A major research effort by the Cranfield Business School involving some 30 sponsoring firms and organisations accounting for 14% of UK total consumer advertising. This identified 17 different ways in which advertisers determine the amount of money spent on advertising. Their conclusion was that 'there is no formula appropriate to all situations'. Mr Middleton observes that 'bearing in mind that the Cranfield work is focused on advertising, not on the whole of marketing, and that it deals mostly with companies who have direct control over their products, prices and distribution, the failure to reduce the effectiveness of tourist marketing expenditure to simple formula was inevitable'.[2] There is a further difficulty for the destination promoter, national or local, state or industry partnerships, in that the end product, the objectives and targets even if economic in character have no direct commercial value. Government, for example, may set some political or social benefit as a prime objective, such as spreading the tourist flow seasonally and geographically, or concentrating traffic growth on poorer regions. Government itself is usually the chief principal beneficiary in the form of taxation and levies on the visitor spend or on the industry. It has been estimated in Britain that Government revenues from indirect taxation paid directly by overseas visitors (VAT, liquor and petrol taxes etc) exceed £800 million a year in foreign currency revenues, and proportionately similar sums accrue to other destination governments. To this must be added the corporate taxes and local taxes paid by industry.

BTA in 1972 invited an American consultant, Leo Kramer, to carry out some original and experimental work examining the substantial promotional spend, largely government financed, in the USA to attract American visitors to Britain.

Detailed analysis of the promotional budgets of 12 European National Offices in the USA 1963–1970 did not lead to any clear pattern. The report stated that 'it is not possible to establish any significant degree of correlation between the amount of promotional expenditure year by year with the number of tourists or their dollar expenditures. There are many extraneous factors which can influence the results.'[3] However Mr Kramer and his expert team were satisfied from their investigations that there does exist a relationship between agency expenditures and the number of tourists, but this relationship is neither direct nor universal . . . the agency budgets cannot be directly translated into measurable numbers of tourists from year to year.

Mr Middleton also drew attention to a study by Mr Heneghan of the Irish Tourist Board, which was claimed as the first systematic statement of the theory and practice of marketing resource allocation in tourism. This involved an outline plan of the marketing activities appropriate to a national (or indeed more localised destination) marketing authority and is included in the Appendix. The plan is a practical checklist for appraisal and evaluation as well as a base for resource allocation.

Although these early and pioneering attempts did not give the clear guidance on performance expected, they proved very valuable and were the first steps towards the development of effective business systems for modern tourism marketing. Certain key lessons were learned, the importance of external factors and the need to evaluate them as well as direct promotion intervention, the importance of the time scale, and consistency of effort, the need to define objectives and targets clearly and resource allocations relative to targets over stated periods of time.

These early researches were followed in Britain by the largest official marketing tests ever launched in international tourism. They benefited from the lessons learnt as the tests were targeted to specific markets and products which must be the bases for such appraisals, in other words a task or specific target or objective approach.

Test marketing campaigns were first carried out in 1972 with a government grant of £350,000, followed by a major experiment in 1973/4 with an expenditure by BTA of almost £1 million. The campaigns involved the selection of test and control areas in the USA, West Germany and the Netherlands. Promotion was planned to assess the impact of marketing a series of 'impulse' package holiday tours to Britain under controlled conditions to selected market segments. When the plans were being developed tourism to Britain had been increasing every year, but unfortunately 'normal' conditions were suddenly and drastically altered in late 1973 and 1974 with political and economic disturbances of a serious nature (the three-day week for example). Details of the results are given in the appendix. Surprisingly in spite of grave difficulties in a time of overall decline in tourist flows to Britain from the USA the fall in holiday movement from the test areas was significantly less than in the control areas. Mr Middleton reports

> that the evidence of volume from the International Passenger Survey is supported by airline statistics, and further supported by evidence from attitude and awareness studies carried out amongst the selected target groups of prospective travellers, and among travel agents. The effect of the reassurance campaigns is particularly striking when comparing test and control areas.
>
> The results available from Germany and the Netherlands are less conclusive. The evidence from the attitude and awareness studies among the selected target groups do not permit the conclusion to be drawn that the BTA test marketing campaigns produced a measurably significant effect. On the other hand, evidence from the International Passenger Survey (IPS) indicates that holiday inclusive tours to Britain did increase significantly from Germany in the first quarter of 1974, against a downward trend for travel abroad generally. There was some increase in the volume of inclusive tours from the Netherlands too, in the first quarter of 1974, compared with a significant drop in non-packaged visits for holiday purposes.

The first task in the audit or appraisal is to examine performance against objectives (see appendix). The following example of the BTA's work will illustrate methods and results. In the BTA Marketing Plan for 1984/5 the results of performance measurement for the previous year are reported as a basis for future planning as follows:

To implement the BTA guidelines from a marketing viewpoint the following are the marketing objectives:

(i)   to optimise overseas earnings;
(ii)   to promote London as 'Britain's biggest single tourist attraction' since its success is vital not only for London but for the rest of Britain;
(iii)   to promote Scotland, Wales and the regions of England, especially in established markets, but also seek to develop out of London traffic from appropriate new markets, wherever possible;
(iv)   to extend the season;
(v)   to further increase revenue for cooperative marketing from the trade, public and private interests.

Performance against objectives: Overseas earnings (£ million)

	1975	1977	1978	1979	1980	1981	1982	1983
Current prices	1,218	2,352	2,507	2,797	2,961	2,970	3,168	3,685
1980 prices	2,560	3,681	3,410	3,310	2,961	2,528	2,566	2,899

Visits in the third quarter were only 38% of the total compared with 44% in 1970.

In 1982 the percentage of overseas visitor nights spent out of London was 61% compared with 57% in 1972.

Revenue from cooperative publicity and sales of publications/advertising in publications has shown a considerable improvement over the past decade.

	1973/4	Income (£) 1982/3	1983/4
Co-op publicity	685,680	6,140,000	8,561,000
Sales of publications	325,341	1,549,000	1,625,000
Sales of ads in publications	172,370	851,000	768,000
Sundry receipts	47,637	452,000	106,000
Total	1,231,028	8,992,000	11,060,000

Resources, marketing operations and organisation

The audit should also be concerned with resources and organisation. Are the resources adequate for the task and targets? Has any market or market approach been left out? There may be concentration on main markets only, neglecting emerging areas.

Consumer advertising may be unaffordable, leaving the operation dependent on print and public relations with substantial opportunity costs. Irrational decisions relating to choice of media and message must be noted. Political influence can have unfortunate results, but these mistakes cannot be avoided unless there is an objective assessment of cost benefits. In 1986 following the sudden collapse of the American tourist movement to Europe, notably to the Mediterranean area, one Government Agency spent $1 million in reassurance promotion to little effect. Research by the European Travel Commission indicated that in the early weeks after the Libyan intervention and following massive media coverage of violence and highjacking in Europe, the travelling public were not prepared to respond to any European promotional message.

Objective testing is difficult and will involve estimation and professional judgement. But there is a second area for test, the marketing operations themselves, which will often provide useful and clear indications of results. These vary according to the media. The simple tests include analysis of replies (particularly coupon replies to advertising). But there are dangers – not all coupon replies are turned into bookings. A second test will measure quality by checking if the enquirer bought the product. Where the destination advertises in partnership with a commercial operator (a tour operator selling a package for example) the tests are easier and more accurate. Sample surveys can show the extent to which the advertisement is read and understood. Similar tests can be carried out for print. Although often neglected this can be a valuable market research exercise showing ways in which the print can be improved to meet the visitor's needs. If print carries advertising, or if sold to the traveller, such research is a necessary investment. Analysis of literature sales and advertising revenue are important performance tests.

Most destinations operate enquiry or information offices, and will have details of enquiries by mail (including reply to advertisements) and by phone. These enquiries and address lists are important not only in offering a measure of effectiveness but as a base for future promotion.

All media can be checked. Public relations activities, such as visits by journalists, should result in press coverage and this can be counted. Travel trade visits can be counted and records made of reports from the trade on new business, and use of the destination material produced for generating sales throughout the trade. Exhibitions and workshops by special sample surveys can show business generated.

While specific operations and campaigns related to selling a particular product will provide helpful guidance and some measurable indication of return on marketing expenditure, the major marketing efforts over the longer term to influence trends, to exploit new markets or to achieve national, local or corporate major objectives are more difficult to evaluate. But consistent effort will produce results and comparison with other operators or products and destinations can be made. For destination promotion a rule of thumb suggests that one per cent of tourism revenue should be reinvested in marketing operations, albeit a mixture of state and commercial funding.

Many commercial operators will spend much more than this, perhaps three or four per cent, depending on their objectives, marketing situation and competition. This is very low compared with other consumer purchases. There are no firm rules. But the resources for the task can be assessed in terms of media and staffing costs. External factors may dictate urgent action to mitigate damage. Governments or corporations may seek rapid results. Breaking into new markets or changing direction can be expensive, and operating on an international scale takes time. There will be mistaken objectives, errors in market intelligence and analysis, resulting in the wrong choice of markets and segments. The marketing operation depends on skilful, and creative presentation especially in a field as human and theatrical as international travel. Mistakes will be made but there will also be successful results, which makes the strictly objective and regular marketing audit of fundamental importance, as the basis for an annual review of the tourism plan and the related marketing operation.

The audit exercise should not be seen as an attempt to uncover failure or apportion blame, but rather as an essential and professional exercise to improve operations and effectiveness in marketing generally. One must start from the assumption that all activities can be improved and one can learn as much from success as from failure.

Techniques unfortunately are neither precise nor wholly reliable, and this is especially true in the public sector when national or local public benefit needs to be assessed.

In the case of commercial operations whether by public or private organisations, the discipline of profit and loss provides a firm measuring rod, but often the financial measures must be related to broader economic assessments and results of marketing campaigns in terms of visitor flows generally. The basic tourist statistics in terms of arrivals and spend may be flawed. Regional and seasonal information, or records by market segment, for example youth or senior citizens, may be imperfect or non existent. It is in these cases that special surveys or enquiries are needed.

Sample surveys are expensive but often omnibus or existing national surveys can be used to provide limited additional information by a piggy back process (ie adding questions to an existing national survey). The industry can be a source of valuable information, e.g. hotel and transport records. It is often possible to carry out a type of retail audit through the travel trade. This should be used more frequently as an understanding of the distribution process is fundamental in marketing. It is essential to know the principal characteristics of the buying habits, for example the type of and proportion of sales through retail agents, time of purchase in advance, and the make up of the clientele. It is important to know if the product is easy to buy, and the extent to which decisions are influenced by the trader. Lack of knowledge of this kind may lead to misdirection of scarce promotional funds and a poor service by the destination 'manufacturers' to the retailer and the prospective customers.

Most market research techniques can be employed in testing for audit purposes. The Delphi type enquiry through in-depth discussion groups made up of industry experts can be valuable. Very little work has been done on a cooperative international basis. But future studies, especially on a market segment basis, could be usefully undertaken by 'regional' destination groups such as the European Travel Commission or the Pacific Area Travel Association and industry associations, national and international.

Changes in spend per day, length of stay (main holidays are getting shorter), and length and frequency of second or additional holidays, are important features to be measured against marketing objectives. There are other qualitative aspects that need monitoring; for example the proportion of repeat visitors compared with first time tourists. In certain cases the majority of visitors may be repeat clients, and some travelling more frequently and becoming regulars. This will greatly influence the marketing approach and may affect strategy and changes in policy. Repeat visitors are not always the most profitable, and may crowd out new entrants into the market clientele.

The audit must be concerned with the adequacy of marketing resources to achieve the targets set. Target setting regretfully and surprisingly is sometimes carried out without reference to marketing funds or plans. A simple estimate will indicate the cost of reaching a desired audience of potential travellers, the potential market. It is not possible or practical to address the entire population. Thus the potential market must be identified through market research, and marketers must aim with a rifle not a shotgun. Indeed good travel marketing will approach the potential travellers in stages, a general invitation to those likely to be interested, and follow up in one or more stages with more detailed information offers and expensive print or personal information services.

The European Year of Tourism 1990

The Year was an initiative of the European Parliament, which in a resolution in January 1988 drew attention to the overall importance of tourism to the European economy, and to the need for a more active Community involvement. The industry organisations fully supported the Parliament and their proposal for a Year's programme in the hope that this would result in a much higher priority for the trade in the Community's policies and programme and that tourism would be treated as an entity in its own right.

The Commission and the Council eventually agreed to the Parliament's suggestion. A Steering Committee was established with industry representation and the EFTA countries (Austria, Finland, Norway, Sweden and Switzerland) were invited to participate. National Committees were set up in member countries to stimulate grass roots action, and experts seconded to the Commission to help manage the Year together with correspondents in each country. But this necessary work force was not recruited until February 1990. There were changes in top management, and a lead time of scarcely a year for such a major event was quite inadequate. The budget, eventually over 8 million Ecus was supplemented by industry and NTO's and much voluntary effort. The industry contributed to the organisation of the Year from the beginning. They fully supported the key objectives:

(a)   to promote the establishment of the single market 1992, and tourism's potential major role in this.

(b)   to develop the integrating role of tourism in creating a people's Europe.

(c)   to promote a better distribution of tourism over time and location.

(d)   to promote Community tourism particularly by encouraging travel from third countries.

Despite the late start, there were valuable initiatives. Substantial world publicity resulted with widespread use of the logo, which provided a rallying point for trade support. The experience of public-private sector partnerships on a pan-European level covering a wide range of interests and services could prove very rewarding for the future. In practice Europe's tourism activity tends to be localised. But there is a European destination and thus a European role.

The Year's programme provided new opportunities and organisational frameworks for cooperation between the member countries, particularly in the target areas:

1.   Youth tourism including a youth exchange programme.

2.   Cultural tourism including cultural itineraries such as the route of St James of Compostella and the Baroque and Celtic routes.

3.   Social tourism. A conference in Gatwick, England, focussed on the holiday needs of the disabled in Europe.

4.   Rural tourism. A big effort was made to involve the principal travel trade fairs in Europe which are seen as key promotion platforms.

A series of seminars and conferences on industry-community cooperation, 1992 the Single Market, conservation and tourism, incentive travel and seasonality with in-depth research, stimulated cooperative action in a number of important fields, and contributed to the work of the Commission's Advisory Committee on Tourism in the review of the Community's Tourism Policy and Programmes announced at the beginning of 1990.

There were inevitable shortcomings. Much of the support funding was distributed for small schemes through the national committees instead of a concentration on European events. But there was much success in a series of competitions to highlight the main objectives. More could have been done with European awards and prizes.

The Commission made a serious effort as recommended by the trade representatives to appraise the results of the Year, so that action could be taken to carry forward successful initiatives, and most important of all, build on the experimental machinery of cooperation and consultation put together with difficulty and delay. The laudable objectives of the Year are ongoing. They cannot be realised in a one year manifestation, and need to be firmly established as tourism priorities in the Community's Tourism Policy.

Summary

A marketing audit is an independent examination of the entire marketing effort of a company (organisation), or some specific marketing activity covering objectives, programme, implementation and organisation (Kotler).

The marketing audit in tourism has a wide as well as a narrow function. Periodic review of strategy and action must lead to appraisals and change in plans accordingly.

There are two basic tasks, appraisal of the strategy and objectives and, secondly, evaluation of the marketing operation through specific campaigns. Performance against objectives needs to be assessed in detail. The audit should also be concerned with resources and organisation. Most market research techniques can be employed in testing for audit purposes. In-depth group discussion with industry experts can be valuable. International cooperative action is needed, together with analysis of basic statistics of traffic flows and expenditures.

Mr Victor Middleton's study of major test campaigns for the BTA and the Department of Trade in London provides helpful guidance. He concludes that 'each aspect of the marketing process is capable of being expressed in terms of specific tasks each involving appropriate methods of monitoring results, each task having a specific cost'.

Appendix

BTA performance criteria can be categorised as primary, secondary and tertiary as follows:

Primary

1   Total visits (International Passenger Survey)

2   Total earnings (International Passenger Survey)
3   Visits and earnings × region (International Passenger Survey)
Europe, N America, Far East, Australasia, Rest of World – percentage
share – spread of markets
4   Brand share seventeen countries of OECD – total spend abroad
provided by OECD members plus International Passenger Survey data
on spend in Britain by residents of each of these countries
5   Seasonal spread – International Passenger Survey quarterly figures
even are borderline according to Department of Employment
statisticians
6   Regional spread – apart from London, Southern England, which are
reasonable standard, error too great for others
7   Non-Government funding as percentage of total marketing spend
and total budget (including 'in kind' support)
8   Any special campaigns, eg Korea, first time visits ex Germany. etc.

Secondary

1   Enquiry figures – 'overseas' offices and British Travel Centre
2   Enquiry figures – advertising coupon response N.B. caveats
– direct mail sales achieved
3   Literature sales
4   Open to View ticket sales *
5   Advertising revenue × publications
6   'In Britain' subscriptions **
7   Addition to direct mailing listings
8   Number media visits
9   Number travel trade visits
10 Workshop research

Tertiary

Individual joint marketing schemes with commercial operators
* A season ticket giving entry to Britain's principal historic properties
** A monthly illustrated consumer magazine describing Britain's
tourist attractions

BTA Test Marketing Campaigns 1973–74

Summary of results by Mr V Middleton, then lecturer at the University of
Surrey and commissioned by BTA as an independent consultant.

The results from all three test countries provide ample proof that
promotion can have a significant influence on travel flows, especially in

The scope of the Marketing Mix in Tourism identified and discussed by Heneghan (1976)[4]

Marketing Variable	Constituent Elements	Specification of Elements as applied to tourism
Price	• Pricing Policy • Price levels, margins • Discounts, etc	• price levels • discounts for off-peak periods
Product	• product range • product quality • depth of product line	• range of 'holiday products' • intrinsic quality of the tourism product • value for money
Advertising	• media used • production costs • cooperative advertising	• advertising • cooperative advertising with transportation companies such as airlines
Print and Distribution	• promotional literature • distribution of literature • storage of literature	• consumer brochures, shell folders, guides, maps, etc. • storage and distribution of literature
Consumer Promotions	• direct mail • promotional aids • advertising and promotional services • word-of mouth communications • consumer promotional campaigns	• servicing enquiries, travel advisory service • promotional campaigns to societies, fishing clubs, etc. • specific mail shots • films, visuals for promotions, representatives
Public Relations and Publicity	• public relations • publicity	• educational tours for journalists • editorial releases • sponsorship of events, etc. • VIPs' visits

Trade Promotions	• trade promotions • trade incentive schemes • shows, seminars, exhibitions • word-of-mouth communications	• promotional calls, 'task force' campaigns, new product promotions • incentive schemes • workshops, 'working breakfast' for agents, etc. • educationals for retail travel agents, wholesalers and tour operators • agents' manuals/product manuals • presentation items to agents, etc.
Distribution Logistics	• means and cost of transporting the goods to the consumer	• charters • subventions to transportation carriers in respect of promotional fares, additional services, etc.
Merchandising	• point of sales displays	• displays, stands for exhibitions, etc.
Consumer Servicing	• after sales service	• tourist information offices • guides, maps of localities • industry standards • complaints investigation
Marketing Administration	• marketing administration costs	• administrative personnel • office space rental, insurance, etc. • shop space rental, insurance, etc.

Source: Heneghan, P, *Resource Allocation in Tourism Marketing* p 4 (16).

terms of particular types of tourist, but it cannot counteract the strength of the other determining factors in terms of overall numbers.

Notwithstanding these observations, and to illustrate the problems involved, it is possible by using the IPS figures provided for the USA test, to attempt crude indications of the effects of the 1973/74 campaigns in test and control areas in terms of the numbers of tourists received in Britain. Taking the IPS data shown for holiday travel, it may be calculated that over the six months October to March 1973/74 inclusive tours from the USA test areas to Britain declined by 18.5% compared to the volume recorded in the same six months period in 1972/73. Other holiday traffic declined by 22.5% in the test areas. By contast, in the USA control areas, it can be calculated that inclusive tours declined by 38.2% in October to March 1973/74 and other holiday traffic was down by 37.2%. If the test areas had declined by the same percentage as the control areas, it can be calculated that the difference in the numbers of holidays (inclusive and other) sold over the six months would amount to 8,000 tourists.

In conclusion, in the least propitious circumstances for off season 'impulse' holiday travel, there is sufficient evidence from the 1973/74 tests to warrant the view that the test money, especially in the USA, has on the one hand helped to minimise the damaging impact of highly adverse conditions for international travel, and on the other hand achieved positive short run results in stimulating the types of travel deemed most advantageous for Britain.

References

1 Kotler, P, *1967 Marketing Management*. Prentice Hall, Inc p 596.
2 Middleton, V, *Test Marketing campaigns* (unpublished)
3 Kramer, L, *A report for BTA* (unpublished)
4 Heneghan, P, *The Scope of the Marketing Mix in Tourism – Resource Allocation in Tourism Marketing*, Irish Tourist Board 1976, p 4.

23 The role of the National Tourist Organisation

The objectives of tourism policy

Tourism is generally recognised as Europe's and the world's largest single trade, with massive social and economic benefits, and a great future potential.

Clearly the incidence of tourism at the regional, national and international level must now be considered as a major factor, for better or worse, in all European countries.

However, in recent years governments have found considerable difficulty in deciding their role and thus their policy and programmes to deal with this area of massive growth. Social and economic policy makers have not regarded tourism as important and so state bodies responsible for tourism activity are often ill equipped to deal with its development.

One reason is due to the fact that tourism represents the 'mobile' as distinct from the 'residential' community in the country. But government politics and related policies are based on the needs and interests of the residents, which may differ very much from those of the visitors. Tourists have no vote, and the tourist service trades cover a wide range of industries which are poorly organised as a collective force for joint action or even consultation.

Tourism requires a partnership between the public and private sectors, linking the planners and regulators for the destination – the public sector interest – (the referees) with the providers of essential services and attractions which visitors want to buy (the players). These key operators are to a large extent in the private sector. They represent a wide range of interests. There is the cooperative as well as the competitive task which is an essential condition for prosperous trade. The state has a fundamental leadership role in setting favourable conditions for competitive international trading, and providing the platform for collective action in consultation, coordination and cooperation.

Although government functions in tourism activity extend across the community, and accordingly across a number of separate departments, coordination within governments at the horizontal level has been historically poor. This is also true between the trades themselves. The result has been a relatively low priority for tourism in government and consequently limited resources and programmes.

The OECD has examined these problems in its recent reports[1] and their findings are directly relevant to the challenge of policy formulation. They conclude that state bodies are in many cases ill equipped to deal with tourism as a major economic force. Yet few other major sectors of government have seen resources and institutional frameworks for tourism so often challenged in recent years. Clearly the weakness is diagnosed but the cure is difficult to find.

The OECD review of government tourism policies in European member countries over the years is instructive. In the 1960s the emphasis was almost entirely on growth, and foreign exchange earnings. This was followed in the 1970s by attempts to channel as well as increase tourism flows, using the trade as an aid to regional policies. This early error unfortunately continued over the years. Tourism is an entity in its own right, and should not be regarded simply as a useful secondary force for some other aspect of government policy. In a changing and competitive world market place the first task is success in attracting the visitors and the consequent enormous revenues, including government revenues, before the community can enjoy the earnings.

Regional development as a state objective was followed more recently in a number of countries by the pursuit of employment, as the service trades are major job creators. Social and environmental aims are now becoming recognised fields for state intervention.

These changes in government's role were accompanied by some important wide reaching political considerations such as decentralised administration by regions or local authorities, and privatisation. But the OECD observed that such steps need to be accompanied by regional planning and integration, albeit broadly, into national policies, as action in the transport field shows. The state cannot avoid the duties of the public sector in such fundamentals as transport (infrastructure) and the provision of leisure and recreational facilities by the local authority. Resorts have a tradition in providing key visitor attractions (including concert and exhibition halls, and in a number of cases, sea and air ports). The state has also an increasing responsibility for conservation and the environment, for regulation and consumer protection, optionally for social services in the recreational field, and essentially for basic marketing services for the destination, which includes information and welcome services and the representative of the host community.

To secure the benefits of tourism in jobs, regional prosperity and massive government revenues through indirect taxation – perhaps the only fully taxed export – the destination marketing platform must be in place. This is a key requirement in state policies since marketing is a wider concept than promotion, and must include visitor satisfaction and thus the consumer interest.

OECD stressed the importance of expertise and effective management in policy making, and the necessary access to or provision of information and statistics. They report 'the state's role in tourism will be increasingly judged on its ability to provide industry and other levels of government with the information they need to draw up their own investment and communication strategies'. They also observe 'the priority that governments give to tourism is also determined by the extent to which all those involved directly or indirectly in tourism make their voices heard'.

A damaging lack of coordination in government policies can be seen in the separation in many cases of transport and tourism policies. The OECD's recent study demonstrated how closely they are linked. It hardly seems necessary to stress this evident fact.

Changing trends in the market must be taken into account so that there is a proper relationship in investment and development policies in each separate sector, for example transport sectors and the other key services of accommodation and attractions. Again this may seem evident but more usually transport, hotels or some other essential component is out of scale and distorting tourism growth.

The European Community and the Commission came relatively late to tourism, reflecting the low priority given to the trade, and the problems of government functions succinctly diagnosed by the OECD.

The reasons given in 1986 for the adoption by the Commission of a tourism programme illustrate the OECD comments on member states' attitudes and the views of individual member governments:

(a) Economic importance of the trade.
(b) Its aid to the expansion of employment.
(c) Its potential for greater understanding and mutual acquaintance.
(d) Advantages in maintaining community members' competitive position in international markets.

The programme itself focused on: Facilitation; seasonal and geographic spread; better use of Community funding in tourism development; better information and protection for tourists; improved working conditions; provision of better information on the sector; and establishing consultation and coordination between the Commission and the member states.

These were and are worthy objectives, although absence of any reference to partnership with the trading sectors was a significant weakness. In the event resources were scarce and progress limited. It was more a statement of broad long term aims than a programme of action.

Thanks to the initiative of the European Parliament the European Year of Tourism 1990 was approved, and warmly supported by the trade sectors, in the hope that it would lead to a higher priority for tourism, favourable conditions in the Commission's policies for tourism growth, better coordination accordingly in those policies, and full consultation and cooperation with industry.

The Commission's statement on the Community's Action Plan in 1991 concentrated on the following key elements:

(a)   strengthening the Commission's horizontal approach by improving industry information, and especially by ensuring that greater account is taken of tourism in the Community's separate policies affecting the service trades concerned in taxation, competition, transport, environment and regional and social development.

(b)   the assurance of consultation with trade sectors and their representative bodies.

(c)   Further action to extend the season, support quality and environmental needs, with rural and cultural tourism interests in particular, training and most important joint promotion.

Europe's tourism prosperity and massive benefits cannot be taken for granted. The effects of the Gulf war indicate clearly the disastrous results of any failure to safeguard international markets.

Although the national organisation is described as the example and pacemaker, the principles apply to all tourist destination authorities, regional and local, the cities, towns and resorts. They have the prime responsibility to act as the inviting host on behalf of the resident community and its visitor resources. There must be a collective or cooperative organisation responsible for providing the forum for the wide range of interests making up the visitor trade, agreeing the tourist development and thus marketing strategy and providing the cooperative base for marketing the destination. There must be a convenor of interests, the stake holder, the inviting host. The particular form of organisation may take differing forms as already explained, governmental, mixed public and private sector, a trade based marketing cooperative with central or local government support. The government role is crucial. No one else can represent the community involved, set the necessary rules and accept public responsibility for fair conditions of trade, welcome and hospitality.

Depending on the form of government, the extent of development and industrialisation, the national or local organisation may have some residual supervisory or development roles. These are not functions unique or essential to the destination tourist organisation. In the case of regional or local bodies, notably resorts, developments in the public sector, sometimes on a partnership basis, may relate to essential infrastructure; roads, parks, gardens, cultural and sporting amenities. These are community services shared with the visitor and properly public sector led.

But specialist departments or partnerships will implement agreed development plans, not the tourist body. Its key role in development relates to strategies, the presentation of professionally studied options, with cost benefits, all firmly rooted in market research and analysis. With the strategies must come outline marketing plans, related to the product market match analysis. The OECD study, Tourism Development and Economic Growth[2] (1966), clearly demonstrated the Government's role, and indicated principal options in formulating a tourism policy. The report commented on the organisation and role of the national tourist body, and the findings are still relevant today.

The role of the national tourist organisation

In formulating its tourism policy, a government will have a number of possible options before it. It will have to decide, for example, the appropriate rate of growth it wishes to see in the tourism sector, whether to encourage mass tourism or to cultivate a slower and more selective growth. It will have to determine what should be the respective roles of the public and the private sector in developing the tourist industry, and similarly, of domestic and foreign capital. It must establish the due importance to be given to the needs of the tourism sector in plans for national and regional development and in so doing must make a decision regarding the time-scale that it considers reasonable for planning forward investments in the tourism industry. There is further the question of whether to treat tourism in the same way as any other growth sector or whether the nature of the industry requires special administrative and credit arrangements.

Tourism involves a number of considerations that are non-economic in nature. Tourism often has significant cultural implications (for example, the restoration of ancient monuments); aesthetic (the preservation of beauties of landscape and the safeguarding of the nation's heritage); social (the provision of recreational facilities for the health and welfare of the people); and political (the improvement of international understanding). These considerations, however, are simply a few of the many alternatives among which a government must choose in deciding the objectives for which it intends to allocate its budget. These are primarily social objectives and, as such, they must be costed and the determination of how much of the national resources should be devoted to them is essentially a matter of social policy. The formulation of the government's tourism programme on the other hand should be determined, primarily, by considerations of economic policy, on the basis of the benefits to the economy which may be expected to follow.

It is important, therefore, that in formulating their tourism policy, governments should clarify their thinking as to the objectives of tourism development. It is also important that they recognise that tourism can represent one of the most hopeful economic resources of the country.

All countries have an official tourism organisation which plays a leading role in both the formulation and implementation of the government's tourism programme. The functions of this body, however, vary considerably according, broadly, to the level of tourism development in the country concerned and the degree of direct intervention that the government wishes to exercise.

These differences of function are reflected in the organisation's structure and constitutional status. Thus in some countries, the national tourism office is a part of the central machinery of government through which the government operates directly in the tourism sector. In others, it has semi-autonomous status and functions not as an organ of government but rather as a professional body outside it. As a general rule, it may be said that this latter conception of the role of the national tourism office is more appropriate to countries where tourism is already fairly advanced and where the private sector is active in it. In countries which are only starting to develop their tourism potential or where it is desired to make a rapid push forward, the government will normally play a more active role itself in promoting tourism development and will use the tourism office as its administrative organ for the purpose.

There is no set formula as to what constitutes the most satisfactory constitutional arrangement for the national tourism body. In some countries, tourism ranks as a full Ministry and in some its Minister enjoys Cabinet rank. Other possibilities include making it semi-autonomous and largely independent of the regular structure of government.

There is clearly a correlation between the standing that the government accords the national tourism organisation and its estimates of the importance of tourism to the national economy, although other considerations, political and psychological, also enter in. Another index of government recognition is the amount of funds that the government makes available to it. In some countries, the activities of the national tourism office are financed in part by means of a direct tax on tourists. As a general rule, however, this is not to be recommended, partly on psychological grounds (it tends to create resentment on the part of the customer) and partly on economic, because through its multiplier effects, tourism is already making a valuable contribution to tax revenue. A special tax on tourists is therefore tantamount to taxing them twice, and, moreover, imposing a surcharge on exports.

At the 1963 General Assembly of the International Union of Official Travel Organisations, it was suggested that the national tourist budget should be not less than 1% of tourist receipts. This however should not be taken as a rigid formula, since for a country whose tourism development is still in its early stages, its yield would obviously be inadequate.

Whatever the constitutional or financial base, the national tourism office in any country will be the officially recognised expert body on tourism matters. As such, it will have the responsibility of preparing the basic studies and forecasts on which the government can prepare the national tourism programme; it will act as spokesman for the interests of the tourism sector; and will assist either directly or indirectly in the implementation of the government's tourism policy. The interpretation of this latter responsibility will, clearly, depend on the government's conception of its own role in tourism development. Thus the functions of the national tourist office may be solely advisory, or regulatory, or they may also be directly operational and promotional.

The administrative structure and composition of the national tourism body will be geared to the functions that it has to perform. A national tourism office would normally include sections to cover the following functions: (1) Research; (2) Information and promotion within the country; (3) Regularisation of standards of lodgings and restaurants; (4) Control of activities of private travel agencies; (5) Publicity overseas; (6) Technical and juridical problems; (7) International relations; (8) Development of selected tourist areas; (9) Overall tourism policy and promotion.

Even where it has a large degree of operational responsibility, it must decide which things it is going to do itself and which it should properly divide with other agencies of government. It has also to decide to what extent it should call in specialists, as for example, for research and forecasting, or for public relations and publicity campaigns. It may also choose sometimes to work in collaboration with the public or the local authorities, as for example in organising a festival.

Whatever the tasks that the national tourism body is called upon to do, what is essential is that it should have the full powers necessary to carry them out. It must, above all, have authority. It must be able to present effectively the case for tourism among the claims of other sectors competing for government support and finance. In a situation where the imperatives of tourism development impinge on those of other sectors and there is a conflict of interests, as in the location of a highway or the priority to be given to a new airport, the head of the tourism organisation should be listened to with as much respect as the Ministers of Public Works or Aviation.

It is essential also that it be technically competent and recognised as such. The wide range of functions devolving upon it require a high degree of experience and professionalism and the calibre and prestige of the senior management of the national tourism organisation can be important factors in the effectiveness with which the government puts through its tourism policy.

Finally, it is essential that the tourism office recognises the limitations of its own mandate, however that may be defined, and maintains close and harmonious liaison with all the other interests that may be involved in tourism development. Three principal interests are concerned. The first is the national planning organisation. In most countries there is regular provision for this liaison at the national level. On the regional level, however, the situation is often less satisfactory and regional planners, and physical planners in particular, often fail to coordinate their work sufficiently with that of the local tourist bodies.

The second is liaison with the other departments of government, partly as a matter of information and negotiation btween different interests, eg labour regulations, taxation, etc, and partly for the infrastructure and services needed for tourism development and which will normally fall to other departments to provide. Thirdly there must be the fullest cooperation with the private sector. This should begin, properly, at the planning stage, when the government should be preparing its programme in consultation with local and private interests. It should continue by means of frequent and informal contacts to ensure harmonious collaboration on the practical problems involved in making the programme into a profitable business.

Five key roles

Burkart and Medlik suggested that the NTO's marketing function is twofold: '. . . in the first place the tourist organisation can formulate and develop the tourist product or products of the destination; secondly it can promote them in appropriate markets'.[3] This is too simplistic. The sophisticated, semi-autonomous agency of government has five key roles, though each role, chameleon-like, spills over into the others. These five roles are:

- Guardian of the image.
- Scene setter.
- Trail blazer.
- Marketing coordinator.
- Monitor of visitor satisfaction.

Guardian of the image

Transporters often forget the very basic fact that people fly on an aeroplane, sail on a ship or ride in a car or bus to get from A to B. Hoteliers do not always remember that people stay in an hotel at B because there is something they want to see or do there. There has to be a reason for going to B – the destination. It is the job of the NTO marketers to determine the images, to create awareness of the destination and position it accurately in the market place. But that is not enough. Images can become tarnished and sullied; they need constant attention to maintain their glitter and glamour. The marketer must use a number of marketing tools to achieve this. Public relations should be designed to create and maintain an image for the destination which is at once appetising and appealing. Advertising is a more precisely-targeted marketing weapon, and performs most effectively when it is projected on a backcloth of receptivity created through a good public relations campaign. Promotional print is used by the marketer in an effort to persuade the reader to select a particular destination. It is the representation of the product or destination, and consequently an important image-maker.

Scene setter

While marketing should be research driven, the marketer, not the researcher, should be in the driving seat. The marketer should devise the research programme's objectives, the researcher should carry out the technical work and help to interpret the findings, and finally the marketer should implement these findings. One of the vehicles for communicating market analysis and trend data to the industry is the strategy document. The NTO's analysis of external factors and trends will point the way for both public and private interests in identifying favourable growth markets as well as gaps in the product range, not only segments which offer future potential, but also those which need remedial action to mitigate damage. The NTO helps the industry to develop the right product for the right market and the right segment within that market. It also helps the industry to target messages more precisely against the backcloth of destination awareness creating campaigns.

Trail blazer

One of the principal roles of any NTO is to develop new markets, new segments and new techniques. In a commercial organisation, marketing appropriations are more likely to be required to secure an immediate return on investment. The trade will very often follow only when the missionary work has been done. The return on investment is in the longer-term and marketing in these conditions becomes an act of faith. In the case of BTA, India and Korea are examples of new market development; senior citizens, special interest travel and incentive travel outside the US market examples of new segments. BTA was a trail blazer in challenging seasonality through its Operation Off-Peak campaign launched in 1985. BRAVO (a switch to link the central reservation offices of the major vendors with the international distribution or computerised reservations systems such as SABRE), was handed over to the industry in 1990, having been developed under the guidance of BTA.

Marketing coordination

The unique and indispensable role is that of the destination marketing authority. Tourism is a market, not a single industry and the market will dominate. The role will involve:

(1)   provision of the cooperative base or focal point for consultation with all the interests supplying services and attractions, and responsible for investment in the future (this will usually mean a public private sector liaison);
(2)   advice to Government and key interests on options for development based on market research and intelligence;
(3)   liaison with Government and key interests on the elaboration of the government tourism policy and identification of cost benefits;
(4)   preparation of marketing strategy to implement the agreed government (local or central) tourism policy, in consultation with the key supplying interests;
(5)   operation of the destination marketing programme in selected markets on a cooperative basis.

It will be essential throughout these operations that the suppliers or producers of services, notably the carriers, accommodation and entertainment or specialist activity interests play a full partnership role. In this way there should be a coordinated approach to marketing, product presentation and development.

The National Tourist Office promotional resources will represent seed money greatly extending promotion for the destination but also the marketing arms of the suppliers, many of whom will be small businesses which could not otherwise enter the international market place. Good examples of this in operation include the European Travel Commission supplements in American newspapers, with full industry advertising support equivalent to $1 million in 1988, more than doubling the Commission's own advertising provision. Participation in foreign travel exhibitions may take the form of a major national destination display space accommodating a number of individual interests, regions and resorts. At the World Travel Market in London some of the larger national exhibits include several hundred separate state, province, resort and company representations. Thus the cooperative base greatly strengthens the total promotion through a collective destination message, which greatly amplifies the local or specific sales approach.

Cooperative action is fundamental in research. Both in the case of the BTA and the European Travel Commission most research is a public private sector partnership, extending the range and scope of the essential market enquiries, and equally important helping to ensure practical results, good and professional interpretation of those results, and appropriate action to implement or use the findings at the destination and trade operational level.

Subsequent appraisals, effectiveness tests, and performance against objective tests will be greatly enhanced if the NTO provides the collective basis for such research. It is rarely possible to evaluate destination only promotion. Like a two stage rocket the destination appeal must be immediately reinforced by easy to buy specific services.

Representational and Educational Roles

The most powerful influence of the National Tourist Organisation or its local counterpart lies in the marketing resources providing a network of contacts with the trade, travel counsellors, public and private and the tourists themselves.

In practice the National Tourist Office is the most powerful motivator for the destination. It concentrates on the national base. Other big promoters, such as air carriers, have many destinations to promote, and do not have the credibility in the public mind of the official government backed services.

The focal point role is not only unique but of prime importance. No other body represents the needs and wishes of the mobile or visiting population. This is the market. If the resident community, national or local, wants to receive visitors and their economic and social benefits, they must listen to the dictates of the market place.

There is therefore a vital representational and educational as well as a promotional role.

This involves representation to central and national government to ensure that conditions for tourism development are favourable. Fiscal and legislative measures may be needed. Reception at ports of entry and frontiers must be satisfactory. BTA's inquiry on reception at ports and terminals in cooperation with government and transport interests is instructive on the necessary representational role from the focal or cooperative base. Tax and social constraints suited to the resident population may need amendment to provide facilities for visitors. In Britain this may affect liquor licensing, shopping hours, health, transport (motoring) and sporting regulation. Standard setting, usually best done for visitors' services on a voluntary or self regulating base, may need some government support or backing (eg currency exchange, control on guides, travel agents, hotel services, transport such as taxis).

The focal point and cooperative base role extends far beyond destination direct interests and commercial activity. There are many state agencies and programmes at national, regional and local level. Although their main purpose will be to add to the national economic and social well being, they may have surplus resources (university accommodation in vacation time, other sports and leisure facilities where there are at times a surplus of provision over resident community need). Regional and specialist development (poorer or declining regions, city centres, failing agriculture etc), employment provision, heritage and cultural preservation programmes can all benefit from a tourism alliance. Governments often have a number of agencies in addition to the official posts (embassies) operating to promote national status and reputation abroad. The state tourist organisation and its industry colleagues, including flag carriers, are in a good position to extend the official arm through cooperation, to add value and benefit to the national and to the tourism programme. Too often there is a degree of separatism and 'water tight compartments' in state operations of this kind. The tourism trade and its interests can often provide a communication bridge and a forum for cooperative action.

This unique and important function of representing all destination interests in a powerful way through appealing to the visitor is often underestimated nationally. Yet for Britain and most developed countries their international visitors provide the greatest medium they have for presentation of national interest. The movement is large (in Britain fifteen million). No single medium press or television could compare. Visitors come prepared to like the country, to be pleased and impressed and wish to return with warm memories and affection. Most do or the ever increasing repeat business would not survive.

Monitoring visitor satisfaction

The national tourist office also has important responsibilities in ensuring the promised quality of service, to watch out for defects and bottlenecks, and to monitor satisfaction through research. These activities, greatly enhanced by the wide ranging contact with a true cross section of the visitor movement, provide a good basis for initiatives to improve product presentation, standards of service and initiation of new services and facilities.

Usually the action will take the form of representation to public (including Government) or private sector bodies and to operators themselves, suggesting improvements or changes. Many examples have been cited in earlier chapters. The NTO should have a formal government liaison and advisory role and the consultative machinery and links to go with it, including interest and support of appropriate government ministers. In many countries the NTO is itself a ministry, but increasingly the practice is to separate the government administrative role from the intensely competitive and internationally commercially related role of the efficient NTO. Either system works provided that the dictates of the market prevail and the government machinery gives appropriate priority for action, following the NTA's advice and guidance in implementing the Tourism Plan agreed with Government.

Product presentation and improvement

There is a further important field for NTO's influence and action. This is in the area of product presentation and improvement. Many new initiatives will need a collective of interests. There may be a need for initiating a new service which the private sector is unable or unwilling to undertake on an individual basis. Examples of this in Britain include the national Britain in Bloom campaign to improve the attractiveness of cities, towns and villages through plants and gardens; to improve cleanliness; the provision of a major travel information and reservation centre for foreign visitors in the centre of London; the launching of major events and festivals (Heritage '84 or the Easter Parade in London); the creation of consortia for accommodation; Commended Country Hotels; the introduction of season tickets; the establishment of interest groups (The Historic Houses Association); codes of conduct (hotels and currency exchange); the specialist services such as training.

Other countries have also demonstrated successful and necessary state initiatives: the Paradores in Spain, the Gites de France, the Meet the Danes home visiting scheme. Opportunities for inspiring the supplies to improve or introduce new products are endless. The NTO is in the best position to point to the needs and provide guidance on the action, through advisory publications, seminars and the like, whether it is on making a video, running a conference or seasonality.

It is important, however, for continuing success, and to ensure best use of resources, that the NTO's role is that of the initiator, the motivator and adviser. The national body should continually seek allies, and like the franchisors bring new resources into the business. This means a policy based on pump priming. There should not be a continuing effort. A good rule of thumb is a three year time-scale to get a new project off the ground. The NTO should not attempt to do other interests' jobs. It should not hold on to successful ventures, a very hard but essential rule to follow. The missionary task is endless.

Summary

The national tourist organisation has the prime responsibility to act as the inviting host on behalf of the resident community and its visitor resources. There must be a collective or cooperative organisation responsible for providing the forum for the wide range of interests making up the visitor trade, agreeing the tourist development plan and thus the marketing strategy, and providing the cooperative base for marketing the destination.

The organisation may have some residuary supervisory or direct development roles but these are not unique or essential functions in a free market economy. Its key role in development relates to strategies, options rooted in market research, and outline marketing plans related to product market match analysis.

The unique and indispensable role is that of the destination marketing authority.

The most powerful influence lies in the marketing resources providing a network of contacts with trade, travel counsellors, public and private, and the tourists themselves. No other body represents the needs and wishes of the mobile or visiting population. If the resident community, national or local, wants to receive visitors and their money, they must listen to the dictates of the market place through the national tourist body.

There is therefore a representational, educational as well as a promotional role . . . This involves advice to central and local government to ensure that conditions for tourism growth are favourable.

The important function of representing all destination interests through appealing to the visitor, a vast market, is often underestimated nationally.

The national tourist organisation has important responsibilities in ensuring the promised quality of service.

Many new initiatives will need a collective of interests in the area of product presentation and improvement.

For best results the national body's role should be that of initiator, a policy based on pump priming and continually seeking new allies. But the Government body should not attempt to do other interests' jobs. The missionary task is endless.

Essentially the National Tourist Office has five key roles – guardian of the image, scene setter, trail blazer, marketing coordinator and monitor of visitor satisfaction.

References

1 *Community Action Plan to Assist Tourism*. Office for Official Publications of the European Communities, Luxembourg, 1991.
2 *Tourism Development and Economic Growth*. OECD 1966, p 13.
3 Burkart, A J and Medlik, R, *Tourism Past, Present and Future*. 2nd ed, Heinemann, 1981, p 256.

24 Future trends

Chapter 7 on forecasts explained the rapid and massive growth in the last two decades in most forms of tourism in industrialised countries, and especially in international travel.

When jumbo jets trumpeted the birth of mass travel in 1970 we saw the beginnings of the great world travel movement. Between 1970 and 1985 international travel movements more than doubled. It grew by six per cent per annum in the 1970s but in fact it has been just over three per cent in the 1980s.

It is generally accepted that it could be around five per cent per annum in the 1990s.

But there will undoubtedly be a change in the great flows and cross currents which could affect Europe adversely.

Many governments now place a higher priority on tourism development – Australia, New Zealand, China and some Latin American countries.

China's latest five year development plan designates tourism as a priority industry. Ten years ago it wasn't even considered an economic activity in China. Many Latin American Governments' attitudes towards tourism have undergone a drastic transformation over the recent past – Venezuela and Brazil especially.

In 1950 visitor arrivals in Asia and the Pacific accounted for less than one per cent of world arrivals. By 1985 its share had increased to over 11%. Many of the world's top hotels are in this region and there has been a dramatic increase in airline services to and from the region over the last decade.

So continuing changes must be expected in the share of travel movements between the world's tourism regions. The Far East, Australasia and Latin America are expanding more rapidly while the traditional tourist areas of North America and Europe, though holding on to their dominant position, will grow more steadily and lose share. This will reflect the levels of competitive spend on both marketing and development – generally reducing in Europe and increasing in these other regions.

European destinations accounted for 72% of world tourist arrivals in 1975; by 1980 it had dropped to 69% and by 1985 it had dropped again to 67%. Europe is, of course, still very significant as a destination for the international traveller, getting about two out of three tourist arrivals.

Europe is also a very important generator of international tourism. Increasingly the destination trend for Europeans will be away from Europe to the Americas and the Pacific.

Tourist arrival figures for individual European countries, show that the majority of their visitors are from European markets. Italy with 92% intra-European traffic, Portugal 90%, Austria 89%, Greece 83%, France 82%. Even Sweden and Denmark with 85% and 87% respectively. Britain gets just 55% of its visitors from Europe and enjoys a good spread of markets.

These figures in the 80% and 90% ranges are unhealthy.

The technology is available now to improve efficiency, safety and cut operating costs of air travel and there will surely be reducd prices in real terms. At the same time marketing by an ever increasing number of new destinations which have 'discovered' tourism will mean the greatest growth on the long haul routes.

Europe will receive fewer Europeans as they increasingly venture further afield.

So on two counts Europe is going to suffer loss of share – unless something is done to counter the trends.

Principal economic determinants are personal disposable income, linked to Gross Domestic Product (GDP) and leisure time.

Both these factors have been highly favourable and the results accelerated by changes in technology notably transport, which have made many forms of travel cheaper in real terms. This is evident in the case of long distance travel. Transatlantic fares are less than half the real price of twenty-five years ago when real incomes were much lower.

The experts suggest that these favourable determinants will continue and that rate of growth may increase as more and more countries grow richer. In fact in recent years Asia and the Far East have shown the greatest rate of growth albeit from a low base.

The WTO estimated world travel movement in 1986 at over 340 million arrivals, and US$115 billion expenditure. All experts predict growth but at varying rates. The European Travel Commission's review of trends suggests a middle way estimate with an annual average growth of 5.15% giving a world arrival figure of 650 million by the year 2000 or shortly after, and a related expenditure of more than $200 billion at 1986 values, and a much higher figure if international fares are taken into account. In fact tourism could represent six per cent of world trade, the largest single item, and nearly 20% of world trade in services. Furthermore the domestic tourist movement must be taken into account, not least because it is becoming increasingly interchangeable with and competitive with international tourism. Domestic movement accounts in most western countries for 90% of total tourism business. Howarth and Howarth pointed out in a recent report that approximately 1.7 million hotel rooms are occupied daily in the USA and only ten per cent are used by foreign guests.

The Japanese government have launched an official programme to encourage Japanese travel abroad called the 'Ten Million Plan', forecasting an annual exodus to foreign destinations of ten million residents within a few years. Not only will the Japanese become better aquainted with other countries and their ways, but spending will help to reduce severe and sometimes embarrassing trade deficits with important customer countries. In many ways the Japanese foreign travel situation is similar to the American pattern after the war. The US government tourist policy, and its aid through the Marshall plan, was to assist Europe to earn American dollars needed to import essential food and supplies for economic recovery. American travel was still in the traditional form of a once-in-a-lifetime package tour of Europe, epitomised in the somewhat cynical joke, 'Tuesday? It must be Brussels'. So the Japanese travel on package trips to Europe, travelling rapidly, sightseeing and taking photographs in an 11 to 12 day period.

The economic determinants create a vast potential market far in excess of current movement. It is astonishing that the USA with its firm roots in Europe's culture, and strong personal links with European people, supports a tourist movement of no more than six million trips (not people, as some travellers are frequent visitors in the course of a year), hardly more than two per cent of the population of the richest country in the world. With relatively cheap air transport, almost all Americans in full time employment could afford a trip to Europe if they wished. So clearly there are other important factors.

Chapter 9 emphasises the power of certain basic external factors, financial, social and political. Their effects will continue and from time to time growth and patterns of travel in certain countries and regions will be reduced or even halted. However tourist flows are generally resilient and long running with an inbuilt stability or tradition of movement. This stability is not as strong as in the past but it is still a factor. Traffic recovers relatively quickly from setbacks. After the serious and sudden decline in American transatlantic travel to Europe in 1986, when a third of the movement (nearly two million trips) was lost, the movement was almost back to normal at the record level of 1985 within two years. The tendency is for traffic to resume growth quickly and in favourable circumstances to reach the anticipated level on the growth curve in a short period.

While the long term outlook seems almost too good to be true, it must be recognised that in an era of growth not every form of travel will grow, nor will every current market expand. There will be winners and losers. There will be new emerging markets, mature markets and declining markets. The same is true of the product and destination. In recent years a number of major tour operators and airlines have suffered and some disappeared. So too new entrants have made their mark and captured their market shares. Probably at the present time the market in its potential and interest is ahead of the trade. Marketing enterprise and the presentation and development of products in a changing world have a long way to go. Furthermore the means and resources, the technological basis for tourism and international travel, are themselves ahead of the market. So unexploited demand and unused or undeveloped resources are the great challenge for the future.

Given the physical and economic resources capable of supporting a massive expansion in travel, key determinants lie more in the lifestyle and behaviour of market segments. This is an age of great change. Traditional ways die hard but they are being modified. Fashion which spreads from the lower as well as the upper levels in industrialised society is changing more rapidly. Main holidays grow shorter and the second or subsequent trips longer. The rigid seasonal divisions are no longer overriding constraints for the majority of international travellers today. Indeed main holidays are no longer necessarily the summer holiday. Seasonality is indeed a challenge and opportunity not a problem, at least in industrialised and developed countries.

Much more attention and research needs to be given to behaviour groups, and the creation in travel and tourism of what might be called many mini mass markets.

Megatrends of tourism in Europe 1990–2000 (ETC) were listed in chapter 7. The most important are:

1.   Global travel spending into and from Europe will increase faster than any other budget items.
2.   Long haul holidays to and from Europe will increase faster than intra-European holidays.
3.   Within Europe, city travel will increase faster than summer and beach vacation holidays.
4.   South–North, East–West and West–East travel will increase relatively faster than traditional North–South holidays.
5.   Traffic across the present intra-European borders will increase faster than domestic travel in most European countries.
6.   Winter sunshine holidays, cultural, winter tours and cruises will probably increase faster than winter sports holidays.
7.   Air traffic will increase faster than other types of transportation. Rail transport will also show strong growth.
8.   Individual packages rather than group travel will become increasingly popular.
9.   Late reservations will increase faster than early bookings as CRS become more comprehensive.
10. Travel by senior citizens and young people will increase faster than other age groups.

11. Demand for cultural and activity holidays will grow faster than other forms of vacation.

12. Groups, including families, will tend to be smaller and more flexible.

13. Price/quality ratios will play an increasing role in the choice of destinations and accommodation. The quality of the environment will become a determining element in attracting visitors.

The potential of the US market for tourism in Europe will continue to grow as the average income and education level rises. More US consumers will become repeat travellers. Additionally, an increased demand for special interest and other non-traditional tourism can be anticipated from this segment, a departure from the US consumers 'capital-hopping' European tour. However, the ultimate factor influencing the tendency for this market to visit Europe remains the strength of the dollar.

Over the next decade or so, it is predicted that the demand for city destinations will grow at a faster rate than the demand for resort destinations. This growth is partially due to the fact that travellers are taking more additional trips for a shorter duration, and partially to the fact that travellers have a better educational background and thus a stronger interest in the cultural experiences available in major city destinations. The growth in demand for city tourism is also augmented by increasingly sophisticated transportation technology such as air travel and such developments as the proposed tunnel to be built under the English Channel.

Additionally the MIC (Meetings, Incentives, Convention) market, an important component of the demand for city tourism, is expected to grow at a faster rate than the level of travel and tourism activity in general.

One important impact of this growth in city tourism will be an increasing demand from visitors for entertainment opportunities and experiences in destination cities.

The development in Europe of the Internal Market in 1992 by the European Community (EC) should have beneficial implications for intra-European tourism. It will represent a market of 300 million population with a high disposable income, and a GDP of 328 billion ECU. The changes should create a single market with free transfers of capital, financial transactions, and the opportunity for business to expand on a European basis and to invest in any part of any tourist region within the European member countries.

Reduction of regulations and restrictions which protect national interests, especially in the field of transport (air and road, eg coaches,) should stimulate new initiatives in routes, services and tourist offers and packages.

But there will be other changes, harmonisation of fiscal measures, VAT, excise duty etc and the abolition of the duty free shops. Where harmonisation means the addition of tax (such as VAT on international transport at present free of charges), there may be in the short term at least some distortion or constraints.

The EC has substantial powers to intervene in policy making, infrastructure development, research and even information and publicity, which if backed by a progressive tourism policy and the full support of the member states, could have a substantial and beneficial effect on tourism and leisure services in Europe. But it must be remembered that the role of the State in tourism development and operation is or should be limited to setting the scene, creating a favourable climate, and providing the necessary destination focal point for cooperative action in liaison, research and promotion.

For Britain there is the special additional interest of the Channel Tunnel in 1993. BTA has reported an estimate of sixteen million British visits to France, Belgium and Germany by 2000, twice the level of traffic achieved in 1987, and comments that a similar level of incoming visits from France, Belgium, the Netherlands and Germany (sixteen million) would mean that traffic will have quadrupled. As explained in earlier chapters, all new routes of any significance create some new traffic and capture from competing routes. The key element remains the reason for the journey, the attraction (and satisfaction) at the destinations. The route is a means to an end, and the results and success will depend on destination marketing in its widest sense. There is of course a marketing task for the transport operators concerned with the tunnel investment and its related transport services. The basic rule is that a route, new or old, will compete successfully with alternatives to the extent in which it dominates in price, time and convenience (comfort, access, timing). Usually dominance in any two of these factors will guarantee success in meeting the competition. There is no intrinsic value in a route or service as such.

It seems unlikely that there will be further technological revolutions as in the recent past such as the growth of wide bodied jets, transport price reductions, mass motor car ownership, with the possible exception of the further development of technological information systems, which are already in place.

There will of course be technical factors. Transport is becoming more efficient. There may be switches between transport forms, greater use of public transport as it offers benefits in the three controlling factors (speed, price and comfort or convenience). Domestic movement grows, often the distinction between day trips and resident community movement (not tourism) is blurred. People are increasingly mobile. Mass movement may afford considerable economies of scale. Tourist use of surplus capacity (left over after residential need is met) can be highly profitable for tourist and producer alike.

Techniques of development will lead to more rapid growth and investment, although mistakes may be also increasingly costly. There is a trend towards mega attractions such as Disney World, the provision of mass assembly centres for multi purpose leisure use (sports, meetings, cultural activity etc). Hotels and accommodation have altered radically in the last three decades. But they may change again, international type large hotels, often chain operated and largely identical in product, are supported by a range of accommodation choice, motels, apartment hotels, holiday centres, villas, cottages and time share. There will be other changes with value for money implications.

But the main area of change will be in demand, fashion and attitude. Work patterns will change, demographics alter, for example the major changes in senior citizen demand. More interest may be generated in the home, and home related leisure. Attitudes to health could be important. Already there are fears about excessive sunshine. In Victorian days, not so long ago, visitors sought the shade in summer. The French Riviera was a winter resort area. The grand hotels in North Africa closed in summer.

It will be more important than ever to study trends by market segment. There are already several mini mass markets behaving differently. These will increase. For example over 50% of international hotel use is through business-related travel. This could change significantly. Specialist travel, already big business in some forms, will increase substantially. But by its nature every specialism must be treated separately.

So the major changes must be sought in human attitudes, fashion and behaviour. The market is truly in charge, and the new techniques must lie in marketing and product development from a marketing base.

Generally speaking, contemporary living patterns for a majority of the population in developed countries are dominated by labour saving appliances and techniques including shopping and food preparation.

There is almost too much leisure time. This reflects the gap between possibilities for activity and purchases in services and the potential demand involving the use of surplus (disposable) income and time away from home for travel orientated people. There are of course home centred people who do not like mobility. There are also segments of the population who do not have either the money or the time to leave home on extended trips. Family burdens for example and home building may for a time preclude other leisure purchase on any major scale.

However, for many other groups and major population segments, senior citizens or more precisely retirees for example, there is an almost insatiable interest in travel services. Elasticity is high; the appetite once whetted frequent purchases follow. Many live frustrated lives, many are lonely, so the appeal of travel, especially foreign travel, new places, new faces, company and excitement, theatrical, and even exotic interest, can have a high priority in consumer choice.

There is a growing trend towards specialist and activity trips, travelling to learn, almost back to the classic origins of tourism. There has always been the urge to travel to improve knowledge and expertise in a particular sport, hobby, art or area of culture. Leisure pastimes are taken more seriously, and the object of substantial purchases in equipment, training and other services. The urge towards face to face contact covers a wide field of human interest not simply in business and the professions. Thus institutions, religious organisations, educational bodies and professional organisations have always played a role in travel. This is likely to expand considerably as demand for life outside the home and in a wider community becomes more pressing.

The travel industry and resorts in particular offer meeting and personal contact services on a major scale. Unused resources are there in abundance.

As disposable income grows and leisure time increases, constraints on frequent travel purchases fall away. The attitudes and behaviour patterns have not adjusted yet to this very new addition to the freedom of choice. It is scarcely a century since annual summer holidays were established in a very rigid pattern to be followed traditionally for two or three generations. The trend to second and more frequent short trips usually for special purpose, to see family or friends, for health or to attend an event, is quite recent.

Increasingly the summer vacation, usually in August in Europe when schools close, can be expected to change, except for families with small children. For the majority of international travellers there are no constraints to choosing any time of the year for journeys away from home. There is a growing trend to avoid peak congested periods, and an interest in off peak movement not for bargains or price reductions, but for quality and value for money. Winter sports may be the objective for the main annual holiday. Sunshine is available year round in suitable geographic locations, and access easier through air transport development at attractive prices. Thus the attitude to holiday taking is undergoing major change, and will have a profound effect on future holiday patterns.

As indicated in the chapter on product development, there will be a massive demand in the longer term for new product development, and re-presentation of former or current attractions. Already spectator events and most forms of leisure are enjoying increasing public and visitor support. Many of these leisure attractions will cater for the resident community, and enjoy year round trade, with the visitor movement an additional but often very profitable source of 'extra' business. Examples can be seen in the popularity of many specialist appeals reaching a rapidly widening and increasing market, such as health facilities and centres, spectator and participating sports, cultural attractions, including the development of new techniques of presenting arts and treasures in theme centres and special exhibitions. The revolution in communication services, both transport and media, notably television, is likely to greatly increase the interest in real life, and places and events outside the home. Educational services and activities, hobbies and personal face to face communication through meetings for business and pleasure will provide new and large scale opportunities for travel.

Tourism and the environment

The rapid growth of mass tourism has led to increasing concern about environmental effects in tourist areas. Forecasts of continuing growth have encouraged public debate and proposals for state intervention. The WTO has indicated an annual average growth rate of about five per cent, which would mean that world tourism would almost double by the year 2000, with some 3,000 million foreign and domestic visitors.

Tourists in European countries have shown increasing interest and sometimes anxiety about quality. The German *Reiseanalyse* survey reported that most tourists going on holiday wanted attractive landscape, unspoilt natural surroundings, and clean and unpolluted water. In the 1985 survey fewer than one third of those interviewed were dissatisfied. But by 1988 one half of the respondents referred to environmental problems.

Recognising a growing demand most sectors of the trade now give some priority to these problems, and they have become major political issues. In the European Community a number of programmes and substantial funding are now being devoted to the subject.

Public opinion supports action to limit acid rain destroying forests, bathing water pollution, and removal of litter, coupled with demand for higher standards in transport and accommodation services.

As with so many aspects of tourism, while the overall problems are visible, and a subject for complaint and criticism, the identification of specific problem areas, cause and effect, and action programmes to remedy damage, is a major difficulty. Too often the individual authorities and sectors of interest blame each other, refuse to accept their own responsibilities for managing their resources and claim that the polluter must pay. Furthermore the separate interests until quite recently never met.

The first task is the objective and professional identification of problems. There are many different kinds of pollution, and thus a variety of ways of dealing with unwelcome pressures. Rather than one environmental policy for tourism, it may prove more practical to build environmental elements into tourism development and marketing programmes. Marketing in practice has one of the largest roles to play. Tourism demand cannot be managed but it can be influenced by those managing the key resources competently.

The first responsibility is that of the state in creating conditions in health, safety and environmental policies to deal with visitors as well as residents. Collective action will be needed by the tourism interests and the environmental authorities. There must be special tourism objectives, for example clean bathing water, the subject of a welcome EC directive, and action to safeguard areas of outstanding natural beauty. Planning controls can be used successfully. Many states have created national parks or nature reserves in this way.

Development controls must be matched in marketing programmes to select and fit traffic to the resources in line with an agreed policy (product–market match). The marketing strategy should be designed to ensure a sustainable flow of traffic, and this will involve some estimation of the area's 'carrying capacity' to avoid saturation. Trade will not be sustained if there is over building or quality loss. The trade will be as interested as the conservators in safeguarding the future. There is no exact formula for deciding sustainable levels, but experience will soon indicate danger.

Marketing techniques include pricing, and the selection and packaging of segments or suitable core markets to shape tourism flows. Promotion of cultural itineraries, organisations of rural or farm tourism, selection of activities in harmony with the agreed development plan, camping, riding, hiking, water sports etc. It may be necessary to set limits to visitor use. But there are costs, not least in lost revenue opportunities. There may be a wish to keep a mountain for oneself, but that is costly in loss of earnings. Tourism spending may offer the principal resource to sustain a poor resident population, and to meet the high price of conservation and environmental qualities. There is a hard choice of traffic to be made; regarding the season and standards (budget or higher spending trade).

The marketing plan must include information and guidance, both in preparing the visitor for the trip and in guiding and informing in the resort area. A travellers' guide to ensure maximum satisfaction should be an important environmental aid.

The host community and authorities must ensure that visitor facilities and welcome are provided, including action to deal with litter. There must be programmes for good hosts as well as good guests.

There are some encouraging examples of good hosting by institutions and the trade. The National Trust in England and Wales, and National Trust for Scotland have a long record of success in managing landscape, beaches, historic buildings for tourism and conservation. Holiday cottages, and even cruises are included in their 'products'. The Gites de

France have a record of success in converting surplus farm and other buildings for holidays in the countryside.

In Spain and Portugal the use of historic buildings by the state as hotels and inns (Paradores and Poussadas) has been admired and appreciated for many years.

The issue is sometimes confused by academic argument and even media campaigns by conservation interests. Terms such as soft tourism, eco-tourism, rural tourism and alternative tourism (as opposed to mass traffic) do not clarify the issues.

Damage must be catalogued, and the specific reasons identified, because solutions will vary. Joint action will be needed by government, the resource owners or managers and the marketers guiding the visitor flows. As part of European Year of Tourism the ICOMOS Conference on Heritage and Tourism in Canterbury, England, brought together conservers, and historic property guardians, public and private sector, and representatives of tourism – tourist boards, local authorities and the trades. Their recommendations underline the essential need for collective effort, although the identification of specific action programmes and the role of marketing needed more attention:

> This conference adopts the following seven points as a basis for the better integration of the interests of tourism and of the heritage:
> 1. Comprehensive tourist development plans are essential as the pre-condition for developing any tourist potential.
> 2. It should be a fundamental principal of any tourist development plan that both conservation, in its widest sense, and tourism benefit from it. This principle should be part of the constitutional purpose of all national tourist agencies, and of local authority tourism and recreation departments.
> 3. A significant proportion of revenue earned from tourism should be applied for the benefit of conservation, both nationally and regionally.
> 4. The best long-term interests of the people living and working in any host community should be the primary determining factor in selecting options for tourist development.
> 5. Educational programmes should assist and invite tourists to respect tourism policy and should take these factors into account.
> 6. The design of buildings, sites and transport systems should minimise the potentially harmful visual effects of tourism. Pollution controls should be built into all forms of infrastructure. Where sites of great natural beauty are concerned, the intrusion of man-made structures should be avoided if possible.
> 7. Good management should define the level of acceptable tourism development and provide controls to maintain that level.

In 1991 The Department of Employment published a report of a task force set up by the Minister to examine the balance of tourism and the environment. Again the main conclusion[1] quoted below emphasises the collective nature of action programmes. The role of marketing was given a special place in the recommendations.

Principles for sustainable tourism

- The environment has an intrinsic value which outweighs its value as a tourism asset. Its enjoyment by future generations and its long term survival must not be prejudiced by short term considerations.
- Tourism should be recognised as a positive activity with the potential to benefit the community and the place as well as the visitor.
- The relationship between tourism and the environment must be managed so that the environment is sustainable in the long term. Tourism must not be allowed to damage the resource, prejudice its future enjoyment or bring unacceptable impacts.
- Tourism activities and developments should respect the scale, nature and character of the place in which they are sited.
- In any location, harmony must be sought between the needs of the visitor, the place and the host community.
- In a dynamic world some change is inevitable and change can often be beneficial. Adaptation to change, however, should not be at the expense of any of these principles.
- The tourism industry, local authorities and environmental agencies all have a duty to respect the above principles and to work together to achieve their practical realisation.

Marketing and information

Marketing aimed at visitors before they arrive can have a substantial impact on visiting patterns. A conscious decision not to market a location can help reduce its profile. Marketing, including pricing, can be used to encourage visitors to come out of season or to visit alternative locations. It can also be used to target particular types of visitor. Information, including pedestrian signing, aimed at visitors once they have arrived can be used to channel visitors in particular directions.

Summary

It is generally accepted that world travel movement can continue to grow at around five per cent per annum in the 1990s, but there will be changes in the great flows and cross currents. Principal economic determinants (Gross Domestic Product and leisure time) will remain favourable and there will be some continuing changes in technology, increasing efficiency and reducing real prices. A vast potential market is expanding far in excess of current movement.

Certain external factors, financial, social and political, will from time to time influence markets, sometimes for the worse, but tourism will remain resilient to short term changes. But in an era of growth not every form of travel nor every market will expand. There will be declining markets as well as emerging markets.

Economic resources and technical abilities are capable of supporting massive expansion in travel. Key determinants will be found in lifestyle and behaviour of market segments. Seasonality is now a challenge, and opportunity not just a problem. The development of the EC Internal Market in 1992 should have beneficial implications for Europe, the world's greatest tourism region, but in the short term there may be some constraint. The role of the state in tourism development should be limited to setting the scene, creating a favourable climate and providing the focal point for cooperative action in liaison, research and marketing.

The Channel Tunnel should also favour travel movement in Britain and Europe.

But techniques of development will lead to more rapid and massive growth and investments, so mistakes may also be more costly.

Major changes must be sought in human attitudes, fashion and behaviour. The market is truly in charge, and the new techniques must lie in marketing and product development from the marketing base.

Reference

1 *Tourism and the Environment. Maintaining the Balance.* English Tourist Board and Department of Employment, 1991.

Index